ORISSA:

ITS GEOGRAPHY, STATISTICS, HISTORY, RELIGION, AND ANTIQUITIES

ORISSA:

ITS GEOGRAPHY, STATISTICS, HISTORY, RELIGION, AND ANTIQUITIES,

BY

ANDREW STERLING, Esq.

TO WHICH IS ADDED,

A HISTORY

OF THE

GENERAL BAPTIST MISSION

ESTABLISHED

IN THE PROVINCE.

BY JAMES PEGGS

GYAN

Published by

GYAN

Gyan Publishing House
5, Ansari Road
Daryaganj, New Delhi-110002
Phone: 011-47034999, 9811692060
E-mail: books@gyanbooks.com

Distribution Network
gyanbooks.com
India, USA, Canada, UK, Australia, France

ISBN:978-81-212-8292-5 (PB)
First Published, 1846

2nd Impression 2023

Printed at: Gyan Press, Delhi.

ORISSA: ITS GEOGRAPHY, STATISTICS, HISTORY, RELIGION, AND ANTIQUITIES

Authors: ANDREW STERLING, JAMES PEGGS

THE TEMPLE AND CARS OF JUGGERNAUT, BULBUDRA, AND SOOBUDRA.

ORISSA:

ITS GEOGRAPHY, STATISTICS, HISTORY, RELIGION, AND ANTIQUITIES,

BY

ANDREW STERLING, Esq.,

LATE PERSIAN SECRETARY TO THE BENGAL GOVERNMENT.

TO WHICH IS ADDED,

A HISTORY

OF THE

GENERAL BAPTIST MISSION

ESTABLISHED

IN THE PROVINCE.

BY JAMES PEGGS,

LATE MISSIONARY AT CUTTACK, ORISSA; AUTHOR OF "INDIA'S CRIES TO BRITISH HUMANITY," &c., &c.

LONDON:

PUBLISHED FOR THE AUTHOR, BY

JOHN SNOW, 35, PATERNOSTER ROW;

SOLD BY BROOKS, LEICESTER; NOBLE, BOSTON; NICHOLSON, HALIFAX.

1846.

PREFACE.

The first missionaries to a country are like the spies which Moses sent to "spy out the land of Canaan," and the writer has often been reminded of the language which Moses addressed to the persons engaged on that important occasion,—"Get you up this way southward, and go up into the mountain: and see the land what it is; and the people that dwell therein, whether they are strong or weak, few or many; and what the land is that they dwell in, whether it be good or bad, and what cities there are that they dwell in, whether in tents or strong holds; and what the land is, whether it be fat or lean; whether there be wood therein or not. And be ye of good courage and bring of the fruit of the land." Numb. xiii. 17—20. The General Baptist Missionary Society, which was formed in 1816, commenced its labours in Orissa in the early part of 1822, and the writer, who has long survived the first missionary, his beloved colleague, the Rev. W. Bampton, has for several years been desirous of laying before the friends of the Orissa Mission both in Britain and America, "the geography and statistics, history, religion, and antiquities of Orissa," with the History of its missionary operations during the first thirty years of its labours. Very few of the Ministers who were present, or living at the formation of the Society have been "allowed to remain by reason of death," and hence the propriety that this effort for "the generation that shall be" should not be long delayed.

It has been in contemplation for some years, by the Committee of the Society, to publish the interesting Account of Orissa by the late A. Sterling, Esq., and the Rev. J. G. Pike had revised it for that purpose, with additional information from Hamilton's Description of Hindostan, Col. Phipps' Description of Juggernaut's Temple, Festivals, &c., &c., but the apprehension of loss from its publication has prevented its appearance. Through the liberality of a few friends, particularly Joseph Sturge, Esq., B. L. Ward, Esq., the Rev. T. S. Grimshawe, W. Evans, Esq., M. P., and the late Sir T. F. Buxton, Bart., the writer has been encouraged to undertake the task, (to him a very delightful one,) of presenting the claims of the Orissa Mission to the present and to succeeding generations. Seeley, in his "Wonders of Elora," thus adverts to this Account and its talented Author,—"A very valuable Essay has lately been presented to the Asiatic Society, on the country about Cuttack and Pooree, by Mr. A. Sterling. This young man when I was at Cuttack, was Assistant to the Commissioner, W. Blunt, Esq. After having stood at the head of all the oriental classes at college, he was selected for an important post. The work has not yet reached England, and the parts in my possession are too long to be inserted: and I feel I should not do justice to the valuable matter by abridging it. I have been sitting with him (in 1821,) while he was conversing in three languages with some Natives of consequence, himself writing in Persian, dictating to a Native Secretary, and at intervals speaking to me, and occasionally giving orders. *The country entrusted to his sole care is probably larger than Ireland.*" An American writer says, "Posterity is eager for details." History supplies these details; and it may be said with peculiar propriety of the historian of a Christian mission, "*He being dead yet speaketh.*" Mr. Sutton's History of the Orissa Mission was prepared by him, aided by his excellent wife, during their voyage from India to America, in the early part of 1833, and was written for publication in America. At that period the brethren began to be cheered by "*the day-spring from on high visiting them, to give light to them that sit in darkness;*" but at this time, it shall be said with admiration and gratitude—"*What hath God wrought?*"

It is of great importance, that the claims of the Orissa Mission should be laid before the Ministers, Officers, and Members of the Churches which sustain it; and likewise the Teachers and youth in our Sabbath Schools, and the young in the families of our people. When Joshua was "old and stricken in years," he had to admonish his people, that "*there remained yet very much land to be possessed,*" saying, "*How long are ye slack to go to possess the land which the Lord God of your fathers hath given you?*" Thus in Orissa, in "*the length thereof, and in the breadth thereof,*" how "*much land yet remains to be possessed!*" More missionaries are required to bring the whole land under the cultivation of the gospel. Who can tell, but "*the God of the whole earth,*" may honour the perusal of this volume, by making it the instrument of stimulating some pious persons to consecrate themselves to the work of God in Orissa? It is designed to send at least one hundred volumes to India for gratuitous circulation, and the profits of the work are devoted to the Orphan Asylums in Orissa.

In conclusion, the writer would adopt the sentiments of an invalid Missionary, in his valuable publication,—"In visiting the churches, the vast importance and the urgent necessities of our Eastern Empire have constituted the great theme of his sermons and addresses; the deliverance of Hindoos from priestcraft and superstition is still the burden of his thoughts, his prayers, and his toils; and whether in the good providence of God he is directed to return to his field of labour, or is obliged to occupy a different sphere at home,—the claims, the welfare, and the conversion of India are bound up with his mortal existence, and must ever have a warm place in his heart. To the gracious care and blessing of that Master whom he desires to serve, the writer commends this attempt to advance the interests of his kingdom; and he hopes a Christian public will receive it, in the spirit of the gospel, as the effort of one who reckons it his highest honour to be a missionary to the heathen, a friend of humanity, and an advocate of the rights, the liberties, and the spiritual interests of India."

Burton-on-Trent, Staffordshire,
November 2nd, 1846.

CONTENTS.

APPENDIX.

REFERENCES TO THE ENGRAVINGS.

ORISSA:

ITS GEOGRAPHY, STATISTICS, HISTORY,

ETC., ETC.

CHAP. I.

Introductory Sketch by Hamilton—General Description—Boundaries Ancient and Modern—Soil—Productions—Geology—Rivers—Towns—Commerce.

ORISSA is a large Province of the Deccan extending from the 18th to the 22nd degree of north latitude. To the north it is bounded by Bengal; on the south by the river Godavery; on the east it has the bay of Bengal; and on the west the province of Gundwana. In length from N. E. to S. W. it may be estimated at 400 miles, by 70 the average breadth. According to the institutes of Akber, Orissa, in its greatest dimensions in 1582, was divided into five districts; viz. Jellasore, comprising Midnapore and the British possessions lying north and east of the river Subunreeka; Budruck; Cuttack; Culling or Cicacole; Rajamundry. Besides this territory on the sea coast, Orissa also comprehended a mountainous unproductive region on the western frontier, making part of the Jeharcund or jungly country, with the districts of Ruttunpoor and Sumbhulpoor; but the two latter properly belong to Gundwana. At present the principal modern territorial subdivisions, commencing from the north, are the following; but there are many other petty states and large zemindaries:—Singhboom, Kunjeur, Mohurbunge, Balasore, Cuttack, Khoordah.

The tracts composing the districts of Ganjam, Vizagapatam, and and a portion of Rajamundry, *are also included within the ancient limits of this Province*, but the five northern Circars have been long a separate jurisdiction. The interior of this province remains in a very savage state, being composed of rugged hills, uninhabited jungles, and deep water courses, surrounded by pathless deserts, forests, or valleys, and pervaded by a pestilential atmosphere. It forms a strong natural barrier to the maritime districts, being only traversed during the driest season, from February to May, by the Lumballies or inland carriers. There are only two passes, properly explored, in the whole length of the great mountainous ridge, extending from the Godavery to the Mahanuddy rivers; the one direct from Chanda to Cicacole; the other oblique from Choteesghur by way of Kalahinki; both uniting at the pass of Saloor or Sauracca. By this pass, during the French possession of the Northern Circars in 1754, a body of Maharattas were introduced; more than half perished from the noxious air of the hills, and the remainder, rather than return by so noxious a road, made a prodigious circuit south by Rajamundry and the Godavery. With such a barrier to the west, and the ocean to the east, the defence of Orissa does not appear difficult; the jealousies, however, of a people subdivided into many petty communities, the absence of civilization, added to the habitual indolence and apathy of the natives, ever rendered it an easy prey to invaders, and they have passed from one yoke to another with scarcely a struggle.

In ancient Hindoo history, Utcala or Udradesa was nearly coextensive with the modern Orissa, the name Utcla, or Udcala, implying the *great or famous country of Cala*. According to tradition, it was then inhabited by a powerful and martial race, who were extirpated by the Karnas or kings of Magadha (Behar.) In more recent times it was governed by a dynasty of Hindoo princes of the race of Gujaputty, who, in 1592, were conquered by Mansingh, the Emperor Akber's viceroy in Bengal; to which dominion it was then annexed as a dependant government, extending from Tumlook on the *Great Ganges* to Rajamundry on the Lesser Ganges, or *Gunga Godavery* of the Deccan. From the accounts of ancient European travellers, fragments of national history, and a few remnants of former splendour, it was probably, at least on the sea-coast, a flourishing country before the Mahommedan invasion, but soon after fell into a comparitive state of depression. It does not appear, however, that the Mahommedans, or any other invaders, ever completely occupied or colonized this province, which, *still remains one of those in which the Hindoo manners are preserved in their greatest purity, and where the smallest proportion of Mahommedans is to be found.* After the expulsion of the Afghans from the province of Bengal during the reign of the Emperor Akber, they retreated into Orissa, and retained possession of the maritime and more fertile portions, and also of the temple of Juggernauth, for many years.

At present *nearly one half* of this extensive region is under the immediate jurisdiction of the British government; the other possessed by tributary zemindars called Ghurjauts or hill chiefs, who mostly pay a fixed rent, and are under British protection, so far as refers to their external relations, and some few are directly amenable to the European courts of justice. The first division comprehends all the low lands trending along the coast; the second the hilly and woody interior. The British half is in general a plain, fertile, but not well cultivated or peopled; the native section is either a barren tract or wild expanse of rock forest, and jungle, thinly inhabited, yet producing a surplus of grain beyond the consumption of its inhabitants. The inhabitants of the first may be estimated at 100 to the square mile; of the second not more than 30 to the same area. The principal articles of produce and manufacture in the British portion are *rice and salt.* The last, although a monopoly, affords much employment to the inhabitants on the coast; the former is the staple commodity of the province, and is so abundant as to admit of exportation. Every sort of grain and vetch is cultivated, and the common manufactures suffice for the frugal habits of the natives. Under such circumstances, and with a mild government, it is highly probable this division of the province is undergoing gradual amelioration, and that the inhabitants, although ignorant of the cause, are gradually advancing in the process of civilization. The tributary part of the province presents the reverse of this picture, a great proportion being unfit for culture, and the lots, under cultivation yielding but a scanty return. In the wilder tracts the necessaries of life are not attainable, and frequently subsistence of any sort is only procurable with the utmost difficulty. Many of the natives are iron smelters and charcoal burners; others make a livelihood by boat building and the felling of timber, thus *protracting a miserable existence under the iron rod of their rapacious chiefs, in whose eyes to be wealthy, or even comfortable, is criminal.*

The territories along the bay of Bengal are subject to frequent hurricanes, which greatly injure the farmer; and the lowlands, in spite of embankments, liable to ruinous inundations from the sudden overflowing of rivers. The buffaloes are a fine large breed, and supply the natives with milk and ghee; but the oxen are of a very inferior description, and the horses mere carrion. The low lands abound with hogs, deer, tigers, and jackals; and the highlands are infested by wild beasts in such numbers, that *they are in many places, regaining the country which had been wrested from them by human cunning and combination!* The rivers and waters swarm with fish, reptiles, and alligators; the plains and jungles with winged vermin. The chief rivers are the Godavery, the Mahanuddy, and the Subunreeka, besides innumerable hill streams of a short course, and small channel. The principal towns are, *Cuttack*, *Juggernauth*, *Ganjam*, and *Vizagapatam*.

The country between the rivers Gaintu and Bamoni is one of the finest parts of the province, and is inhabited by a considerable number of weavers, chiefly of coarse muslins for turbans; sanaes are also a staple manufacture. The best bamboos for palanquins come from the pergunnahs of Tolchan and Hindole. They grow near the summit of the rocks, and spring in July, when the people who collect them, having selected the strongest shoots, tie them to stakes driven into the ground, and thus direct their growth to the proper shape. In this manner they grow from ten to twenty yards long, by the setting in of the dry season, when their tops are cut off. If suffered to stand longer, the hollow part increases, and they become weaker.

Some of the native Ooreas in the back parts of this province still retain their semi-barbarous manners, are a fierce people, and possess a considerable degree of personal courage. They commonly go armed with bows and arrows, or swords; the latter being generally carried naked, and are of a shape which is broad at the end, and narrow in the middle. Between them and the Maharattas a rooted antipathy has long existed. The Ooreas within the British territories, having been long accustomed to peaceful, inoffensive habits, are good cultivators, and tolerably industrious, their chief characteristic being an effeminate timidity accompanied by much low cunning and dissimulation. The great body of them are Hindoos, distinguished into the castes usually found in other parts of Hindostan. In a specimen of the Lord's prayer in the Orissa or Utcala language, examined by the missionaries, thirty-one of the words could be traced as being the same with those used in the Bengalee translation of that prayer; but notwithstanding its close affinity to the Bengalee, its peculiar terminations cause the whole specimen to differ much in sound.*

* Hamilton's Hindostan, vol. ii. pp. 31-4.

The extent and boundaries of Orissa have undergone many changes at different periods of its history, and remain to this day very ill-defined and imperfectly understood. The corresponding Puranic division of Utkala Desa or in the vulgar tongue Utkal K'hand reached on the north to Tumlook and Midnapore, taking in a portion of Rarha Des in Bengal, and south to the Rasikulia or Rasikoila Nadi which flows into the sea at Ganjam. On the east it was bounded by the ocean and the river Hoogly, and on the west by Sonpur, Bunay, and other dependencies of Sumbulpoor and Gondwana. *Or Desa*, or *Oresa*, the old original seat of the *Or* or *Odra* tribe, had anciently less extended limits, the Rasikulia river marking its southern and the Kans Bans which passes near Soro, in latitude about 21°. 10'. N. its northern extreme; but in the progress of migration andconquest, the *Oreah* nation carried their name and language over a vast extent of territory, both on the sea shore and in the hills, including besides Orissa properly so called, a portion of Bengal and of Telingana. During the sway of the Princes of the Ganga Vasa line, for a period of nearly *four centuries*, the boundaries of the Raj or kingdom of Orissa may be stated as follows, with sufficient accuracy for a general description. *North*, a line drawn from the Tribeni or Terveni ghat above Hoogly, through Bishenpur to the frontier of Patkum; *east*, the river Hoogly and the sea; *south*, the Godaveri or Ganja Godaveri; and *west*, a line carried from Sinhbhum to Sonepur, skirting Gangpur, Sumbulpoor and its dependencies, and thence through Bastar to Jayapur, and the Godaveri. Thus in the more prosperous days of the Orissan monarchy, and that too at no very remote period, it comprised within its limits four of our modern zillahs entire, and portions of three others, viz. Midnapore, Cuttack, Ganjam, and Vizagapatam, with parts of the Jungle Mehals, Hoogly, and Rajamundry, besides a portion of the hills and woodland country of Gondwana. The degree of authority exercised by the sovereign power throughout this extensive territory, fluctuated of course greatly at different periods, depending on the personal character of the reigning Prince, the circumstances of the times, and the conduct, resources, and dispositions of the numerous dependant Rajas and feudatories, whose principalities or jurisdictions have at all times formed so remarkable and important a feature in the political geography of Orissa. Occasionally the conquests of the Gajapati Princes extended into the more remote parts of Telingana, and even to the Carnatic, but it appears that they never obtained a firm footing in any acquisitions, South of the Godaveri, and during the last century of their independence, their possession even of Rajamundry was much contested and disturbed by the Bahmini sovereigns of the Deccan. One of the first arrangements of the ministers of Akber on annexing Orissa to the Dewani of the Mogul empire, was to join Hoogly and its ten dependant Mehals, to Bengal. The Mogul Subah of Orissa then comprised the whole country stretching from Tumlook and Midnapore on the north, to the fort of Rajamundry south, divided into the five unequally apportioned Sircars, called Jellasore, Budruck, Cuttack, Calinga, Dundpat, and Rajamundry. The vast range of hilly country bounding the Subah to the westward, from Bishenpur down to the neighbourhood of Karronde, Bastar and Jayapur, was classed under a separate head in the revenue accounts of the empire, and was allowed for many years after the Mahommedan conquest, to remain entirely under the management of its native Chiefs, subject either to the condition of military service or to the payment of a light quit rent. Very early after the settlemennt of the Emperor Akber, if not indeed at the moment of its formation, the Circar of Rajamundry and that portion of Kalinga Des which lies south of Tikali Raghunat'hpur were dismembered from Orissa, by the successful encroachments of the Mahommedan Kings of Golconda, called the Kutteb Shahis, but of this event, no distinct account is given in the history of the country. At the opening of Mahommed Tacki Khan's administration, A. D. 1726, who governed as the Naib or Deputy of the Nazim of three provinces, the most authentic Revenue records exhibit the Subah of Orissa as extending from Radha Dewal seven coss beyond the town of Midnapore to Tikali* Raghunat'hpur, one of the estates in or near the Mahendra Mali range of hills in Ganjam, a computed distance 176 coss, and on the west from the sea at False Point to the Bermul Pass, 85 coss. Before the close of his government its limits had become much reduced. The Officers of the Nizam of Hyderabad intriguing with the powerful Zemindars of the Ganjam district, contrived to alienate from the Province the whole of the country south of the Chilka Lake. On the Bengal side, views of financial convenience induced the Nawab Shuja Uddin Mahommed Khan to annex the mehals included in the old Jellasore Circar, as far as the Subunreekha, to the territory immediately dependent on the Moorshedabad Government with the exception of Pergunnahs

* Mr. Grant in his Political Survey of the Northern Circars calls this place "Teckaly or Rogonaut'hpore on the sea coast 43 miles N. E. from Cicacole, the inheritance of Juggut Deo another descendant of the royal family of Orissa but more immediately branching from that of Kimedy."

Pattaspur, &c. It was bounded by the Subunreekha and Pergunnah Pattaspur, &c. north, and by the Chilka Lake on the south ; East, by the ocean, and west by the Bermul Pass, that Orissa was relinquished to the Berar Mahrattas, by the famous Aliverdi Khan in A. D. 1755-6 in lieu of the sums which he had stipulated to pay as Chouth : and it is to this tract, the modern zillah of Cuttack, which may not inaccurately be called *Orissa Proper* from its comprising the ancient original country of the Uria or Odra nation, and from the circumstance of its retaining amongst the natives of the present day the exclusive appellation of *Or Desa* or *Oresa*, that the following description is intended chiefly to apply.

The Purans and Upapurans are lavish in their praises of *Utkal K'hand*, "The famous portion or country," and not, the famous country of Kala, as rendered by a very high authority. It is declared to be the favourite abode of the Debtas, and to boast a population composed, *more than half, of Brahmins.* The work called the Kapila Sanhita, in which Bharadwaja Muni explains to his inquiring pupils, the origin, history, and claims to sanctity of all the remarkable *Khetrs* or holy places of Orissa, opens with the following panegyric: "Of all the regions of the earth Bharata K'hand is the most distinguished, and of all the countries of Bharata K'hand, Utkala boasts the highest renown. *Its whole extent is one uninterrupted Tirt'h* (place of pilgrimage!) Its happy inhabitants live secure of a reception into the world of spirits, and those who even visit it, and bathe in its sacred rivers, obtain remission of their sins, though they may weigh like mountains. Who shall describe adequately its sacred streams, its temples, its khetrs, its fragrant flowers and fruits of exquisite flavor, and all the merits and advantages of a sojourn in such a land? What necessity indeed can there be for enlarging in the praises of a region, which the Debtas themselves delight to inhabit?" The Annalists of Orissa are fond of relating, that when the famous Sivai Jay Sinh, the General of Akber, marched with an army into the country in A. D. 1530, he was struck with amazement at the sight of its sacred river Mahanadi, its vast crowds of Brahmins, its lofty temples of stone, and all the wonders of the ancient capital Bhuvaneswar, and exclaimed, "This country is not a fit subject for conquest, and schemes of human ambition. It belongs wholly to the gods, and is one entire Tirt'h." He accordingly interfered little in its affairs and soon returned to Hindustan, leaving a large share of authority in the hands of its Native Princes. The importance of establishing Christianity in a country so highly esteemed by the inhabitants of Hindostan, must strike every intelligent and pious mind.

The Hindus of modern times however, freely admit, that the estimation in which Orissa is or was held, is to be ascribed entirely to its temples, places of pilgrimage, and its brahminical institutions. At all events, the European observer will soon discover, that notwithstanding its puranic celebrity, the soil of the country is generally poor and unfruitful, all its natural productions of an inferior quality, and that its inhabitants rank the lowest, in the scale of moral and intellectual excellence, of any people on this side of India. This circumstance may probably be ascribed to the debasing influence of idolatry on a country so peculiarly devoted to its baneful sway.

Modern Orissa or Cuttack, comprises, as is well known, an extensive, imperfectly explored region, on the west, consisting chiefly of hills and forests, intersected by many fertile plains and valleys; and a plain level country, extending from the foot of that barrier to the sea, evidently of alluvial formation, the uniform surface of which is not disturbed by a single rocky elevation throughout its whole extent—nor does a single stone occur between the beds of iron clay lying on the western frontier, and the ocean, if we except the curious spheroidal concretions of calcareous matter or limestone nodules which are found very generally dispersed. The Province may be considered as divided both naturally and politically into *three regions*, distinguished from each other by their climate, general aspect, productions, and the institutions prevailing in them, viz: The *marshy woodland tract* which extends along the sea shore, from the black Pagoda to the Subunreekha river, varying in breadth from five miles to twenty: the *plain and open country* between this and the hills, whose breadth on the north is about ten or fifteen miles, and never exceeds forty or fifty; and the *hill country*. The first and third are known to the natives as the Eastern and Western Rajwara or Zemindara,* that is, the country occupied by the ancient feudal Chieftains or Poligars† of Orissa; and the second, as the Mogulbundi, from which the native sovereigns and the Mogul conquerors of the country derived the chief part of their land revenue, and which at present pays a revenue to the British Government of Sicca Rupees 1,264,370; whilst the tribute yielded by the other extensive portions is fixed in perpetuity at Sicca Rupees 1,20,411.‡

* The Zemindars are landholders—Zemindara or Zemindares, the estates of such landholders.

† The Poligars are small tributary landholders in the south of India, who were never thoroughly subdued by the Mahommedans.

‡ Khurda belongs to the Rajwara, but is at present under the immediate management of the English Revenue Officers, and is not included in this statement of Land Revenue.

It will be convenient to describe the *soil*, *productions*, and *geological* formation of the country in the order just noticed.

The first region has much of the character of the Sunderbands, in its swamps and marshes, innumerable winding streams swarming with alligators, its dense jungles and noxious atmosphere; but wants entirely that grandeur of forest scenery, which diversifies and gives a romantic character to many parts of the latter. The broadest part of it is divided amongst the Rajas* of Kanka and Kujang, and the Khandaits of Herrispur, Merichpur, Bishenpur, Golra, and others of less note. The Killah or Zemindari estate of Al likewise comes in for a share. Northward of Kanka the quantity of jungle diminishes up to the neighbourhood of Balasore, but the whole space is intersected by numberless nullahs which deposit, and creeks which retain, a quantity of fine mud, forming morasses and quicksands highly dangerous to the unwary or uninformed traveller. The surface of the whole is covered with coarse reedy grass, and brushwood, valuable as fuel to the salt manufacturers. Much of the Jhao or Tamarix Indica is interspersed with quantities of a stunted dwarf Palm, called Hintal (Phœnix Paludosa.) Generally, where pure sand appears, more especially about the black Pagoda, the surface of it is covered with a thick net work, formed by the interlaced stalks of a creeping convolvulus, with succulent leaves, which are for half the year loaded with large gay looking flowers of a bright reddish purple. The natives call it Kynsarilata. A delicate succulent plant with small bright green leaves growing thickly together, is also very common; and the summits of the sand hills are for the most part crowned with tufts of the Asclepias Gigantea and a stiff thorny gramineous plant known by the name of Goru Kanta. The prevailing timber is the Sundari. Extensive thickets of the thorny bamboo render travelling impracticable in most parts of Kujang, Herrispur, &c., except by water. The whole of the jungles abound with leopards, tigers, and wild buffaloes, and the rivers at the flowing of the tide are perfectly surcharged with large and voracious alligators of the most dangerous kind. The climate seems to be hurtful even to the natives, who are peculiarly subject to two formidable diseases, the *Elephantiasis*, and a species of dysentery called the *Sul*, besides the more common complaints of *fever* and *ague*.

In this wild inhospitable tract however *the finest salt of all India is manufactured*, which under the monopoly system, yields annually to the Government a net revenue little short of *eighteen lacs of*

* Raja, a king, prince, chieftain.

rupees. The produce, distinguished for its whiteness and purity before it has passed into the hands of the merchants, is of the species called Pangah procured by boiling. The process observed by the Molunghees or manufacturers is rude and simple in the last degree. The sea-water which is brought up by various small channels to the neighbourhood of the manufacturing stations, is first mixed and saturated with a quantity of the salt earth, which forms on the surface of the low ground all around, after it has been overflowed by the high tides; and which being scraped off by the Molunghees, is thrown into cylindrical receptacles of earth having a vent underneath, and a false bottom made of twigs and straw. The strongly impregnated brine filtering through the grass, &c., is carried, by a channel dug in the ground, to a spot at hand, surrounded with an enclosure of mats, in the centre of which a number of oblong earthern pots, generally about two hundred, are cemented by mud into the form of a dome, under which is a fire place or oven. The brine is poured into this collection of pots, and boiled until a sufficient degree of evaporation has taken place, when the salt is taken out as it forms, with iron ladles, and collected in heaps in the open air. The heaps are afterwards thatched with reeds, and remain in this state until sold, or removed by the officers of the agency.

Occasional patches of rice cultivation are to be met with in this portion of the Rajwara producing sufficient grain for local consumption, and the Raja of Kanka exports a considerable quantity both to Calcutta and Cuttack. The sea all along the coast of the bay of Bengal yields *abundance of fine fish*, of which upwards of *sixty-one* edible kinds are enumerated, by the natives. Those most prized by Europeans are the *Sole* or Banspatti, *Tapsiya* (Mango Fish,) *Phirki* (Pomfret,) *Gajkarma* (Whiting,) *Hilsa* (Sable Fish,) *Kharanga* or *Mullet*, a fish called the *Bijay Ram* something resembling Mackerel, and the *Sal* or Salia. The Chilka Lake produces noble *Bhekti* or Cockup. The value of the excellent *Turtle*, *Oysters*, *Crabs*, and *Prawns*, found off *False Point*, and in other parts, was unknown to the natives prior to their subjection to the British rule, but they are now of course eagerly sought after, to supply the stations of Balasore, Cuttack, and Juggernauth. The great season for fishing is in the winter months, from October to February, whilst the wind and the surf are moderate. At this time all along the northern coast the fishermen go out in parties of from twenty to thirty each, with large nets, which they set up before the commencement of flood tide, with the aid of bamboo poles, in the form of a vast triangle, having the base open towards the shore. As the tide retires the fishermen take in and close up the nearest nets, thus driving the fish into the apex of the triangle where there is a net placed with a large pouch ready for their reception. The quantity obtained at a haul in this way is often prodigious. The produce is taken to the neighbouring villages for sale, after reserving a sufficiency for home consumption; and a large quantity travels far into the interior, unprepared in any way, which it of course reaches in the last stage of putridity, but not on that account a bit the less palatable or acceptable to the nice and scrupulous Hindu.

On emerging from the insalubrious and uninteresting tract just described, you arrive at the second and most important division of Orissa, called the Mogulbandi, which is divided into 150 Pergunnahs, and 2361 estates of individuals, recorded in the public account of the British Government as Zemindars and proprietors of the soil. Though this region in general is highly cultivated, and produces most of the grains and vegetables common in Bengal, its soil is certainly for the most part of a poor and unfruitful description. South of the Mahanuddy it may be characterised as generally light and sandy. Beyond that river, and especially in the neighbourhood of the hills, it acquires a clayey consistency, and appearance, and is often remarkably white. Often too, for miles together it has the surface strewed with a thin sprinkling of gravel or limestone concretions, called by the natives Gengti. This description of soil extends nearly to Midnapore. It is generally speaking unproductive, particularly near the hills; and large plains occur, as about Dhamnager and Budruck, which are wholly unfit for cultivation, growing nothing but low stunted brushwood, chiefly the wild Corunda and tufts of the Bena grass.

Rice is the great article of produce, and consequently of food, throughout Orissa Proper. In the Pergunnahs north of the Byterini river, it is almost the sole object of agricultural labour. The grain is in general large and nutritious, but coarse, and is considered far inferior to the average produce of Bengal and Behar. The two great rice crops of Cuttack are called the *Sared* and *Beali*. Of these the first and principal is sown in May, and June, and reaped from the middle of November to the middle of January. The land which grows it rarely yields a second crop. The second in importance called the *Beali* is sown about the same time on the higher lands, and the produce is obtained from the end of August till the end of September. Afterwards a plentiful crop of the *Rubbee* grains is derived from the same fields. There is another less abundant crop called *Satkia*, put into the ground in August and September, and reaped in November; and an inferior description of rice which is sown in low marshy spots at the opening of the cold weather, and by frequent transplantation and irrigation is rendered fit for cutting, in the following April. The cultivation of the latter sort called *Dalo*, takes place chiefly in the Pergunnahs between Khurdah, the Chilka Lake and the sea.

In the northern Pergunnahs the Sared rice cultivation is occasionally but rarely diversified with a few patches of Sugar-cane, Tobacco, and Palma Christi, in spots suited to their production. In the Central and Southern parts however, abundant crops of pulse, millet, and vegetable oils, are raised during the cold weather. Next to rice, the culture of the Arend or Palma Christi is perhaps the most abundant. The natives use the oil in their common cookery, mixed with a small quantity of mustard seed oil, which latter they prefer for burning as being the most economical. Cotton, Sugar-cane, and Tobacco, are every where common South of the Byterini, but the produce is of a poor description. The richer natives will not condescend to use the *Desi* Tambaku and the cotton formerly required for the manufacture of the finer fabrics was nearly all imported from Berar. Good wheat and a small quantity of barley are grown in Pergunnahs Saibir and Asseresser. There is but little of the vegetables producing materials for dyeing, cordage, &c., reared in the district, the *Safflower*, *Pat* (Hibiscus Cannabinus,) and *Kasmira* or *Sana* (Crotolarea Juncea,) being the only kinds that are commonly met with. The culture of the Poppy, Mulberry, and Indigo, is unknown in the plains of Orissa. Nor, were the peasantry acquainted with the method of cultivating the Betle vine, until taught by the natives of Bengal some generations back. The Piper Betle now flourishes in the gardens around Pooree and in the neighbourhood of a few Brahmin villages, but the produce can be adequate only to the supply of a very limited consumption, notwithstanding the assertion of the author of the work called the *Ayeen Akberi*, or Institutes of Akber, that "they have a great variety of the Betle leaf in Orissa." The spots which are destined for the cultivation of Betle as also of Turmeric, Sugar-cane, &c., require laborious preparation and the application of a large quantity of manure, for which latter purpose the oil cake or Pire made of the refuse of the sesamum, mustard, and other seeds of the same family is generally used. An occasional sprinkling of rotten straw, cow-dung, and ashes, is the only manure expended in the fields which yield the other kinds of produce.

Orissa has little to boast in the produce of its *gardens*, though praised by Abulfazl for the excellence and abundance of its fruit and flowers. There is no deficiency however of the humbler kinds of pot herbs, and cucurbitaceous plants, with the *Hibiscus esculentus*, the *egg plant*, the *sweet potatoe*, and *Capsicum annuum*. The native lists likewise comprise most of the ordinary garden produce of India. The more common fruits are as elsewhere, the *Mango*, the *Phalsa*, the *Jam*, the *Guava*, *Custard Apple*, the *Harphaleri*, the *Chalta*, the *Kendhu*, the *Pomegranate*, the *Cashewnut*, the *Jack*, the *Bel*, the *Kath-Bel* or *Wood Apple*, and the *Kharanj*, from whose fruit an oil is extracted, used for burning by the natives. The *Wine palm* and the *Khajur* abound in particular quarters. We rarely meet with the *Cocoanut* and *Supari* except near Brahmin villages, though they would thrive every where in Cuttack, more especially the former. In all times Cuttack has been famous for its abundant produce of the fragrant *Keora* or Ketaca (Pandanus Odoratissimus.) It grows every where wild, and is much used, jointly with several kinds of Euphorbia and Mimosa, for making hedge-rows. The fruit borne in quantities by the female plant has much of the rich and tempting appearance of the pine apple, but the inside proves to be hard, stringy, and tasteless. Its pith is used when boiled, as an article of food by the poorest classes, but seems to be little prized even by them. An intoxicating spirit is distilled from the strongly scented flowers of the male plant, to which the lower orders have no aversion.

The surface of the Mogulbandi is in most parts south of the Kans Bans embellished and diversified with fine shadowy groves of *Mangos*, dense thickets of *Bamboo*, and the most magnificent *Banyan trees*. The better cvltivated gardens are loaded with *Jessamines*, *Sambacks*, *Marigolds*, *Bauhinias*, the *Hibiscus*, *China Rose*, *Michelia Champaca*, &c. About the huts of the natives we generally find in great quantities the *Hyperanthera Morunga*, *Melia azadirachta* and *Sempervirens*, *Æschynomene Sesban*, and grandiflora, the *Bombax Heptaphyllum*, *Nauclea* orientalis, &c., with the usual proportion of *Plaintains*.

The inferior quality and limited growth of many of the most valuable products of agriculture in Orissa, are owing in a great degree to something unfavourable in the soil and climate, is clearly evinced by the indifferent success attending the efforts of the European residents in gardening. Much however must be ascribed to the general poverty, ignorance, and want of enterprize of its peasantry and agriculturists. No one can enter the enclosures of the

Villages held at a light quit rent by colonies of a particular class of Brahmins, without being instantly struck with the wide difference, which their precincts exhibit, as contrasted with the aspect of ordinary Ooreah villages. The higher description of cultivation which prevails on those lands, the superior value of their produce, and the flourishing groves and gardens which extend all around, evince what may be effected by intelligent industry, secured in the enjoyment of an adequate return and undisputed proprietary possession, even in this little favoured soil and climate. It is in such situations only and in the neighbourhood of some of the well endowed temples, that the eye of the botanist is gratified by the presence of those graceful trees and plants, which constitute the chief ornament of the Indian Flora, such as the Nagacesara (Mesua Ferrea,) the Moulsari (Mimusops Elengi,) the Jonesia Asoca, the Ochna Squarrosa, the Sultan Champa or Calophyllum Inophyllum, the Jarool, (Lagerstrœmia Flos Reginœ,) and the finer kinds of Ixora, interspersed with Cocoa and Areca nut trees, and plantations of the betle vine, turmeric, and ginger. The Sasan Brahmins indeed are the only land proprietors of Orissa, who manifest any symptoms of a disposition to improve their system of agriculture, or to raise any plant or produce beyond what the wants of nature absolutely demand.

The *Domestic Animals* do not rank higher in the scale of excellence than the produce of its soil. The *horned cattle, sheep,* and *goats,* are a miserable diminutive breed. A few fine *buffaloes* are domesticated on the eastern frontier for the sake of their milk, but they are not at all used as beasts of burden. There is little *Game* to be met with, excepting *grey partridges, hares, snipes, jungle fowl,* and *ducks* of various kinds, and that little is difficult to be obtained from the nature of the jungle. Few districts in India perhaps possess fewer attractions for the sportsman. The mention of the wild animals will more properly come under the description of the hill portion of the district.

The third region to be described is that of the *Hills* which bound the Mogulbandi to the westward from the Chilka Lake to the Subunreekha river. A few groups extend into the plains, as at Derpen, Alemgir, Khurdah, Limbai, &c. In latitude about 21° 20' N. the hills take a direction considerably to the eastward for some miles, then turning north they compress the Balasore Chucklah within very narrow limits. The distance between the high land and the sea is no where more than from *sixty to seventy miles.* At Balasore a group of fine rocky hills project boldly forth, to within sixteen or eighteen miles of the shores of the bay of Bengal, which were known to the old navigators as the Nilgiri mountains, and between Ganjam and the Lake a low ridge appears actually to run out into the sea, though in reality separated from its waters by a wide sandy beach. The whole of this region, reaching west as far as Sonepur, Gondwana, and its Dependencies, in breadth about one hundred miles, and from Sinhbhum adjoining Midnapore, north, to Goomsur in Ganjam south, a distance of certainly not less than two hundred miles, is, *parcelled out amongst sixteen Khetri or Khandait Zemindars,* who have been recognized by the British Government as tributary Rajas. They mostly pay a fixed rent, and are under British protection as to their external relations. Along the feet of the hills extends *a chain of twelve more Khundaitis* held by a similar class, some of whom pay a light tribute, but are subject to the British laws and regulations, whilst others have been assessed at the ordinary rate. Their estates or feudal jurisdictions are entered in the revenue accounts, under the Mogul designation of Killah* or castle. The greater killahs within the hills, are subdivided again into a vast number of dependant Gerhs or estates, which are held by hereditary officers, called Khandaits, Dulbrehras, Naiks, subordinate to the chief Zemindar.

The hills visible from the low country between the Brahmani river and Ganjam, are chiefly a granite formation remarkable for its resemblance to sandstone, and for its containing vast quantities† of imperfectly formed garnets disseminated throughout, with veins of steatite considerably indurated. They occur generally in irregular scattered groups, having peaked summits, which seem to cross each other at all angles; or in isolated conical and wedge-shaped hills wholly disconnected at their bases, and are all covered with vegetation to the very top. The greatest height of those seen from the Mogulbandi may be about 2,000 feet. Their ordinary elevation varies from 300 to 1200 feet. Ranges occur further in the interior of greater loftiness and regularity, but I believe that an extended,

* The original meaning of *Killa* was a fort or strong place *on a hill* or mountain, though in latter times it has become applied to all kinds of places of defence. The class of estates here referred to always comprized some strong hold, difficult of access, and more or less fortified. The term properly designating the principal residence of the chief, gradually became applied to his whole country in the revenue accounts.

† Having enjoyed an opportunity of submitting an extensive collection of Cuttack specimens to the examination of Mr. H. Voysey, Surgeon and Geologist to Col. Lambton's survey, I am enabled by his assistance to express myself with some confidence in the little which I have to offer regarding the mineralogy of the province.

continuous chain of mountains is no where to be met with in the Rajwara of Orissa. The prevailing colour of the principal rock is red. As far as my observation goes it never occurs stratified. Its texture often approaches to slaty, and from its generally decomposed aspect, the quantity of red spots which it contains, being the ill-formed garnets above noticed, and the frequent veins of red and white steatite intersecting it, it presents altogether a most remarkable appearance. The same rock I apprehend extends throughout the Northern Circars and far into the Deccan.

The rock most abounding in this division of the Province next to the granite, is that singular substance called Iron Clay by Jamieson, and Laterite by Dr. Buchanan. It lies in beds of considerable depth on the feet of the granite hills, often advancing out for a distance of ten or fifteen miles into the plains, where it forms gently swelling rocky elevations, but never rises into hills ; sometimes it is disposed in the manner of flat terraces of considerable dimensions which look as if they had been constructed with much labour and skill. The composition and aspect of the Cuttack iron clay are very remarkable, from the innumerable pores which it contains, filled with white and yellow lithomarge, and from the quantities of iron ore pebbles and fragments of quartz imbedded in it. By far the most interesting circumstance is, its complete and intimate mixture with the granite, which has been traced in several instances, exhibiting one rock entirely invested by the other, though it is not easy to pronounce which is the inclosing substance. We have here an instance of a rock of the Wernerian newest Fœtz trap formation, resting upon the oldest primitive rock and in actual junction with it. The granite, at the place where the specimens were principally collected, appears to burst through an immense bed of the laterite, rising abruptly at a considerable angle. Numerous broken fragments are strewed all around the line of junction, and in some specimens the two rocks are so mixed as to form a sort of coarse breccia or rather conglomerate.

South of the Mahanuddy, in Khurda, a few isolated hills of white and variegated sandstone occur, curiously interspersed among the granitic ones. An indurated white lithormage is found in company with them from which the natives prepare a white wash to ornament their houses.

In the estates of Keonjher, Nilgiri, and Moherbenj, which constitute the northern portion of the hilly division of the Cuttack Province, the half decomposed granite above described passes into fine white granite and gneiss rocks containing micaceous hornblende as a constituent part, many of which differ little in composition and general appearance from specimens collected on the highest accessible summits of the Himalaya mountains. The whole of the region now adverted to, furnishes a great variety of valuable mineral productions, and is well worthy of attentive exploration by a geologist qualified to describe adequately its most striking features and peculiarities. The granitic rocks are here highly indurated and destitute of vegetation, and present a bold and varied outline with frequent sharp peaks and abrupt craggy faces. They are moreover in many parts curiously intersected by trap veins, which seem to consist chiefly of green stone approaching often to basalt and hornblende rock. In company with these rocks, talc slate, mica slate, and chlorite shist passing into serpentine and pot stone, are found in great abundance. Several of the chlorites are scarcely distinguishable from the latter mineral, and are much used under the general denomination of Mugni, for the manufacture of culinary vessels, *idols*, and sculptured slabs which decorate the temples and finer edifices of the Oreahs. The granites and gneiss rocks being too hard for the tools of the quarriers in this quarter, and the shists, with the exception of the chlorite, not being of a description applicable to any useful purposes, the natives have adopted a very summary and comprehensive geological classification. They style the Mugni, *karma*, or useful, and all other rocks they banish into the class of *akarma*, or useless; concerning the situation and history of which they are as provokingly indifferent as they are ignorant. Besides the substances above enumerated, a variety of corundum, or *corund*, is found in the Nilgiri hills, called by the quarriers *Sila Dhar*, which as the name implies, is used for sharpening their tools; also steatite, and Meerschaum in the state of a remarkably pure white powder, occur abundantly in Keonjher. The natives know no use for the latter substance, except to form the *tika* or *streaks which particular classes draw on their foreheads.**

Iron is abundantly diffused throughout the whole of the Cuttack hills, in the state chiefly of pisiform iron ore, earthy red ditto, and ochry red ironstone. It is smelted principally in the estates of Dhenkanal, Angol, and Moherbenj. Some of the rivers of Dhenkanal and Keonjher are said to have golden sands, but the report

* This custom gives the natives a ridiculous appearance. It has been remarked of the late Mr. Ward, of Serampore, that when Hindoos came to him thus disfigured, he has sent them away to wash themselves before he would do business with them. The Author's Pundit one day asked a Native in his study, whether a bird had dirtied his forehead. The laugh naturally turned against the man.

wants confirmation, and I have not been able to ascertain the existence of any metal except iron in this Province. The only *limestones* are the calcareous nodules which occur abundantly in beds and nests, both within the hills and in the open country adjoining them, consisting of a ball of tolerably pure limestone enveloped in a yellowish coating of indurated marl.

The Hill estates vary much in the proportion of arable land which they contain, but, in most, a considerable quantity of rice is grown, and a few of the rubbee grains. In patches of jungle which have been recently cleared, and on the slopes of some of the minor hills, the Jowar and Bajera and the Mandia *(Eleusine Corocana,)* thrive with great luxuriance. Moherbenj, Beramba, Dhenkanal, and Keonjher, grow a small quantity of *indigo*, and on the latter estate the *poppy* is cultivated. Keonjher (during the expedition against the Coles,) was found to be for nearly one hundred miles, an open cultivated country only occasionally interrupted by ridges of hills and patches of jungle. Generally speaking, the land fit for tillage bears a very trifling proportion to the vast extent of rocks, hills, beds of torrents, and forests which occupy this region.

The woods of the interior produce abundance of *fine timber*. A few teak trees are found in Despalla, but that valuable timber does not form forests nearer than the banks of the Tel river which flows into the Mahanuddy at Sonepur. The Sal trees of Angol, Dhenkanal, and Moherbenj, are particularly sought after from their size. They are said to form forests of great depth and grandeur, throughout a large porportion of the latter estate. Good Oranges and Mangos are produced in many of the hill estates. The *Mango* tree occurs frequently in situations where it is obviously growing wild, and the natives are fond of ascribing the existence of this highly esteemed fruit, under such circumstances, to the benevolence or caprice of the debtas or gods.

The trees seldom attain to a large height or luxuriant growth in the decomposed soil covering the granitic hills, which border the Mogulbandi, or in the woods that stretch along their bases. The jungles in the latter situations abound to a remarkable degree with trees and plants yielding drugs and medicinal articles,* or at least fruits esteemed such by the natives. The following trees likewise very commonly occur, viz., Asin (Pentaptera tomentosa,) Geringa, a species of Pterospermum, Lodh, (query, Phyllanthus Longifolius?) Patali (Bignonia Suaveolens), besides the steady

* In Rennell's MS. of Orissa, the names of 265 medicinal plants are given, the virtues of which are much extolled by the Natives.

companions of all Indian sylvan scenery, the *Tamarind, Mango, Bamboo, Bur*, and *Peepul* (Ficus Indica and Religiosa.) The produce of the above trees is collected by the wild inhabitants of the jungles for sale in the Cuttack market, by which traffic chiefly they gain a livelihood. A gigantic climbing Bauhinia forms a very conspicuous object in these woods. The name given by the natives is Siahri. The leaves are much used for thatching their miserable huts, and the fibres of the bark serve to bind down the thatch, and to make mats. The fruit is a huge legume of a wooden consistency, containing from four to six round flat seeds, which have a sweetish pleasant taste not unlike the flavour of almonds, and are eaten with great relish by the hill people. Amongst the underwood one observes, in great quantities, several species of Mimosas, Euphorbias, and Justicias, the Jataopha Curcas, Capparis trifoliata, a Cassia with a pale yellow flower, the wild Corunda which at most times of the year is loaded with delicate white blossoms, the Samalu, and a vast number of thorny shrubs, which probably have never yet been honoured with a name and place in any system of botany. It is remarkable, that *the natives have a name for almost every plant, however humble or devoïd of beauty;* which may arise perhaps from the circumstance of their consuming the wild berries and fruits, to a very great extent, in aid of their limited means of subsistence. The Calamas Rotang, or ground Cane, is every where common, and seems in many parts to form a sort of nucleus, about which the other brushwood and jungle collect in small patches. During the hot months and the rains the rich and gaudy flowers of the Capparis trifoliata, called by the natives Baran, and the scarlet blossoms of the Palas (Butea frondosa,) interspersed with quantities of the Gloriosa superba, which grows quite wild, lend an air of splendour even to these cheerless and uninviting tracts of jungle. In the cold weather they receive another brilliant tinge of colouring from a parasitical plant the Loranthus Bicolor, of scarlet and yellow hue, which covers the larger trees in great profusion, and from the young floral leaves as well as the flowers of a sort of creeper, the Combretum Decandrum, which ascends and overhangs the whole woods in large whitish masses, distinguishable by the contrast of their hue from a considerable distance. Amongst the bulbous, monandrous, and gramineous plants, which bedeck or clothe the surface of the ground, a species of Pancratium, the wild turmeric, and the Andropogon aciculatum and muricatum occur most frequently. In the pools and marshes, water-lilies of all colours, and also the true Lotus, sacred Bean Lily, are found in abundance.

The *vegetable dies* procured from the hills, are chiefly the Bacam or Sappan wood, the Aal or Achu (Morinda citrifolia,) the culture of which is little attended to in the plains, and the flowers of the Butea frondosa. Lakh, or *wild silk*, *wax*, *honey*, *and Dhuna* or Indian pitch, are reckoned the most valuable articles of forest produce, and are procurable in great quantities on nearly every hill estate. The Cocoons of the wild silk, are much larger than those of the real worm, and are found generally attached to the leaves of a tree called the Asin (Pentaptera tomentosa.)

The *woods* which skirt the western frontier of Cuttack, as well as the forests of the interior, are filled with wild animals, such as Tigers, Leopards, Panthers, Hyenas, Bears, Buffaloes, Deer, Antelopes, Hogs, the wild Dog called Balia, the Ghoranga an animal resembling the Nilgao, and the wild Ox denominated here the Gayal, a ferocious beast of immense size with a noble pair of horns, which has been well described in the Asiatic Researches, vol. viii. Wild Elephants infested the jungles of Moherbenj and did great injury to the surrounding country, until very recently, the Raja, after having failed in every other attempt, hit upon the following method of getting rid of them. By the advice of a scientific byragee or religious mendicant, he caused a quantity of mineral poison to be mixed up in balls of rice such as are usually given to tame Elephants, which were strewed about in the places chiefly haunted by the wild animals. The bait took effect; a great number of the Elephants were destroyed by the poison ; it is said that upwards of *eighty* dead carcases were found, the rest decamped in alarm, and have since made their appearance in the jungles of another quarter. From the inconsiderable size of the herds which frequented Moherbenj, it seems highly probable that the Elephant is not indigenous to the Province, and it is said that the breed had its origin in the escape of some of the tame animals from their keepers in former ages.

As it respects the *ornithology* of the Province it may suffice to say, of all the feathered tribe that I have seen, I have been most struck with the Dhanesa or Indian Buceros, which is found in large flocks in Khurda, and is there called the *Kuchila-khai* or Kuchila-eater, from the circumstance of its delighting to feed on the fruit of the *Strychnos nux vomica*. The bird has a most singular appearance, particularly when flying, with its long neck stretched out horizontally, aud the huge protuberance rising from the upper mandible of the bill distinctly visible from a great distance. This protuberance or horn, in the Khurda species, measures often seven inches from base to peak, and about two and a half in height from the upper mandible. The flesh is much prized by the natives, who consider it a sovereign remedy for the rheumatic pains called *Bat*, and is often kept prepared in a particular way, with spices, for four or five years. The loud screaming and chattering noise which announce always the presence of the Indian horn bill, well entitle it to its place in the Linnæan order *Picæ*.

The Province of Cuttack is watered by innumerable streams, which swell into rivers of magnitude during the rains, but few of them have any current throughout the whole year. I shall mention only the *principal rivers*, as it would be tedious to attempt an enumeration of the almost countless ramifications, which strike off from the larger channels about the centre of the Mogulbandi, and assume new and independent names. The chief stream in name, importance, length of course, and the associations connected with it by popular superstition, is the Mahanuddy, which is said to rise near Bastar, and after passing Sumbulpoor and Sonepoor, (at which latter place it receives the waters of the Tel river,) enters the Mogulbandi division at the city of Cuttack, where it throws off its principal arm the *Cajori* inclining to the southward, and another on the north-east face of the town called the *Berupa*. Afterwards pursuing an easterly course verging to south, it sends off to the northward another large river called the *Chittertola*, and numerous smaller arms, until at Paradip, it divides into two or three considerable branches, and empties itself by two principal mouths into the bay of Bengal a little south of False point, having completed a course of more than 500 miles. The breadth of this river at Sumbulpoor, 160 miles distant from Cuttack, is nearly *a mile during the rains*, and opposite to the town of Cuttack *its bed measures full two miles across*. After this, the main channel narrows very considerably. It deposits universally a coarse sand (intermixed with numerous fragments of different coloured quartz and scales of Mica,) destructive of course to the fertility of any land on which it may be carried by inundation, and its bottom is singularly irregular and uneven. During the rains the Mahanuddy may be navigated nearly as far as Ryepur, distant 300 miles from the point of confluence with the sea, though the passage is rendered difficult in the higher parts by rocks. A great portion of the bed however is dry for five or six months of the year, and it is fordable from January to June, even at Cuttack.

The principal channel of the *Cajori* terminates in the Alankar which is deep and narrow, and pursues a singularly tortuous course until it is lost amidst a variety of smaller ramifications. About half way between Cuttack and the sea, the Cajori sends off a large branch which after dividing, doubling upon itself, and again branching out in indescribable intricacies, enters the sea at last in a broad channel about *forty miles north of the Black Pagoda*, under the name of the *Deb Nadi.* Another large stream leaves the above opposite to Cuttack, and subsequently divides into three principal rivers, the *Bhargabi, Dava, and Kusbhadra*, which flow south, inclining a little to the east. The latter enters the sea between the Black Pagoda and Pooree. The two former uniting again into one stream, discharge their waters into the Chilka lake, called by various names at different stages of their course, and finally the *Harchandi.* All these deposit coarse sand like the parent stream.

Next to the Mahanuddy, the *Brahmani* and the *Byterini* are the most important rivers. The former, soon after entering the Mogulbandi, throws off a branch called the *Karsua* which equals either in size. All the three, after frequently dividing and branching off, unite with the Berupa at different points of their courses, and flow into the Mahanuddy in two or three large channels forming the *Kanka Island* or Delta near Point Palmyras. Some of these rivers deposit a portion of fertilizing mud near the mouth, as well as much coarse sand. To the northward of the above, the *Solandi, Kans Bans, Burabalang*, and the *Subunreekha*, are all respectable rivers, more especially the latter two. They deposit near their mouths a considerable quantity of fine mud as well as sand. "This river," says Hamilton, "has its source in the province of Bahar, district of Chuta Nagpoor, whence it flows in a south-easterly direction, until, after a winding course of about 250 miles, it falls into the bay of Bengal. For many years prior to the conquest of Bengal by the British, this river had formed the southern boundary of that soubah under the different native governments, and continued to mark the boundary until 1803, when the acquisition of Cuttack brought the Bengal and Madras Presidencies for the first time into contact."*

The whole of the country between the Chilka lake and the Brahmani river, is *peculiarly subject to inundation from its proximity to the hills*, and the astonishing rapidity with which the torrents descend in the rains; the strange conformation of the channels of some of the principal rivers, which are very broad within the hills, but divide soon after leaving them into a number of narrow streams; and also from the practice which has existed from very old times of using embankments. As an instance of rapid rise, it deserves to

* Hamilton's Hindostan, vol. ii. p. 34.

be recorded that, during the heavy rains of 1817, *the waters of the Cajori rose in one night a height of eighteen feet*, as ascertained by careful measurement. This immense volume of water, which was then perhaps *one and a half mile in breadth by thirty or forty feet depth, over-topped the general level of the town by a height of nearly six feet*, and was only restrained from overwhelming it, by a solid embankment faced with stone and supported by buttresses, the work of former governments. The defence alluded to, however, called the revetment, has yielded in places within the memory of man, and the consequences were of course most tremendous. The Cuttack rivers are generally swollen to an extreme height about three times during each rainy season, and at such periods the crops and villages in many parts are exposed to imminent hazard. To guard against the evil as much as practicable, embankments have been always maintained by government, at a large expense. Such works are indispensably necessary in the state to which things have been brought, but they obviously only aggravate the evil, and sometimes occasion direct mischief, by being injudiciously constructed to suit the interests of particular parties, without a due advertence to the general welfare. The embankments or *bunds* are solid mounds of earth well sloped and turfed on either side, the principal ones measuring from *forty to fifty and sixty feet in breadth, and eight to sixteen in height*. The havoc occasioned by the bursting of one of these large *bunds* is generally most serious. The torrent rushes with a frightful roar and velocity, tearing up trees by the roots, prostrating houses, and washing away every trace of the labours of the peasantry. The devastations of the flood too are in general more permanently commemorated, by a deposit of coarse sand, which renders the soil in the neighbourhood of the breach unfit for tillage for several years.

The Rev. A Sutton, Missionary at Cuttack, thus describes what he witnessed during a great swell of the river in 1826. He writes, —"In a few days the Cajori has risen from an insignificant stream to a river as large as the Thames. This rise is principally occasioned by the torrents of water which pour down the celebrated blue mountains, which we can see very plainly, though many of them are at a great distance. These torrents are again augmented by several rivers overflowing their banks and uniting with the regular stream. Trees of all sizes are seen floating down the stream, with the utmost rapidity, towards the sea, and the poorer class of people are busy enough swimming after them; some go an amazing distance before they can overtake them, or get sufficient command over the force of the current, to get them ashore. It is a very amusing and picturesque scene from our verandah, (from our friend Peggs' house.) The river rises to an alarming height, it is now within an inch of overflowing the embankments opposite to our house; the people begin to grow much alarmed, and numbers are watching the rise or decline of the water. The country on the other side of the river is inundated for a considerable distance, and I have heard and seen that many houses have been washed away, and in some cases inhabitants and cattle altogether; several roofs of houses have been seen floating down the river with the families on the top of the thatch, and have thus been saved. A sacrifice has been offered to day by some people of the shoemaking cast, for the purpose of appeasing the wrath of the river, which they imagine is angry with them, and threatens to deluge the town. It was a long unmeaning piece of business; the man set out from his house, attended by a great concourse of people, accompanied by the usual wretched apology for a band of music. A black he-goat of about a year old headed the procession, then the music, next the priest, and offerings consisting of sweetmeats, little ornaments such as paltry rings, necklaces, &c., and a looking-glass for the goddess, some red powder, different sorts of fruit, a remnant of red, and another of yellow, silk, some rice, spices, combs, and several other trifling articles. The man threw himself in the dust every step from his house to the river, he every time lay flat on his face, muttered something, often knocked his head aud arms; of course he proceeded but very slowly. When they arrived at the waterside, the brahmin first arranged the articles, then kindled a small fire, into which he threw incense the whole time of the ceremony; he afterwards went through the tedious formulas of presenting the offerings, sanctifying the offerer and his family by touching their foreheads, pouring water into their hands, &c.; five lamps were then lit and waved before the river, the people took some grains of rice, and other trifles, after they had been sanctified, and threw them into the river, they then lay down flat on their faces, and worshipped the river. The principal offerer was in such a state of perturbation that he was obliged to be supported, his knees trembled like Belshazzar's. The principal part of the ornaments were then placed on a plaintain-tree stage and let down into the water, but the sweetmeats were taken away, I suppose by the brahmin. The things floated for some distance down the river before they were upset; some red and yellow powder was then smeared on the head of the goat, the man then presented it to the goddess, and when all was ready a man with a sword severed the head from the body at a stroke, the blood was then poured in the river, and afterwards both head and body were thrown in after it. The struggling body appeared for a few moments, and then sunk, the people shouted their deafening hurre bol, saying it was well done, and dispersed. All night the people were assembled on the river banks with torches, &c., but the river began to decline the next day, the rain having ceased on the mountains. The alarm then subsided, and the people were satisfied that the goddess had been duly propitiated."*

The *Chilka Lake* forms too material a feature in the geography of Orissa, to be passed over unnoticed. The general opinion of Europeans, has been that it was formed by an irruption of the ocean, and it is worthy of remark that the native histories record the occurrence of such an event, about the beginning of *the third century of the Christian era*, to which they universally ascribe the formation of the Chilka. It is separated from the sea for many miles by a long narrow strip of sand, seldom more than *three hundred yards in breadth*, and discharges its waters by an outfall, which has been lately excavated about a mile north of Manikpatam, the old one having become nearly choked up with sand. Its form is very irregular, the greatest diameters measuring from N. E. to S. W. *thirty-five*, and from E. by N. to W. by S. *eighteen miles*. To the southward, it is divided into numerous narrow channels by large inhabited islands, and for a long way it can scarcely be distinguished from the channel of the Harchandi, which flows into it. The general depth is about four or five feet, greatest depth six feet; and it is considered to be rapidly filling up from the sand and mud brought into it by the Daya, Bhargabi, and various smaller streams, which empty their waters into this basin. The Pergunnahs Rahang, Seraen, Chowbiskud, Killahs Roreng, Kokla, Khurda, and the Jagir of Kerar Mahommed, encircle or touch its shores for nearly two thirds of the whole circumference. On the Ganjam side the hill estates of Calicote and Palur occupy the remaining interval. The lake is valuable for the salt which it yields, called Karkach, obtained by solar evaporation, of which nearly *two lacs of maunds*† *are obtained annually*, on the Jagir of Kerar Mahommed; and to the inhabitants of its vicinity for its fishery, the produce of which when dried, forms a considerable article of export. On the Cuttack

* Gen. Bap. Repository, 1827, pp. 141-2.

† Maund, a measure of weight,—at Madras, 25 pounds; at Bombay 28. The factory maund in Bengal may be computed at 80 pounds.

side its shores are flat, marshy, and destitute of picturesque beauty, but the opposite banks from Banpur to Rhamba exhibit scenery of a very romantic and diversified character. The hills of Khurda, Goomsur, and Calicote, are seen extending along the whole of the south western face in irregular chains, and groups of moderate elevation, some of which jut into the lake, forming low rocky points or promontories. The Chilka itself, north of Palur, expands into a majestic sheet of water, interspersed with a few rocky Islands, and enlivened by boats sailing along before the wind, or forced on by punting with bamboo poles called laggis, or stationary for the purposes of fishing. If the visitor is curious enough to approach these islands, he will be struck with their singular conformation. They consist entirely of huge rounded blocks of a highly indurated porphyritic granite, containing large crystals of felspar, on which the hammer will scarcely make any impression, tossed and piled on each other in the wildest confusion, and exhibiting every symptom of violent convulsion. Some of the masses are arranged in the form of fortresses with huge round bastions, and others present much the appearance of some grand edifice of ancient days, in ruins. A scanty soil which has formed on their summmit, by what process one cannot readly conceive, gives nourishment to a few peepul trees. mimosas, euphorbias, and gramineous plants. They are the resort of numerous aquatic birds, chiefly of the Saras kind, which enjoy undisturbed possession, except when roused occasionally by the approach of a chance visitor.

The principal towns in Orissa Proper are, Cuttack, Balasore, and Juggernaut. Jajpur, though a place of great sanctity in the estimation of the Hindus, and the site of an ancient capital, is merely a large village. The more important Kesbehs, or head Villages of Pergunnahs are, Budruck, Soro, Kendrapari, Asserajasar, Harriorpoor, and Pipley, but these are of small size; and nearly all the rest of the Cuttack Mouzahs are mere hamlets, if we except the villages of the Sasan Brahmins. The country of Rajwara does not, I believe, contain a single respectable village.

The extent, appearance and population of the Town of *Cuttack*, are not unsuitable to its rank as the capital of a large Province. Its situation on a tongue of land or peninsula, near the bifurcation of the Mahanadi, is commanding both in a political and commercial point of view; though these advantages have been in some degree counterbalanced, by the outlay incurred in defending it by stone revetments, from the encroachment of the rivers which wash two of its sides. The hilly country of Rajwara seen from its environs furnishes a pleasing and picturesque prospect. The real etymology of the word Cuttack is *Katak*, signifying in Sanscrit a *royal residence*, or *seat of empire*. It was one of the five Kataks, or Capitals of Gangeswara Deo, the second prince of the Gang Bans line, and is still distinguished by the natives as Katak Biranasi or *Benares*, by which name also it is mentioned in Ferishteh's *History of Bengal*, and in the *Ayin Akberi*. The denomination Biranasi, has been in latter times confined mostly to a village, or Patna, which stands near the point of separation of the Mahanuddy and Cajori rivers, about four miles distant from the town. Authorities vary as to the date of the foundation of the Katak Biranasi, but there seems good reason to think that it became a capital city as early as the end of the *tenth century*, during the reign of the Kesari princes. Chowdwar, Jajpur, and Pipley, divided with it at different periods, the honour and advantage of accommodating the Hindu court of Orissa.

The only monument of the Gajpati Rajas which their ancient capital exhibits, is the fortress of Barabati, built probably in the fourteenth century by Raja Anang Bhim Deo. Some ascribe its erection to Telinga Mukund Deo, the last of the independent sovereigns of Orissa, and others refer it back to a period as early as the times of the Kesari dynasty. However that point may stand, its square sloping towers or bastions, and general style, bespeak clearly a Hindu origin. The Mahommedan or Marhatta governors added a round bastion at the N. W. angle, and constructed the great arched gateway in the eastern face, which alterations are alluded to in a Persian inscription, giving for the date of the repairs and additions, according to the rules of the Abjed, the fourth year of the reign of Ahmed Shah or A. D. 1750. The fort has double walls built of stone, the inner of which enclose a rectangular area measuring 2150 by 1800 feet. The entrance lies through a grand gateway on the east, flanked by two lofty square towers, having the sides inclining inwards, from the base to the summit. A noble ditch faced with masonry surrounds the whole, measuring in the broadest part, *two hundred and twenty feet across*. From the centre of the fort rises a huge square bastion or cavalier supporting a flag staff. This feature, combined with the loftiness of the battlements on the river face, give to the edifice an imposing, castellated appearance, so much so that the whole when seen from the opposite bank of the Mahanuddy, presented to the imagination of Mr. La Motte, who travelled through the province in A. D. 1767, some resemblance to the west side of Windsor Castle. No traces of the famous palace of Raja Mukand Deo nine stories in height, mentioned in the Ayin Akberi, are to be found within the walls of fort Barabati, but the fragments of sculptured cornices, &c., which have been dug up at different times, and more especially a massive candelabra, or pillar furnished with branches for holding lights, formed of the fine grey indurated chlorite or pot stone, are probably the remains of some large and splendid edifice.

The only Mahommedan monuments worthy of notice at the capital, are a small neat mosque built by Ikram Khan, a governor during Arangzeb's reign, towards the centre of the town ; and the Kadam Rasool, an antique looking edifice standing in the midst of a fine garden, which contains certain reliques of the prophet commissioned from Mecca by the Newab Nazim Shujaa ud Din Khan, or his son Mahommed Taki Khan, the latter of whom lies buried within the enclosure. The Mogul and Marhatta Subadars always resided in the palace of the Lal Bagh on the banks of the Cajori, which we must suppose to be the "Stately Court of Malcandy," described by Mr. Cartwright, who visited the "Governor of *Coteke*" in 1632, though there are no traces of splendour remaining to warrant the high wrought description of the palace, given in Bruton's Narration.

The Town contains a population of about 40,000 souls, residing in 6,512 houses, exclusive of cantonments, amongst which are several fine mansions of stone that belonged formerly to the Gosain and Parwar merchants, who engrossed all the trade and principal official employments of the province under the Marhattas. It is divided into a number of Mehallas and Bazars, named after the Sirdars who founded, or the trades or classes residing principally in them, as the Tatar Khan, Ali Shah, Uria, Telinga, &c., Bazar. The Chandni Chouk is a fine broad street, consisting of neat stone houses, disposed with much regularity, but owes its respectable appearance chiefly to European interference. There is of course no deficiency of small modern temples in and about the town, amongst which that dedicated to Seta Ram is the most conspicuous both in size and form ; and from its existence having been officially recognized by the British Regulations. Reg. XII. 1805, sec. xxx.

Balasore, distant about 100 miles from Cuttack, is a large straggling Town, containing several small brick houses inhabited by merchants, who carry on an inconsiderable traffic with Calcutta. Its situation is extremely unfavourable, on a low dreary plain, deformed by numerous unsightly ridges and ant hills, near the muddy banks of the Bura Balang, and it is considered in consequence unhealthy during the rainy season. The number of inhabitants does not exceed 10,000. It is surrounded by an infinity of little hamlets; the whole neighbourhood is covered with numerous little villages, which send forth an immense population, and which give it the character of the most populous part of the province. Balasore is the principal port of the district, and is provided with dry docks on the banks of the river, to which sloops, drawing not more than fourteen feet water, can be floated during the spring tides. It is frequented chiefly by three descriptions of country craft, viz., Maldive vessels, the boats employed in transporting the Company's salt to the Presidency, and a class of sloops built at Contai and Hidgelly called Hollas, which come in great numbers during the cold weather to carry off rice to Calcutta.

The importance attached to this station, in the infancy of the commerce between the western hemisphere and Bengal, is attested by the remains of the factories of four European nations, *English, French, Danish,* and *Dutch.* Traces of a Portuguese establishment are also to be observed, in the ruins of a small Roman Catholic Chapel in the town, having a wooden cross over the principal doorway. The Dutch seem to have been settled here prior to 1660 A.D. at least that date is discoverable on two curious monumental pyramids of masonry, which rise near the Factory. The English formed their first Bengal establishment at Pipley on the Subunreekha in 1640 A. D., and the date 1684 A. D. is to be observed on a tomb in the English burying-ground at that place. The magnitude of the Company's establishment here, may be estimated from the number of large obelisks and obituary columns still standing in the burying-ground, erected to the memory of our predecessors who ended their days in this remote corner. The English had likewise a fine country house surrounded with gardens, at a place called Balramgerhi near the sea, the remains of which may still be seen, and will always be viewed with interest from its having afforded a temporary shelter to several of the Company's servants, when Calcutta was captured by the armies of Seraj ud Dowlah in 1756 A.D. "On the 29th of November, 1688, during a rupture between the East India Company and Aurengzebe, Captain Heath landed a body of troops and seamen, attacked and took a battery of 30 pieces of cannon, and plundered the town of Balasore. The English factory was burned by the governor, and the Company's servants carried prisoners up the country, from whence it does not appear that they ever returned. On the breaking out of the war with the Nagpoor Maharattas in 1803, an expedition was dispatched against this place, when the troops and stores were conveyed in vessels to within four miles of the town, where they were landed, and the fort and factory captured after a long contest, but with little loss on the part of the assailants."*

The trade of the place was formerly important, from the Sannahs and fine Muslins manufactured there, and likewise at Budruck and Soro, the demand for which has now almost entirely ceased. The drugs and dies imported from the hills, may have constituted also a considerable article of export. Balasore, doubtless derived its principal consequence as the site of a factory, from its convenience for carrying on commerce with Bengal Proper, before permission had been obtained to establish settlements within that province.

The Town of *Pooree Juggernaut* owes its size and importance entirely to its connection with the temple, It is situated on the sea coast in lat. 19° 49' N. long. 85° 54' E. 47 miles S. by E. from Cuttack. Travelling distance from Calcutta 311 miles; from Benares 512 miles; from Madras 719; from Delhi 910; and from Bombay 1052 miles. It contains 5741 houses. Every span of it is considered holy ground, and the whole of the land is held free of rent, *on the tenure of performing certain services, in and about the temple.* Respecting the value attached to this reputedly holy ground, a resident in Orissa observes,—'For about one hundred yards from the temple every square cubit is worth a row of rupees eight deep; the space for the next hundred yards is worth a row seven deep; the next diminishes to six deep, and so proceeds till you get beyond the ground subject to these regulations.' The principal street is composed almost entirely of the religious establishments called Mat'hs, built of masonry, having low pillared verandahs in front, and plantations of trees interspersed. Being very wide, with the temple rising at the southern end, it presents by no means an unpicturesque appearance; but the filth and stench, the swarms of religions mendicants, and other nauseous objects, which offend one's senses in every part of the town, quite dispel any illusion which the scene might otherwise possess. Fine luxuriant gardens and groves enclose the town on the land side, and produce the best fruit in the province. The stately and beautiful *Callophyllum Inophyllum*, called by Dr. Ainslie the Alexandrian Laurel, grows here in great abundance, and the *Cashew-nut* thrives with peculiar luxuriance. The environs exhibit some fine tanks, as the Indra Daman, Chandan, Markandeswar Talao, &c., which are supposed to be very ancient; and the inquisitive stranger who may be

* Hamilton's Hindostan, vol. ii. p. 37.

disposed to explore amidst the sand hills situated between the sea and the town, will find many ancient and curious looking religious edifices, nearly overwhelmed with sand, to excite and reward attention.

The climate of Juggernaut, is the most agreeable and salubrious probably in all India, during the hot months from March to July. At this season the south-west monsoon blows from the sea in a steady and refreshing breeze, which seldom fails until the approach of the rains, and every door and window is thrown open to court its entrance. A visit to Juggernaut has in some cases proved as beneficial to the European constitution as a sea voyage.

Buddruck is situated on the north bank of the Cowah, or Solundee river, which at one season of the year is here 300 yards broad, and at another, fordable. Lat. 21° 7' N. long. 86° 26' E. 38 miles S.S.W. from Balasore. From this part of Orissa, come most of the people termed in Calcutta, Balasore bearers.*

Singboom, a town in the province of Orissa, governed by a Raja, independent within his own territories, but under political subordination to the British government. It is bounded on three sides by the districts of Chuta Nagpoor, Midnapoor, and Moherbunge; and on the south by that of Kunjeur. The zemindars in this and other districts on the frontiers of Midnapoor, were formerly many of them robbers by trade, kept robbers in their pay, and have still a hankering after their old profession. While tributary to the Maharattas, they were under no external control, and were, at home, magistrates, with unlimited powers of life and death, and accustomed to make predatory inroads on British territories. The town of Singboom stands in lat. 22° 31 N. long. 85° 40' E. 105 miles W. from Midnapoor, and notwithstanding the etymology of the name of the pergunnah, it is notorious that there never was a lion seen within its limits.

The town of *Kunjeur* stands in lat. 21° 31' N. long. 85° 32' E. 92 miles N.N.W. from Cuttack.

Ogurrapoora, a town in Orissa, 77 miles N.N.W. from Cuttack. Lat. 21° 21' N. long. 85° 24' E.

Andapoorghur, a town in the Orissa province, 48 miles west from Balasore. Lat. 21° 34' N. long. 86° 5' E.†

Harriorpoor, the capital of the large zemindary of Moherbunge, and residence of the zemindar. It is situated in lat. 21° 51' N. long. 86° 42' E. 28 miles N. by W. from Balasore.‡

* Hamilton's Hindostan, vol. ii. p. 38. † pp. 34-5. ‡ p. 37.

Burwa, a town in Orissa, 27 miles N.N.E. from Cuttack, in lat. 20° 45' N. long. 86° 21' E.

Caulahandy, a town in Orissa, 95 miles S. by W. from Sumbhulpoor. Lat. 19° 49' N. long. 83° 12' E.

Jeghederpoor, a town in Orissa, 20 miles south from Bustar. Lat. 19° 14' N. long. 82° 28' E. Under this town a considerable river runs, named the Inderowty (Indravaty,) the bed of which at this place is very rocky, and not fordable at any time of the year. There is a small fort on a peninsula formed by the winding of the river, which in the rainy season overflows its banks, and forms a lake of considerable dimensions.

Narlah, a town in Orissa, 37 miles E. from Bustar. Lat. 19° 37' N. long. 83° 2' E.

Jyapoor, a town in Orissa, 70 miles N. W. fJom Vizagapatam. Lat. 18° 25' N. long. 82° 43' E.

Aul, a town in the province of Orissa, district of Cuttack, 50 miles from the town of Cuttack in a north-east direction.

Jagepoor, a town in the Cuttack district, 35 miles N.N.E, from the town of that name. Lat. 20° 52' N. long. 86₀ 24' E. It stands on the south side of the Byterini river, which is here in the rains nearly half a mile broad. This is a large straggling town, in which a good deal of cloth is made. During the Mogul government, it was a place of importance, and the remains of several Mahommedan edifices are still visible. The mosque was built by Abou Hassir Khan, who, in an inscription, is very extravagant in the praises of his own mosque, although it is remarkably ill proportioned, having a large dome and small pillars. The country around is much intersected with small rivers and water courses. The principality of Jagepoor in Orissa was invaded by Toghan Khan, the Mahommedan governor of Bengal, in A.D. 1243, at which period it appears to have been a state of some strength, as the Raja not only defeated Tohban Khan, but pursued him into Bengal, where he besieged Gour, the metropolis. The approach of reinforcements from Oude compelled him subsequently to retreat. The Mahommedans were again totally defeated by the Raja of Jagepoor, in 1253. There is no record at what time this place fell finally under the domination of the Mahommedans, who possessed it until expelled by the Maharattas.

Kunka, a town in the province of Orissa, district of Cuttack, 80 miles N. E. from the town of Cuttack. This is the capital of one of the tributary estates in Cuttack subject to the British regulations, the exact limits of which have never been ascertained, but which have been roughly estimated at 75 miles from north to south, by 50 from east to west. Prior to the acquisition of Cuttack by the British, the Raja of Kunka, who possessed this inundated and unhealthy tract of country, had long baffled the Maharatta generals in all their attempts to subdue him. The Maharattas had been accustomed to embark troops and artillery on large unwieldy flat bottomed boats, unmanageable in large streams or near the sea; in consequence of which, their ill-constructed fleets always fell a prey to the Raja's light armed vessels, which were long, narrow, with barricadoes to cover the men, and some of them having 100 paddles or oars. When these squadrons met, the Ooria boats moved quickly round the heavy Maharatta armada, and picked off the men with their matchlocks, until the remainder were compelled to surrender, when they were carried into a captivity from whence they seldom returned, the pernicious atmosphere of these morasses permitting none to live but the aborigines.

Point Palmiras, a small town and promontory in the province of Orissa, district of Cuttack. Lat. 20° 43' N. long. 87° 5' E. In favourable weather, Bengal pilot schooners for the river Hooghly are frequently met with as soon as this cape is passed.

Deknall, the capital of a tributary zemindary in the province of Cuttack, 40 miles N. N.W. from the town of Cuttack. Lat. 20° 58' N. long. 85° 48' E.

Bamraghur, a town in the Orissa province, 80 miles N. W. from Cuttack. Lat. 21° 3' N. long. 85° 2 E. To the south of this place are some iron mines and forges.

Autghur.—This place stands in the midst of a wild and woody country, about 14 miles N. W. from the town of Cuttack. On the north it is bounded by the tributary state of Durpun, and on the west by the fortress of Tigria. Owing to the quantity and density of the jungle, the country is reckoned very unhealthy, and its extreme dimensions are 15 miles east to west, by 12 from north to south.

Narsingah, a town in Orissa, 60 miles W. by N. from Cuttack. Lat. 20° 37' N. 85° 11' E.

Ongologur, the capital of a large zemindary in the Cuttack district, situated 59 miles W. from the town of Cuttack. Lat. 20° 32' N. long. 85° 11' E.

Bankee, a town in the province of Cuttack, the capital of a tributary zemindary, 30 miles west from the town of Cuttack.*

* Hamilton's Hindostan, vol. ii. pp. 46-7-8-9.

Khoordah.—The Khoordah Raja is hereditary high priest of Juggernauth, and keeper of the idol's wardrobe. Khoordahghur his residence, is situated about 20 miles S. W. of Cuttack, and 15 west of Piply. It is enclosed by a depth of impervious forest to the extent of many miles, carefully trained to grow in a close matting of the most thorny thickets, the only avenues to the interior being through defiles strongly fortified. The principal entrance in 1804 was from the eastward, communicating with the road leading to Piply, which was also strengthened in the native manner; and there were two other accessible entrances, one from the north-west, and the other from the west.

Soon after the conquest of Cuttack, this pergunnah became remarkable for its hostility to the British government; and at length became so turbulent, that to preserve the tranquillity of the district, it became necessary to secure the person of the Raja, Mukund Deo, then 18 years of age, and retain him in custody at Midnapoor. For the accomplishment of this object, in 1804, three separate attacks were made on Khoordahghur; on which occasion, the route pursued by the troops was along the banks of the Mahanuddy, through a picturesque country, diversified by hill, dale, and water scenery. After penetrating, with much physical difficulty but little loss, through a great depth of forest, the detachment reached a vale of an oval form, about three miles long by two in width, the whole under rice cultivation, and ready for reaping. This vale contained also a mango grove and neat village; but the Raja resided on a hill at the south end, the approach to which was strongly stockaded and fortified with several barriers, and a well constructed stone wall surrounding a portion of the summit, within which dwelt the Raja and his family, with their principal officers and domestics. By a series of well concerted operations, the whole multitude were here pent up, and a scarcity of provisions ensuing, a great proportion of them dispersed, leaving only a garrison of 1000 men. After three weeks' endeavours, rendered difficult by the complicated and unintelligible form of the enemy's works, the external defences were stormed under a heavy but ill-directed fire, until at length the base of the stone wall and gateway were attained, leading into the body of the place, on the summit of the hill. Another party which had gone by a more circuitous route, having got over the wall, proceeded to the gateway, and let in the rest, when they all proceeded against the Raja's dwelling, he having recently fled through another gateway at the foot of the hill. With this terminated the siege of Khoordaghur, but the troops being much exhausted were unable to pursue, the Raja, who however, a short time subsequent, voluntarily came in and surrendered himself.

Marickpoor, a town in the province of Orissa, district of Cuttack, 40 miles S. E. from the town of Cuttack.

Ahmedpoor, a town in Orissa, 11 miles north from Juggernauth. Lat. 19° 58' N. long. 85° 54' E.

Piply, a town in Orissa, 27 miles south from Cuttack. Lat. 20° 5' N. long. 85° 58' E.

Boad, a large fenced village in the province of Orissa, situated on the south-side of the Mahanuddy river, which at this place in the month of October is one mile and a half broad. Lat. 20° 32' N. long. 84° 10' E. 124 miles west from Cuttack. The face of the whole country, in this neighbourhood is mountainous, interspersed with valleys, from four to sixteen miles in circumference. The villages are fenced with bamboos to protect the inhabitants and their cattle from wild beasts; and in the fields the women are seen holding the plough, while the female children drive the oxen. The Boad territory commands some of the principal passes into the Cuttack division. By the engagements concluded with the Boad Chiefs, in 1803, they were liberated from the payment of any tribute to the Maharattas, and guaranteed in the possession of their estates, on condition that they faithfully discharged their duties as tributaries to the British Government.

Ramgur, a town fortified in the native manner in the province of Orissa, situated in the south-side of the Mahanuddy river, 106 miles west from Cuttack. Lat. 20° 26' N. long. 84° 26' E. By the arrangement made during the Marquis Wellesley's administration, in 1803, the chief of this place was exempted from the payment of tribute to the Maharattas, and had his territories guaranteed to him, on condition of faithfully fulfilling his duty as a tributary to the British government.

Cooloo, or Kontiloo, a town in Orissa, 80 miles S. E. from Sumbhulpoor. Lat. 20° 31' N. long. 84° 39' E. This is a considerable mart for the inland trade, the Berar merchants bringing their cotton to Cooloo, from whence they return to the interior with a load of salt.

Judimahoo, a town in Orissa, 58 miles W. by S. from Cuttack, Lat. 20° 16' N. long. 85° 13' E.*

The following Towns are not within the limits of modern Orissa, yet some information respecting them may be useful.

Midnapoor is a considerable town situated on the south side of

* Hamilton's Hindostan, vol. ii. pp. 50-9.

the Booree Bellaun river, 70 miles W. S. from Calcutta, but travel-distance 141 miles. The fort has recently been converted into a prison.

Hijelle is situated on the west side of the Hooghly river, 55 miles S. S.W. from Calcutta, and formed a part of the province of Orissa.

Tumlook is about 35 miles S. W. from Calcutta. Major Wilford supposes there were kings of this place, one of whom, in A.D. 1001, sent an embassy to China.

Ganjam is situated near the sea coast, lat. 19° 21' N. long. 85° 10' E. An awful epidemic raged in 1814, which occasioned the removal of the European residents to Berhampore and Chicacole. It has been considered more healthy of late years.

Sumbhulpoor is the capital of the district of the same name, which is a part of the Gundwana province. It is situated on the eastern side of the Mahanuddy, 167 miles W. N. W. from Cuttack. Lat. 21° 8' N. long. 83° 33' E. Of this district, Hamilton observes,—"To the north it is bounded by Choteesghur and Gangpoor; on the south by various petty states in the province of Orissa, dependent on the British government; to the east it has Orissa; and on the west Choteesghur or Ruttunpoor. The climate of Sumbhulpoor is very unwholesome, owing to the quantity of jungle, and the vicissitudes of heat and cold. The soil in the valleys is said to be a rich loam, in which grain or pulse will thrive well, and the mountains have the reputation of containing diamonds. The natives wash the sand of the rills that descend from them, and procure considerable quantities of gold. The diamonds are found about 13 miles beyond the town of Sumbhulpoor, near the junction of the river Hebe with the Mahanuddy, at which spot, after the rains, the natives search in the river for red earth, washed down from the mountains, in which earth the diamonds are discovered. The matrix containing the diamonds is a clay, which appears burned red, nearly to the degree that bricks usually are."*

Some interesting circumstances connected with this town, are related by Mr. Lacey. When he mentions the distance from Cuttack he probably refers to the travelling distance. His statements are—

"Sumbulpoor lies about 300 miles west of Cuttack; and stands in a part very little cultivated, or indeed little known by Europeans. The road to it lies through a dense jungle, which renders the place almost inaccessible. The inhabitants, however, being removed from the idol at Pooree, are much less superstitious and violent than the people in these parts; which, last year, induced me to attempt to visit them by water. After seven days' journey we were attacked with fever and were obliged to return. Under

* Hamilton's Hindostan, vol. ii. p. 20.

these circumstances, *to send Tracts* were the only means left to us of communicating the precious knowledge of Christ to the people. I soon found a trading company returning to Sumbulpoor, and to one of the merchants, a respectable Brahmin, I committed a good number of tracts, and he promised to distribute them. I afterwards met a professed Christian and gave him a number more, and he made the same promise; and we pursued our homeward journey somewhat relieved, hoping and praying for the divine blessing on the books; and the following incident will show that our hopes were not groundless.—

"About a month ago, as I was preaching in the open bazar to the Oreahs, and speaking particularly of Jesus Christ, three strangers exclaimed, with apparent pleasure, 'O, that is the name! that is the name! And this is also the person who sent the books.' It was a circumstance so rare and so pleasing that such unusual joy should be manifested by these people at the name of Jesus Christ, that I immediatly questioned them where and how they had heard of him; when their reply was, that they had heard about Jesus Christ from *some books* that had been sent to Sumbulpoor, and would I be so kind as to give them some for themselves? I of course complied with their request, and furnished them with books for themselves, and a few others for distribution. I asked the men particularly as to the use that was made of the books I had sent? and they answered that *they were read*, and their contents had become a subject of interest among their countrymen, but that *they wished for more full and complete instruction from us.* The truth of the above account seems clear from the men being familiar with the name of Christ."

The *Manufactures and Trade* of Orissa Proper are very inconsiderable and unimportant. A sufficiency of the coarser cloths is made for the use of the inhabitants, in all parts of the district. The calicos of Balasore, Soro, Budruck, Janjipoor, and Harihurpoor, were once much prized and sought after under the name of Sannahs, but the demand for the finer fabrics of that description having long since greatly declined, the quantity now manufactured is very trifling. At Piply Niur a good sort of quilt is made.

The province must certainly, *a century or two since*, have afforded some encouragement to the resort of European traders, as besides the large establishment at Balasore, the English had inferior factories at Cuttack and Harihurpoor. At present the whole value of the exports and imports, which pay duty, is only Sa. Rs. 2,97,285, and the customs and transit duties collected at the several small ports and inland chokies from the Subunreekha to the Dhamra river, do not exceed Sa. Rs. 30,000 per annum. The exports liable to duty are as follow :—Piece goods, bees' wax, iron, kut'h (the inspissated juice of the khayar or mimosa chadira,) oil, lac, stone plates, sal timber, congni wood, kurbeli, shurbeli, and petty articles.

A considerable exportation of rice takes place from the several small ports along the coast to Calcutta. The *horned cattle* and *swine* of the district also are carried out in large herds for the supply of the Presidency market. The quantity of salt now transported by private individuals, in the course of legal and open traffic, does not perhaps exceed 20,000 maunds annually; but formerly salt was an important article of export by way of the great road leading along the Mahanuddy to Sumbhulpoor and Berar, and likewise by that of the Bamangati pass in Moherbunje, more than three lacs of maunds being exported annually. The *dried fish* and *prawns* of the Chilka lake may be noticed as an article of traffic, between the inhabitants of the hills, and those of the low country in that quarter.

Piece goods, silk, good *tobacco,* and every thing in the shape of a luxury, are imported from the adjoining districts of Bengal, and a small supply of *couris, cocoanuts, coral,* and *dried fish* is obtained from the few Maldive vessels, which resort annually to Balasore and Dhamra, to take on board cargoes of rice and earthen pots. Dhamra is a village situated at the mouth of the river, by which vessels sail for Patamoondy, with freight for Cuttack.

CHAP. II.

Casts—Character—Manners and Customs of the Plain—Description of the Hill People—Coles—Khunds—Sours—Language—Population—Revenues—Land Tenures and Institutions.

The four great casts or tribes into which the Hindoos are divided, are of course the same in Orissa as elsewhere, and have the same origin ascribed to them. The ordinary cast and professions of the province are known by the name of thirty-six Pathaks "*Chattis Pathak*;" the individuals composing which are all either *Sudras,* or of what is called the "Sankara Verna," that is, a mixed, impure race, proceeding from the promiscuous intercourses of some of the four tribes in the first instance, and again from their commerce with the desendants of such a connection, or the indiscriminate cohabitation of those descendants amongst one another. Pathak signifies literally *a learner,* it being the duty of the whole of these casts either to perform service to the three higher tribes, or if they cannot gain a livelihood in that way, to *learn* the various arts and trades which are useful to society.

The proper, genuine Khetris, are considered to be extinct, and those who represent them are by the learned held to be only Sudras. There are eight classes or families who claim to represent the military and regal tribe, known by the affixes or titles of Dhir, Dhal, Towang, Mal, Bhanj, Rai, Rawat, and Khandait. The only professions of the pure Vaisya tribe, in Cuttack, are the two classes of Baniyas, called the Gandha Baniya, or druggist, and Swerna Baniya, or money changer. The following are considered apparently genuine Sudras, viv., The Gowala (Gopa) milkman; Bhandari (napita) barber; Gowria (Gourakara) vender of sugar; the Chasa (Krishhakara) or husbandman; and the Talica or seller of Areca nut. The designation of *Or* or *Odra* is applied as it were *par excellence* to the class of husbandmen, who are commonly called Or Chasa. Such of that tribe who perform the duties of Paiks in the hills, and of sirdar village watchmen in the plains, are called Or Paik and Or Khandait.

The first set of the mixed casts springing from intermarriage of original tribes, chiefly Byse and Sooder, and which with exception to the last two, rank next below the pure Sudra, is composed as follows; viz.—

Ooria.	*Sanscrit.*	*Occupations.*
Mali	Malacara	Gardener.
Lohar	Karmakara	Iron smith.
Sankari	Sanc'hacara	Worker in Shells.
Tanti	Tantraaya	Weaver.
Kumhar	Cumbhacara	Potter.
Kansari	Cansacara	Brazier, or worker in bell metal.
Barhai	Sutracara	Carpenter.
Chitrkar	Chitracara	Painter.
Sonar	Swernácara	Goldsmith.
Kewat	Caiverta	Fisherman.
Bed	Vaidya	Physician.
Mainti	Carana	The Writer or Secretary Class.
Bawari	Berbera	Labourers.
Chandal	Chandala	Performs the lowest offices.

The last mentioned, the Chandal, is described to be the offspring of a Sudra father and Brahmin mother, and is considered here as elsewhere, to be the most degraded of the human species. Some make the founders of the first nine trades to have sprung from Viswakarma by a Sudra woman; and the physician they derive from the god Aswinikumar and a Brahmin female. The Pathariya or stone cutter and Kutwya or sawyer are likewise introduced into some enumerations, as forming separate trades, of the same origin with the carpenter and iron smith.

A second set is derived from the promiscuous intercourse of the above casts with each other, and are as follow:

Ooria.	*Sanscrit.*	*Occupations.*
Teli	Tailica	Oilman.
Tiur	Tivara	Fisherman.
Chamar	Charmacara ..	Leather dresser.
Sundi	Sundika	Wine seller.
Dhobi	Rajaka	Washerman.
Magora	Vyadhi	Huntsman.
Naik	Jyotishi	Astrologer.
Shewala.. ..	Madhuka ..	Confectioner and toddy seller.
Dom	Dombha	Matmaker.
Patra	Patucara.. ..	Cloth seller and weaver.
Tula Bhania..	Tula Bhedara..	Cotton beater.
Kandra	Danda Pasika..	Village watchman.
Chunari	———	Lime maker.
Pandra or Pan	———	Cane maker.
Shiputi	———	Tailor.
Baldia Teli, Charia Mar, Bindhani, Hari	———	Perform the lowest offices.

In some lists, the Rupacara or *maker of gods*, appears amongst the mixed classes, as the follower of a separate trade. The Patra or cloth seller and weaver, branches out into the following subdivisions, viz., Sakuli, Pagani, Hansi, Matia, Ashti, Gola, Sara, Bona; and the fishermen as follows, Rarhi, Khatwa, Newnlea, Kartiya, Gokha, and Panua. The three tribes called Dom, Pan, and Hari, furnish the village musicians. They are termed in Sanscrit *Antavasi*, or those who live in the most abject state.

The remaining caste are the wild tribes of the hills, called *Kole*, *Khand*, and *Sour*, by the Oorias, and in Sanscrit "*Pulinda*" (a word signifying mlechcha and barbarian) who scarcely belong to the great Hindoo family.

The Odra or Utcala Brahmins, are one of the ten original races of Saca Dwipa Brahman, taking their names from the countries which they inhabit, viz., Gaura, Saraswati, Canyacubja, Cannouj, Mait'hila, *Utcala*, Tailanga, Carnata, Maharashtra, and Dravira. Their duties are said to be *Yajana*, *Adhyayan*, and *Dan*, or sacrificing, reading the Vedas, and giving alms; and their regular means of subsistence *Yajan*, *Adhyapan*, and *Pratigraha*, or officiating at sacrifices, teaching the Vedas, and receiving charity. If they cannot gain an adequate livelihood by the regular modes, they may eat at a feast in the house of a Sudra, or receive charity from one of that class; also, they may cut firewood from the hills and jungles, and sell it. Should these resources fail, they may, after

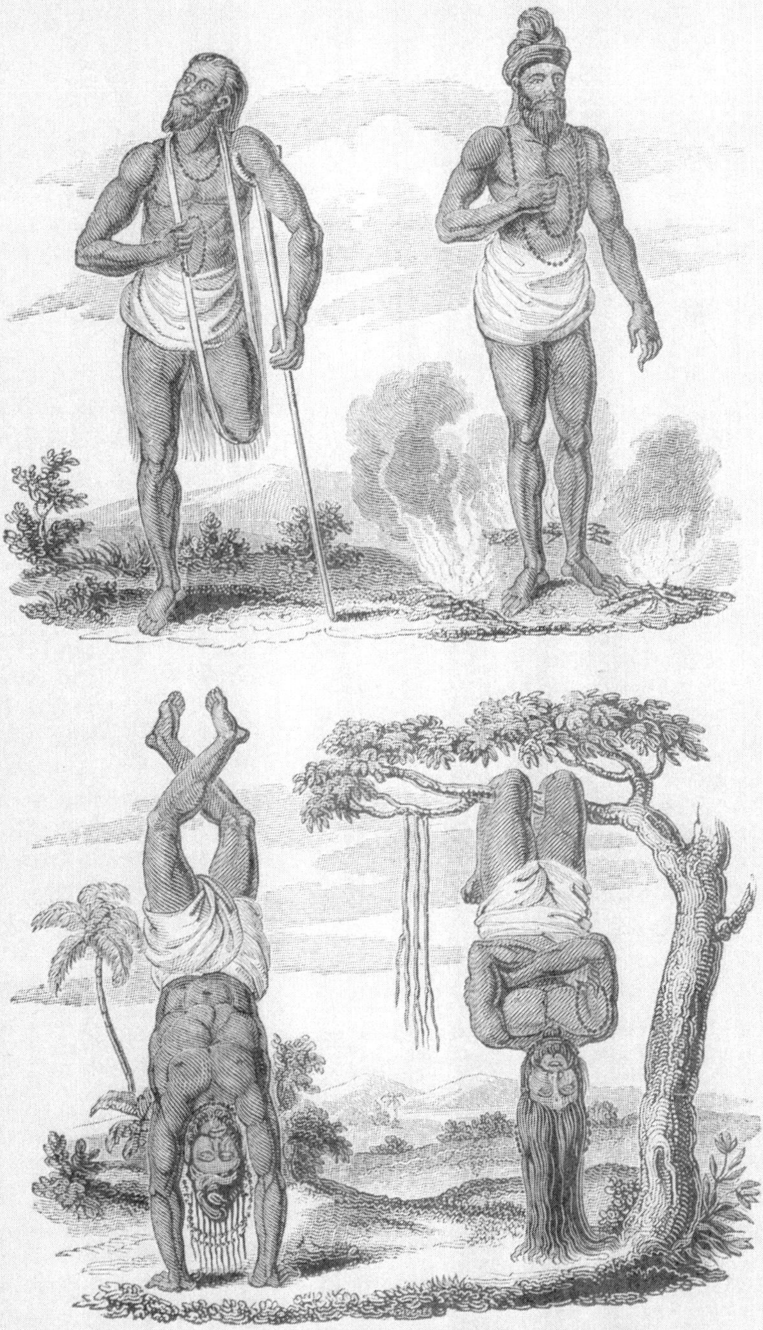

HINDOO DEVOTEES.

fasting for three days, *steal* a little rice from the house of a Brahmin or any other, in order that the king hearing of their distress by this means, may assign something for their maintenance! Should all these expedients prove insufficient, they may engage in the duties of the Cshatriya and Vaisya, but as soon as they have collected a little property, they must repent and return to their original occupations. The Brahmins who confine themselves to the *six duties and employments above noticed*, are of course the most honoured and esteemed. Inferior Brahmins are those called Devalaca, and Grama Yajaka, who attend the village gods, and perform funeral obsequies for hire. There is another class known commonly in Orissa by the name of Mahast'han or *Mastan* Brahmins, who form a very considerable and important class of the rural population. Besides cultivating with their own hands, gardens of the kachu (Arum Indicum,) cocoanut, and Areca, and the piper beetle or pan, they very frequently follow the plough, from which circumstance they are called Halia Brahmins, and they are found every where in great numbers in the situation of Moqeddems and Serberakars, or hereditary renters of villages. Those who handle the plough glory in their occupation, and affect to despise *the Bed or Veda Brahmins, who live upon alms.* Though held in no estimation whatever by the pious Hindu, and although not free from some of the vices of the Brahmin character, audacity, stubbornness, and mendacity, they are unquestionably the most enterprizing, intelligent, and industrious of all the ryots or renters of land, in Orissa. Their moral and intellectual worth indeed, seems to rise exactly in proportion to their emancipation from those shackles of prejudice and superstitious observances, which narrow the minds, and debase the nature of the higher and orthodox class. I have not been able to trace satisfactorily the origin and history of these Mastan Brahmins, who I am informed resemble exactly the cultivating Brahmins of *Tirhoot* and *Behar,* but the point is one well worthy of investigation.

The Oorias as a nation are justly described by Abul Fazl to be very effeminate; that is, they are extremely deficient in manly spirit, their figures are slight and delicate, and the costume of the males has little to distinguish it from that of the females, except the different manner of wearing the cloth fastened about the loins. They are moreover equally ignorant and stupid. Orissa might be termed the *Bœotia* of India, with reference to the intellectual dultess of its inhabitants, as compared with the people of any other rovince. A striking proof of the estimation in which their capacity has ever been held, is the fact, that in all ages and under all governments since the fall of the Orissan monarchy, the principal official employments throughout the province have been engrossed by foreigners—by Bengalees, north, and Telingas, south of the Chilka lake; owing I really believe in a great measure to the difficulty of selecting from its indigenous population, persons properly qualified for trusts of difficulty and importance. The mass of the people are little prone to the commission of crimes of a daring and heinous character, as might be inferred from the feminine spirit above ascribed to them; but they are well versed in all the arts of low cunning, dissimulation, and subterfuge; and the love of intrigue forms a prominent feature in their character, however clumsy many of their attempts to mislead or circumvent. Their manners are sufficiently dissolute, a failing not to be wondered at considering *the obscene character, and impure symbols, of the demoralizing religion which they profess.** In justice however to the bulk of the agricultural population, it must be said that the *ryots* of Cuttack are extremely industrious, though they work with little spirit or intelligence; and altogether the Oorias of the plains, whatever their faults, are certainly the most mild, quiet, inoffensive, and easy managed people in the Company's provinces. They furnish a valuable class of servants known as the Balasore bearers, in whom the virtues of fidelity and honesty (according to their own conception of those qualities) are conspicuous.

The inhabitants of *the Hills, and of the Jungles on the sea shore,* differ chiefly from the rest of population, in that they are more shy, sullen, inhospitable, and uncivilized than the latter. Their chiefs, the Khandaits or ancient Zemindars of Orissa, who claim to represent the regal and military class, are grossly stupid, barbarous, debauched, tyrannical, and slaves of the most grovelling superstition. Whatever the cause of the degradation ascribed to them in a very curious passage of the Institutes of Menu, if *subjection to Brahmins* could redeem their lost dignity, they have long since entitled themselves to the recovery of their station amidst the four great classes of the Hindu nation. The passage above alluded to is this,—"The following races of Cshatriyas by their omission of holy rites, and by

* "This witness is true." The figure of Seeb, or Maha Deb, the great god, the impure figures on Juggernaut's temple, the character of the dancing girls attached to it, the representations formerly on the car of Juggernaut and still on other cars, the obscenities of the Doorga pooja, and the insufferably vile images in stone seen at some of the temples and bathing places, are demonstrations of the cause and depth of that moral degradation which has suffered such abominations to exist from age to age. *Auth.*

seeing no Brahmins, have gradually sunk amongst men to the lowest of the four classes, viz. Paundracas, *Odrus* and Draviras, Cambojas, *Yavanas* and Sakas; Paradas, Pahlavas, Chinas, Ciratas, Deradas, and Chasas." The Paiks or landed militia of the Rajwara, combine with the most profound barbarism, and the blindest devotion to the will of their chiefs, a ferocity and unquietness of disposition, which have ever rendered them an important and formidable class of the population of the province. They comprehend all casts and classes, chiefly perhaps the Chasa or cultivating tribe; occasionally individuals of the lowest casts are found amongst them, as Kandras, Pans and *Bawaris* (*Sanscritice* Berber or Barbarians:) and the fashion has often prevailed of adopting into their order some of the more savage inhabitants of the remote hills, called *Kands*, as also even Mussulmans and Telingas. It is well known that they are paid by service lands, which they cultivate with their own hands in time of peace, subject to the performance of military and rude police duties whenever called upon by their chiefs. Abulfazl states the number of Paiks or zemindari militia (in the original, *Sipah-i-zemindari*) liable to be required for the service of the state according to the conditions of the tenure of the zemindars, at about 1,55,000 for the present districts of Cuttack and Midnapore, which probably formed but a small part of the entire force maintained by those chiefs. The Paiks of this part of the country are divided into three ranks, distinguished by names taken from their occupations, or the weapons which they use chiefly, viz:—

The *Pahris*, who carry a large shield made of wood covered with hides and strengthened by nobs and circles of iron, and the long straight national sword of Orissa, called the khanda. They are stationed chiefly as guards.

The *Banua*, who use the matchlock principally now (in lieu of their old missile weapons,) but have besides a small shield and sword. It was their duty to take the field principally, and go on distant expeditions.

The *Dhenkìyas* who are armed with bows and arrows, and a sword, and perform all sorts of duties.

The *war dress* of the *Paiks* consists, or did consist, of a cap and vest made of *the skin of the tiger or leopard;* a sort of chain armour for the body and thighs; and a girdle formed of the tail of some wild animal. Besides the terror inspired by these unusual habiliments, they farther heightened the ferocity of their appearance by *staining their limbs with yellow clay, and their countenances with vermillion*, thus exhibiting as savage and fantastic an air, as one can well conceive to invest the national army of any country or people. However wild and motley their appearance, they certainly did not fight badly, when encouraged at least by the proximity of their jungles, since we find them constantly sustaining the most bloody battles with the Moguls, and it may be doubted whether they were not superior to any infantry which the Berar Marhattas ever brought into the field during their government of the province.

Exclusive of the regular Ooria population of the Brahminical persuasion, there are three remarkable races inhabiting the hilly region, the *Coles*, *Khands*, and *Sours*. They are quite distinct, the two former at least, in language and features, manners and religion, from the Hindus of the plains; and the supposition seems plausible that their ancestors may have been the aboriginal inhabitants of the country, prior to the arrival of the Brahmin colonists from the north who now possess India. No such tradition or belief however exists. These three tribes should perhaps be considered merely as branches of the same original stock, but as the offsets, found under different names and circumstances in different parts of the province, it will be convenient to mention them separately.

The *Coles* are divided into *thirteen* different tribes, viz., Kol, Lurka-kol, Chowang, Sarvanti, Dhurowa, Bahuri, Bhunian or Bhumiah, Khandwal, Santal, Sour, Bhumij, Batholi, and Amavat. Their original country is said to be *Kolant Des,* which the natives describe as a hilly tract lying between Moherbanj, Sinhbhum, Jynt, Bonye, Keonjher, and Dalbhum. They have however for many years gained possession of parts of Chota Nagpore, Jaspur, Tymar, Patcura, and particularly of Sinhbhum; their encroachments upon Moherbanj have been felt as serious. Some tribes are found settled in the back parts of Nilgiri, and from their restless disposition and constant endeavours to extend their possessions, they have proved troublesome neighbours even to the powerful Keonjher Raja. The Coles are a hardy and athletic race, black and ill-favored in their countenance, ignorant and savage to the last degree; but their houses, built entirely of wood, are said to exhibit a considerable degree of neatness and comfort, and they carry on a very extensive cultivation. Their arms are the bow and arrow, and a small iron battle-axe called *Tangi*, in the use of which they display much spirit and dexterity. This people own ***none of the Hindu divinities, and indeed seem scarcely to have any system of religious belief;*** but four things are held by them in high veneration, ***the Sahajna tree (Hyperanthera Morunga,) paddy, oil expressed from the mustard seed, and the dog!*** In all their contracts and negociations, the leaf of the former is always introduced, and they rub each other with oil which is considered to give solemnity to the proceeding. They have also a curious method of striking a bargain or concluding a pacification, which will not fail to remind the classical reader of the origin of the word *stipulation.* I allude to the circumstance of their breaking a straw *(stipula)* between the disputants, a practice which always follows or precedes the final adjustment of any compact. The Coles are passionately fond of fermented liquors, and eat all kinds of flesh and grain, as well as various roots which grow spontaneously in their jungles, called the Buenjkarba, Charmika, Tanka, Pachali, Pani Alu, Massia and Manhachu. The flesh of the hog is particularly prized by them, so much so, that almost every house of the Coles is said to have the appendage of a piggery. They are governed chiefly by numerous petty sirdars, or heads of villages, called Manki and Munda, but acknowledge allegiance, and in some cases pay tribute, to the hill zemindars in whose countries they are settled.

The *Kands* are found in great numbers in all the hill estates south of the Mahanuddy. They form the principal part of the population of Killah Ranpur which has thence been called the Kandreh Dandpat. The natives also have the idea of a district situated between Daspalla, Boad, and Goomsur, inhabited entirely by this tribe of hill people which they call *Kandra.* I apprehend that the vast unexplored tracts of mountain and forest lying at the back of the Ganjam and Vizagapatam hill estates, as far as the Godaveri, are peopled chiefly by Kands in a very savage state, who probably differ little from their neighbours the *Gonds,* though Captain Blunt observes on the authority of the Jaghirdar of Malud and Manickpatam, (vide Journal of his route from *Chunar* to *Yertnagoodum,*) that the Coands and Goands are to be considered quite distinct races.*

The *Sours* are found chiefly in the jungles of Khurda, from Banpur to Cuttack, and in the woods of Atgerh, Daljora, &c.,

* The passage is as follows: "Having afterwards heard of a people who in the northern Sircars are called Coands (Kands) and whose depredations into those provinces are attended with similar acts of cruelty, I naturally conceived them to be the same tribe, but in conversation with Kumal Mahommed, the officer in charge of the Marhatta Pergunnah of Manickpatam, and who appeared to be well acquainted with the different tribes of mountaineers subject to the Berar government, he informed me that these are a different race from the Goands. The latter he said are much larger men, and had in many instances been made good subjects, but the Coands are inferior in stature and so wild, that every attempt which had been made to civilize them had proved ineffectual."

which skirt the foot of the hills for some way to the northward of the Mahanuddy. They are in general a harmless, peaceable race, but so entirely destitute of all moral sense, that, *they will as readily and unscrupulously deprive a human being of life, as any wild beast of the woods, at the orders of a chief, or for the most trifling remuneration!* Thus during the insurrection which prevailed in Khurda, they were the agents employed to carry into execution most of the schemes of revenge planned by its instigators, whenever helpless individuals were to be the sacrifice; and the quantity of blood shed by the hands of these ignorant savages without motive or remorse, during the above period of anarchy and disorder, is almost incredible. In ordinary times they are considered very useful both by the zemindars and villagers, in clearing the jungles and providing fuel which are their chief means of gaining a subsistence. They likewise collect the produce of the woods, and dispose of large quantities to the druggists and fruit sellers, in the neighbouring bazars. They are distinguishable from the other natives of the province, by their inferiority of stature, mean appearance, and jet black colour, as well as by an axe for cutting wood, the symbol of their profession, which they always carry in their hand. Their language little resembles that spoken by the Oorias, and is scarcely intelligible to any but themselves. They are said to worship certain rude forms of Devi and Mahadeo or rather the Hindus so interpret the adoration paid by them to a few natural objects, as stumps of trees, masses of stone, or clefts in rocks, in which an impure imagination may discern some resemblance to the Lingu. Some dwell in small villages called Sour Sais; others lead a migratory sort of life, clearing annually spots in the jungle, where they erect huts of sticks, leaves, and grass, and sow different sorts of grain of the Millet kind, which sprout up with extraordinary luxuriance in such situations. They will eat almost any kind of food, whether animal or vegetable. A great part of their subsistence is derived from the roots and produce of the jungles. The flowers of the Madhuka (*Bassia latifolia,*) and the Keora, yield them an intoxicating liquor; in lieu of rice they consume the seed of the bamboo, a very heating and indigestible food; the wild yams, arums, and other roots, furnish a nutritious and not unwholesome substitute for bread; and for a desert they have the wild mangoe, the fruit of the Bela every where abundant, and the seeds of the *Bauhinia racemosa,* served up on the large ribbed leaf of the Ravya, which answers the purposes of a dish. "The Puttah Soar (says Rennell) cover their nakedness with Saul leaves, and inhabit the mountains. They do not cultivate grain, but subsist on wild herbs, roots, berries, and such like, and hold no communication with the villagers."

The author of the work called *Kholaset ul Towarikh*, places in the neighbourhood of Orissa, the country called the Triya or Stri Raj, where females exercise the powers of government, and have the superiority in society, and in the management of all affairs. The fable of the existence of such a country in this part of India, seems to be a purely gratuitous invention of the Mahommedan writers, and is unsupported either by the histories or the current belief of the natives.

The *language* of the *Or* or *Odra* nation is a tolerably pure dialect of the Sanscrit, resembling closely the Bengali, but far remote apparently from any affinity with the Telinga. Most of the titles of which the natives are so fond are pure Sanscrit; more than *three-fourths* of the nouns and roots of verbs may be traced to that language, and its few simple inflections are obviously founded on the rules of the Vyakaran or Grammar. The basis of the alphabet is the common Hindi or Nagari character, somewhat disguised however by a peculiarity in the mode of writing it. In the direction of Bengal, the Ooria language is used tolerably pure, following the line of the coast as far as the Hijellee and Tumlook divisions at least: I have been credibly informed that in the Mysadal Pergunnah, all revenue accounts are written on tal patr or leaves of the palmyra tree in that dialect. On the western side of the Midnapore district, the two languages begin to intermingle, at Rani Sarai about twenty miles north of the Subunreekha. A very mixed and impure bhasha is used by the Zemindari of Naraingerh and the hill estates beyond it, which improves a little at Midnapore, and at that town becomes more decidedly Bengali. The inhabitants of the country on the north of Keerpoy (officially termed the Jungle Mehals) probably speak the language of the Bengal province quite correct and unmixed. To the westward the Gond and Ooria languages pass into each other on the estate of Sonepur, the Raja of which country informed me, that *half his people speak one and half the other dialect*. On the south we find the first traces of the Telinga about Ganjam, where a different pronunciation may be observed. The people there call themselves *Oodiahs* and *Wodiahs*, instead of Oorias; Gerh becomes Gadda, Juggernaut, Jagannada, &c. The language of Orissa Proper still however prevails at Barwa, forty-five miles south of Ganjam, on the low lands of the coast, and as far as the large estate of Kimedy in the hills, beyond which the Telinga begins to predominate; at Cicacole it is the prevailing dialect, and in Vizagapatam, Telinga only is spoken in the open country. In the mountains of the interior, however, the dialect of the Odras is used by the bulk of the inhabitants, from Goomsur down to Palcondah, Bastar, and Jayapoor. The Oorea language thus prevailing from Tumlook to a considerable distance beyond Ganjam, or over an extent of country from three to four hundred miles in length, a wide field is furnished for the labours of missionaries who acquire that language.

I know of no original composition deserving any notice in the language of Orissa, excepting the Epic Poem called the *Kanji Kaviri Pothi*, which celebrates the conquest of Conjeveram, one of the most distinguished events in the modern history of the country. There is no deficiency however of translations of the more esteemed writings of the great Hindu authors, both religious and scientific, and every temple of importance has its legend or *Sthan Puran*, every almanac maker his Panji, and Bansabali, composed in the local tongue.

In estimating *the amount of the Population* of the Cuttack Province, we have no means of forming even a tolerable conjecture of the number of inhabitants in the hill countries. Information on that subject could be procured only from the hill Rajas or zemindars; and such are their jealousy, contumacy, and untractableness, that we might be sure, even if they condescended to furnish any returns at all, that they would be entirely false. The estimate given for the Mogulbandi, and that portion of the Rajwara which lies between it and the sea, though mostly conjectural, is founded upon data of a nature which warrant some confidence in its accuracy. The total of villages has been tolerably well ascertained.

The eighteen Police Thanas* of the Mogulbandi including the Rajwara estates of Aul, Kanka, Kujang, Herispur, Marichpur, and Bishenpur, with the whole of the smaller Killajat, contain 11,915 villages (Mouzahs and Patnas,) and 243,273 houses, exclusive of the towns of Cuttack, Balasore, and Pooree. This enumeration yields an average of about *twenty houses to a village*, which although low compared with the Bengal average, is corroborated by actual observation of the very small size of such villages of Orissa as ordinarily meet the eye. In the three northern Thanas which comprise the poorest and most unproductive portion of the Mogulbandi, the average is scarcely nineteen; in the twelve central

* They are thus named:—Basta, Balasore, Soro, Churaman, Badrak, Mattu or Talmal, Janjipur, Patamandri, Asserassar, Arackpur, Cuttack, Puharajpur, Taran, Harihurpur, Gope, Piply, Pooree, Khurda, Banpur.

ones it is nearly twenty; and in the three southern ones which contain the pergunnahs adjoining Pooree, filled with the large villages of the Sasan Brahmins, it is thirty.

In the first mentioned division, the ascertained number of inhabitants, men, women, and children, in 1678 houses, is 9576; yielding an average of rather more than five and two-third inmates for each house. In the southern division, 19,930 houses have been ascertained to hold 130,871 inmates; viz., men 33,518, women 33,903, infants 36,450, that is five and a fraction of about one-fifth per house. Adverting to these data which have been prepared with much care and accuracy, more especially in the southern division, an average rate of five persons per house, for the whole district, would not appear too high. On this calculation, the entire population of the district will stand as follows:—

Village inhabitants	12,16,365
Population of the town of Cuttack	40,000
——— Pooree..	30,000
——— Balasore	10,000
Total,	12,96,365

This calculation does not, as has been observed, include the inhabitants of the hill country, by some supposed perhaps as many more: nor does it include various districts in which the Oorea language is spoken, but which are not now reckoned parts of the province, as Ganjam, Tumlook, &c.

The area of the tract now under consideration, has been estimated with tolerable accuracy at about 9,000 square miles, by counting the squares into which Captain Sackville's map is divided. The result of the above calculation therefore gives to *the open and cultivated part of Orissa, a population of* 135 *souls per square mile.* That the estimate for Cuttack should fall much below that suggested for Bengal, viz. 203 per square mile, will not surprise those who have attended to the picture drawn in the preceding part of this history, of the general poverty of the people, and the paucity of large towns and villages.

The statements for the pergunnahs Raheng, Saraen, Choubiskud, Uldhar, and Rorang, which are by far the most to be relied on, yield the following proportions of the principal classes, viz:

Total number of Householders..	19,930
Chasas or Husbandmen	7,432
Brahmins	3,565
Mahtis (Carana or Writer cast)..	611
Gowalas (Cowherds)	537
Baniyas, both Druggists and Shroffs	232
Artisans, Manufacturers, Shopkeepers, &c.	4,887
Low casts, as Fishermen, Kandras, Pans, Bawaris, Chandal, &c., or common labourers, coolies, village watchmen, &c.	2,420
Balance composed of Mussulman, foreigners, mendicants, and casual residents	246

It will not be altogether uninteresting to compare this estimate of the population of Cuttack, with the sales of salt for the supply of the district. Salt is sold on the part of government at several golahs or store-houses in the interior, in quantities of not less than one maund, at the fixed monopoly price of Sicca Rupees two per maund, increased by charges of transportation, storing, commission, &c., which raise the price according to circumstances to from 2 Rs. 3 As. to 2 Rs. 6 As. per maund, at the storehouses. The average retail rate varies from about 2 Rs. 8 As. to 3 Rupees per maund. This system of supply has been established since the beginning of 1818. During the last four years, the average of the public sales for consumption within the Mogulbandi, has been 2,00,000 maunds. Mr. Colebrooke considers the quantity of one-fourth of a chittack per diem to be an ample allowance for an inhabitant of Bengal. In Cuttack, an allowance of half a chittack is insisted upon by the people themselves as the usual average, when salt was cheap; and the larger individual consumption of the article in this district, is explained by a reference to the peculiar diet of the people, the villainous insipidity of which must necessarily require to be relieved by an additional mixture of salt. Abulfazl has observed of the Oorias, "After boiling their rice they steep it in cold water, and eat it the second day." This stale and unpalatable species of food is still universally used under the name of *Panbhatta*. As the enhanced price of salt under the British government, certainly amounts to from 400 to 500 per cent, may have somewhat reduced the former consumption by the poorer classes, that is the mass of the community, we shall perhaps arrive near the truth by taking a medium between the Cuttack and Bengal allowances. Some deduction too must be made on account of children under ten years, whose numbers, adopting the average suggested by the Raheng returns, may be estimated at about one-third of the whole population. The calculation of the quantity necessary for the Cuttack people will then stand as follows in round numbers:

Eight and a half lacs of adults, at between one-fourth and one-half chittacks per diem, consume annually .. *Mds.*	1,75,000
Four and a half lacs of infants, at rather less than one fourth ditto .. .. *Mds.*	56,000
Total consumption ..	2,31,200

The balance required of about 30,000 maunds, may be supposed to be obtained by smuggling, independent of the government sales.

The accounts remaining to us of the most important operation in modern Indian finance, Raja Toral Mall's settlement, called the Taksim Jamma and Tankhah Raqmi, are as imperfect and deficient in Orissa as in every other part of India with which I am acquainted. There can be no doubt but that a *jarib* or measurement of the lands of the three sircars Jelasore, Budruck, and Cuttack, was made, under the orders and superintendence of that distinguished minister, with what is termed the Bareh Dasti Padika or rod of twelve spans, and all the Ruqbeh accounts in the offices of the Sudder Canungos and their Gomashtehs, are stated to be founded on that measurement. The subsequent corrections and alterations that have taken place, are said to have been made by *Nezir Andazi* or guess work. What is curious, the standard of the bigah, which was originally uniform, is now found to be different in every part of the district, to such an extent indeed, that in some pergunnahs the bigah is four times the size of that nominal measure in other divisions, and all the intermediate variations frequently occur. By what rule the other great step in the settlement was adjusted, viz., the determination of the rates of rent to be paid by the husbandmen for a bigah of each description, I can find no evidence or information whatever. Abulfazl in describing the Emperor's settlement for Hindostan generally, says, that an average of ten years' collection was struck. But whether in this province which had then only recently been conquered from its Hindu sovereigns, and rescued from the destructive anarchy of the Bengal Afghans, the ancient rates were maintained, or heavier ones imposed, I cannot venture to offer any assertion. My general impression is that the fixed and regular assessment of the Moguls was heavier than that of the Hindu Rajas, but the indigenous princes of Orissa seem to have had so many methods of extorting a large revenue from their subjects, by extra demands, occasional requisitions, and irregular claims under various heads and pretexts, that the burthens of the ryot may be presumed to have been pretty much the same under either administration.

I shall now proceed to furnish abstract statements of the *land assessment of Cuttack* according to its present dimensions, translated from revenue accounts in the private possession of the family of the former Dewan of the Marhatta government, the authenticity of which I see no reason to doubt; and it is on these only I should be disposed to rely, in forming any comparison between the former and present productiveness of the revenues of Cuttack.

Taksim Jamma of the Moguls.

Thirteen Sircars contain	Mehals	297
Deduct Tehsil Bengaleh, or collected under Bengal.. ..	Mehals	27
	Remain, Mehals	270

		Kahans.	*Pans.*
Tankhah Raqmi or Jamma of the above	Couris	59,61,499	8

Under the Marhattas.

Tashkhis Bhoonsla, or fixed Jamma under the government of the Nagpore Raja	Rupees	2,42,236	10
	Couris, *Kahans*	47,36,803	0

viz.

	Rupees.	*Couris. Kahans.*
Mehalat and Thanehjat (Khaleseh Land).. ..	2,24,079 7 0	36,42,978
Tribute of the Zemindareh or Killajat Estates..	18,157 3 0	10,93,825
Rupees,	2,42,236 10 0	47,36,803

Dakhil Sircar or remitted to the Raja's Treasury at Nagpore, calculated in Rupees of sorts	6,00,000
Kharch Sipahan o ghyreh, expenses of Troops and management	9,00,000
Total Rupees,	15,00,000
Equal to Sa. Rupees,	13,50,000

The sum of Sicca Rupees 13,50,000, may be assumed as the standard revenue of Cuttack under the Nagpore government, and was certainly the highest amount ever realized by the Marhattas from the district, though their assessments were sometimes rated higher. The collections indeed I suspect very frequently fell short of the above standard, more especially during the last ten years of the Marhatta administration. The proportions between the net expenditure, and the remittances to Nagpore, I take to have been in a great measure nominal.

The following are the results of settlements formed by different Subahdars, taken from authentic accounts which are still extant. Some indefiniteness must attach to the statements, from the uncertainty of the rate of exchange between couris and silver, which fluctuated tó from three to four kahans per deh masha rupee, during the whole of the Marhatta administration.

The settlement of Sheo Bhat Sautra for 1167 A. is entered as follows.

Gold Mohurs		231	0
Rupees, of sorts		3,82,829	8
Couris	Kahans,	27,82,446	0

Another settlement by Sambha Ji Ganesh in 1178 A. is entered.

Ashrafis		11	0
Rupees, of sorts		5,01,394	15
Couris	Kahans,	42,37,666	0

Another by Raja Ram Pandit.

Rupees, of sorts		1,10 318	14
Couris	Kahans,	53,37,685	0

Another by Inkaji Suk'h Deo.

Rupees, of sorts		1,51,435	9
Couris	Kahans,	57,78,224	0

On the subjugation of the province by the British government, in 1803, a rate of conversion of four kahans of couris per Sicca Rupee was assumed, and the *revenues* have been invariably demanded and paid entirely in silver, at least since 1807. The assessment of the British government has been raised by two successive and gradual augmentations, to the amount of 14,45,950 rupees.

Mogulbandi (exclusive of pergunnah Pataspur, &c., assessed under the Marhattas, at Rs. 30,000)	12,64,370
Killah Kurdah, held khas for political reasons, which paid latterly to the Marhattas a Peshcash of Sicca Rupees 10,000	61,169
Fixed tribute of *thirty-one Khandaitis* or Zemindaris of the Military Chiefs of Orissa, styled Rajas	1,20,411
Total, Sa. Rs.	14,45,950

"The Mogulbandi (says Hamilton,) or that portion of Cuttack paying revenue to government, and the rents of which are not yet fixed, is distributed into 83 pergunnahs or revenue divisions, of different and capricious magnitudes. The total amount of the Cuttack revenue termed Mogulbandi, is 1,363,668 rupees. The estimated measurement of the assessed lands in cultivation and arable, is only 1,200,220 bigahs; the number of estates 2349; and of inhabitants 737,922, of which number only 21,932 are Mahommedans. The tributary estates, their annual payments to the revenue, and extreme dimensions, are given below, and those not subject to the British laws and regulations are marked with an asterisk (*).

List of the twenty-nine Ghurjaut or Tributary Estates.

	Dimensions.	Tribute, per ann.
Mohurbunge	150 miles by 100	1,001 rupees.
Kunka	75 by 50	19,132
*Autghur	15 by 12	6,848
Marickpoor	9 by 6	3,120
Aul	20 by 10	26,680
*Deknal	112 by 87	4,780
*Bankee	30 by 25	4,162
*Khandeapurah	25 by 12	3,948
*Jenmoo	17 by 9	620
*Neyaghur	75 by 25	5,179
*Nursingpoor	.. .. ..	.. ..
*Neelgur	.. .. ..	3,656
*Ongologur	125 by 10	1,550
*Hindole	17 by 12	516
Koorjung	50 by 25	7,034
Harrespoor	80 by 5	34,083
Sookundah	8 by 5	1,272
*Koonjeur	182 by 125	2,790
Muddoopoor	15 by 13	5,813
Chedra	3 by 2½	2,134
Demparah	7 by 5	776
Durpun	15 by 13	5,853
Buttoo Dumparah	.. .. ..	.. ..
*Runpoor	15 by 10	1,313
*Talchere	15 by 15	974
*Tegrah	13 by 12	826
Burmba	12 by 8	1,310
Bissenpoor	5 by 3	1,740
Kulkulla	1½ by 1	123

The annual demand on the above 29 zemindaries is fixed at the above sums. The sum total annually accruing to the British government, from this source, amounts to 118,687 rupees; the supposed surplus of clear profit remaining to the landholders is estimated at 525,250 rupees, which is a mere trifle considering the immense tract of country from which it is derived. All these tributary zemindars assume the title of Raja in their respective territories, and admit each others claim to that dignity. They also exhibit the insignia, go abroad with the retinue, and observe the forms and state of independent princes, according as their income suffices for covering the consequent expenditure.

Some of the principal zemindars, to the number of sixteen, are at present exempted from the operation of the British regulations; the remaining thirteen are within the jurisdiction of the laws. The exemption of the first sixteen, from the operation of the Bengal code, was not founded on any claim which the proprietors of these tributary estates had to the exercise of independent authority; on the contrary, it originated entirely from the opinion that was entertained of the barbarous and uncultivated manners of these zemindars and their subjects, combined with the impervious nature of the country, consisting mostly of hills and jungles, which local circumstances would have rendered it extremely difficult to execute any process of the courts of judicature, or to enforce the orders of the public functionaries. Experience, however, has demonstrated, that the liberality of this arrangement has not exempted it from much inconvenience and embarrassment. On the contrary, the tribes thus left to their own guidance have habitually addicted themselves to the perpetration of crimes of the blackest dye, and the zemindars who ought to have been the conservators of the public peace, and distributors of justice, have been the very persons most suspected of these atrocities, more especially of assassinations committed for the purpose of usurping estates, and acts of extreme cruelty exercised on the persons of their tenants.

The Bengal government, however, not being prepared to extend the regulations generally to those estates, which without an efficient police might tend rather to aggravate than alleviate the sufferings of the inhabitants, determined to appoint a special officer to control the conduct of the Rajas; both to serve as a check on their proceedings, and with the view of obtaining an accurate knowledge of the country, a necessary step towards the introduction of an improved system of administration. A superintendent of the tributary estates was accordingly appointed, and invested with a general control over the conduct of the proprietors.

A great outlay is annually necessary in Cuttack, for the purpose of keeping the embankments in good order; the expense incurred by government on this account, in 1814, having amounted to 40,514 rupees. Some of the principal embankments, especially that at the town of Cuttack, are indispensable; but the utility of many of the inferior ones is by no means equivalent to the disbursements they involve. More than *one fourth* of the circulation of the district is carried on by cowries; copper one tenth, gold one fortieth, and silver three fifths. Formerly, the revenue was calculated in cowries, and annual importations of these shells are still made from the Maldives in return for grain exported.*

The excess of regular receipts under the head of land revenue alone, may be stated at from one to two lacs per annum in favour of the British government, which increase may be fairly ascribed to the improved and enlightened system of management now pursued. The country has unquestionably prospered under our administration, though much suffering was long experienced in particular quarters from injudicious measures, the errors of which have been perceived and remedied: cultivation has greatly increased in every part: and if the ryot or husbandman has not benefited by the change of government, in proportion to the superior importance of that class of the community to which he belongs, and to the benevolent intentions of the legislature, his condition must certainly be considered on the whole better than it was under the native system, whilst the higher classes connected with the soil (now acknowledged as proprietors) have undoubtedly attained to a state of comfort, independence, and comparative opulence, quite unknown at any former period of the history of the country.

The revenue derived from the salt monopoly, exceeds the total amount of the land rents paid to the state, and is entirely the creation of the British government. The salt sold within the province yields a net return of about 3,00,000, and the quantity annually exported to Calcutta for public sale at the salt office, produces little short of from rupees 15,00,000 to 16,00,000. Under the heads of customs, tax on spirituous liquors, and *tax on pilgrims*,† a further net revenue of about one lac per annum is obtained. The value of Cuttack, after deducting expenses of management, may be fairly assumed at upwards of *thirty lacs of rupees per annum*. If a revenue of 3,00,000 rupees annually is derived from the people,

* Hamilton's Hindostan, vol. ii. pp. 41-2-3.

† Repealed by Regulation, April 20, 1840.

how imperative the duty that something upon a large scale should be attempted for the intellectual and moral improvement of the people.

In surveying attentively the ancient Political Institutions of Orissa as connected with *the tenure of land*, it is impossible not to be struck with the marked resemblance which many of their features exhibit to the system of European policy called the *feudal*, at certain stages of its progress. I am strongly inclined to think that the comparison might be extended to India generally, and that a careful enquirer would not fail to discern in every part of the country, obvious traces of the former existence of such a system, however irregularly defined, and liable to variation in the details, from local peculiarities. The subject has not hitherto met with that attention which its importance, more especially when viewed in connection with the much disputed question of Zemindari rights, unquestionably merits. Some writers indeed have treated with utter contempt and derision, the notion of the existence of any analogy whatever between the ancient institutions of India, and the feudal system of Europe. Others, however, of equal or greater authority, have not been able to resist the striking evidence of such affinity which presents itself in every province of India, where the Hindu form of government has been little impaired or modified. Thus, Sir J. Malcolm, page 375 of his valuable *Report on Malwa*, observes, "The principle of this part of a Raj or *Rajput* principality, differs little from that feudal system which formerly existed in Europe, and is liable to the same vicissitudes in the relations and powers of the respective parties." But every one knows that the Rajput, is only one branch or epithet of the great Regal and Military caste amongst the Hindus, called the Cshetriya (*Khetri,*) and anciently *all* principalities and kingdoms might in one sense be designated *Rajput*. Captain MacMurdo in an excellent Paper on the province of Cutch, in vol. ii. *Bombay Transactions*, states, "The government of Cutch is that of a pure aristocracy, in which the power is vested in a variety of Chiefs on their respective territories, which bear a strong resemblance to the feudal baronies. These Chiefs have a head who is entitled Rao, to whom they owe the duty of military service with their relations and followers." The Chiefs in question are afterwards described to be Rajputs. Colonel Wilford expressly applies the title of *Barons*, to the inferior Khetris, in his historical Essays on ancient India. In the essay on Anugangam we find the following curious and apposite passage,—"Like Parasurama he (Maha Bali) either destroyed or drove out of his dominions the remnant of the Cshetris or Military tribe, and placed Sudras in their room. These were the *Barons* of the land who often proved troublesome. Raja Balwant Singh, the predecessor of Cheyt Singh did the same in the district of Benares with the *Zemindars,* who represented the *Cshetris,* and even pretended to be really so ; from an idea, that it was impossible to improve the revenues arising from the land tax under their management."

In the preceding part of this account of Orissa, I have noticed generally the great territorial divisions, both natural and political, which exist in this province. The extensive hilly regions and forest tracts, jungle Pergunnahs and Mehals, as they are now termed, reaching nearly from Bishenpur to the Godaveri, together with the woodland country on the sea shore of Orissa Proper, have been in all ages parcelled out among and occupied by a number of Chieftains of the Military class. These Chiefs may be safely considered as de facto proprietors of their possessions under the native governments, that is, they held them hereditarily, exercised uncontrolled territorial jurisdiction within their limits, and appropriated the entire revenues subject to the condition of preforming Military service, or other offices and duties, at the court of their superior Raja, the Gajapati, residing mostly at Cuttack, which services have in latter ages been generally commuted for a light tribute or money payment. The more fertile and productive division of the province formed the Kot, Khaliseh, or domain of the prince, from which the Hindu sovereigns of Orissa like their successors the *Moguls, Marhattas,* and *English,* derive their principal revenues. There can be no question, but that this other great territorial division was the landed estate or property of the sovereign. It may be observed that such a state of things as above indicated, conforms exactly with the declaration contained in a well known passage of the digest of Hindu law translated by Mr. Colebrooke: "By conquest the earth became the property of Parasurama: by gift the property of the sage Casyapa, and committed by him to *Cshatriyas* for the sake of protection, became their protective property, successively held by powerful conquerors and not by subjects cultivating the soil." So strikingly and universally true indeed is the maxim of the property of the soil vesting in the Cshstriyas, that we find them always either asserting a title to ownership in the land, which they occupy hereditarily, or in the actual enjoyment of the proprietary right, even when reduced to the situation of '*cultivating subjects*'—witness the various casts and classes of Rajput village Zemindars in every quarter of Hindustan, and the western provinces.

The feudal Lords of Orissa, for such certainly may the Military

Chiefs referred to, be termed, are known and described by several different titles both in history, in official records, and in the common language of the country, and these are quite indiscriminately applied, whence has resulted a corresponding confusion of ideas. They are called simply *Khetris* (Cshetriyas,) from their caste; *Khandaits*, an Orissa name for a branch of the same class, signifying literally persons entitled to wear the *Khanda* or national sword of Orissa; *Bhunia, Bhuyan or Bhumi* derived from *Bhu*,* the earth, and synonymous with *Bhupati* (Lord of the soil:) *Poligar*, a Telinga word, derived from *Pollam*, a fief: *Sawant*, in Persian, *Sirdar*, meaning Chief and Lord: *Sevakan Arni Dar*, or servants and vassals holding tracts of country hereditarily, on the condition of service; and finally *Zemindars*. Many of them were descended from the supreme Rajas of the country. We have Orme's authority in a remarkable passage of the 8th book of his History, for the belief entertained by the Poligars south of the Chilka lake of their origin as above intimated. He says, "These conquests (made by a Raja of Orissa, some centuries before Mahommedanism,) were distributed in many portions to his relations, officers, and menial servants, from whom several of the present northern Poligars pretend to be lineally descended, and to govern at this very time the very districts which were then given to their ancestors." It is not improbable that many of the Orissan Khandaits and Bhunias first received estates during the 12th century of the Christian era, in Raja Anang Bhim Deo's time, who is said to have created sixteen Sawants or great Lords, but the tenure of the majority no doubt reaches back to a very remote antiquity. To describe a little more particularly their duties and offices, it may be observed, that they were posted all round and along the frontiers of the Raj, with the view to defend it from the irruptions of neighbouring powers, or the incursions and devastations of the savage inhabitants of the wild regions in the interior, such as the Kands and Coles, who to this day give serious annoyance in many parts of the hill estates, and if the belief of their origin and ancient situation be well founded, were doubtless in former ages far more numerous than at present.

In this point of view their situations and duties resembled much that of the Lords of the Marches in Europe. Nor is the above the

* Mr. Elliot, in his observations on the inhabitants of the Garrow hills transmitted to the Asiatic Society, observes, "The head people of the villages are called *Booniaks* a name used by the *head Rajas* of *Bengal* when the king resided at Gour." In the Ayin Akberi, the word Boomi, derived from *Boom*, the soil, is continually used as synonymous with Zemindar.

only striking feature of analogy between the feudal lords of India and the western hemisphere. The estates or jurisdictions of that class in Orissa were always called by the Hindus, *Gerhs*, and by the Mussulmans, killahs or *Castles.* A certain part of the lands under the head Officer were parcelled out amongst several military retainers and dependents called Naiks, Dalais, Dalbehras, and sometimes Khandaits, who held of their superior on much the same principle, as he did of the supreme Raja, though generally speaking by a more limited and imperfect tenure. Under these again, a portion of the lands of each subordinate Gerh, were assigned as service land to the feudal militia of the country, called Paiks, who following equally the occupations of soldier and cultivator, were obliged at any moment when called on by their leader, to take up arms, and accompany him to the field. In time of war the Khandaits or nobility of Orissa at the head of their respective contingents of this landed militia, ranged themselves under the standard of their sovereign, and formed the main part of his military array. Thus we frequently read of the Gajapati assembling his chiefs to attend on a warlike expedition, and we find that the Sunnuds, granted by the Mogul government (in cases where they exercised the right of investiture,) always contained a condition that the Khandait should be ready to attend with his *contingent*, when summoned by the Military Officer of his division. The Paiks are the local Infantry constantly referred to in the Ayin Akberi. The author observes, speaking of the imperial army; "The Zemindari troops alone are in number upwards of *four million and four hundred thousand*, as will hereafter be particularized"—a fact which shews the extensive prevalence of the military tenure throughout the country, even as late as the 16th century. The proportion of landed militia set down for Orissa Proper in the same work, is about *one hundred thousand.* Besides the general obligation of military service, the Indian feudatories were bound to do homage, and to perform certain nominal duties or offices resulting from their tenures, when in actual attendance on their liege lords, called by the expressive word *Sewa, Seva*, or service, (in Persian *Khidmat*,) a consideration of which, reminds one strongly of some of the ancient forms of the Germanic constitution. Thus it was the business of one to bear *the sword of state;* another held *the shield;* a third carried the *umbrella or royal standard;* a fourth presented the *Raja's slippers;* a fifth *fanned him with the regal chouri*, &c. The above services are to this day performed in the presence of the Khurdah Rajas, by several of the hill Zemindars, as often as they visit Pooree, though the distinctive character of the office appropriated to each, has become a good deal merged in the simple duty of holding the chouri and pankha, in the presence of the representative of their ancient Lords Paramount.

The estate of the Chief Khetri, or Lord Paramount, comprised the fairest and most fertile portion of the monarchy of Orissa. In every part of India it would seem that, even under the Hindus, the domains reserved for the crown constituted, if not the largest, at least the most valuable and productive share of the whole territory, and it was the uniform policy of the strong government of the Mahommedans, constantly to enlarge this share by the gradual subjugation and absorption of the possessions of the lesser chiefs and princes. As it is the above-mentioned estate or concern, with the management of which the Officers of the British government are chiefly occupied, and from which nearly all its revenues are derived, it is of course of particular importance to enquire respecting *the system and the rights anciently prevailing and still existing, in the tract known by the modern appellation of the Mogulbandi or Khaliseh.* Whilst it yields to the state a revenue of between *twelve and thirteen lacs*, in its real character of proprietor, the Rajwara or division occupied by the feudal chiefs, pays a light tribute of only 1,20,000, the difference between that and the actual net produce, which is at the lowest calculation in the ratio of one to ten, being enjoyed by the several Zemindars, in virtue of *their* proprietary rights.

In the Cuttack territory, obvious traces exist to this day of a subdivision of lands into tracts held by military retainers, and those of the common ryots. Tenants of the former description are called at present Paiks, and lesser Khandaits, and the estates on which they are found are entered in the revenue accounts as "*Khurdiah Gerjat*," but whatever may have been their number anciently, they are now too few and unimportant to claim a particular notice. The ryoti land, paying a full rent to the sovereign, demands our principal attention. According to the uniform system of India generally, it was partitioned into numerous *grams*, townships, or village societies. The larger revenue allotments or circles of villages known to the Hindus of Orissa, were denominated *Khand* and *Bisi* or *Bishe*; words meaning literally a portion or district. Each of these petty districts was under the management and control of two descriptions of hereditary officers, vested with police and revenue functions, viz. the *Khand Adipati* and *Bishuya* or *Bissoee*, (words signifying chief of a division,) who was the principal man; and the *Bhoi Mul* of the Karan or writer cast, who had the more particular charge of keeping all the accounts and registers connected with the land. In parts of the Deccan, the same description of officers still exist, and are called the Des Mukh and Des Pandiah, terms of precisely corresponding import. They seem to have acted jointly in the discharge of some of their functions, and separately and independently in regard to others. One perhaps had the more especial duty of administering the police, the other of collecting the revenue; whilst they both watched generally over the fiscal interests of the state, and acted as umpires and moderators of Punchaits, in investigating and adjusting disputes between inhabitants of different villages, or between the people of a village and their head man. Every respectable village had its chief and accountant, called the Padhan and Bhoi—but frequently several of the smaller hamlets of Orissa were associated under one set of officers of this name; much oftener the same individual performed both functions in a village; and sometimes none of the kind existed, in which case the charge of the village affairs attached more immediately to the division officer. Where the Padhan and Bhoi existed, they discharged respectively much the same duty in regard to their individual village or villages, as the superior officers exercised in regard to their circle of villages. The Padhan looked after the police with the aid of the village watchman, who made his reports to a Sirdar or Sirdars called the *Or* Khandait, stationed with the Bisoi; the Bhoi kept the village accounts and furnished information to the Bhoi Mul or chief accountant. All these functionaries held their situations *hereditarily*, and were in the habits of mortgaging or even selling the whole or shares of them, with the sanction of the ruling power, just as we see *the priests and officers in the temple of Juggernaut at this day, disposing constantly of their several shewas or services, with the emoluments thereunto annexed.* To infer from these circumstances any right of property *in the soil,* would seem equally rash and absurd. It is a nicer question, whether *under the old Hindu system the actual occupants of the soil were considered to possess any subordinate title of ownership in land.* There are no obvious traces of such a right now remaining in Cuttack, as we read of in Canara and Malabar. I have never yet been able to discover any well anthenticated instance of the *sale* or *mortgage* of land by a Malguzari ryot of the province. The thani or fixed cultivators, however undoubtedly possessed under the old Rajas the privilege of hereditary occupancy; their fixed assessment was light and easy; and there was then no one to dispute the matter with them, excepting the despotic uncontroled sovereign of the country, who, whatever his claims in theory, of course required nothing from the land but an adequate revenue.

The changes consequent on the subjection of the province by the *Mogul* government come next to be considered. It is well known that after the defeat of the Afghan usurpers, who had gained temporary possession of Orissa, by the armies of Akber under the command of his General Khan Jehan and others, the celebrated Dewan Tural Mall visited the province A. D. 1580, to superintend the introduction of his settlement of the crown lands, founded on a measurement and valuation called the *Taksim Jamma* and *Tankha Raqmi.* The arrangements for the annexation of the Suba of Orissa to the empire, did not, however, receive their final completion until the arrival of Raja Man Sinh, the Imperial Lieutenant, who assumed charge of the government in 999 Amli, or Mahommedan era.

Under his administration the heads of the existing branches of the Royal family were acknowledged as Rajas; they were invested with the rank and titles conferred by the Mogul Court on officers of distinction; and extensive portions of country were assigned to them as hereditary fiefs in Zemindari tenure. No regular tribute appears to have been required from them on account of their own lands, but the right of investiture was reserved to the ruling power, with the privilege of levying such contributions on the accession of a new Raja, as it might be thought expedient, according to the circumstances of the times, to demand. The reigning prince was styled the Raja of Khurda, with the rank of a Commander of 3,500 "*Mansabi Seh Hazar Panjsad,*" and his estate was composed of the jurisdiction called Killah Khurda, with the Mehals Rahang, Limbai Pursottem Chetter, &c., alienated from the Khaliseh. To the two sons of Telinga Mukund Deo (the last independent monarch,) were assigned respectively with the title of Raja and rank of five hundred, Sarangher, Pattia, Sailo, Saibir, &c., and Al with Derabissi, and Uthar. A certain number likewise of the great Chiefs of Orissa were placed under the control of each of the above Rajas, who collected the tribute before due from them, or then for the first time imposed. *Zemindar** is the obvious translation of

* Even the powerful Rajas of Joudpoor, Bhartpoor, &c., were called Zemindars by the Mogul government down to the latest period, and we know from history the nature of their tenures. They were bound to attend in succession on the person of the Emperor at the head of a fixed quota of Troops. Their own countries were and are still subdivided into the lands of the Military retainers or Thakurs, and the revenue lands, on the same principle that prevailed under the Hindu government in the empire at large.

the word Bhunia, Bhyan, or Bhupati, the common title of the ancient feudatories of this province, whose offices now received a *Persian* name, as well as their jurisdictions, the Hindi word *Gerh*, being exchanged for *Killah.* The more distant Zemindars were separated from the control of the superior Raja, and placed under seven principal Zemindars or Sawants, viz: the Zemindars of Keonjhar, Moherbenj, Bishenpur, Futtihabad, Naraingerh, Karrangher, and Nag or Bagbhum. The jurisdiction thus left to the Raja of Khurda, extended from the Mahanuddy to the borders of Kimedy in Ganjam, comprising 129 Killahs, Gerhs, or hill estates, exclusive of those situated within his own Zemindari. The above number agrees exactly with that given in the Ayin Akber,—"In Cuttack are *one hundred and twenty-nine brick forts* (killahs,) subject to the command of Gajapati." The other two Rajas had under them altogether *fifty-two* Zemindaris and *seventy-nine* killah divisions; and the seven Zemindars mentioned *fifty-six* ditto, containing *one hundred and one* killahs—all exclusive of their own estates, and the dependent killahs situated within them.

Extract from Documents in Persian.

Statement of Killajat, in the jungles and hills under Zemindars, subject to tribute (Peshkash) according to the allotment of Raja Man Sinh in 999 Amli, (Mahommedan era.)

Under the Raja of Khurda whose Manseb is that of 3500, are placed exclusive of Mehals, *thirty-one* Zemindars, and *two hundred* killahs.

The Raja's own estate of Khurda, one Zemindari, contains *seventy-one* killahs, viz: Khurda, Rathipur, Ber Gerh, Sissupal, Jharpareh, Kupliperrsad, Paterpareh, Nonepur, Jamkhely, Tapang, Chatarma, Lal Sinh, Gangpareh, Malipareh, Dumduma, Palih, Ramesar, Manibandh, Mankgora, Mangoi, Kormati, Kalamatiah, Kondlogerh, Mangalajuri, Jaripareh, Rorang, Karm, Mallipareh, Narsingpersad, Baran Gerh, Karang, Mirtunjay Gerh, Kaimattia, Usna, Baranda, Balbhadderpersad, Nowailee, Banjgiri, Tarkai, Seraen Gerh, Matiapareh, Bangro, Bhingro, Koklo, Karki, and eight killahs, in Limbai; Andharua, Darutang, Kolapokhar, Tirah Sowri thirteen killahs, Nakhikot, Kaipadda, Bolgerh, Gumhapur, and Muljher.

Under the Raja's command are *thirty* Zemindaris of Hindu Sirdars, containing *one hundred and twenty-nine* killahs.

Under the Raja of *Surangerh*, whose Manseb is that of 500, (exclusive of Mehals,) are placed *thirty-one* Zemindaris, containing *fifty* killahs.

The Raja's own estate with Balanta, *two* Zemindaris contains *twelve* killahs, viz: Killah Sarangerh, Bajgiri, Talgiri, Gowaligerh, Raghunathpur, Pattiah, Kalabank, Atagerh, Motri, Garukun, Balanta, and Nurkantiah. Dependent Hindu Sirdars, holding *twenty-nine* Zemindaris and *thirty-eight* forts under the Raja's orders.

Under the Raja of Al with the rank of 500 are placed *twenty-four* Zemindaris, containing *forty-two* killahs.

The Raja's own estate of killah Al, one Zemindari and one killah. Dependent Hindu Sirdars, *twenty-three* Zemindaris, containing *forty-one* killahs.

Under the Zemindar of Keonjhar are *fifteen* Zemindaris and *fifty-five* killahs. His own estate one Zemindari, containing *eleven* killahs, viz: Anandpur, Sikri, &c., *four* killahs, Mitagher, and others name unknown. Dependent Chiefs *fourteen* Zemindaris, having *twenty-four* killahs.

Under the Zemindar of Moherbenj *twelve* Zemindaris containing *forty-two* killahs. His own estate, one Zemindari containing *eighteen* killahs, viz: Bhunj Bhum, Mantri, Harriorpoor, Dewalia, Purnia, Karkachna, Bamanhatti, Sirhonda, and small insignificant forts, ten. Dependent Chiefs, eleven Zemindaris having *twenty-four* killahs.

Under the Zemindar of Bishenpur, are *twelve* Zemindaris and *twenty-nine* killahs. His own estate, one Zemindari comprising *fifteen* killahs. Dependent Chiefs, eleven Zemindars, having fourteen killahs.

Under the Zemindar of Futtihabad, *seven* Zeminders containing *seventeen* killahs. His own Zemindari, Futtihabad, &c., containing two killahs. Dependent Zemindars *six*, containing *fifteen* killahs.

Under the Zemindar of Naraingerh, six Zemindaris, containing *seventeen* killahs. His own Zemindari contains four killahs. Dependent Zemindaris *five*, containing *thirteen* forts.

Under the Zemindar of Karan Gerh *six* Zemindaris, having *eight* killahs. His own one Zemindari, containing two killahs. Dependent *five*, containing *six* killahs.

Under the Zemindar of Nag or Bagbhum. His own one Zemindari, containing two killahs.

Badshahi Thanehs under Cuttack	21
———— under Bengal	4

Establised in old times by Raja Man Sinh 999 Amlee. Cuttack, Piply Nour, Talmal, Pacherah, Jajipoor, Budruck, Soro, Ramna, Bastah, Jellasore, Futtihabad, Narain Gerh, and Midnapore; the last four under Bengal.

Under Kam Garkhan: Malud, Telingapenth, Santrapur, Chattiah, Sarangerh, and Mahulpur. Under Hazim Beg Khan: Naltigri, Alemghir, Shirgher.

Under Shujaa-ud-din, Fatteh Gerh, Shujaa Gerh, Paikani, Ahmedpur, Andiyari, Tiran, Gope, Kujang, and Rynto, both of which latter ones were broken up by the Zemindars. Mohammed Taki Khan, after the seizure of Raja Ramchander Deo, planted twenty-two thanehs for the protection and subjugation of Rajwara from Bulwanta to Banpur, but they were all removed excepting Balanta, when Bir Kishore Deo succeeded to the Raj by order of the King.

Whilst the ministers of Akber thus wisely left the turbulent feudal chiefs or Khetri Zemindars, to the management of those who from their local rank and hereditary influence were best qualified to control them, they considered it expedient to adopt also, with very little variation, the system which they found existing for the administration of the affairs of the *Kot*, or as they called them the *Khaliseh* lands, that is, the country annexed to the Imperial Dewanni. The only marked change which they introduced, indeed, was that of translating all the uncouth and harsh sounding Oorea designations of things and offices, into more familiar Persian terms of corresponding import.

The *Khands* and *Bissees* now became *Pergunnahs;* the Police and Revenue Officers, Chowdris* and Vilaity (Mofussil or Provincial) Canungos, or generally Talukdars, the heads of villages Mokaddams; and the villages themselves Mouzas. The larger territorial division of Sircar was perhaps arbitrary, suggested by considerations of financial convenience, or may have been copied from the Oorea *Dandpat.* The term Mehal, or plural Mehalat, by which the Revenue lands were designated in contradistinction to Killajat or the Military ditto, comprised in Akber's time, each, several Pergunnahs, and answered nearly to the modern Chakleh, though it is now applied to every petty estate or interest separately engaged for with the Collector.

* The author of the Ayin Akberi says, speaking of the Subeh of Berar, —"In this country they call the *Chowdri*, Desmookhee; the *Canungoe*, Despondiah: the *Mokaddum*, *Putayl* and the *Putwaree*, *Koolkurnee*.

Until the conquest of Orissa by the British arms, the functions and situation of the Chowdri and Canungo, Talukdars and the Mokaddams, remained precisely as I have generally explained them. All Pergunnahs in the Marhatta accounts (with very few exceptions) are found entered as divided into the Taluks of Chowdris and Canungos named after the holder, and the separated or Mazkuri villages of such Mokaddams as had been entirely emancipated from their control, with certain alienated lands known by names and revenue terms which it is unnecessary here to mention. On the introduction of the British Government and regulations, all parties whose names appeared in the public accounts of the preceding administration as answerable for or intrusted with the collection of the public dues, were forthwith acknowledged not only as *Zemindars*, but *as proprietors of the land comprised in their Zemindaris.* Whatever may be thought of the policy of this admission and the advantages that have resulted from it, that it was founded on an erroneous view of the state of things under the native Government, seems to me to be beyond all question. How did this error, which seems to have been as generally prevalent every where else as in Cuttack, originate? I think its origin and prevalence may be ascribed chiefly to three causes; 1st, the want of a proper distinction being made between the rights and circumstances of the real ancient Zemindars of the country, and those officers called by the Moguls Talukdars or by whatever other name, who exercised hereditarily the management and collection of the domains of the state; 2nd, the confused and inaccurate application of the term Zemindar by the natives of the country themselves, long before the accession of the British Government, which was probably a principal cause of the want of discrimination above noticed; 3rd, the failure to distinguish between the inheritance and sale of an office (a practice probably peculiar to the Hindus) and the inheritance and sale of the land with which that office was connected and concerned.

Under the Mogul Government persons denominated Talukdars and Mokaddams held offices connected with the collection of the revenues derived from the land. In Cuttack, the offices of Talukdar and Mokaddam, were, in conformity with the universal Hindu practice, *hereditary;* the rent or revenue of the lands payable to the state had been fixed with reference to the capability of the soil, and the established rules for the division of the crop; and certain perquisites were allotted to all parties concerned in the business of collection and management, which rendered those situations, though less valuable than at present, still objects of ambition to the class who alone were likely to hold them, under the native administration. Such being the case, it was a frequent practice of the Mogul Government, to oblige the Talukdars or Mazkuri Mokaddams, when they had embezzled the revenues, or otherwise fallen into arrears, to dispose of a portion of what they held, when the price obtained was invariably paid into the local treasury in discharge of balances. The custom may be considered to indicate a recognition of property, on the part of those classes of functionaries in their *offices*, but certainly cannot be held to establish any title of property in the soil itself. In most cases, the thing sold is carefully defined to be the whole or a share of the Talukdari and Chowdrahi, or of the Mokaddami of a village. Occasionally there is some ambiguity, where a single village only is disposed of, but I am persuaded that no person could rise from the perusal of a number of such deeds of sale of the old times, without being satisfied, that they transfer nothing more than a hereditary official tenure in a village or villages, or portion of a Taluk, the profits attaching to which are defined in the margin or endorsement, as well as the fixed revenue assessed. I observe, that, in the very first of the cases brought forward in the appendix to Sir J. Shore's Minute, on the permanent settlement, as an instance of the sale of *lands* in Bengal, the thing disposed of is distinctly stated to be, two sixteenths of the *Chowdrahi* of Kismat Pergunnah Fattehjanjpur, sold by Kamal Chowdri, to Hari Sircar.

In like manner, I apprehend that the sense of the words *Malik* and *Milkiat*, which occur generally in the Cuttack deeds of sale, as in those of a similar nature in Bengal and elsewhere, must, in any consistent and intelligible view of the case, be held to apply only *to the office and perquisites of the seller*, implying that he enjoyed them hereditarily, by a tenure independent of the will of any local superior, in contradistinction to an office held by a mere Gomashteh, or ephemeral agent at the pleasure of another. Indeed, the *Milkiat*, or right of property asserted, is most commonly and distinctly stated to refer to the Chowdrahi, Canungoi, and Mokaddammi. If such were not the case, it would follow that the same land might have two different kinds of absolute proprietors.

The difficulty vanishes when we view them, as, what they unquestionably were, offices connected with the land, of different degrees of authority and importance, each having its distinct duties and perquisites. In the southern Pergunnahs, formerly under the Khurda Rajas, where the heads of villages and accountants retain their old Hindi appellation of Padhan and Bhoi, we find them constantly selling shares of their *Padhanee* and *Bohi Giri*, or offices of chief and accountant, with a proportionate allotment of the service lands and Rassum attached; and these transfers, the real nature of which it is impossible to mistake, serve to throw a strong light on the character of similar transactions in other parts, where the use of terms of doubtful import, has invested the subject with a degree of ambiguity which probably will never be altogether dispelled.

Actual sales of *land* were not however unknown under the native administration of Cuttack, and wherever it was clearly intended to sell such, so many bigas are plainly stated in the Qobalehs to be the subject of transfer, without any periphrasis as to the Zemindari, Talukdari, or Mokaddammi right in them. Such sales however were confined to a particular description of land called *Arazi Banjar Kharij Jamma*, or ground, waste, unoccupied, and unassessed, in the disposal of which the Talukdars and Mokaddams were allowed by prescription to exercise considerable privileges. If only two or three bigas were sold for the building of a house, patna, &c. or disposed of as rent free, the individual Talukdar or Mokaddam executed the deed, with the sanction of the ruling power, implied by the necesary attestation of the *Sadder* Canungo, or his agent: if a large quantity as a batti, or so, was to be assigned away, the deed of transfer was executed jointly by the Chowdris, Canungos, and Mokaddam. This mode of transfer gave rise to a curious tenure in the district of Cuttack, called Kharideh or *purchased*, and Milk Kharideh, which often comprised much valuable land, owing to good land being fraudulently alienated, instead of the *Banjar*, which the deeds set forth, and they formed a constant subject of scrutiny and resumption on the part of the Officers of the native government. The purchasers of such property often again transferred it to others, and the privilege of sale likewise seems to have been conceded to those who enjoyed rent free lands, under grants of the government, as milk, ayma, and madadmash.

The following are translations of a few deeds of sale selected.

Sale of a Chowdree's Talook attested by the Seal of the Cazee, and Signature of the Sudder Canoongoe's Goomastah.

I who am Ruttum Mum Gujinder Chowdree, son of Hurdee Ram Gujiuder Chowdree, son of ——— inhabitant of Ma Shamsoonderpore, in Pergunnah Byaung Sircar *Budruck*. Since I am altogether unable to pay the balances due from the Biswa Talook, including Mouzahs Shamsoonderpore, &c., in the above Pergunnah, and have been placed in confinement on that account by the Ohdedar Mirza Bengalee Beg, I do of my own free will and consent sell for the sum of 104 K. 10 P. as per margin to Rasbeharee Mahapatar, son of Oordhub Nurrinder Raee, son of Moorlee Dhur Hurrichundun, inhabitant of Mouzah Byaung Pergunnah ditto, the aforesaid four Biswa Talook, together with the Duftur Chowraee which I have held to this day in proprietory possession. Let the purchaser as long as he lives, and after him his sons and his son's sons exert themselves in bringing the same into cultivation and be careful to discharge the Government dues. He will enjoy the profits and make good any losses that may ensue. Neither I, nor my heirs, nor my brothers, nor their heirs, will hereafter have any right or title in the Talook. Should any one advance a claim, it will be false and unfounded. This is written as a Sunnud Kobaleh Talookdaree. Dated 28th of the month Kubbee Ool Awwul 1168 Umlee.

2 Mouzahs or Villages and 13 Biswas, Mokurree Rudpa. .. .. Arazee Battees,	540	2	12	0
	Sa. Rs.	*A.*	*G.*	*C.*
Mokurrureh Tunka Ruqmee	Rs. 937	11	0	0
Jumma Kemal Cowris	K. 547	4	0	0
	Kahuns	*P.*	*G.*	*C.*
Ryottee	524	5	0	0
Moojraee..	22	15	0	0

Total two Mouzahs 13 Biswas, and the *Dufter* of 4 Biswas of the Pergunnah, viz. Shamsoonderpore 1 Mouza—Kath Moonda 1 ditto—Kistmut Husanabad 8 Biswas—Kismut Roopa 5 Biswas.

Deed of Sale of Ground.

I who am Sudahund Mahapater, son of Gopee Mahapater, son of Moorley Mahapater, Chowdree of Pergunnah Byaung, in the Sircar of *Budruck*, in the full possession of my senses, of my own free consent declare that I have sold a parcel of about 11 Bigas 19 12 of land *Bunjur Kharij Jamma* 26 Dustee measurement on the Rudba of Mouza Dhurinkuntpore, my Talooka, (or dependent on me) which as specified below, has to this day been in my possession, with every thing on and belonging to it to the revered Saeed ood Deen Mohummud. for the sum of Sicca Rupees 19 3, the fair and current price. Let him dispose of it as he likes; should the Hakim ever claim a Jumma from it, I will be answerable.

Here follows a specification of boundaries. Dated 10th Rejeb, 1144 Umlee.

Deed granting Ground free of Rent, by Talookdars of a Pergunnah or District jointly.

We who are Futteh Khan Chowdree, Bamdoe Canoongoe and Kishen Canoongoe Zemindars of Pergunnah Saced Abad in the Sircar of Cuttack, declare as follows: Since Bishnoo Churn Doss Birjabashee, inhabitant of Mouzah Nujal in Pergunnah Deogaon Bissee has no means of subsistence, and is unable to give food to the numerous Fakirs and Byshnoos, who are constantly resorting to him, and thereby suffers extreme distress, we have therefore of our own accord and free will appointed 7 Battees 7 Bigas* 11 Ghoonts Arazee Bunjur kharij Jumma, from the Rudba of the Mouzahs attached to our Talooks as below, to be hereafter held by him as Khyrat. Let the above-mentioned take possession of the Land and bring into cultivation and expend the profits in maintaining himself and other

* A biga is about a third of an English acre; 20 bigas or 6 acres two thirds form a battee. In Orissa, however, the standard of the biga, which was originally uniform, varies greatly in different parts of the country.

Fakirs and Byshnoos; should we or our heirs ever attempt to resume it may we go to hell. This is given as a Sunnud Khyrat.

Here follows a specification of the Villages in each Talook from which the Land was granted. Dated 16th Jumadool Awwul, 1155 Umlee.

Deed of Sale of the Zemindaree of a Village.

I who am Busunt Raee, son of Sudashib Raee, son of Jeet Raee, inhabitant of Kusbeh Pergunnah Hurrihurpore, in the Sircar of Cuttack, in the full possession of my senses declare in this Mujlis, that the Zemindaree and Talookdaree and Moquddumee of Mouza Naroo, in Pergunnah Athaees has been heretofore in my possession. Being unable from land falling out of cultivation to pay the public assessment, I have of my own free consent disposed of the Zemindaree of the said Mouza, for the sum of 500 Kahuns of Cowris of Luchmun Raee, son of Hur Raee, son of Baboo Raee, and have received the amount from the Tehvil of Narain Dutt Gundooah. Let the purchaser take possession of the Zemindaree, &c. of the above Mouza, the Bhaghat, Khanabaree Land, the Cocoanut Plantations, &c. whatever in short attaches to it, and exerting himself to extend cultivation, and let him pay regularly the Government dues. Neither I, nor my heirs will hereafter advance any claim on the above Mouza. This is given as a Kobaleh and Kubzool Wusool. Dated Rubee ool Awwul, 1208 U.

Deed of Sale by Pudhans of Village Odeypore in Pergunnah Limbaee.
[*Oorea.*]

Dated Wednesday, 27th Assin, in the 43rd Ank or year of the reign of Raja Beer Kishore deo Maharajah.

We four persons, Dhurnee Das, Koornee Das, Kesub Das, and Seba Das, Pudhans of Mouza Odeypore in Pergunnah Limbaee, having this day received from Kishen Patjoosee Mahapater, inhabitant of Putna Kishen Sarunpore *Hat* Delang in the above Pergunnah, the sum of Rs. 76 8 in cowris, or at the current rate of exchange of 2k. 4p. per rupee, altogether 172 kahuns, which is a fair price, execute the following deed of sale. We sell to you our Pudhanee or right of management in the whole of the said village of Odeypore, the Ruckba of which is about 15 battees, 10 bigas, and also our Hita Pudhanee or service lands, which are 3 bigas Dehee, 3 bigas Kala, and 7 bigas Sarud, altogether 13 bigas. You will hold the Pudhanee of the village as long as the sun, moon, and earth last. Should any Sawunt or chief, or our heirs or any other claimants advance a claim, we will be responsible, so long also you will enjoy the Hita Pudhanee or service lands, which we have sold, with every thing above and beneath, water, dry land, mineral productions, wells, wood, stones, fruit trees, &c. You may cut down and plant trees on the ground and act as you please with the above Hita, also you will receive the customary Sarbee (Siropa) of Sri Juggunnath Jeo. This Deed will stand for ever as a Kiria Putr and Bishodun or receipt.

Witnesses, several Pudhans and Bhooees.

Deed of Sale by a Bhooee or Village Accountant.

Dated Monday, 25th Assin, in the 17th Ank or year of the reign of Biresree Raja Dirb Sing Deo Maharajah.

I who am Rugoo Nath Maintee, Bhooee of Mouza Gowree Pot Matiapara in Pergunnah Limbaee, execute in behalf of Sunkur Putnaik, inhabitant of Monza Odeypore the following Deed of Sale, having this day received from you the sum of 35 rupees in cowris or kahuns 83-2 at the rate of 2-6 per rnpee, which is a fair and even price, I hereby sell to you in exchange for that sum the Bhooee Giri or Office of Bhooee of the said Mouza, which was formerly purchased by my father with the sanction of the Maharaja. The Ruckbah of the village is about 85 battees (or bigas 1,700.) I sell you likewise my Hita lands which are established at the customary rate of 12-8 per battee, with my Dustooree and Russoom. You will enjoy the office of Bhooee and the Hita land as long as the sun, moon, and earth last. Should any Sawunt or Huqdar, or neighbour or heirs of mine advance any claims, I shall be responsible for satisfying them. Till the day of resurrection you will possess the Hita land, and every thing above and beneath it—water, dry land, mineral productions, ponds, wells, trees, stones—you may cut down and plant trees at your pleasure. This is given as a Deed of Sale and receipt.

CHAP. III.

The Chronology and History of Orissa.

THE learned Natives of Cuttack maintain, that, in latter ages, upon the decline of that great monarchy of upper India, whose history seems destined to remain for ever buried in the darkness of fable and uncertain tradition, four principal thrones or races of Hindoo Princes ruled over the country, viz: the Narapati, the Aswapati, the Chatter or Chatrapati, and the Gajapati. By the first they understand the Ram Rajas or Sovereigns of Telinga and the Carnatic, who opposed the earlier Musselman invaders of the Deccan, under Sultan Ala-ud-din ; the second throne they place in the Marhatta country, and intend to designate by the epithet, the old and powerful Rajas of Deogir or Tagara, of whom frequent mention is made in Ferishteh ; by the third, the celebrated line of Rajput Princes, whose descendants are found at Ambher and Jyepoor; the fourth is the title given to the Monarchs who ruled over Orissa, from the earliest times of which any authentic records are preserved. The origin of these sovereignties, they trace to the four great feudal vassals of an empire, which they believe to have extended over the whole of Hindustan, from the commencement at least of the Çali yuga;* and they explain their titles by reference to the nominal offices held, or services performed by them, when in attendance on the Lord Paramount or supreme Raja at the court of Hastina (Hastinapura) and Delhi. Thus the Narapati† is supposed by some to have been the commander of the armies: the Aswapati, the lord or master of the horse; the Chatrapati, the bearer of the imperial umbrella or standard of state: and the Gajapati, the master of elephants. Others suppose the epithets were derived from the designations of the four gates of the palace, at which the chiefs in question took their stations, when present at the capital.

The recollections preserved of these races of Princes are by no means confined to Orissa. In the Canara *Raja Padhati* translated by Dr. Buchanan, the fabulous monarchs are first described as usual beginning with Yudhisht'hira, and the author then states, "After this Narapati, Gajapati, and Aswapati, three thrones were established." He then details the Princes of the Narapati line, who ruled over that portion of the Deccan. They are now probably forgotten in Upper India, but seem to have been perfectly well known and familiarly spoken of, even at Delhi, only two centuries

* The Hindoos have four joogs or ages. The *sutya joog*, the golden era, they pretend lasted 1,728,000 years, and produced four incarnations. It was the age of merit, and virtue was without alloy. Men died when they wished; their stature was 31½ feet; they lived to the age of 100,000 years! dined off golden vessels; and the name by which men obtained *mooktee*, or final deliverance, was Narayn. The *treta joog* lasted 1,296,000 years, and produced three incarnations. Actions of merit were then in comparison of sin, as three to one; the human stature was 21 feet; men lived to the age of 10,000 years, and dined off silver dishes! Ram was the name by which men obtained deliverance. The *dwarpur joog* lasted 864,000 years, and produced two incarnations. Merit and sin were in equal proportion. The human stature was reduced to 10½ feet; men lived 1000 years, and dined off copper dishes! The *kalee joog*, the iron and present age, will last 432,000 years. Of this period 4,926 years are past. There will be one incarnation, the genius of degeneracy; merit will be reduced to one fourth, while sin will rise to three fourths. Men will be three cubits and a half in stature, live a hundred years, and dine from dishes without rule. *Friend of India (Quarterly Series)* Oct. 1825.

Infidels once seemed to hope for much aid from Hindoo records or chronology. Their earlier records are mere fable and fiction, and their chronology has been proved false and absurd to an extreme degree. The authenticity of the chronology of Scripture, is quite unaffected by the absurdly long periods attached to the Hindoo ages of the world. Major Wilford says—"With regard to history, the Hindoos have really nothing but romances, from which some truths may be occasionally extracted." Sir W. Jones also remarks to the same effect—"The dawn of true Indian history appears three or four centuries only before the Christian era, the preceding ages being clouded by allegory or fable."

† The titles imply respectively, "Lord of Men"—"Lord of Horses"—"Lord of the Umbrella"—and "Lord of Elephants," or as we should say, "Master of, &c."

since. There is a highly curious passage in the *Ayin Akberi*, where treating of the game of cards with which the Emperor Akber recreated his royal mind, the writer observes, "This is a well-known game. At first the pack consisted of twelve kings with eleven cards dependent upon each in the following order. First, *Aswaput*, the king of the horses. He is painted on horse back like the king of Delhi, with the Chutter, Alum, and other ensigns of royalty. Second, *Gujput*, the king of elephants, is mounted on an elephant like the king of Orissa. Third, Nurput, the king of men. Like the king of Vijayapur, he is seated on a throne and has different kinds of soldiers attending him on foot," &c. &c.

It is the account of the fourth and probably least important race of Hindu monarchs of the middle ages, the Gajapatis* of Orissa, that is here narrated; but to render the chapter complete, a sketch is added of the history of the province to the date of the British conquest, A. D. 1803.

The earlier native histories of the country are of the legendary or fabulous class, copied from the Puranas, but embellished or disfigured by a plentiful admixture of local traditions. Their later annals assume an air of authenticity about the date of the accession of the family called the Kesari Vansa, 473 A. D., prior to which the accounts are so replete with obvious falsehoods and contradiction, inconsistency and anachronism, as to be equally unintelligible and unworthy of notice. The memory of a few great names and events, only, has been preserved up to the fourth and fifth centuries of the Christian era, and to adapt these to their favourite system of chronology, the brahmins, who will never admit want of information on any subject, have been obliged to give an expansion to the reigns of their traditionary Rajas, in some cases of five or six hundred years, and in all, far beyond the natural or possible term of the human life. Yet these are the men whose tales infidels would with unblushing effrontery, still oppose to the consistent and rational records of the Bible. As, however, it will not be uninteresting to those curious in researches into Hindoo antiquity, to learn what traditions the natives have preserved regarding their history in the earlier ages, I shall begin my sketch of the contents of their annals from the remotest period to which they profess to go back.

The sources from which my information has been chiefly derived are, 1st. A work in Sanscrit called the *Vansavali*, belonging to a learned brahmin of Pooree, said to have been originally composed

* Derived from Gaja, an elephant, and pati, a master or potentate.

by some of his ancestors three or four centuries since, and continued in the family to the present date. 2nd. The chapter of the *Mandala Panji* or Records preserved in the temple of Juggernaut, called the *Raj Charita* or "Annals of the Kings" in the Oorea language, which records are stated to have been commenced upon more than *six centuries*, and to have been since regularly kept. 3rd. Another *Vansavali* or Genealogy written in Sanscrit on leaves of the Palmyra tree, procured from a brahmin living in the family of the Raja of Puttia Sarengerh, one of the branches of the royal house of Orissa. Less certain and trustworthy guides than the above, are to be met with in the numerous Genealogies possessed by nearly every Panjia or almanac-maker in the province. They in general abound with errors and inconsistencies, but occasionally a few facts or illustrations may be gleaned from them.

Conformably with the notion, above stated, of the existence of a great empire at Delhi, to which all other Rajas stood in a feudatory relation, *the annals of Orissa commence with the death of Krishna, the opening of the Cali yuga or evil age*, 3001 B. C. and the reigns of Jojishtee Deo, or Yudhisht'hira, Parikshita, and Janamejaya. Twelve years after the setting in of the Cali yuga, in the month of Cheyte, when the moon was in the lunar mansion called Purv Asarh, at the moment of the rising of the seven Rishis, or constellation, called the Great Bear, Parikshita the son of Abhimanyu and grandson of Arjun, is said to have ascended the imperial throne of India. He reigned 757 years, and his son Janamejaya 512 years!! There is an ancient temple at Agrahat in killah Daljura about eight miles north of Cuttack, which the brahmins of the place say was visited by this Raja Janamejaya during his progress over India, with all the feudatory Rajas of the country in his train; and they point out the spot where he performed the sacrifice for the destruction of serpents, to revenge the death of his father. The circumstance merits notice from its agreeing with a somewhat similar tradition, recorded in an inscription at Bednore, communicated to the Asiatic Society by the late Colonel Mackenzie (vide Researches vol ix.); and what is further curious connected with the place, is, that the ground around is strewed with numerous stone pillars, shaped like temples in miniature about three feet long, exactly resembling those found in Khurda at an acknowledged seat of Jain worship, which the brahmins of Agrahat say amounted formerly to several hundreds, and were set up by Raja Janamejaya to commemorate the great sacrifice there performed; or according to other accounts, to stand as substitutes for those Rajas or Vassal Lords of India, who were not in attendance at the ceremony.

After these celebrated heroes of Indian antiquity, we have a list of other Princes, whose names I have nowhere else met, viz: eight Rajas who reign for the moderate space of 1636 years! Many of them are obviously merely Rajas of the province, but in relating the succession of reigns, no distinction is drawn between those personages who were local or dependant princes, and those whom it is intended to represent as the monarchs of a large part of India. Goutama Deo, the second in succession from Janamejaya is said to have added the country from the Mahendra Mali hills in Ganjam, as far as the Godaveri, to his dominions. Mahendra Deo, his son, founds Raj Mahendri or Rajamundry. Shewak Deo, a very religious Prince, is assiduous in his devotion at the temple of Juggernaut. In the reign of Bajranath Deo, the Yavanas are said to invade the country in great numbers from Babul Des, explained to mean Iran and Cabul, but they are finally driven back. Then follows an incomprehensible story, involving some strange anachronism, about Imarut or Himarut khan, who comes from Dehli, with a large army and fights the Raja. His successor, Sarsenkha Deo, a warlike prince, is attacked by another Khan, whose name is variously written, and always so incorrectly spelt, that it is impossible to unravel it. The Raja defeats the invader and emboldened by his success, advances upon Delhi, and reduces a great part of the country. In the reign of Hanas or Hangsha Deo, the Yavanas again invade the country in great force from Cashmir, and many bloody battles ensue.

Respecting these Yavanas, who are so often mentioned in the legendary portion of Orissan history, it may be observed that the word in all the original Ooria accounts is written *Jaban*, and the natives whom I have employed to translate both these and the Sanscrit Vansavalis, always render it *Mogul.* Who they really were, if they ever entered the country at all, may be plausibly guessed in some instances from their being said to come from Babul Des and Cashmir, by which the Hindus understand generally Persia, Affghanistan, and part of Tartary. Nothing however can exceed the looseness and confusion of authorities, in speaking of countries and nations beyond their own immediate frontier. They often bring the Yavanas from Delhi, by which appellation they seem to point to some great monarchy or monarchies lying to the northward and westward, of which they have preserved an indistinct notion, rather than to the particular city so named. Dr. Buchanan has remarked a similar degree of confusion on this same point in the historical recollections of the brahmins of the southern countries of India. He observes—"Who were these Yavanas? The word properly signifies an European, but as the Hindus speak with great confusion concerning the northern and western nations, it is often confounded with the Mlechchas and Turks, Arabs or Tartars, and all these terms are frequently applied to the Mussulman." (Vol. iii. chap. xv, page 113.)

Next in the series of kings, comes Raja Bhoja, who is made to reign 127 years, that is from about B. C. 180 to B. C. 53. He was, according to the Orissan Chronicles, a brave, liberal, just and merciful prince. He conquered the whole of India and took tribute from all the Rajas of it. His Court was adorned by the presence of 750 eminent poets, the chief of whom was Calidasa, author of the 752 Ashloks called the Chanak or Chataka, and Maha Nataka. Raja Bhoja invented boats, the weaver's loom, and wheeled carriages, or at least in his time the use of them first became common. In this reign the Yavanas from Sindhu Des invaded the country in great force, but Bhoja discomfited and destroyed them, and afterwards captured many of their possessions and cities.

Sri Bickermajit or Vicramaditya succeeded to the throne, and reigned 153 years. He was master of all sciences and a great magician. Having subjected the Ashta Vetala or eight demons to his control, he could perform many miraculous feats, such as travelling one hundred jojuns or four hundred cos per day, extinguishing fire, and stopping the current of water by the force of his incantations. So great was the fame of his wisdom, that he was on one occasion taken up to the heaven of Indra,* to settle a fierce dispute which had arisen amongst the Debtas, respecting the relative merits of two of the heavenly Choristers, named Rembha and Urvasi! His decision in the important matter submitted to his arbitration, obtained great applause, and the gods dismissed him with a present of the famous magic throne called the *Sinhasana*. On returning to the "*Martyaloka*," or region of mortals, much edified by what he had seen above, he became sole and undisputed Maha Raja of the whole face of the earth, and received the title of Raja Adhiraj or Supreme Raja of Rajas. Through fear of his power, the Yavanas all left the country. At last came Salivahana from the Deccan, who attacked and conquered Vicramaditya, put him to death, and assumed the

* Indra is the king of heaven in the Hindoo mythology. His body is full of eyes, a transmutation of the punishment of a crime, the account of which cannot be narrated in the ears of Christians.

reins of empire. From that period the era called the Sacabda prevailed, and was introduced into all the Panjis.

I cannot pass over the above most important event in Indian history, marked by the introduction of a new epoch into all the southern countries, without specifying precisely how my different authorities express themselves regarding it, though they throw no new light on who this mysterious personage Salivahana really was, and whence he came? The extract from the *Mandali Panji* says, "After many years Saca Deo Brahma Raja of Pratishthanapura, came with a large army, attacked the Maha Raja Vicramaditya, and having conquered and destroyed him, fixed the seat of his empire at Delhi." The author of the Vansavali states, "With the assistance of the Yavanas, a person named Nri Nikas Salivahana Saca Hera fought many battles with the Raja, and deposed him from the throne of Delhi. From that period begins the era called the Sacabda."

It will be curious, and not altogether unprofitable, to compare these relations with a passage in Major Wilford's distinguished Essay on Vicramaditya and Salivahana. He says, page 123,—"In the seventh section of the Vrihat-catha, we read, that there was a king of Pataliputrapura, called Vicramaditya, who hearing of the growing power of Nrisinha, king of the consecrated city or *Pratishtana*, called to his assistance the *Gajapati*,* (lord of the Elephants or king of Thibet,) and the *Aswapati*, (lord of Horses or Horsemen, or the king of Persia.) The confederates took the field but were defeated by Nrisinha Nripa or Salivahana with an incredible slaughter. Vicramaditya fled with the utmost precipitation," &c. In another part it is observed that Vicramaditya "obliged Cataca (Cuttack) to submit;" probably brought it into a dependant and tributary relation to his government, which may account for his being classed amongst the ancient Sovereigns of the province.

From the commencement of the Cali yuga to the fall of Vicramaditya, thirteen Rajas are made to reign the monstrous term of years 3173! viz:—

	Years.
Yudhisht'hira Deo	12
Parikshita	757
Janamejaya	516
Sambar or Sancara Deo	410
Gautama Deo	373
Mahindra Deo	215
Ashti Deo	134
Shewak or Ashok Deo	150

* Query, the Raja of Orissa and the Sovereign of the Marhatta country?

Bajra Nath	107
Sarsankh	115
Hansh or Hansa	122
Bhoja	127
Vicramaditya	135*
Total	3,173 years.

After that event, the era of Salivahana which dates its commencement from A. D. 77 in Orissa, is used in all the accounts, and we now come to reigns of a probable and moderate duration, the first dawning of an approach to the authentic period of the native history.

The Raj Charitra goes on to state, "Afterwards Karmajit, son of the *above*, (Query, Vicramaditya ?) ruled over *Or Desa* or Orissa. He was devoted to the worship of Juggernaut and died A. S. 65." Then follow four unimportant reigns remarkable only for mention of invasions by the Yavanas. The Rajas names are as follows :—

Bata Kesari, reigns	51 years.
Tirbhobun Deo	43 ,,
Nirmal Deo	45 ,,
Bhima Deo	37 ,,

In the time of Subhan Deo the next in the series of kings, who succeeded to the Raja A. D. 318, relation is given of an extraordinary and incomprehensible occurrence, of which I am quite unable to offer any explanation. It has obviously been strangely distorted by popular tradition, though in all probability possessing a foundation in fact.

The following is an outline of the story. A Yavana, or foreigner, named Rakta Bahu, (the Red-Armed,) having assembled a large army with the intention of invading Orissa, embarked his troops on vessels with numerous horses and elephants, and having made the coast, anchored at a distance from the town of *Jagannath*,

* It may be observed that a list of this description uniformly introduces the genealogies of every race of princes in the Deccan, and originates with an attempt to fill up a blank in the local histories, with persons borrowed from the Puranas or from tradition. The age of Bhoja is now well established as being assignable to the ninth or tenth century, this being made therefore anterior to Vicramaditya who lived before our era, shews with what imperfect knowledge of dates and persons these lists are compiled; neither was a son of Bhoja named Vikrama which might form a plausible excuse for the confusion, it being ascertained by inscriptions, older probably than these lists, that the son and successor of that prince was named Kalabhoja. In point of history and chronology however, neither Vicrama nor Bhoja have any connexion with the dynasties in which the Chroniclers of the Peninsula have enrolled them.—*Note by the Secretary of the Calcutta Asiatic Society.*

hoping to take *Pooree* by surprise. The dung, straw, &c. of the horses and elephants, happening to float ashore in quantities, attracted the notice of some of the people of the town. They immediately reported the unusual appearance to the Raja, who guessed that some powerful enemy was coming to attack him. Seized with a panic, he took the image of Sri Jeo or Jagannath out of the temple, lodged it in a covered cart with all its jewels and utensils, and fled away to Sonepur Gopalli, the most remote town on his western frontier! The Yavanas landed, and not finding the prince, plundered the town and temple and committed great excesses every where. The Raja's alarms increased on receiving intelligence of the proceedings of the invaders; he now buried the image, planted a *ber* tree over it, and himself fled farther into the jungles. The Yavanas, unable to understand how he had escaped them, began to institute enquiries on the subject, when some of the low people of the coast informed them of the way in which their approach had been discovered. Enraged with the ocean for disclosing his secret, Rakta Bahu drew out his armies to chastise its waters. The sea, on observing such formidable preparations, retreated for nearly a cos—the infatuated Yavanas rushed on—when the tide suddenly returning with tremendous noise and fury, swallowed up a great portion of the army and inundated the whole country to a frightful extent! The flood reached inland as far as the Baronai Pahar of Khurda, taking with it immense quantities of sand. It was at this time that the Chilka lake was formed by the irruption of the waters of the ocean. The Raja died shortly afterwards in the jungles. His son Indra Deo succeeded to the title, but was captured and murdered by the invaders. A Yavana dynasty then ruled over Orissa for the space of 146 years. Thus were completed years 396 of the Sacabda.

Possibly the tradition may have some connection with the fierce religious disputes, which raged between the worshippers of Brahma and Buddha about the period in which the invasion of foreigners, and the flight of Juggernaut is placed, and which as is well known terminated in the expulsion of the latter from the continent of India. A real irruption of the ocean may have occurred in the same age, and this natural calamity, the ever active invention of the Brahmin Chroniclers chose to ascribe to the authors of the bloody wars, revolutions, and other moral evils, which afflicted the country at the time. But it were vain to speculate farther on the origin of an account which is perhaps the work of imagination.

We come now to the accession of the Rajas called the Kesari *Pat* or Vansa, A. D. 473, from which period I should be disposed to date *the commencement of the real history of the province;* but before entering upon the account of their reigns I should observe that there is nothing in the preceding relation to explain what is meant by the "eradicated race of Utcala," alluded to in the inscription on the pillar at Buddal, which Major Wilford refers to the expulsion of a martial race of Princes from Orissa by the Carna Emperors of Behar, prior to the accession of the Gujapatis; but it would obviously be easy enough to imagine a space for the occurrence of such a revolution, in some of those chasms of upwards of a century's duration, which intervene between many of the early reigns.

No information is afforded as to the origin and pedigree of the Princes called the Kesari Vansa or Kesari Bans. The founder of the dynasty of Kesari Vansa was Jajati Kesari, a warlike and energetic prince, but who he was or whence he came we are not apprized. He soon cleared his dominions of the Yavanas who then retired to their own country. His court was held at Jajepur where he built a palace and castle, called Choudwar, or the mansion with four gates. The most important event of his time was, *the recovery of the image and the restoration of the worship of Juggernaut.* Directed by what was esteemed certain omens and supernatural appearances, he proceeded to the Purushottem Khetr to institute enquiries regarding the idol and the temple, when the brahmins of the place informed him, that a tradition existed amongst them of Sri Jeo (Jagannath) having been carried off, upwards of *a century and a half* before, to Sonepur Gopalli, on the invasion of a person called Rakta Bahu, where the former had ever since remained concealed from mortal eyes! This intelligence induced the Raja to make a visit to the jungles of Sonepur. He discovered after some search the place where Sri Jeo had been buried, cuts down the ber or banyan tree which overshadowed the sacred spot, and finds the image or images encased in a stone vault, much decayed and disfigured.

His next care was to search out the officiating priests, descended from those who formerly fled from Puri, and having discovered several of them in the Rattenpur country, he consulted with them how the worship of Juggernaut should be revived in all its ancient splendour. The formation of a new image being considered an indispensable preliminary, the priests proceeded into the woods to look for a proper piece of timber; and having found one with all the requisite qualities indicated by the shastras, they brought it to the

Raja, who clothed both it and the old images in rich robes, and conducted them in great state to Puri. A new temple was then erected on the site of the old one, which was found to be much dilapidated and covered with sand. The four images were afterwards duly prepared and set up on their throne with much pomp and solemnity on the 5th of Kakara (Cancer) the thirteenth year of the Raja's reign, amidst the shouts and rejoicings of the multitude. At the same time the necessary officers were appointed, feasts and festivals established, sasans founded, and the whole country around Puri assigned as endowments for the maintenance of the temple. On this memorable occasion the Raja received by general acclamation the title of the second Indradyumna.

Towards the close of his reign, Raja Yayati Kesari began the buildings at Bhuvaneswar, and died A. D. 520.

The reigns assigned to his two sucessors, Suraj Kesari and Ananta Kesari, are probably of too long duration, being altogether ninety-seven years, and are distinguished by nothing remarkable, excepting that the latter prince began the building of the great temple at Bhuvaneswar.

He was succeeded A. D. 617 by Lalat Indra Kesari, a personage of high repute in the legends of the Bhuvaneswar temple, in consequence of his having built or completed the great pagoda at that place sacred to Mahadeo under the title of the Ling Raja Bhuvaneswara, in the year of Salivahana 580 and A. D. 657. He also founded there a large and populous city containing seven *sais* and forty-two streets which became the capital of the Raja.

An uninteresting series of *thirty-two* reigns of the Kesari Princes follows, extending through a period of 455 years, of the history of which little is given excepting the characters of the Rajas, and some absurd stories connected with the temples of Juggernaut and Bhuvaneswara. A few particulars worth noticing however may be gleaned from the accounts, such as that the rate at which the ryots were taxed by the sovereign was five kahans of cowris per batti, or about one anna per biga. One of the Rajas named Bariya Kesari, in a time of emergency, raised the demand for revenue as high as one kahan of cowris per biga, or four times the former amount, but his successor Suraj Kesari reduced it to the old rate. Raja Nirupa Kesari, a martial and ambitious prince, who was always fighting with his neighbours, is said to have first planted a city on the site of the modern Cuttack about A. D. 989. The reign of Markat Kesari was distinguished for the construction of a stone revetment, or embankment faced with that material, (probably the ancient one of which the remains are yet to be seen), to protect the new capital from inundation A. D. 1006; and Madhava Kesari has the credit of building a fortress of vast dimensions at Sarangher.

Different stories are related of the extinction of the Kesari family. The Raj Charitra says, that the last of the line died childless, when at the suggestion of the deity, another family were brought from the Carnatic by Basudeb Banpati and placed on the throne. The Vinsavali ascribes the change of dynasty to a dispute between the Raja and this same Basudeb Banpati, a brahmin and powerful officer of the court; who having been driven with indignity from the royal presence, went to the Carnatic and instigated a person named Churang or Chor Ganga to invade Orissa. He conquered Cuttack, on Friday, the 13th of Assin, A. S. 1054 or A. D. 1131, and thus acquired the sovereignty of the country. Both accounts agree in giving the above as the date of the accession of Raja Churang Deo. This personage, whatever his real origin, is fabled to have been the offspring of the goddess Ganga Sana or the lesser Ganges (Godaveri) by a form of Mahadeo. With him began the race of princes called the Ganga Vansa, or Gangbans line, who ruled the country for about four centuries; a period fertile in great names and events of importance, and which forms unquestionably the most interesting portion of Orissan history, if such terms may be applied to the annals of a hitherto unknown dynasty, governing one only, of the many provinces which now constitute the British empire in India.

Churang, or Sarang Deo, held the reins of government for twenty years, and conformably with his supernatural origin is believed to have been a skilful magician. It is said of him that he established the records of the Juggernaut temple called the Mandala Panji, and was a great worshipper of certain forms of Devi to the neglect of all the other gods and goddesses. The memory of his reign and of his singular name, which is certainly not an Oorea one, is preserved in a Sai or quarter of the town of Pooree, with a tank called the Churang Sai. Tradition also ascribes to him the building of forts and palaces both at Sarengher and Cuttack Choudwar.

His son Gangeswara Deo succeeded A. D. 1151. His dominions reached from the Ganges to the Godaveri. He had five kutuks or royal metropolises, viz., Jajpoor, Choudwar, Amravati, Chatta or Chatna, and Biranassi, the modern Cuttack. The account which places Amravati, a town near the Kistna in the heart of the Deccan, amongst the capital cities of this Raja, is one of the commoner genealogies to which I attach no great degree of credit. It is not improbable, however, that the place may have formed part of a principality held by Churang Deo when invited to ascend the throne of Orissa, which thereby became annexed, temporarily to the latter Raj ; and claims and political relations arising out of the possession of it, may have been one cause of the frequent expeditions south of the Godaveri and the interference in the affairs of Telingana and the Carnatic, which we shall find to be henceforwards exercised by the Ganga Vansa Rajas.

As a specimen of the morals of the Court of Orissa in this age it should be mentioned, that Raja Gangeswara Deo committted incest with his own daughter; to expiate which offence, he dug a superb tank by the advice of the brahmins, called the Kousala Ganj, which is still pointed out between Khurda and Pipley.

After two short and unimportant reigns, Raja Anang Bhim Deo, one of the most illustrious of the Princes of the Ganga Vansa line, ascended the Gajapati Sinhasan or throne A. D. 1174. He resided during the early part of his reign in the palace called Choudwar at Jajepur, but was induced by some omen, to build a magnificent palace on the site of Fort Barabatti, adjoining the town of Cuttack, where he afterwards held his Court chiefly. The construction of the present castle of that name should in all probability be referred to this period, though a later date is generally assigned to it. Raja Anang Bhim Deo may be called the Firoz Shah of the age and country, from the number and variety of public works executed by his orders for the benefit or ornament of his dominions. Having unfortunately incurred the guilt of killing a brahmin, motives of superstition prompted him to construct numerous temples as an expiation for his offence, whilst the suggestions of a noble and princely spirit urged him to a large expenditure on works of more direct public utility, as tanks, wells, and bridges. He is said to have built sixty stone dewals or pagodas, ten bridges, forty wells, one hundred and fifty-two ghats, and to have founded four hundred and fifty sasans or villages, containing colonies of brahmins, besides excavating *a crore* or ten millions of tanks ! He more especially filled the whole khetr of Jagannath with sacred edifices, and the great temple was erected by his orders under the superintendence of Paramahans Bajpoi, at an expense of about thirty or forty lacs. The date of its completion was A. D. 1196. He at the same time enlarged considerably the establishment, added fifteen brahmin and fifteen sudra Shewaks or officiating priests, and gave fresh splendour to the worship of the idol of the place, by the institution of numerous bhogs and jatras (feasts and festivals.)

The most remarkable feature of Raja Anang Bhim Deo's reign, however, is the measurement undertaken by him of the whole of the land comprised within his dominions, and the arrangements connected with that procedure. We are informed that under the superintendence of the principal ministers Damodar Bar Panda and Isan Patnaik, the whole country from the Ganges (Hoogley) to the Godaveri, and from the sea to the frontier of Sonepur, was measured out with the rods called Nal and *Padhek*. The results were as follows, viz.

Total contents, (each batti containing 20 bigas).. *Battis*	62,28,000
Deduct, ground occupied by sites of hills, beds of nullahs, towns, &c., and land irreclaimably waste ..	14,80,000
Remains,	47,48,000

Of this quantity 24,30,000 battis* are stated to have been reserved as the Raja's *Nijkarch*, khaliseh or royal domain, and the remainder 23,18,000 battis were assigned for the support of his chiefs, armies, officers of state, brahmins, elephants, &c.

Connected with and illustrative of the above proceeding, a highly curious speech of the Raja's is given in the annals of the Pooree temple, of which the following is an abstract translation. Having been warned in a dream by Parameswara (Sri Jagannath,) that it was proper he should offer his devotions at Pooree, the Raja proceeded to that place in the 12th year of his reign. After performing the usual worship with great pomp and solemnity, he collected about him the princes of his family, vassal lords, and chief officers of state, and held the following discourse: "Hear, Oh Chiefs and Princes, the arrangements which I have established for the management of my empire, the expenses of state, the pay of my armies and religious establishments, and the support of the royal treasury, and attend to the counsel which I give you. It is known to you that the Rajas of the Kesari line ruled from the Kans Bans river on the north, to the Rassikoilah south, and from the sea on the east to the Dandpat of Bhimnagar west, from which tract of country they derived a revenue of fifteen lacs of *marhs* of gold. By the grace of Sri Jagannath, the Princes of the Ganga Vansa have, after subduing

* The amount of the estimate in square yards or miles, must depend on the size of the biga, which is not indicated. If we assume it at the present average of the province, the dominions of the Gajapatis included at that period more than 40,000 square miles.

the khetris and bhuniyas, added to the Raj the following extent of country, viz., on the north that lying between the Kans Bans and the Datai Borhi river; south the country from the Rassikoilah down to the Dandpat of Rajamundry; and west to the confines of Boad Sonepur, from which an increase of revenue of twenty lacs has been obtained: my total gross revenues therefore are thirty-five lacs of *marhs* of gold. Out of this amount I have assigned stated sums for the payment of the Sawants (Commanders,) Mahawats and Rawats (chiefs of horses and elephants,) priests, brahmins, and the worship of the deity. For the maintenance of the Paiks, Shewaks (vassals or officers,) and other servants of the state, lands have been duly set apart. Oh Princes and Chiefs, respect my arrangements, and beware that you never resume the above grants and allowances, lest you become liable to the penalty denounced in the shastras against those who take back what has been given. Above all in the management of the country under your charge, be just and merciful to the ryots, and collect revenue from them according to the fixed and established rate. As I have by my own good fortune and exertions accumulated a large treasure, viz., forty lacs of marhs of gold taken from the countries of the conquered bhuniyas, and jewels to the value of seven lacs eighty-eight thousand marhs, it is now my intention to devote a portion to the service of Jagannath, by building a new temple one hundred cubits high, and bestowing a quantity of ornaments and utensils. Let me hear your opinions on this point." The ministers and courtiers all replied that so good a work could not too soon be taken in hand, and that after the sagacity aud prudence displayed by his majesty, any advice on their parts must be superfluous. An officer named Paramahans Bajpoi was therefore directed to take the work in hand forthwith, and twelve lacs and fifty thousand marhs of gold with jewels to the value of 2,50,000 were set apart for the purpose.

The marh of gold is stated to be equivalent to five mashas weight, a valuation which would raise the amount of the revenues of Orissa according to the above statement, far beyond what we can believe them ever to have realized, even allowing, as offered in explanation, that the gold of that age was very impure, and that the statement includes the gross rents of the whole of the lands of the country, both the royal domains and those now held by the hill Zemindars and Poligars. It appears unaccountable too, why the sum total of the revenues should be stated in gold, when we know that cowris always formed the principal currency of the district. As I am unable to furnish any satisfactory elucidation of these points, I must leave the statement as it stands, content with having presented a faithful translation.

On the occasion of building the temple, a new coin and seal were struck by the Raja's orders, with the titles which are used to this day by the Khurda Rajas, who claim to represent the majesty of this once powerful race. Their pompous nature may amuse those who are unacquainted with eastern ostentation, and with its displays of the pitiful pride of dying men. They run thus,—"Vira Sri Gajapati, Gaureswara navakotikernatotkalavergeswaradhirai, Bhuta bhairava deva, Sadhusasanotkarana, Rawat Rai, Atula balaprakarmasangrama Sahasra bahu, Kshetriya Kuladhumraketu," &c. "The illustrious Hero, the Gajapati (Lord of Elephants,) Sovereign of Bengal, Supreme Monarch over the rulers of the tribes of Utkala, Kernata, and the nine forts, a divinity terrible as Bhairava to the wicked, the protector of the grants enjoyed by the pious; king of kings; like the lord of a thousand arms in the field of battle by his unequalled might, and a comet to the martial race."

His son Rajeswara Deo reigned thirty-five years and was succeeded A. D. 1236 by Raja Narsinh Deo, surnamed Langora, a prince of great celebrity in the annals of Orissa, as well as in its legends and romances. His great personal strength, and skill in athletic exercises, seem to have invested him with a sort of supernatural character in the eyes of his subjects; and popular tradition has exaggerated some peculiarity in his figure or dress, into the fable of his being provided with a tail, whence is derived the epithet Langora. He is said to have been of a very martial turn, and to have waged a long war to the southward.

It was this Raja who built the famous temple of the sun at Kanarak, called by the Europeans the Black Pagoda, "thereby," observes the author of the Ayin Akberi, "erecting for himself a lasting monument of fame." The work was executed chiefly under the superintendence of the minister Shibai Santra, and is stated to have been completed in the year of the Sacabda 1200, answering to 1277 A. D.

After Raja Langora Narsinh Deo, five other princes named Narsinh and six with the title of Bhanu, whom some describe as a separate family called Suraj-bansi, ruled over Orissa, until A. D. 1451. Their reigns are for the most part undistinguished by events of importance, but they have left some public works which coupled with other monuments of the Ganga Vansa Rajas, give a favourable impression of the public spirit and munificence of that race. Amongst these is the bridge at the entrance of Pooree called the

Athara Naleh, said to have been built A. D. 1300, by Raja Kabir Narsinh Deo. A dreadful scarcity is recorded to have happened early in the 14th century, when paddy rose to the (then) enormous price of 120 kahans of cowris per bharan—about *three* times its present *average* rate calculated in the same currency, but nearly *sixty times* the ordinary selling price of that age, if an account in my possession is to be credited, which states, that under the Bhanus, rice in the husk sold for two kahans per bharan, clean rice at ten cowris per ser, and cotton one pan ten gandas per ser.

The last of the Rajas surnamed Bhanu, being childless, he adopted as his son and successor a youth, named Kapila or Kapil Santra, of the Suraj-bansi tribe of Rajputs. The boy became afterwards a prince of high renown under the title of Kapil Indra Deo, and the native chroniclers have not failed therefore to embellish the history of his early life, with flattering fictions and stories of supernatural occurrences, prophetic of his future rise and greatness. It is said, that when a child, he gained his livelihood by tending the cows of a brahmin. One day his master found him fast asleep on the ground at mid-day, and a huge snake standing erect near him, with its hood spread out and held in such a manner, as to shelter him from the fierce rays of the meridian sun. This indication satisfied the brahmin that he was destined to become something great. Shortly after, the Raja, whilst passing one day to the temple, took notice of him, enquired his name, and being struck with his answers and appearance, finding moreover that he was by caste and descent a rawat or leader of the Suraj-bansi Rajputs, he attached him to the royal household, where he speedily became a favorite. He was soon directed by Mahadeo in a dream to adopt him as his son and successor. The lad was now called Kapil Bhowarbar, and rose rapidly through several offices to the post of Pater or Prime Minister. The Moguls having come into the country from the north with a large army to demand tribute, the Raja feeling himself unable to cope with them in the field, sent his favorite to negociate a treaty of peace. He was detained as a hostage for the payment of the sum agreed upon, but was well treated by the King or Nawab, and on the death of his patron soon after, he was allowed to return to Orissa, when he assumed the government, A. D. 1451, under the title of Kapil Indra Deo. His reign is described to have been one continued series of wars, sieges, and expeditions. He visited in person every quarter of his widely extended dominions, but was occupied chiefly to the southward, and resided a good deal at Kimedy and Rajamundry. He also visited the city of Vijianagara and founded there several Sasans, more especially one called Damoderpur Sasan. The Raja afterwards pursued his conquests as far as Rama's bridge, opposite Ceylon, which the natives call Set Band Rameswara.

Ferishteh relates, that in the time of Humayun Shah Bahmini, about A. D. 1457, the Telingahs prevailed on the Rajas of Orissa and Uria to afford them assistance against the Mohammedans, who sent a large army to their aid, with many war elephants. The confederates completely defeated the armies of Islam, and pursued them from the field of battle for many miles. Under Nizam Shah, son of the above, the Rai of Orissa in conjunction with the powerful Zemindars of Khetris of Telingana, again invaded the territories of the Deckany sovereigns by way of Rajamandry and plundered as far as *Kolas.* The Rai of Orissa is said to have advanced in great state and splendour, with the declared intention of conquering the whole of Telingana from the Mussulmans, aud compelling them to pay tribute. When he had arrived however within ten miles of the Mohammedan capital Ahmedabad, the ministers taking courage sent him a message of defiance saying that "their king had long intended to subjugate Orissa and *Jehannagar* and render it tributary, but the idea of the distance of that country had hitherto deterred him from the undertaking: however as the Raja had now come so far to throw himself into the jaws of destruction, much trouble would be saved to the victorious armies of Islam." This bravado was followed up by a spirited sally of Patan horse, which cooled a little the ardour of the Hindus, and induced them to fall back. They were finally glad to purchase a secure retreat to their own frontier, by paying down a sum of five lacs of rupees.

The Bahmini king, who had always wished to obtain a footing on the Godaveri, agreed to Himber's proposal, marched an army into Uria, defeated the usurper Mangal Rai, and restored the principality to his ally, taking for his own share the forts of Rajamandry and Condapilly.

After some time Rai Uria seems to have repented of his connection with the Mohammedans, and to have become desirous of returning to his old allegiance. One of those destructive famines noticed in the accounts of Raja Kapil Indra Deo's reign, having spread general ruin and consternation throughout the Deccan, the conjuncture appeared to him favourable for making an effort to throw off the Musselman yoke, and he accordingly dispatched a message to the Rai of Orissa, saying, that "if he wished to recover his *hereditary dominions* in Telingana, now was the time." About A. D. 1471, the Raja of Orissa collected together an army of 10,000 foot and 8,000 horse, and summoning all his tributary chiefs to attend him, proceeded into Telingana without delay. Mohammed Shah hastened to oppose the combined forces of Orissa and Uria, and soon compelled the Rais to retreat across the lake of Rajamandry. He then, says Ferishteh, resolved to punish the Idolater for his insolence and aggression, and taking with him a chosen body of 20,000 men, made a dash into Orissa, and penetrated as far as the capital, plundering and laying waste the country on all sides. The Raja unable to withstand the fury of the storm which he had so rashly raised, fled before the invaders, and was soon obliged to sue humbly for peace; which was granted on condition of his paying a large sum of gold and silver, and surrendering twenty-five celebrated elephants which he valued next his life. The Musselman prince then retired, with the same degree of rapidity as he advanced, to Condapilly, where he humbled his other opponent Rai Uria.

The reign of Raja Pursottem Deo who came to the crown A. D. 1478, is rendered memorable by the most striking exploit recorded in the annals of Orissa, viz. the expedition to and conquest of Conjeveram, 48 miles S. W. from Madras. The circumstances of that transaction deserve to be rescued from oblivion, as well for the curious picture which they afford of the manners and opinions of the age and nation, as from their connection with an historical incident of some importance. The fullest account of the expedition is to be found in the poem called the Kanjikaveri Pot'hi.

The story runs nearly as follows: "In the country of Dakhin Kanouj Kernat Sasan, there lived a powerful Raja who had a vast fortress and palace built of a fine black stone, called Kanjinagar (Conjeveram,) and a daughter so beauteous and accomplished, that she was surnamed Pudmavati or Padmini.* The fame of her charms having reached the ears of Maharaja Pursottem Deo, he became anxious to espouse her, and sent a messenger accordingly to the Chief of Conjeveram to solicit the hand of his fair danghter. That Raja was well pleased with the prospect of having for his son-in-law so great and powerful a prince as the Gajapati of Orissa, but considered it advisable, to make some enquiries regarding the customs and manners of that Court before consenting to the alliance.

* This was the name of a Princess, whose amours with Khosru Perviz, are celebrated in several Indian and Persian Romances, and is in Sancrit indeed the general name of a particular class of beauties.

He soon found that the Maharajas were in the habit of preforming the duties of a *sweeper* (Chandal) before the image of Jagannath, on its being brought forth from the temple annually at the Rat'h Jatra. Now the Kanjinagar Raja was a devoted and exclusive worshipper of Sri Ganesh (Ganesa), and had very little respect for Juggernaut, the divinity of Orissa; and conceiving the above humiliation to be quite unworthy of, and indeed utterly disgraceful to a Khetri of such high rank, he declined the alliance in consequence. The Gajapati monarch became very wroth at the refusal, and swore, that to revenge the slight cast on him, he would obtain the damsel by force and marry her to a real sweeper. He accordingly marched with a large army to attack Conjeveram, but was defeated and obliged to retire. Overwhelmed with shame and confusion, he now threw himself at the feet of Sri Jeo, and earnestly supplicated his interference to avenge the insult offered to the deity himself in the person of his faithful worshipper. The god promised assistance, says the author of the poem, directed him to assemble another army, and assured him that he would this time take the command of the expedition against Conjeveram in person. When the Raja had arrived, during the progress of his march, at the site of the village now called Manikpatam, he began to grow anxious for some visible indication of the presence of deity. In the midst of his cogitations on the subject, a milkmaid named Manika, came up and displayed a ring which she said had been entrusted to her, to present to the monarch of Orissa, by two handsome Cavaliers, mounted the one on a black, and the other on a white horse, who had just passed on to the southward. She also related some particulars of a conversation with them which satisfied the Raja, that the promise of assistance would be fulfilled; and that these horsemen were no other than the two brothers Sri Jeo (Krishna) and Baldeo (Baladeva.) Full of joy and gratitude, he directed the village in future to be called, after his fair informant, Manikpatana, and marched onwards to the Deccan secure of success. On the other hand the chief of Conjeveram, alarmed at the second advance of the Gajapati in great force, appealed for aid to his protecting deity Ganesh, who candidly told him that he had little chance against Jagannath, but would do his best. The siege was now opened and many obstinate and bloody battles were fought under the walls of the fort. The gods Juggernaut and Ganesa, espousing warmly the cause of their respective votaries, perform many miracles and mix personally in the engagements, much in the style of the Homeric deities before the walls of Troy; but the latter is always worsted. In reality, after a long struggle, Conjeveram fell before the armies of Orissa. The Raja escaped, but his beautiful daughter was captured and conducted in triumph to Puri. A famous image of Gopal, called the Satbadi Thakur, that is, the "*truth speaking god*," was brought off at the same time and set up in a temple ten miles north of Pursottem, where it may still be seen, a monument of the Conjeveram expedition.

Conformably with his oath, Raja Pursottem Deo made over the fair Padmavati or Padmini to his chief minister, desiring him to wed her to a sweeper. Both the ministers, however, and all the people of Puri commiserated her misfortunes; and at the next Rath Jatra, when the Maharaja began to perform his office of *Chandal* (sweeper), the individual entrusted with the charge of the lady brought her forth and presented her to him, saying, "You ordered me to give the Princess to a sweeper; *you* are the sweeper upon whom I bestow her." Moved by the intercession of his subjects, the Raja at last consented to marry Padmavati, and carried her to the palace at Cuttack. The end of this lady's history is as romantic as the preceding portion of it. She is said to have conceived and brought forth a son by Mahadeo, shortly after which she disappeared. All the circumstances were explained to the husband in a dream, who acknowledged gratefully the honor conferred on him, and declared the child thus mysteriously born his successor in the Raj.

Pursottem Deo died after a reign of twenty-five years, and was succeeded by Pertab Janamuni, the son of Padmavati, under the title of Pertab Rudra Deo, A. D. 1503. The wisdom and learning of this prince soon became the theme and admiration of the whole country. He had studied deeply all the shasters, was very fond of disputing and conversing on points of theology, and introduced many curious constructions of his own, and doctrines that were altogether new. He was also devout, and built many temples. His skill in the arts of war and civil government, were eminent; he was equally celebrated as an able, learned, warlike and religious prince. A very curious anecdote is related of his conduct, which seems to shew that the followers of Buddha continued to form a sect of importance in this part of India until the beginning of the sixteenth century.* It is said that a serious robbery happened in the Raja's

* As this is contrary to received opinions, to the inferences warranted by the works of Madhavacharya in the 13th century and the statement of Abulfazl in the 16th, it seems likely that the original authorities have confounded, as is very commonly the case, the Bauddhas and Jains, and that the latter are here intended.—*Note by the Secretary C. A. S.*

palace, and that he being anxious to discover the perpetrators, assembled together all the wise men, both of the Bauddhist and Brahminical persuasion, to obtain their assistance in prosecuting an investigation. The brahmins could tell nothing, but the followers of Buddha, through their knowledge of the occult art, were enabled to point out both the offender and the place where the stolen property was concealed. The Raja was induced by this incident to form so high an opinion of the learning and skill of the Bauddhists, that he became for some time a warm supporter of that sect. His Rani on the other hand espoused zealously the cause of the brahmins. It was at last determined to make another formal trial of their relative skill as men of science, or rather magicians. Accordingly a snake was secretly put into an earthen jar, the mouth of which being covered up, the vessel was produced in a great assembly at the palace. Both parties were then asked what the jar contained. The brahmins answered, "it contains only earth," and sure enough when opened it was found to contain nothing but earth. This specimen of skill entirely changed the Raja's opinion, and he now became as violent against the Bauddhists as he had been before prejudiced in their favour; so much so that he not only withdrew his protection and countenance, but violently expelled the whole sect from his dominions, and destroyed all their books except the pot'his called the Amer Singh and Bir Singh. About this time Chytunya or Chytan Mahaprabhu came from Naddia in Bengal to visit the temple of Jaggannath, and preformed various miracles before the Raja. The key of the whole story is probably to be found in the visit of this celebrated Vyshnavite reformer or secretary, who doubtless had some share in creating the hostile disposition of Raja Pertab Rudra Deo, towards the followers of the heretical Budha.

Another of those famines which have so often afflicted India, occurred early in the sixteenth century in Orissa. The Raja who could find leisure for schemes of conquest and ambition amidst his religious enquiries and controversies, marched with his army down to Setu Band Rameswara, reduced several forts, and took the famous city of Vijayanagara. The Mohammedans of the Deccan also gave abundant occupation to his arms on the southern frontier of the Raj, and whilst he was occupied in repelling or provoking their attacks, the Afghans from Bengal made an inroad into the province in great force. They advanced as far as Cuttack, and pitched their camp in the neighbourhood of the city, when the Governor Anant Singhar finding himself unable to oppose any effectual resistance, took refuge in the strong fortress of Sarangerh, south of the Katjuri.

After satiating themselves with the plunder of the capital, they proceeded towards Puri, where they committed dreadful devastations; but the grand object of their search, *the Idol or Deo of Orissa,* had been removed out of their reach, the priests having taken the precaution, so soon as they heard of the approach of the invaders, to carry off Sri Jeo and the other images in boats across the Chilka in order to conceal them amongst the hills. Raja Pertab Rudra Deo on receiving intelligence of these disastrous occurrences, hastened back from the Deccan; and preforming a journey of months in a few days, he came up with the invading army before they had left the khetr, gave them battle, and destroyed a great number. He was however himself so much crippled by the contest, that he was happy to conclude a peace nearly on the enemy's terms, when they retired and left the province.

This prince died A. D. 1524, having reigned twenty-one years. With him terminated all the glories of the Ganga Vansa dynasty, and the royal house of Orissa. The race itself became extinct soon after the demise of Raja Pertab Rudra Deo, and the independence of the country was not destined long to survive. Pressed at both extremities by the vigourand enterprize of the Mohammedan governments of Bengal and Telingana, now in the full maturity of their strength, the downfall of the Orissan monarchy was further hastened by intestine commotions, disunion amongst the chiefs, and a series of bloody and destructive contests for the supreme dignity.

Soon after the death of Raja Pertab Rudra, the powerful minister Govind barbarously murdered *thirty princes* of the royal house, and waded through blood to the throne. Various individuals succeeded him; and in 1550 A. D. the last independent Raja ascended the throne with the title of Telinga Mukund Deo.

All the native accounts concur in describing their last independent Raja as a man of courage and abilities. He has been honored with a notice in the work of the Jesuit Tieffenthaler, who extends our knowledge of his character by informing us, that "the last king of the Orissans was called Mukund, who was very polite to strangers and had four hundred women." The early part of his reign was employed chiefly in constructing monuments of public utility or superstition, as temples, tanks, and brahminical sasans. Amongst other works of the kind, he founded a ghat and temple at the sacred spot called Tribeni, on the Hoogly, north of the town of that name which formed the extreme verge of his dominions; and whilst so occupied, frequent communications are said to have passed between him and the king of Delhi, or rather the officers of the emperor.

Soliaman Gurzani, the Afghan king or governor of Bengal, having assembled an army to invade Orissa, the Raja built a strong fortress in some commanding situation, and for this time opposed his endeavours successfully. At last however came Kala Pahar General of the Bengal forces, the conqueror of Orissa, with his wonder working kettle drum, at the sound of which it is said the ears and feet of the idols would drop off for many coss all around. The Hindus say of this dreaded enemy of their images and superstition, that he was originally a brahmin, but lost caste through a contrivance of the princess of Gaura, who was smitten with the manly beauty of his person. He then married her, turned Musselman, and became a relentless persecutor of the adherents of the faith from which he had apostatized. Many dire omens preceded and announced his arrival in the province; amongst others a large stone fell from the summit of the great tower of the temple at Puri, and when he entered the precincts of the khetr, a general darkness overspread the four corners of the land. In short, Kalapahar invaded Orissa on the part of the king or governor of Bengal with an army of Afghan Cavalry, defeated and killed the Raja or drove him from the country, and finally overthrew the independent sovereignty of Orissa, A. D. 1558. Two titular princes were set up after the expulsion of Mukund Deo, who both fell into the hands of the conquerors and were put to death by them. An anarchy of twenty-one years duration then ensued, during which the Afghan Mohammedans possessed the whole of the open country, and there was no Raja.

The several accounts which have been handed down of Kalapahar's invasion of Orissa, differ widely in the details, though the main facts are well known and established. The story told by the Musselman writers is that, Mukund Deo, apprehending the designs of the king or governor of Bengal, encamped with a large part of his army on the Ganges; but Kalapahar turning his position got a-head of him into Orissa, and began to plunder the country and attack the temples of the Hindus with relentless fury, before any force could be brought to check him. A battle at length took place at Jajipur in which the Raja lost his life. The Afghan chief then went on to Sumbhulpoor, where he was killed by some of the Bhuyans. Others say that on his passing the great temple of the Ling Raj at Bhuvaneswara, a swarm of bees issued from the throne of the idol and stung him to death. The Puri Vynsavali makes the Raja to have been busy in Khurda when the Afghan army suddenly advanced upon Cuttack, defeated the Governor Gopi Sawant Sinhar, and plundered the palace and treasury, alarmed at which news, Mukund Deo fled out of the province not daring to oppose so powerful a force, and died shortly after in the king of Delhi's dominions.

All the native writers agree in speaking with horror of the cruel excesses committed by their Afghan conqueror, and the wide destruction of images and temples occasioned by his unrelenting persecution of the Hindu faith. Many demolished idols seen at various temples demonstrate the devastation caused by these invasions. Their conquerors gloried in the destruction of idols, and even made them stepping-stones to their mosques.

The adventures of the great Idol form a curious episode in the history of this period. According to the Mandala Panji, when the priests at Pooree saw the turn which matters were taking, *they again for the third time in their annals, hurried away the helpless god in a covered cart, and buried him in a pit at Parikud, on the Chilka Lake.* Kalapahar was not however to be defrauded of so rich a prize, and having traced out the place of concealment, he dug up Juggernaut and carried him off on an elephant, as far as the Ganges, after breaking in pieces every image in the Khetr. He then collected a large pile of wood, and setting fire to it, threw the idol on the heap. A bystander snatching the image from the flames, threw it into the river. The whole proceeding had been watched by Besar Mainti, a faithful votary of Juggernaut, who followed the half-burnt image as it floated down the stream, and at last, when unperceived, managed to extract from it the sacred part, (Brahm or spirit in the original,) and brought it back secretly to Orissa, where it was carefully deposited in charge of the Khandait of Kujang.

After twenty-one years of anarchy, the principal men of the country chose for their chief a person named Ranai Raotra, whom they raised to the rank and dignity of Maharaja of Orissa, A. D. 1580, under the title of Ramchander Deo. With him begins the *third* and titular race of sovereigns called the Bhoi Vansa, or Zemindari race. The election was confirmed by Sewai Jye Sinh, the general of the Emperor Akber, who came into the province about the time, with his army, to look after the imperial interests. The sight of Bhuvaneswara, its numerous temples, the crowds of brahmins, and the sacred character of every thing in Utcala Desa, is said to have impressed him with feelings of so much reverence and admiration for the country, that he determined to interfere very little in its affairs, and retired shortly afterwards, leaving a large share of authority in the hands of its Native Princes. The town of Midnapore was at this time made the northern boundary of Orissa.

Raja Ramchander Deo's first care was to recover the sacred relics belonging to the old image of Jagannath, which duty being accomplished with the assistance of their preserver Besar Mainti, the *Daru Murat*, or image made of the wood of the *Nim tree*, was fabricated according to the rules of the shaster, and again set up in the temple, on a propitious day, with much pomp and solemnity. The worship of Sri Jeo was now fully restored, all the feasts and endowments of the temple put on their old footing, and a number of sasans were founded in honor of the memorable event. It was disturbed again however almost immediately afterwards, by an invasion of Musselmans from Golconda, whose king or *Adipati*, as the Hindu writers call him, seems to have given the Raja a severe defeat.

Ramchander Deo enjoyed his station and dignities for twenty-nine years. He was an able and respectable prince, and his memory seems to be much venerated by the natives of the province. From his time, the field embraced by the Orissan annals, becomes greatly narrowed, though they still afford a vast deal of curious local information. The necessary limits confine me to an exhibition of 1st. A list of the names of the several Rajas and the duration of their reigns; and 2nd, a brief outline of such part of their history, as has any connection with the general affairs of the *Subah* of Orissa. The materials for an historical account of the country, under this new denomination, are very scanty and imperfect. The slender information extant of the proceedings of the Mogul officers from the retirement of Raja Man Sinh in A. D. 1604, to the dewanship of the famous Nuwab Jaffer Khan Nasiri (A.D. 1707 to 1725,) has to be gleaned from a few scattered notices in Persian histories of Bengal and scarcely intelligible revenue accounts; though the century in question must be regarded as a most important period in the annals of the country, when we consider the deep and permanent traces impressed on the state of affairs, by the arrangements, institutions, offices, and official designations, introduced by the imperial government during that interval. Subsequent to the elevation of Jaffer Khan, we meet with tolerably full and detailed journals and records both of the Mohammedan and Marhatta administrations, composed in the Persian language.

List of Khurda Rajas.

Ramchander Deo, succeeds	A. D. 1580
Pursottem Deo	1609
Narsinh Deo	1630

Gangadhar Deo	1655
Balbhadder Deo	1656
Mukund Deo	1664
Dirb Sinh Deo	1692
Kishen or Harikishen Deo	1715
Gopinath Deo	1720
Ramchander Deo	1727
Bir Kishore Deo	1743
Dirb Sinh Deo	1786
Mukund Deo	1798

The southern part of Orissa Proper must have suffered much from the constant wars, insurrections, and internal commotions, that prevailed during the early times of the Musselman government. The Moguls seem to have been actuated by peculiar rancour and ill will towards Jagannath, and lost no opportunity of annoying and disturbing the Hindus in the performance of their devotions at his temple. To say nothing of other fruitful sources of jealousy and animosity, this interference alone was sufficient to produce many bloody encounters between the two nations, in which success was often doubtful. On the whole however, the native Princes suffered the most severely, and gradually sank before the superior energy and civilization of the Moguls. The Rajas had at first established their residence at Pipley; afterwards they retired to Rathipur; and finally built their fort and palace in a naturally difficult part of Khurda, where they were found settled in 1803. During these contests in and about Pooree, the images so much venerated by the one party and abhorred by the other, were twice or thrice carried away across the Chilka lake, and concealed amidst the hills, until the times appeared favorable for again setting them upon their thrones in the temple. This religious warfare was at last set at rest by the institution of the *tax on pilgrims*, which, if we may credit the author of the work translated by Gladwin, under the title of History of Bengal, yielded to the Mogul government *a revenue of nine lacs.* Under such circumstances, religious antipathies however strong on the part of the ruling power, must have yielded gradually to considerations of self-interest.

The Afghans did not disappear from the field as disturbers of the peace of Cuttack, until 1611 A. D., when having again risen under Osman Khan the son of Kattali, they were defeated with great slaughter on the Subunreekha by Shujat Khan from Bengal, and compelled finally to submit. They then settled peaceably in many of the principal villages of the district, and their descendants at this day form a Musselman population, under the general denomination of Pathans.

But the greatest of all their calamities overwhelmed the unfortunate Orissans about A. D. 1743. After some alarming demonstrations in the year preceding, the Berar Marhattas suddenly made their appearance in the Province, in large force. There being no power adequate to oppose them, they swept the whole country up to the walls of fort Barabatti at Cuttack, plundering whatever they could lay their hands on without mercy,—and the same scenes were repeated the year following, by a still larger army under Ragoji Bhonsla himself, and the famous adventurer Habib Ullah. Aliverdi Khan made astonishing efforts to relieve the Province, as well as to protect the adjoining districts from these destructive inroads, but the people of Midnapore and Cuttack enjoyed little respite from the Marhatta incursions and depredations until 1750. A fresh army invaded Orissa in 1753, under the command of Raja Janoji Bhonsla and Mir Ḥabib Ullah, who in the same year, in their camp at Choudwar, near the Mahanuddy, projected and arranged a partition of the Province between themselves, for the maintenance of their respective armies. Its resources on this occasion were estimated at only ten lacs.

Things remained in this miserable state till the next year, when a fresh treaty was entered into, between the Marhattas and Aliverdi Khan, at the instigation of the whole body of the Zemindars of Midnapore and neighbouring districts, who, worn out by the repeated incursions of the Berar Marhattas, offered to pay any sum which might be agreed to as a composition for the Chout or tribute. Masalih ad Din was in consequence dispatched by the Court of Moorshedabad to Nagpore, with full powers to treat, and the following arrangements were determined on—" The Chout of the three Subas was now settled at 12,00,000 annually. The Suba of Orissa from Pergunnah Pattaspur to Malud to be managed by a Subadar appointed from Bengal, who should yearly pay the surplus revenue of that Province, estimated at four lacs, to an agent of the Bhonsla stationed at Cuttack. The remaining eight lacs were to be made good from Moorshedabad, Patna, &c., by Hundis or Bills of Exchange. The Marhatta armies forthwith to evacuate the Province." On the conclusion of the treaty, Raja Janoji quitted Orissa, Mohammed Masalih ad Din received the appointment of Naib Subadar and Sheo Bhat Santra, an eminent Gosain merchant, was named the agent for the Court of Berar to receive the four lacs from

Cuttack, and to look after the annual remittance of the balance of the Chout from Moorshedabad.

The administration of the Marhattas in Cuttack, as in every other part of their foreign conquests, was fatal to the welfare of the people and the prosperity of the country, and exhibits a picture of misrule, anarchy, weakness, rapacity, and violence combined, which makes one wonder how society can have been kept together under so calamitous a tyranny. All the head offices of the district, as those of Subadar, Dewan, and the Killadarship of fort Barabatti, were openly bought and sold at Nagpore. It frequently happened that appointments were given to two or three persons at the same time, and still oftener the individuals in charge refused to retire under various pretexts. The different claimants, assembling their followers, would fight the most obstinate battles, and lay waste the country with their dissensions, before the right to succeed was settled. Pressed by the urgent irregular demands of the Court of Nagpore for remittances, and by the necessity of reimbursing themselves for the expences incurred in obtaining office, the most ruinous expedients were perpetually resorted to, to wring a higher revenue from the lands, whilst their resources declined in proportion to the tyranny exercised over the cultivators. Notwithstanding that large military bodies were posted all over the district, the Marhattas were quite unable to retain the Khandaits and their paiks in any sort of order. Those of the sea shore and the hills, not only laid the whole of the pergunnahs bordering upon them under regular contribution, but frequently the Paiks of several small killahs, combining together, advanced into the heart of the district, and committed the most ruinous depredations up to the very walls of Cuttack. Every year regularly after the Dassera, the Marhatta armies took the field under the Subadar in person, and advanced into some part of the Rajwara, to chastise some insolence, or to enforce the demand for tribute. When successful, the most sanguinary punishments and destructive ravages were inflicted,—but they were frequently defeated, and their weakness exposed, by the Paiks of killahs which now scarcely retain a name. Besides, the continued marches and countermarches of a licentious disorderly Marhatta soldiery, in every direction across the Province, were in themselves evils of no trifling magnitude. Matters improved a little towards the close of the Marhatta period, during the long administration of Raja Ram Pundit; but if the ryots were in a small degree better protected by his measures, he reduced, to the lowest stage of poverty and degradation, a powerful and important class, the hereditary Talukdars of the Mogulbandi, who were ejected by him, very generally, from the management of their Taluks, and left with scarcely even the means of subsistence.

It would be impossible to render interesting to the general reader, the never varying detail of oppression, mismanagement, and suffering displayed by the Marhatta annals in this fourth stage of Orissan history.

The first and most energetic of the Marhatta Subadars, was Sheo Bhat Santia, who exercised a disputed and precarious authority for a period of about eight years, from 1163 to 1171 Amli, and may be said to have been in full possession of the powers of government for about half that period. He made a settlement of the revenues of the Province, nominally at 18,00,000 of Arcot Rupees, of which 14,00,000 were entered as regular land revenue, and the remaining 4,00,000 as imposts under various heads. During his administration, a farther dismemberment took place of the territories of the Maharajas of Khurda. In 1167 Amli, Narain Deo, the famous Zemindar of Kimedy,* a descendant of the royal family of Orissa, who had before asserted his preferable title to the Khurda Raj, invaded that district by way of Banpur, with the avowed intention of taking possession of it, and drove the reigning prince Bir Kishore Deo before him. Unable to resist his powerful rival, the latter was thrown upon the dangerous expedient of claiming the assistance of the Marhattas, which was granted on condition of the payment of a large sum, to defray all expenses, in return. The aid of the Subadar proved effectual in clearing Khurda of the pretender's army, but the Raja being unable to discharge the money bargained for, he was obliged to mortgage or surrender temporarily for its liquidation, the best portion of his dominions, viz. the Mehals, Limbai, Raheng, Pursottem Chatter, &c.,—in short, the whole country lying between the Dya river, the lake and the sea, with the tribute of the fourteen Rajas or Khandaits of the hills, still subject to his control. The Marhattas were allowed to appoint their own Amils, and having thus gained a footing in the tracts in question, they never afterwards relinquished possession. The benefit of the acquisition seems doubtful, as the usurpation of Raheng, &c., involved them in a

* Mr. Grant in his Political Essay in the Northern Sircars, says of this person: "Kimedy, fifty miles N.E. by N. from the town of Cicacole, is the capital of another tributary but more accessible dependant principality vested in a Raja of the royal family of Orissa, who actually bears the titular designation of that ancient house under the proper name of Gujipati Deo, through the refractory imprudence of Narain Deo, father of the present occupant, in opposing the Company's authority."

state of unceasing hostility with the Khurda Rajas; and the claim to levy the tribute of Rajwara brought them yearly into disputes and battles with the hill Chiefs, in which, to say nothing of the expenditure of blood and treasure, they were nearly as often worsted as they were successful.

Raja Ram Pundit, who had for many years filled the office of Deputy to the local governor, and had taken a leading part in all the arrangements for the management of the interior, succeeded to the office of Subadar, about 1185 Amli. His personal qualities and abilities were respectable, and, coupled with his extensive local knowledge, lent a character of dignity and stability to his administration, with which no preceding one had been invested. The chief measure ascribed to him, is that of setting aside all the hereditary Chowdris and Canungos, in other words the Talukdars of the Mogulbandi, and collecting the revenues through officers of his own appointing, either from the ryots direct, or through the agency of the head men of villages, where such existed. He was also the first governor who imposed a tribute on the Maharajas of Khurda. Raja Bir Kishore Deo, after a long reign of forty-one years, fell into a state of furious insanity, and committed such frightful excesses, even to the extent of murdering four of his own children, that a general outcry was raised against him throughout the country. The Marhattas did not neglect so favorable an opportunity of interfering. They secured the Raja's person, threw him into confinement in fort Barabati, and refused to acknowledge his grandson Dirb Sinh Deo as successor, until they had obliged him to agree to the payment of a yearly tribute of Sa. Rs. 10,000. The expense of collecting this, must have been far greater than its value, for the Raja would never pay until compelled by the presence of a military force; and so low had the character and efficiency of the Marhatta Infantry sunk, that the Paiks of Khurda often presumed to measure their strength with them, even in these last days of the power of the Rajas of Orissa.

Chimna Ji Bapu's visit to Cuttack, with a large army in 1781 A. D., is described as intended to enforce the claims of the Berar government against Bengal, for arrears of Chout. Having cantooned his force at Kakkar, opposite to Cuttack, he sent on Raja Ram Pundit with Bissembher Pundit Vakil to Calcutta, who is said to have negotiated a treaty with Mr. Hastings, by which the English government agreed to the payment of 27,00,000 Rs. on condition of all farther claims being relinquished.

THE TEN HINDOO AVATARS,

BEING DESCENTS, OR INCARNATIONS, OF THE GOD VISHNOO, IN VARIOUS FORMS

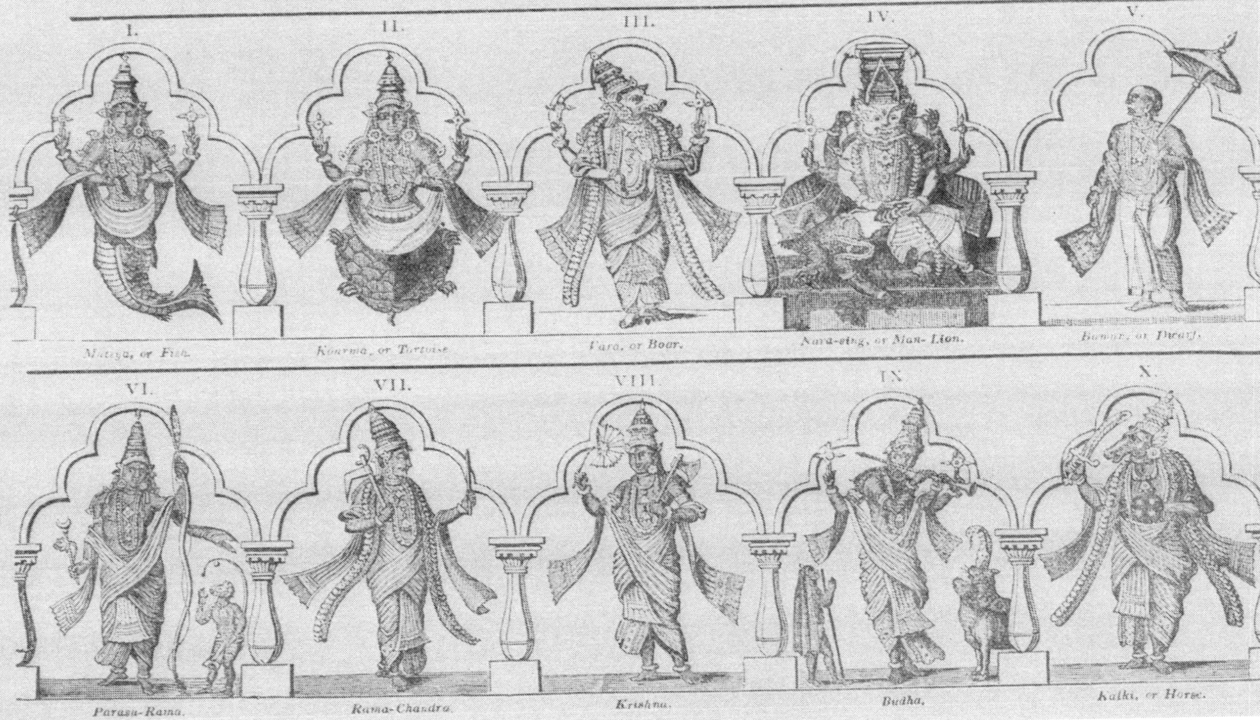

In 1803, the Province was conquered by the English armies. The dominion of the Khurda Rajas was not finally extinguished till 1804, when a most unprovoked rising against the newly established English Government, drew down upon Raja Mukund Deo the vengeance of the British power. He was driven from his fort, seized, sent a prisoner to Midnapore, and his remaining territory of Khurda was brought under the management of the British collectors.

Since that period the proud but insignificant representatives of the Maharajas of Orissa, have been officially acknowledged only as private landholders; but the liberal policy of government has conferred on them a sufficient pension, and an office of authority connected with the temple, in the enjoyment of which they pass their days in retirement, within the limits of Jagannath Pooree. The complete subjection of the Province terminated in 1805, by the conquest of Kunka.

CHAP. IV.

Religion, Antiquities, Temples, and Civil Architecture.

UTCALA DESA which is believed or fabled to be itself so holy a region throughout its entire extent, contains four places of pilgrimage of peculiar sanctity, called the Hara Khetr, the Vishnu or Pursottem Khetr, the Arka or Padma Khetr, and the Vijayi or Parvati Khetr, within the limits of which will be found nearly all that is curious and interesting in its Religious Antiquities.

The Hara khetr, sacred to Mahadeo Seeb under the titles of the Linga Raja Bhuvaneswara, and thence called by the vulgar Bhobaneser, contains several very ancient and remarkable monuments of the native princes of the country, and their system of religious belief. At Balwanta, on the new road, sixteen miles from Cuttack, the attention of the traveller is attracted by a lofty massive tower of stone, rising from amidst the thickets which skirt the adjoining frontier of Khurda. A path leads through the woods towards this object of curiosity, and conducts, at the end of about six miles, to a gently swelling rocky elevation or Tangi formed of beds of the iron clay, on reaching which you find yourself, with astonishment, in the centre of a ruined city, consisting entirely of deserted and dismantled towers and temples sacred to the worship of Mahadeo, under the innumerable titles, which absurd legends or the fancy of his votaries have assigned to that deity. From amidst the whole, the great Pagoda of the Ling Raj, or Lord of the Lingam, lifts its singular form, eminently conspicuous both for size, loftiness, and the superior style of its architecture.

Bhobaneser is the site of a capital city founded by Raja Lalat Indra Kesari, the third of the princes bearing that surname, who reigned from A. D. 617 to A. D. 660. If we are to judge of its extent and populousness, during the period that it formed the seat of government of the Rajas of the Kesari Vansa, from the almost countless multitude of temples which are crowded within the sacred limits of the Panj Kosi, we might pronounce it to have been, in the days of its splendour, one of the greatest cities which India ever saw. Standing near the chief Pagoda,* one cannot turn the eye, in any direction, without taking into the view upwards of forty or fifty of these stone towers. The natives say that there were originally more than seven thousand places of worship consecrated to Mahadeo, within and around the city of Bhobaneser, containing no less than a crore of lingams, and the vestiges that remain, fully warrant a belief, that the place may have comprised some *hundreds* of buildings of this description, when in its most flourishing state. A considerable number of the temples are still in a tolerable state of preservation, though *entirely neglected and deserted.* Many more are now screened from the view by the luxuriant foliage of the surrounding jungles, or present merely shapeless masses of stone buried amidst tangled brushwood and rank vegetation.

Nor is the astonishing number of the Bhobaneser temples the only remarkable feature of this place. The style, size, and decoration of these singular buildings, add greatly to the wonder and interest of the scene. They are all constructed, either of reddish granite resembling sandstone, or else of the free stone yielded plentifully by the neighbouring hills, in the form of towers rounded towards the summit, with other edifices attached rising from a square enclosure, the wall encompassing which is now generally in ruins. Their height is never less than fifty or sixty feet, and the loftier towers reach to an elevation of from one hundred and fifty,

* Mr. Ward mentions it in is work on the Hindus under the name of Ekamrakanuna, "a place, he says, on the borders of Orissa, containing Six Thousand temples dedicated to Shiva." Ekamra or Ekamber is the name given to the surrounding woods.

to one hundred and eighty feet. Not a wooden beam it may be observed has been used throughout. The stones are held together with iron clamps. Iron beams and pillars are used where such aids could not be dispensed with; but in general the architects have resorted, in the construction of their roofs, to the method of laying horizontal layers of stone, projecting one beyond the other like inverted steps, until the sides approach sufficiently near at the summit to admit of other blocks being placed across. The exterior surface of the buildings is in general adorned with the richest and most elaborate sculptured ornament, and the ruined courts which surround them, are strewed with a vast variety of curious relics, as bulls, lingams, and other symbols appropriate to the worship of Mahadeo, representations of Ganesa, Hunuman, and various forms of Siva and Parvati, Durga, or Kali, Carticeya the god of war with his peacock, the female or energy of the same called Caumari, and the Narasinha and Baman Avatars. The more finished temples have frequently large well polished slabs of the grey chlorite slate, or pot stone, let into three of their sides, on which are sculptured, in alto relievo, nearly as large as life, some of the above personages, executed with no mean degree of skill and symmetry. Carved in the coarser stone of which the walls are constructed, one observes figures of Apsarasas, or dancing nymphs in groups or solitary; forms of Mahadeo and Parvati sitting or standing together, generally in the most obscene attitudes; representations of warriors, horses, and elephants, engaged in combat or arranged in state processions: monsters resembling lions, with grim grotesque countenances, in various attitudes; and groups of a peaceful character exhibiting a Muni, or philosopher, imparting instructions to his pupils. The architrave of the door-way of every temple of Orissa is ornamented with the nine figures in a sitting posture, called the Nava Graha or nine planets, of which seven represent the divinities presiding over the days of the week, and the two remaining ones the brahminical ascending and descending nodes, Rahu and Ketu.

The forms and character of all the principal temples at Bhobuneser, and indeed throughout the province, being exactly similar, a more particular account of the plan and distribution of the great Pagoda will answer the purpose of a general description. The edifices which compose it, stand within a square area, enclosed by a substantial wall of stone, measuring six hundred feet on a side; which has its principal gateway guarded by two monstrous griffins, or winged lions, in a sitting posture, on the eastern face. About the centre, the great tower, Bara Dewal, or sanctuary, in which the images are always lodged, rises majestically to a height of one hundred and eighty feet. It is composed of a cluster of stone ribs, alternately flat and semicircular, eight principal and eight inferior ones, springing from a square ground plan, which towards the summit curve inwards, without, however, meeting. They bear, as it were on their shoulders, a cylindrical neck, and this, with the aid of brackets in the form of eight immense griffins or lions, supports the ornamented crest or head piece, shaped somewhat like a turban, which forms so distinguishing a feature in the temple architecture of Orissa. It consists of a huge solid circular slab, called the Amla Sila, from some fancied resemblance to the fruit of the Amlika (*Phyllanthus Emblica,*) on which rests another circular ornament, in the form of a large inverted earthen dish, and thence indeed called the "*Dihi Bandhi.*" Sometimes the two ornaments are repeated. On the summit stands, either an urn, or the Chakra or wheel of Vishnu, according to circumstances, surmounted by an iron spike, to which pendants are attached on occasions of ceremony. The best illustration that can be given, of the shape and appearance of the generality of these towers, is to compare them to a medicine phial, or comfit bottle with the stopper inserted; though the comparison does not do justice to the picturesque effect of the grand and massive building which I am now describing. From each face of the building, at different degrees of elevation, a huge monster projects to a distance of several feet, which has the body of a lion, but a most grotesque and unnatural countenance, resembling nothing in the catalogue of terrestrial animals. The figure on the eastern face is by far the largest, and it has between its feet, an elephant of comparatively diminutive size, on which it is trampling. This, it may be observed, is the common mode of representing the lion of Hindu mythology, one of the epithets of which is, Gaja Machula, or the destroyer of the elephant. The entrance to the tower lies through a large square vestibule or antichamber, crowned with a pyramidal roof, and surmounted by the crest or series of ornaments above described, which is joined to the eastern face of the sanctuary, and rises to about three fourths of its height. It is called the Jagamohana, or that which delights the world, because it is from thence that the idol is generally seen and worshipped by pilgrims. These two buildings form the essential and most sacred part of the temples of Orissa. Farther in advance of the Jagamohana, and connected with it by a sort of colonnade, is another square edifice of precisely the same form, but smaller dimensions, which is called the Bhag Mandap, or apartment in which the idol's food is served up, and afterwards distributed amongst the officiating priests, &c. The Court of the Ling Raj contains many other towers and temples apart from those already enumerated, in which a variety of the inferior deities, or less esteemed forms of the greater ones, are worshipped, and which add, by their style and number, to the general grandeur of its appearance, but do not need a separate description. The whole are adorned with a profusion of sculptured work, consisting of elaborately wrought cornices, beadings, arabesque and reticulated ornaments, and clusters of pilasters, with figures of men, animals, serpents and flowers intervening, arranged in such an infinite variety of devices, that the eye is absolutely bewildered in endeavouring to trace out any particular pattern or design. Amongst the ornaments on the great flat central ribs of the Bara Dewal, there is one peculiarly remarkable from its resemblance to some armorial, bearing or heraldic device. The brahmins explain it to be a compound of the Gada, Padma, Sankh, and Chakra, or Mace, lotus, conch-shell and discus of Vishnu, and it would seem therefore rather out of place, in the conspicuous position which it occupies on the walls of the Ling Raj ; but, it may be observed generally, of these edifices, that the sculptors have by no means confined themselves, in their choice of ornaments, to emblems peculiar to the deity of the place.

The temple of the Ling Raj at Bhobaneser is both the finest monument of antiquity which the province contains, and likewise indisputably the most ancient. It took *forty-three years* to build it, and local tradition as well as the histories of the country, concur in fixing the date of its completion, as A. D. 657. We have no particular accounts, of the period and causes of the decline of the city of Bhobaneser, and the worship of Mahadeo. Nearly all except the great temple, have been long since completely deserted ; and the establishment kept up there, is on a very small and inadequate scale, under the patronage of the Khurda Rajas, whose ancestors granted all the lands and endowments, by which the brahmins attached to it now subsist! It is occasionally visited by the Bengalee pilgrims on their way to Jagannath, and every year, at the Sheo Ratri, a considerable collection of Desi, or country pilgrims, are gathered together under its walls, to hold a mela or fair.

The ruins of two extensive palaces, belonging to the Rajas of the Kesari line, are shewn at or near Bhobaneser. There is likewise a very superb tank, lying north of the temple, called the Bidu Sagar, which forms a conspicuous object in the scenery of the place, and another, faced with stone, on the east, remarkable for its being bordered all round with rows of small antique looking temples, about thirty on a side, just large enough to contain the human figure in a sitting posture, in which *sixty female ascetics, who had devoted themselves to the worship of Devi, are said to have lived and died many ages back.* Amongst the curiosities of the environs, the attention of the visitor is generally directed to a huge figure of the lingam, *forty feet* in height, at the temple of Bhaskăresar Mahadeo. It is formed of a single shaft of sandstone, situated partly in a subterranean vault, and part rising into the centre of a great tower, of the usual form, which is said to have been built round this impure and degrading object of worship, after it had been set up and consecrated.

About five miles west of Bhobaneser, near the village of Jagmara, in the Char Sudhi Khandaiti of Khurda, and still within the limits of the khetr, a group of small hills occur, four in number, from one hundred and fifty to two hundred feet in height, which present many objects of interest and curiosity. These hills called severally the Udaya Giri, Dewal Giri, Nil Giri, and Khand Giri, (by which latter name the spot is now generally designated,) are composed of a silicious sandstone of various colour and texture, and are all curiously perforated with small caves, disposed in two or three irregular stories. Each of the caves is large enough to contain from one to two human beings in a sitting posture. Some of them appear to be natural cavities, slightly improved by the hand of man; others have obviously been excavated artificially; and the whole are grotesquely carved and embellished. In one part, a projecting mass of rock has been cut into the form of a tiger's head, with the jaws widely distended, through which a passage lies into a small hole at the back secured by a wooden door,—the residence of a secluded ascetic of the Vyshnavite sect. The ridiculous legend which the natives relate to explain the origin of these isolated hills, bears a resemblance to the tales of Popery, another kind of Paganism, respecting angels carrying to Italy the house of the lady of Loretto. The Popish tale is well known; the Pagan one is, that these hills formerly constituted a part of the Himalaya, at which time they were inhabited by numerous Rishis, who dug the caves now found in them. They were taken up bodily, ascetics and all, by Mahabir Hunuman, with other masses of rock, to build the bridge of Rama, but, by some accident, were allowed to drop in their passage through the air, when they alighted in their present position.

The summit of the highest rock, is crowned by a neat stone temple of modern construction, sacred to the worship of Parasnath; all around, and in the neigbourhood of which, are strewed a quantity of images of the Nirvanas, or naked figures worshipped by the Jain sect,* executed chiefly in the grey cholorite slate rock. At the back of these temples, a highly remarkable terrace is shewn, called the Deo Sabha, or assembly of gods, which is covered with numberless antique-looking stone pillars or temples in minature; some standing, others lying on the ground, about two or three feet long, having, on each of the four sides, a figure of the naked Jain deity rudely sculptured. The place is still frequented by the Jain or Parwar merchants of Cuttack, who assemble here in numbers, once every year, to hold a festival of their religion.

A short way up the Udaya Giri hill, the Nour or palace of the famous Raja Lalat Indra Kesari, is pointed out as the chief curiosity of the place. It consists of a sort of open court formed by a perpendicular face of sandstone rock, about forty feet in height, with shoulders of the same projecting on either side. Rows of small chambers having been excavated in each face, arranged in two stories, and divided by a projecting terrace. Both the exterior surface and the inner walls of the chambers are decorated with cornices, pilasters, figures, and various devices, very rudely sculptured, and the whole exhibits a faint and humble resemblance, in miniature, to the celebrated cavern temples in the south-west of India. The rude and miserable apartments of the *palace*, are now occupied by byragis

* Mr. Ward thus describes this sect. "They take their name from jimi (*ji* to conquer,) he who has overcome the eight great crimes, viz., eating at night; slaying an animal; eating the fruit of those trees which give milk, pumpkins, young bamboo plants; tasting honey, flesh; taking the wealth of others; taking by force a married woman; eating flowers, butter, cheese; and worshipping the gods of other religions. The sect is said to owe its rise to Rishubbu Devu, a Hindoo, who is said to have been incarnate thirteen times. The last of the Jain jogees was Muha Veeru, who is said to have been incarnate twenty-seven times. The earth, say they, is formed by Nature, that is, by inherent properties existing in itself. As the trees in an uninhabited forest spring up without a cultivator, so the universe is self-existent: and as the banks of a river fall of themselves, so there is no supreme destroyer. There are no such beings as creator, preserver, and destroyer. The world is eternal; it exists from itself, and decays of itself. Man does not possess an immortal spirit. The highest virtue consists in refraining from injuring sentient creatures. Every species of pleasure may be called heaven. Absorption is realized in death. The entire absence of desire or affection is the highest state of happiness. Their precaution to avoid injuring any being, is inculcated in the orthodox religion, but carried by them to a ludicrous extreme. They are spread all over India, but are not numerous anywhere except in Tooluvu. Formerly many powerful princes were their followers."

and mendicants of different sects, who state that the place had its origin in the time of Buddha, and that it was last inhabited by the Rani, or Queen of the famous Raja Lalat Indra Kesari, favourer of the Buddhist religion.

Farther up the same hill, on the overhanging brow of a large cavern, we met with an ancient inscription cut out of the sandstone rock, in the very identical character which occurs on the pillars of Delhi, and which as yet has been only very partially decyphered. There are I think two eminently remarkable circumstances connected with the character used in the above inscription. The first is the close resemblance of some of the letters to those of the Greek alphabet, and the second the occurrence of it on sundry ancient monuments situated in widely distant quarters of India. The Greek *ou*, *sigma*, *lambda*, *chi*, *delta*, *epsilon*, and a something closely resembling the figure of the digamma. With regard to the second, any reader who will take the trouble of comparing the Khandgiri inscription with that on Firoz Shah's Lat at Delhi, on the column at Allahabad, the Lat of Bhim Sen, in Sarum a part of the Elephanta, and a part of the Ellora inscriptions, will find that the characters are identically the same.

A portion of the Ellore and Salsette inscription written in the above character, has been decyphered by the learning and ingenuity of Major Wilford, aided by the discovery of a key to the unravelling of ancient inscriptions in the possession of a learned brahmin, vide the eleventh article of vol. v. *Asiatic Researches;* and it is to be regretted that the same has not been further applied to decyphering the Delhi and other characters. The natives of the district can give no explanation whatever on the subject. The brahmins refer the inscription with shuddering and disgust, to the Budh Ka Amel, or time when the Buddhist doctrines prevailed, and are reluctant even to speak on the subject. I have in vain also applied to the Jains of the district for an explanation. I cannot however divest myself of the notion that the character has some connection with the ancient Pracrit, and considering that it occurs in a spot for many ages consecrated to the worship of Parasnath, which the brahmins are pleased to confound with the Buddhist religion, and that the figure or characteristic mark which appears in company with it, does in some sort seem to identify it with the former worship, I am persuaded that a full explanation is to be looked for only from some of the learned of the Jain sect.

The Vishu or Purushotama Khetr or Juggernaut extends, properly from the Bytarni to the Rassikoila river at Ganjam, but the more sacred part of it is comprised within a range of five coss, in the centre of which, termed fantastically the Sank'h Nabhi Mendel, and on a low ridge of sand hills dignified with the title of the Nilgiri or Nilachal (blue mountain), stands the famous temple of Jagannath, "*that mighty Pagoda or Pagod, the mirror of all wickedness and idolatry.*"* The building in its form and distribution resembles closely the great Pagoda at Bhubaneswar; nor do the dimensions of the two edifices greatly differ, but the Jagannath one has the advantage in point of situation. Altogether its appearance is certainly imposing from its loftiness and the mass of masonry which it comprizes, but the execution is extremely rude and inelegant, and the form and proportions of the principal object, the Bar Dewal or great tower, are, it must be acknowledged, by no means pleasing to the eye. The present edifice was completed A. D. 1198, at a cost of from *forty to fifty lacs of rupees*, under the superintendence of Param Hans Bajpoi, the minister of Raja Anang Bhim Deo, who was unquestionably the most illustrious of all the Gajapati princes of Orissa; and it seems unaccountable that in an age when the architects obviously possessed some taste and skill, and were in most cases particularly lavish in their use of sculptured ornament, so little pains should have been taken with the decoration and finishing of this stupendous edifice. Its appearance has farther suffered of late years from the exterior having been covered with a coating of chunam which has all been washed off excepting a few stains and patches, and still more from the barbarous practice now in force of marking out parts of the sculpture with red paint. The material used for the construction of the temple is chiefly the coarse granite, resembling sandstone, found abundantly in the southern part of Cuttack. The following is a sketch of the plan of it. The edifices composing and connected with the temple which are very numerous, stand in a square area enclosed by a lofty stone wall, measuring about six hundred and fifty feet on a side. A broad

* Whoever thus describes the temple of Juggernaut, describes it justly. The name of the town signifies good men; but every intelligent candid man, whether Christian, Mahommedan, or Hindoo, who is acquainted with the character of its inhabitants, knows it to be a great misnomer. The figures on the walls of the temple, the well known character of the Idol's attendants, male and female, the oppression of the deluded pilgrims practised within its walls, the probable murder by poison of the individuals employed to remove the contents of the old Idol into the new one, the effrontery shewn to the true God by the prostration of millions in past ages before its mishapen gods, and the poverty, want, suffering, and death, occasioned by pilgrimages to it from all parts of India, awfully confirm this description of Juggernaut's temple, as—"the mirror of all wickedness and idolatry."—*Auth.*

flight of twenty-two steps leads from the Sinh Darwazeh or principal gate of entrance, on the east, to a terrace twenty feet in height, enclosed by a second wall four hundred and forty-five feet square, on which occurs the first apartment called the Bhog Mandap. In a line, and connected with it by a sort of low portico, is the great antichamber of the temple called the Jagmohan, which adjoins and opens into the tower or sanctuary. The tower itself rises to a height of one hundred and eighty feet from the terrace, or two hundred from the ground. The ground plan is a square measuring thirty feet on a side. Most of the other principal deities of the Hindoo Pantheon have temples at this place situated between the two enclosures. The eastern gate is flanked and guarded by colossal figures of lions, or more properly griffins, in a sitting posture, and by smaller images of the mythological porters Jaya and Vijaya resting on their clubs, sculptured on the side posts. In front stands a column of dark coloured basalt, with a base of the mineral resembling pot-stone, remarkable for its light and elegant appearance and the beauty of its proportions, which supports a figure of the monkey-god Hunuman. One might guess that this is the work of artists of a different class and era from those who raised the temple of Jagannath, and the fact is really so; it having been brought from the famous, but now deserted, temple of the sun at Kanarak, about sixty years ago, by a brahmachari inhabitant of Pooree, of great wealth and influence.

Some ingenious speculations have been hazarded upon the origin and meaning of the worship of Jagannath and the causes of the peculiar sanctity of the place, but amidst the conflicting and contradictory legends and traditions which prevail, it seems scarcely possible to arrive at any satisfactory conclusion on the subject. The accounts given in the writings of the Hindus, more especially the Kapila Sanhita and the Khetr Mahaytmya of the temple, are simply as follows, divested of the load of declamation and repetition which embarrass the perusal of them. From the beginning of all things until the expiration of the first half of the age of Brahma, Parameswara, Sri Bhagwan, or Jagannath, in other words Vishnu, dwelt on the Nilachal in Utcala Desa, in the form of Nil Madhava. The fame of this form of the deity having reached the Court of Indradyumna, Maharaja of Avanti or Oujein,* an eminently pious

* Oujein a city of great celebrity in the Malwa country, Lat. 23°. 11'. N. long 75°. 52'. E. By Abul Fazel in 1582 it is described as follows "Oujein is a large city on the banks of the Sopra, and held in high veneration by the Hindoos. It is astonishing that sometimes this river flows with milk."

FESTIVAL OF THE SWINGING OF KRISHNA, IN THE TEMPLE OF JUGGERNAUT, IN ORISSA, ON THE BAY OF BENGAL.

prince in the Satya Yuga, he conceived a desire to perform worship at the sacred shrine, and accordingly set out on a journey to Orissa, with a large army, after having first dispatched a brahmin to make enquiry. Just as he reached the spot, on the expiration of a three months' journey, it was reported to him that the image of Nil Madhava had disappeared from the face of the earth. The Raja was overwhelmed with disappointment at this intelligence, and fell into a state of the deepest melancholy and affliction until comforted in a dream by the deity, who informed him that although he had abandoned his former shape, he would soon reappear again, (or that a fresh Avatar would take place), in a still more sacred form, that of the Daru Brahm which would remain to all ages. Shortly after, the Maharaja was apprized that a Daru,* or log of wood of the Nim tree (*Melia Azadirachta*) was to be seen floating to the shores of Pursottem Chetr from the quarter of the Sitadwip island, adorned with the Sankha, Gada, Padma, Chakr, or several emblems of Vishnu, viz. the *conch shell*, *mace*, *lotus* and *discus*, and bearing a most divine and beautiful appearance! Transported with joy the prince ran to the sea shore, embraced the sacred log, which he was satisfied from the above symptoms must be a real form of Vishnu, and proceeded to deposit it with great ceremony in a consecrated enclosure. He then through the advice of Narad Muni, who had accompanied him, obtained the aid of Visvakerma, the architect of the gods, to arrange the image in its proper form. At the first blow of the sacred axe of the Hindu Vulcan, the log split of itself into *the four-fold image* or Chatur Murti. A little colouring only was necessary to complete them, and they then became recognized as Sri Krishna or Jagannath distinguished by its *black* hue, Baldeo, a form of Siva, of a *white* colour, Subhadra, the sister of these brothers of the colour of *saffron*, and a round staff or pillar with the chakra impressed on each and called Sudersan. The Raja's next care was to erect a temple and to establish the worship on a suitable scale of splendour. On the great day when all was ready for consecrating the temple, Brahma himself, and the whole company of the deities of Indra's court, came down from heaven on their several appropriate vehicles to offer up worship at the shrine of the lord of the universe, which, say the Urias, has since that period, and especially in the Kali yuga, maintained a rank and celebrity such as

* Some accounts say that the Maharaja had first to preform a hundred thousand Aswa Med'h Jagya or *sacrifices of the horse*, before favored with a view of this choice form of the deity, but as usual with every Hindu fable there is prodigious discrepancy in the several versions of it.

even Kasi, or Benares, Brindraban, or Setu Band Rameswar, cannot boast.

Mr. Ward in his valuable work, thus describes the origin of the worship of Juggernaut. "The image of this god has no legs, and only stumps of arms; the head and eyes are very large. At the festivals the brahmins adorn him with silver or golden arms. Krishnu in some period of Hindoo history was accidentally killed by Ungudu, a hunter; who left the body to rot under the tree where it fell. Some pious persons, however, collected the bones of Krishnu and placed them in a box, where they remained till Indru Dhoomu, a king, who was performing religious austerities to obtain some favour of Vishnoo, was directed by the latter to form the image of Juggernaut, and put into its belly these bones of Krishnu, by which means he should obtain the fruit of his religious austerities. Indru Dhoomnu inquired who should make this image, and was commanded to pray to Vishwukurmu, the architect of the gods. He did so, and obtained his request; but Vishwu-kurmu at the same time declared, that if any one disturbed him while preparing the image, he would leave it in an unfinished state. He then began, and in one night built a temple upon the blue mountain in Orissa, and proceeded to prepare the image in the temple; but the impatient king, after waiting fifteen days, went to the spot, on which Vishwu-kurmu desisted from his work, and left the god without hands or feet. The king was very much disconcerted; but on praying to Brumhu he promised to make the image famous in its present shape. He now invited all the gods to be present at the setting up of this image. Brumhu himself acted as high priest, and gave eyes and a soul to the god, which completely established the fame of Juggernaut. This image is said to be in a pool, near the present temple at Juggernaut-kettra in Orissa."

The Hindus of Orissa endeavour, though with little foundation, to ascribe to the worship of Jagannath a more *spiritual* character than is generally claimed for their superstition elsewhere. They refer to the common title of the divinity of the place, which implies the Brahma or Divine spirit that pervades and sustains the universe, and are fond of quoting a passage in the legendary account of the temple, which runs thus, "Hear now the truth of the Dara Avatar, (the appearance of the deity in the form of Nim tree log). What part of the universe is there which the divine spirit does not pervade? In every place it exults and sports in a different form. In the heaven of Brahma it is Brahma; at Kylas it is Mahadeo; in the upper world it is Indra; on the face of the earth it is to be found in all the most renowned Khetrs, at Baddrika as Badrinath; at Brindaban and Dwaraka as Krishen; at Ayodhya (Oude) in another shape; but in the Khetr of Pursottem it appears in its true and most sacred form." The brahmins also have a practice of dressing up the figure of Sri Jeo in a costume appropriate to the occasion, to represent the principal deities, on the occurrence of the yearly festivals held in honor of each, which are termed the different Bhues, or Phases, of the Thakur. Thus at the Ram Navami, the great image assumes the dress and character of Rama; at the Janam Ashtami, that of Krishen; at the Kali Puja, that of Kali; when the Narsinha Avatar is celebrated, that of Narsinh; when the Baman Avatar, that of the mighty dwarf. This would seem to evince some symptoms of a belief that in offering up worship to Jagannath, his votaries do not confine their adoration to any particular deity, but adore the whole host of Hindu heaven, or rather the spirit which animates them, whilst at other Khetrs the divinity of the place alone is worshipped. Mr. Paterson's hypothesis refers the worship now under consideration to the adoration of the mystical syllable, A, U, M, coalescing into Om, and is certainly the most ingenious and plausible that has been suggested, but goes far beyond the knowledge or comprehension of the most learned and intellectual of the present day. All the explanation which the more intelligent brahmins can or will afford on the subject, is, that they worship at Jagannath Bhagwan or the supreme spirit itself, and not any subordinate deity; that the images are shapeless, because the Vedas have declared that the deity has no particular form; and that they have received their present grotesque and hideous countenances, with the view to terrify men to be good. The same fancy which has invested the Khetr of Jagannath with superior sanctity, is the cause, of course, of the unusual virtue ascribed to the Mahaprasad, or food cooked for the deity, and consecrated by being placed before images. The Khetr Mahatmya says, that Maha Lukshmi herself prepares and tastes it. He who eats it is absolved from the four cardinal sins of the Hindu faith, viz. *killing a cow, killing a brahmin, drinking spirits, and committing adultery with the female of a Guru or spiritual pastor.* So great is its virtue, that it cannot be polluted by the touch of the very lowest caste, and the leavings even of a dog are to be carefully taken up and used. The most tremendous and inexpiable of all crimes, is to handle and eat the Mahaprasad, without a proper feeling of reverence.

Without going into any profound speculation as to the origin, nature, and meaning of the worship of Jagannath, there is one cause sufficiently obvious why all sects should hére unite in harmony in the performance of their religious ceremonies, viz. that the temple instead of being consecrated exclusively to some form of the deity Vishnu alone, is in fact occupied, in joint tenancy, by forms of three of the most revered divinities of the Hindu faith. Balbhadra or Baldeo, (Balarama,) the elder brother, who is treated with the greatest respect, though not so popular as his black relation, is clearly identified with Mahadeo, both by his white colour, and the figure of the serpent Shesha or Ananta* which forms a hood over the back part of his head; and Subhadra is esteemed a form of Devi or Kali, the female energy of the above. The precedence is always given to the elder brother; he has a rath or chariot of equal size with that of Jagannath, and altogether the veneration paid to him is quite sufficient to conciliate the votaries of Siva, who are the only violent or bigoted sectaries. All the idol deities are allowed to occupy niches or temples within the precincts of the great Pagoda, and are treated with so much respect, that the most obstinate sectary could not with any decency or consistency refuse to join in the general worship of the place. Juggernaut's temple thus becomes in effect a Pantheon of the Hindoo idols.

The legend above quoted regarding the establishment of the worship of Jagannath, does not provide for or explain the sacred deposit which popular belief, sanctioned by the brahmins, places in the belly of the image. Some conjecture it to be *a bone* of Krishna, but how it came there is not explained. As the image has been often remade of the wood of the Nim tree, it seems not improbable that it may be a relic of the wood of the old original idol which is thus preserved. Col. Phipps who was stationed at Juggernaut in 1822, in his account of Juggernaut's Temple (see *Mis. Register* Dec. 1824,) thus describes the formation of a new Idol. "When two new moons occur in Assur (part of June and July,) which is said to happen, about once in seventeen years, a new idol is always made, a Nim tree is sought for in the forests on which no crow or carrion bird was ever perched! it is known to the initiated by certain signs. This is prepared into a proper form by common carpenters, and is then intrusted to certain priests who are protected from all intrusion: the process is a great mystery. One man is selected to take out of the idol a small box containing the spirit, which is conveyed inside the new; *the man who does this is always removed from this world before the end of the year!*"

* Both these words in Wilson's Sancrit Dictionary are explained to mean a serpent and a name of Baladeva.

The memory of Raja Indradyumna is perpetuated by a superb tank which bears his name. Either the author of the Ayin Acberi, or his translator, has confounded things together, in calling him Raja Indra Dummun or Nilkurpurbut (Nilgiri Parvat,) instead of stating that he visited the sand hills at Puri called by that name in the Hindu writings. The assertion also of Abulfazl that the image of Jagannath is made of sandal wood, is founded apparently on some confusion between the material appropriated to that purpose, and a bar of timber used for closing the entrance of the temple during the Chandan Jatra, thence called the Chandan Daru or sandal wood.

The monstrous idols of the place may be seen daily, with few exceptions, seated on their Sinhasan, or throne, within the sanctuary; but they are publicly exposed to view on two occasions only in the year, the *Asnan* and the *Rath Jatras.* At the Asnan or festival of the bath, Jagannath and his brother, after undergoing certain ablutions, assume what is called the Ganesh Bhues or form of the elephant-headed god, to represent which the images are dressed up with an appropriate mask. Thus arrayed they are placed on a high terrace overlooking the outer wall of the temple, surrounded by crowds of priests who fan them to drive away the flies, whilst the multitude below gaze in stupid admiration.

At the Rath Jatra, the images, as is well known, are indulged with an airing on their cars and a visit to the god's country house, a mile and a half distant, named the Goondicha Nour, after the Rani of Maharaja Indradyumna who founded the worship. The display which takes place on this occasion has often before been described, but some brief notice of it will naturally be expected.

On the appointed day, after various prayers and ceremonies have been preformed within the temple, the four images are brought from their throne to the outside of the Lion gate—not with decency and reverence, seated on a litter or vehicle adapted to such an occasion—but, *a common cord being fastened round their necks,* certain priests to whom the duty appertains, drag them down the steps and through the mud, whilst others keep the figures erect and help their movements by shoving them from behind, in the most indifferent and unceremonious manner, as if they thought the whole business a good joke! In this way the monstrous idols go rocking and pitching along through the crowd, until they reach the cars, which they are made to ascend by a simular process up an inclined platform reaching from the stage of the machine to the ground. On the other hand, a powerful sentiment of religious enthusiasm pervades the admiring multitude of pilgrims assembled without, when the images first make their appearance through the gate. They welcome them with the loudest shouts of joyful recognition and stunning cries of *Jye Jagannath*, victory to Jagannath; and when the monster Jagannath himself, the most hideous of all the figures, is dragged forth the last in order, the air is rent with plaudits and acclamations. These celebrated idols are nothing more than wooden busts about six feet in height, fashioned into a rude resemblance of the human head resting on a sort of pedestal. They are painted white, yellow, and black respectively, with frightfully grim and distorted countenances, and are decorated with a head dress of different coloured clothes shaped something like a helmet. The two brothers have arms projecting horizontally forward from the ears! The sister is entirely devoid of even that approximation to the human form. Their Raths* or cars have an imposing air from their size and loftiness, but every part of the ornament is of the most mean and paltry description, save only the covering of striped and spangled broad cloth furnished from the EXPORT WAREHOUSE of the BRITISH GOVERNMENT, the splendour and gorgeous effect of which compensate in a great measure for other deficiencies of decoration!† After the images have been lodged in their vehicles, a box is brought forth containing the golden or gilded feet, hands, and ears of the great Idol, which are fixed on the proper parts with due ceremony, and a scarlet scarf is carefully arranged round the lower part of the body or pedestal. Thus equipped and decorated, it is worshipped with much pomp and state by the Raja of Khurda, who performs before it the ceremony of the Chandalo, or sweeping, with a richly ornamented broom. At about this period of the festival, bands of villagers enter the crowd dancing and shouting, with music playing before and behind, each carrying in his hand a branch of a tree. They are the inhabitants of the neighbouring Pergunnahs, Raheng, Limbai, &c. called Kalabetiahs, whose peculiar duty and privilege it is, conjointly with the inhabitants of Puri, to drag the Raths. On reaching the cars, they take their station close to them, and soon as the proper signal has been given, they set the example to the

* Jagannath's Rath, called Nandi Ghos, measures forty-three and a half-feet high. It has sixteen wheels of six and a half feet diameter each and a platform thirty-four and a half feet square. The Rath of Baldeo, called Thala Dhaj, is about forty-one feet high and has fourteen wheels. The Devior Subhadra Rath called Padma Dhaj is forty feet high, the platform thirty-one square, and fourteen wheels of six and a half feet diameter.

† This has ceased by the abolition of the Pilgrim Tax.

multitudes assembled, by seizing on the cables, when all advance forwards a few yards, hauling along generally two of the Raths at a time. The joy and shouts of the crowd on their first movement, the creaking sound of the wheels as these ponderous machines roll along, the clatter of hundreds of harsh sounding instruments, and the general appearance of so immense a moving mass of human beings, produce, it must be acknowledged, an impressive, astounding, and somewhat picturesque effect, whilst the novelty of the scene lasts; though the contemplation cannot fail, to excite the *strongest sensations of pain and disgust in the mind of every Christian spectator.* At each pause, the Dytahs or Charioteers of the god advance forward to a projecting part of the stage, with wands in their hands, and throwing themselves into a variety of wild and frantic postures, address some fable or series of jokes to the multitude, who grunt a sort of response at the proper intervals. Often their speeches and actions are grossly and indescribably indecent and obscene! The address generally closes with some peculiar piquant allusion, when the gratified mob raise a loud shout as the final response, and all rush forward with the cables. The progress made varies greatly according to the state of the roads, the care used in keeping the Raths in a proper direction, the zeal and number of the pilgrims, and the will of the priests, or as they say of the god, the former having some method of choking the wheels, and thereby preventing the movement of the cars, notwithstanding the utmost efforts of the credulous multitude to advance forward. Generally from two to three days are consumed in reaching the Gondicha Nour, where the images are taken out. Before even this period has elapsed, the curiosity and enthusiasm of the pilgrims have nearly evaporated, they steal off in numbers, and leave Sri Jeo to get back to the temple as he may. Without indeed the aid of the villagers before described, and of the population of Puri who hold their ground free of rent on condition of performing this service to the deity, the Raths would now-a-days infallibly stick always at the Gondicha Nour. *Even the gods' own proper servants will not labour zealously and effectually without the interposition of authority. I imagine the ceremony would soon cease to be conducted on its present scale and footing, if the institution were left entirely to its fate and to its own resources, by the officers of the British Government.*

Hamilton enumerates the festivals at the Temple. At Juggernaut there are 13 annual festivals; viz.

1.	Chandana	A sweet-scented powder.
2.	Snana	The bathing festival.
3.	Ruth	The car festival.
5.	Bahura	Ditto returning.
5.	Shayana	The lying down festival,
6.	Janma..	The birth festival.
7.	Kojugara	The waking festival.
8.	Rasa	The Rasa festival.
9.	Urana..	The warm clothing festival.
10.	Abhishaca	The anointing festival.
11.	Macura	A sign of the zodiac festival.
12.	Dola	The swinging festival.
13.	Rama Narami	Rama's birth-day festival.

Such Hindoos as perform this pilgrimage contrive to arrive at four particular times, when the swinging, the sweet scented, the bathing, and the car festivals take place; but much the greater number at the swinging and car festivals: some go and return immediately, while others sojourn for two or three months. After the preliminary ceremonies are gone through and the fees paid, the pilgrim goes and looks at the image; he next bathes in the sea, and then returning to the temple, purchases some rice which has been recently offered to Juggernauth, and with it performs the obsequies of his deceased ancestors. During his stay he attends the daily solemnities, and makes offerings through the Brahmins of rice and other articles to Juggernauth. For payment the officiating priests supply him with food ready dressed, which is particularly nutritious, as having been first presented to Juggernauth, *who eats (by proxy) 52 times each day!!* The penitent also feasts the Brahmins, and eats with all descriptions of pilgrims, of whatever caste. Various reasons are assigned, and stories told, all equally irrational, to account for the singular exception of permitting an act to be done here, which performed anywhere else would render the individual a miserable outcast. All Hindoos eagerly accept whatever has been offered to an idol, hence it is common to observe flowers which have been so offered stuck in their hair, and the water which has been offered to Juggernauth is preserved and sipped occasionally as a cordial. The appellation of Juggernauth is merely one of the 1000 names of Vishnu, the preserving power, according to the Brahminical theology.

The concourse of pilgrims to this temple is so immense, that at 50 miles distance its approach may be known by the quantity of human bones, which are strewed by the way. Some old persons come to die at Juggernauth, and others measure the distance by their length on the ground; but besides these voluntary sufferings, many endure great hardships both when travelling, and while they reside here, from exposure to the weather, bad food and water, and other evils. Many perish by dysentry, and the surrounding country abounds with sculls and human bones; but the vicinity of Juggernauth to the sea, and the arid nature of the soil, assist to prevent the contagion which would otherwise be generated. When this subject of their misplaced veneration is first perceived, the multitude of pilgrims shout aloud, and fall to the ground to worship it."*

That excess of fanaticism, which formerly prompted the pilgrims to court death by throwing themselves in crowds under the wheels of the car of Jagannath, has happily long ceased to actuate the worshippers of the present day. During four years that I have witnessed the ceremony, three cases only of this revolting species of immolation have occurred, one of which I may observe is doubtful and should probably be ascribed to accident; in the other two instances the victims had long being suffering from severe excruciating complaints, and chose this method of ridding themselves of the burthen of life, in preference to other modes of suicide so prevalent with the lower orders under similar circumstances. The number of pilgrims resorting to Jagannath has I think been exaggerated, as well as the waste of human life occasioned thereby; though doubtless, in an unfavourable season, or when the festival occurs late, *the proportion of deaths caused by exposure to the inclemency of the weather, is very melancholy.* The following is a statement of pilgrims of all classes who attended for the last five years at the three great festivals, procured from the most authentic sources, viz.

1817-18,	Paying Tax 35,941,	Exempt 39,720,	Total 75,641
1818-19,	 36,241,	 4,870,	„ 41,111
1819-29,	 92,874,	 39,000,	„ 131,874
1820-21,	 21,946,	 11,500,	„ 33,446
1821-22,	 35,160,	 17,000,	„ 52,160

The Khetr of Jagannath or Vishnu contains temples innumerable sacred to the worship of all the other principal deities, and some secondary ones rarely met with elsewhere, as the god Cuvera or Plutus, who has a curious antique looking temple amongst the sand hills on the coast. Shiva and his female energy are likewise fabled to reside constantly within its limits, in sixteen different

* Hamilton's Hindostan, vol. 2. p. 53, 54.

forms, eight male and eight females. The male ones or Sambhus figured by images called Yameswara, Visveswara, Gopal Mochan, Markandeswara, Nilkantheswara, Trilochan, Bhuteswara, and Pataleswara; the female figures or Chandis have the apellations of Mangala, Bimla, Sarvamangala, Kali, Dhatri, Kamakhya, Ardha Asti, and Bhawani. There is also a small Sikh* College amongst the sand hills, inhabited by three or four priests of that sect. The horrid practice of self-immolation of widows prevails less at Pooree than might perhaps have been expected, with reference to the general character of the place and the numerous families that resort there to pay their devotions, the average of Suttees not exceeding six per annum for the police division in which it is comprized. The concremation both of the dead and the living bodies takes place on the sea shore, close to the civil station, at a spot impiously called the Swarga Dwara, or passage to heaven. There is this peculiarity in the rite of Suttee when performed here, that instead of ascending a pile, the infatuated widow lets herself down into a pit, at the bottom of which the dead body of the husband has been previously placed, with lighted faggots above and beneath. The latest returns shew the whole number of victims who destroy themselves annually in the above revolting manner, to average from twenty to thirty for the entire district of Cuttack.†

The Arka or Padam Khetr at Kanarak is distinguished by its containing the remains of the celebrated temple of the sun, called in our charts the black Pagoda, which is situated amongst the sand hills of the sea shore, near the site of the old village of Kanarak, eighteen miles north of Jagannath Puri. The Jagmohan or antichamber is the only part of the building which exists in tolerably

* The Sikhs are so called from Shishy a disciple; their founder was Nanuk, a Hindoo born in 1469, and at his death left 100,000 followers. He maintained the divine unity, that God dwells in the devout, and that this divine inhabitation renders the ascetic an object of reverence and even of worship. Their works advise the Sikhs to seek absorption in God, rather than the happiness enjoyed in inferior heavens, from whence the soul descends to enter on a succession of births. As long as the soul is confined in the body, it is in chains, and whether the chains be of gold or iron, it is still a prisoner and enduring punishment. Nanuk taught—He who serves God, the fountain of all good, will obtain his blessing. God is served, by listening to his excellences, by meditating on them, and by celebrating their praises, the method of which is to be obtained from a spiritual guide, who is above all gods, and who is in fact God himself. God has created innumerable worlds. The period of creation is not laid down in any writing; it is known only to God. There are said to be a hundred Sikh Chiefs possessing separate districts in the Punjab.—*Ward's View*, vol. ii, p. 431.

† The Suttee was abolished by Regulation of the Bengal Government, Dec. 4th, 1829.

good preservation. The great tower has been shattered and thrown down by some extraordinary force, either of an earthquake or lightning, and in its fall seems to have injured that side of the adjoining edifice which looks towards it. A small section however still remains standing, about one hundred and twenty feet in height, which viewed from a distance gives the ruin a singular appearance, something resembling that of a ship under sail. The whole of the outer enclosures of the temple have long since disappeared, and nothing is left of the edifice called the Bhog Mandap but a heap of ruin, completely buried under a sand hill.

The black Pagoda even in its present imperfect and dilapidated condition, presents a highly curious and beautiful specimen of the ancient Hindu temple architecture; and as it has long been completely deserted, we may here study at leisure and without interruption, some of the most striking peculiarities of that style.

The deity of the place is called by the vulgar Soorju Deo (Surya) and at full length, Chunder Soorju Birinji Narayan.* The origin of the worship of a divinity so little honored in India, generally speaking, is ascribed to Samba, the son of Krishna, who having been afflicted with leprosy, and banished from his father's Court at Dwarka, as a punishment for accidentally looking in upon the nymphs of the palace whilst sporting naked in the water, was cured at this spot by the Sun, to whose service he in gratitude raised a temple. The present edifice it is well known was built by Raja Langora Narsinh Deo, A. D. 1241, under the superintendence of his minister Shibai Sautra. I cannot discover any authority for the assertion of the author of the Ayin Acberi, that the entire revenue of twelve years was expended on the work, but doubtless

* "The Brahmins consider Surya, or the Sun, one of the greatest of the gods; and he is at present worshipped daily by them, when flowers, water, &c., are offered, accompanied with incantations. On Sunday, at the rising of the sun, in any month, but especially in the month of Maghu (part of January and February,) a number of persons, chiefly women, perform the worship of Surya. Surya and the other planets are frequently worshipped, in order to procure health. This the Hindoos call a sacrifice to the nine planets, when flowers, rice, water, a burnt sacrifice, &c., are offered to each of these planets separately. The origin of obtaining relief from sickness (by worshipping the sun,) is ascribed to Shambu, the son of Krishnu, who was directed in a dream to repeat, twice a-day, the twenty-one names of Surya, then revealed to him. The persons who receive the name of Surya and adopt this god as their guardian deity, are called Souras: they never eat till they have worshipped the sun, and when the sun is entirely covered with clouds they fast. On a Sunday many Souras, as well as Hindoos belonging to other sects, perform, in a more particular manner, the worship of this idol, and on this day some of them fast. Surya has two wives Suvurna and Chaya (Shadow.) There are no temples dedicated to him in Bengal." See Ward's View, vol. ii. pp. 42-6.

the cost was very serious compared with the state of the Raja's treasury. The natives of the neighbouring villages have a strange fable to account for its desertion. They relate that a Kumbha Pathar or loadstone, of immense size, was formerly lodged on the summit of the great tower, which had the effect of drawing ashore all vessels passing near the coast. The inconvenience of this was so much felt, that about two centuries since, in the Mogul time, the crew of a ship landed at a distance and stealing down the coast, attacked the temple, scaled the tower, and carried off the loadstone. The priests alarmed at this violation of the sanctity of the place, removed the image of the god with all his paraphernalia to Puri, where they have ever since remained, and from that date the temple became deserted and went rapidly to ruin. As above intimated, the origin of its dilapidation may obviously be ascribed either to an earthquake or to lightning, but many causes have concurred to accelerate the progress of destruction, when once a beginning had been made. To say nothing of the effects of weather on a deserted building, and of the vegetation that always takes root under such circumstances, it is clear that much injury has been done by the inhabitants of the neighbourhood, in forcing out the iron clamps which held the stones together, for the sake of the metal; and it is well known that the officers of the Marhatta government actually beat down a part of the walls, to procure materials for building some insignificant temples at Puri.

Abulfazl's quaint, but lively and picturesque, description of the temple of the Sun, is of course familiar to those who have perused the Ayin Acberi with attention. Although however it affords a good general idea of the character of the building, it is strangely inaccurate in respect to measurements, no less than in the description of the emblems and ornaments which embellish it. Without noticing its several errors in detail, I shall first insert the description above alluded to, and then offer an account of the place as it appears to the visitor in the nineteenth century.

The author of the *Ayin Acberi* observes, (vide Gladwin's translation,) "Near to Jagannath is the temple of the sun, in the erecting of which, was expended the whole revenue of Orissa for twelve years. No one can behold this immense edifice without being struck with amazement. The wall which surrounds the whole is one hundred and fifty cubits high and nineteen cubits thick. There are three entrances to it. At the eastern gate there are two very fine figures of elephants, each with a man upon his trunk. To the west are two surprizing figures of horsemen completely armed, and over the northern gate are carved two lions who having killed two elephants, are sitting upon them. In the front of the gate is a pillar of black stone of an octagonal form fifty cubits high. There are nine flights of steps, after ascending which, you come into an enclosure where you discover a large *dome* constructed of stone, upon which are carved the sun and stars, and round them is a border where are represented a variety of human figures, expressing the different passions of the mind, some kneeling, others prostrated with their faces upon the earth, together with minstrels, and a number of strange and wonderful animals, such as never existed but in imagination. This is said to be a work of 730 years atiquity. Raja Nursinh Deo finished this building, thereby erecting for himself a lasting monument of fame. There are twenty-eight other temples belonging to this pagoda, six before the northern gate, and twenty-two without the enclosure, and they are all reported to have performed miracles."

The wall which formed the outer enclosure may have measured about two hundred and fifty yards on a side; within this was a second enclosure having three entrances called the *Aswa* or horse, the *Hasti* or elephant, and the *Sinha* or Lion gate, from the colossal figures of those animals, which surmounted the several side posts. The horses and elephants on the north and south, have long since been precipitated from their bases, but the lions, or rather griffins, still retain the attitude and position assigned to them by Abulfazl, except that they are standing, instead of sitting, on the bodies of elephants, and have one paw lifted in the act of striking. Fronting the Sinh gate, stood the beautiful polygonal column, formed of a single shaft of black basalt, which is now placed at the entrance of the Puri temple. It supported, at that time, the appropriate emblem of Aruna, the charioteer of the sun, which has since given place to Hanuman, and measures about thirty-three feet in height, instead of fifty cubits.

From the eastern gate of the inner enclosure, a flight of ruined steps leads to the only tolerably perfect part of the building now remaining, called the Jagmohan, or Antichamber of the Sanctuary. No one, certainly, can behold the massive beams of iron and the prodigious blocks of stone used in the construction of this edifice, without being struck with amazement. The ground plan is a square, measuring sixty feet on a side, or, if we take in the four projecting doorways, it should rather be called a cross. The walls rise to a height of sixty feet, and have in some parts the unusual thickness of twenty feet. They support a noble and curiously constructed pyramidal roof, the stones comprizing which overhang each other, in the manner of inverted stairs, until they approach near enough towards the summit to support iron beams laid across, on which rests a prodigious mass of solid masonry, forming the head-piece or crowning ornament. The slope measures about seventy-two feet, and perpendicular height, sixty-three or sixty-four. The total altitude of the building, from the floor to the summit, is about one hundred feet or a little more. The outside of the roof is divided into three tiers of steps, formed by slabs projecting curiously from the body of the building, which are all bordered with a very fine pattern of elephants, birds, and various figures executed with considerable skill and spirit. Each of the terraces between the tiers, is decorated with statues, placed at intervals, nearly as large as life. One of the two lower ones, are figures of nymphs and heavenly choristers, dancing and playing upon sundry instruments, but with countenances expressing very little passion or feeling of any kind. The third story has the usual mythological animals, more nearly resembling lions than any thing else, which support on their shoulders the outer rim of the huge turban-shape ornament on the top; besides these, there is a four-headed statute over each of the door-ways, the crowns and sceptres of which, mark them as intended to represent the majesty of Brahma.

Each face of the Jagmohan has a fine rectangular door-way, with a porch projecting considerably beyond and lined with superb slabs of the grey indurated chlorite, many of which measure fifteen feet high by a breadth of six or eight feet. The architrave of the door-way, as well as the roof of the passage leading to the interior, and an enormous mass of masonry resting upon it, are supported by nine iron beams, nearly a foot square by twelve or eighteen long, which are laid across the side ways in the most rude and inartificial manner. The whole fabric is held together by clamps of the same metal, and there is no appearance of any cement having been used.

If the style of the black Pagoda betrays, in the rude and clumsy expedients apparent in its construction, a primitive state of some of the arts, and a deficiency of architectural skill, at the period of its erection, one cannot but wonder at the ease with which the architects seem to have wielded and managed the cumbersome masses of iron and stone, used for the works, in an age when so little aid was to be derived from any mechanical inventions; and it must be allowed that there is an air of elegance, combined with massiveness, in the whole structure, which entitles it to no small share of admiration. There is much, however, about this remarkable building, which it is difficult either to describe or comprehend. The interior is filled, to a height of several feet, with large blocks of stone, which seem to have fallen from above, and what purpose they answered, in their former situation, is a matter of great doubt and discussion. Amongst the heap are to be seen, two iron beams, measuring twenty one feet in length by about eight inches square, absolutely crushed beneath a superincumbent mass of stone, many of the blocks composing which, measure fifteen and sixteen feet in length, by about six feet of depth and two or three in thickness. It seems probable that they formed part of an inner or false roof, but neither is it easy to assign any precise place for such a ceiling, nor can one divine the motive or object of elevating such prodigious blocks of stone to a great height in the building, when lighter materials would have been so much better adapted to the work.

The exterior of the side walls, as of the roof, is loaded with a profusion of the richest sculptured ornaments. A remarkably handsome cornice or border occupies the upper part, all round, for a depth of several feet. Below this, the surface is divided by another fine cornice, into two tiers of compartments, parted off into inches by clusters of pilasters, in each of which are placed figures of men and animals, resting on pedestals with a sort of canopy overhead. The human figures are generally male and female, in the most lewd and obscene attitudes, * * * * * * * Amongst the animals, the most common representation is that of a lion rampant treading on an elephant or a prostrate human figure. Generally speaking, the style and execution of the larger figures, are rude and coarse, whilst the smaller ones display often much beauty and grace; but it should be observed that the whole have suffered materially, from the corrosion or decomposition of the stone, of which the building is chiefly composed, viz. the coarse red granite of the province, which is singularly liable to decay, from exposure to the weather.

The skill and labor of the best artists, seems to have been reserved for the finely polished slabs of chlorite, which line and decorate the outer faces of the door-ways. The whole of the sculpture on these figures, comprizing men and animals, foliage, and arabesque patterns, is executed with a degree of taste, propriety, and freedom, which would stand a comparison with some of our best specimens of Gothic architectural ornament. The workmanship remains, too, as perfect, as if it had just come from under the chissel of the sculptor, owing to the extreme hardness and durability of the stone. A triangular niche, over each door-way, was once filled with a figure cut in alto relievo, emblematic of the deity of the place, being that of a youth in a sitting posture, holding in each hand a stalk of the true Lotus or *Nelumbium speciosum*, the expanded flowers of which are turned towards him. Each architrave has, as usual, the Nava Graha, or nine brahminical planets, very finely sculptured in alto relievo. Five of them are well proportioned figures of men, with mild and pleasing countenances, crowned with high pointed caps and seated cross-legged on the Padma *(Nelumbium speciosum)*, engaged in religious meditation—one hand bears a vessel of water, and the fingers of the other are counting over the beads of a rosary, which hangs suspended. The form of the planet which presides over Thursday, (Vrihaspati or Jupiter,) is distinguished from the others by a flowing majestic beard. Friday, or Venus, is a youthful female, with a plump well rounded figure. Ketu, the descending node, is a triton whose body ends in the tail of a fish or dragon; and Rahu, or the ascending node, a monster, all head and shoulders, with a grinning grotesque countenance, frizly hair dressed like a full blown wig, and one immense canine tooth projecting from the upper jaw; in one hand he holds a hatchet, and in the other a fragment of the moon. These are doubtless the "sun and stars" mentioned by the author of the Ayin Acberi. Why they occupy, so uniformly, a position over the door-way of every temple in Orissa, sacred to whatever deity, I have never been able to learn.

The walls of the interior are, as usual with Hindu temples, entirely plain and devoid of ornament; but each of the projecting steps in the square pyramidal roof, has been curiously rounded, and formed into a sort of cornice, which gives a slight finish to that part of the building.

From the fragment remaining of the great tower, it would seem to have been covered with rich and varied sculptured ornament, in the style of the Bhubaneswar temple. Like all edifices of the kind, too, it had evidently an inner false roof, of pyramidal shape, formed of the inverted stairs used by the old architects of the province, as a substitute for the arch.

The Rev. A. Sutton thus describes this Pagoda. "I set off to the *Black Pagoda* about half a coss distant, where I expected to meet with a great many people, and get a sight of this ancient monument of idolatry, and was not disappointed, except in having my expectations far exceeded. There was a very large assembly of people sitting round about the temple, and quite at liberty. This is by far the best spot for missionary purposes, and would amply repay the trouble of an excursion another year. I preached to the people in different places, and distributed the remainder of my books to very eager applicants. I had entertained the mistaken idea that Hindooism originally was comparatively a pure system to what we see it in our day; and if any one entertains the same opinion, I would recommend them to visit the Black Pagoda on the Orissa coast. Here is one of the oldest temples in India, so old, that no account can be given of its origin or antiquity; the natives believe, and told me repeatedly, it was the work of the gods. It is very magnificent in many respects. The carving in stone and marble work, is laboured and various to an astonishing extent; *but this skill and cost is principally bestowed on figures the most beastly that can be conceived, and altogether, presents a mass of obscenity which beggars all description!* The temple is now little better than a heap of ruins. The Idol, they told me, was stolen away, and it is now at liberty for any one's minutest inspection. On my entering it, the stench was extremely disagreeable, occasioned by the swarms of bats, bears, and other noxious creatures, which had taken up their abode in the holy place. It must have been a noble building once. The stones of which the interior is built are many of them of an immense size, and excited my wonder and admiration how the Hindoos could have managed them. I measured one on which I stood, that lay clear of the heap, and on my return home found it to be twelve feet long, and nearly the same in girth. This stone had fallen with the inner roof or dome, and I have no reason whatever to suppose it one of the largest. The Temple however served me for a very different purpose to that for which it was originally intended; for, as there were many people inside looking about, our conversation led me to discourse at some length on the universal destruction of Idolatry, and the spread of the glorious soul-restoring gospel of the Son of God. They listened with attention, and seemed to think I spoke the truth. I was afterwards struck at the idea of making a preaching-house of an Idol's temple. Before I left I clambered nearly to the top of this mass of obscenity. One of the beastly representations over which I crawled, and which had fallen down, was large as life, and there were many others like it."

The Birjai or Parbati khetr, comprizes the country which stretches for five cos around the village of Jajipur (Yajyapura) on the banks of the Bytarini, as a centre. The sanctity of the place is, as usual, founded on a variety of fanciful notions and wild traditions, which it would be tedious to detail at any length. In the first place, its name, the "City of Sacrifice," is derived from the circumstance of Brahma having performed here, in ancient days, the great sacrifice called the Das Aswamed'h, at the ghat so called, to which all the gods and goddesses were invited. Amongst others, Gangaji was prevailed on to attend, and has since flowed through the district in the sacred form of the Bytarini, which, *descending to the infernal regions by an opening near Jajipur, becomes there the Styx of the Hindu Tartarus.** At this same sacrifice, a particularly holy form of Durga, or Parvati, sprung up from the altar on which the burnt offering was laid, and adopted the title of Birja, whence the name of the khetr: from her, again, issued the eight Chandis, or representatives of the Sacti of Mahadeva; and their appearance was followed by that of the eight Sambhus, or lords of the Linga, who with their dependent lingas, amounting in all to no less than a crore, are stationed at different points, over the whole khetr, to guard it from the intrusion of Asurs, Rakshases, and other malignant demons. The titles of the female energies above noticed, are Koth Vasini, Sidaheswari, Nibakhi, Uttareswari, Bhagavati, Kotavi, and Bhimaki; those of the males, Trilochana, Someswara, Trilokeswara, Pranaveswara, Isaneswara, Akandeswara, Agniswara, and Siddhiswara, which the learned reader may compare with the epithets of the same divinities who protect and sanctify the Bishen Khetr.

Besides the afore-mentioned claims to veneration, Jajipur is farther esteemed, from its being supposed to rest on the navel of the tremendous giant or demon, called the Gaya Asur, who was overthrown by Vishnu. Such was his bulk, that, when stretched on the ground, his head rested at Gaya,† his navel (nabhi) at this place, and his feet at a spot near Rajamendri. There is a very

* "The dead in going to the judgment hall of Yumu or death, cross the Byturunee, the India Styx, the waters of which like those of Phlegethon, the fourth river of hell, which the dead were obliged to cross, are said to be boiling hot. This river encircled the infernal regions nine times. Byturunee encircles this hall six times."

† This is the modern capital of Behar. It is situated in Lat. 24° 49' N. Long. 85° E. 55 miles south of Patna, a celebrated place of Pilgrimage, to release the souls of the dead out of purgatory. The Pilgrim Tax was abolished here April 1840.

sacred well or pit within the enclosure of one of the Jajipur temples, called the Gaya Nabhi or Bamphi, which is fabled to reach to the navel of the monster, and into it the Hindu pilgrims throw the *Pinda*, or cake of rice or sweetmeats, which is offered, at particular conjunctions, as an expiation for the sins of their ancestors. The priests and inhabitants of Jajipur insist, that in 1821, a sudden rise of water took place in the well, which forced up the accumulated mass of sour rice cakes that had been there fermenting for months or years, and deluged the whole area of the temple with filth. The occurrence was regarded both as a miracle, and as the forerunner of some great calamity.

The numerous stone temples on both sides of the Bytarini river executed mostly in a very respectable style of architecture, bespeak the ancient importance of the place; and history informs us that it was formerly one of the capitals of the Orissan monarchy. The Rajas of the Kesari dynasty held here their Court occasionally, as well as those of the Ganga Vansa line, and the remains of their palace, at present an undefinable heap of ruin, are still shewn. The Musselman writers seem sometimes to mention Jajipur as a separate principality, in the time of the Ganga Bans Rajas, but I can discover no ground whatever for such a territorial division. Mohammed Taki Khan, the Deputy of Shujaa Khan Nazir of Bengal, held his Court at Jajipur, and built a fine palace and mosque on the banks of the Byterini, early in the last century, out of the materials of some dilapidated Hindu temple, the sculptured ornaments of which may be still observed in many parts of the walls. His palace, again, has been in great part destroyed by the officers of the present government, to obtain materials for the construction of public works in the neighbourhood. The environs of Jajipur, present much to interest the curious, in its temples, khambas or columns in various styles, and fine remains of statuary. On one of the pillars, an inscription has been discovered, which is said to be of the same character exactly as that on the brow of the Khandigiri cavern of Khurda. The most eminently curious objects of the place however, are, the images of certain Hindu goddesses, carved in stone, which I shall now more particularly describe.

At the back of a high terrace supporting the cenotaph of Syyed Bokhari, a Musselman saint, three colossal statues of the Hindu divinities, are shewn. They lie with their heels uppermost, on a heap of rubbish, in precisely the same position apparently that they assumed, when tumbled from their thrones above, by the Musselman conquerors of the province, who destroyed a celebrated temple at the spot, and further desecrated it, by erecting on its ruins a shrine and mosque of their own worship. The images are cut in alto relievo, out of enormous blocks of the indurated Mugni, or chlorite slate rock, and measure about ten feet in length. They represent Kali, Varahi the wife of the Boar Avatar, and Indrani the lady of Indra; and though the subjects are grotesque, the execution is distinguished by a degree of freedom, skill and propriety, quite unusual in the works of Hindu sculptors. The first is a disgusting, but faithful, representation of a ghastly figure, nearly a skeleton, with many of the muscles and arteries exposed to view, invested with the distinguishing marks and attributes of the goddess Kali. She is seated on a car, or vahana, supported by a kneeling diminutive figure of Mahadeva. The second has a boar's head, and a huge pot belly, like that of Ganesa, and rests on a buffalo. The third is a well proportioned female figure, seated on an elephant, the animal consecrated by the Hindu Mythology to Indra, the lord of the Debtas

On the banks of the river, we meet with a sort of raised gallery, filled with mythological sculptures, amongst which seven large colossal figures of the female divinities called the Matris, are particularly remarkable. They are said to have been recovered, lately, out of the sand of the river—where they were tossed by the Moguls on their shrines being destroyed—by a mahajan of Cuttack, who built the edifice in which they are now deposited. They differ little in style and dimensions, from those above described, but appear to be cut out of blocks of basalt, or greenstone, instead of chlorite shist. They are styled respectively, Kali, Indrani, Caumari, Rudrani, Varahini, Vaishnavi, and Yama Matri. The figure of Kali is sculptured in a very spirited manner; she is represented with an axe in one hand, and a cup full of blood in the other, dancing in an infuriated attitude, after the destruction of the giant Rakta Vija, and trampling unconsciously on her husband Mahadeo, who, as the fable runs, had thrown himself at her feet, to solicit her to desist from those violent movements, which were shaking the whole world. That of Jam Matri, the "mother of Yama," is also a very striking and remarkable piece of sculpture. Her form is that of a hideous decrepid old woman, seated on a pedestal, quite naked, with a countenance alike expressive of extreme age, and that sourness of disposition which has rendered her proverbial as a scold. There are likewise fine representations in this mythological gallery, of the Narasinha Avatar, and the Giant Ravana, with his hundred heads and arms.

Under the head of *Civil Architecture*, I shall, in conclusion, mention the Bridges of Orissa, which are certainly the most creditable, though not the most magnificent, monuments remaining of its indigenous princes. Many of these works are to be found in different parts of the province, still in excellent state of preservation. The principal bridges which I have seen, are, that between Simleah and Soro, of fourteen nalehs or channels: the Athareh or eighteen naleh bridge, at Puri; the Char naleh, in the same neighbourhood; the bridge at Delang, and another over the Dya, between Khurda and Pipley. They are generally termed indifferently by foreigners, Mogul and Marhatta bridges; but the latter race during their unsettled and disturbed government in Cuttack, certainly never constructed works of so useful and durable a character; and besides the fact that the history of some of the principal ones is well known, it is quite obvious from a consideration of their style and architectural ornaments, that they are of pure Hindu origin, and belong to an age ignorant of the use of the arch. A short description of the Athareh naleh bridge at Puri, will serve, to illustrate sufficiently this part of the subject. It was built of a ferruginous colored stone, probably the iron clay, early in the fourteenth century, by Raja Kabir Narsinh Deo, the successor of Langora Narsinh Deo who completed the black Pagoda. The Hindus, being ignorant how to turn an arch, substituted in lieu of it the method, often adverted to above, of laying horizontal tiers of stones on the piers, the one projecting slightly beyond the other in the manner of inverted stairs, until they approach near enough at top, to sustain a key stone or cross beam; a feature so remarkable in Hindu architecture, that it seems strange it should not have been hitherto particularly noticed, in any description of the antiquities of the country. The bridge has eighteen nalehs or passages for the water, each roofed in the way described. Its total length is 290 feet, and height of the central passages eighteen feet, and its breadth fourteen ditto; of the smallest ones, at each extremity, thirteen and seven respectively; and the thickness of the piers, which have been judiciously rounded on the side opposed to the current, eight and six feet; the height of the parapet, which is a modern addition, is six feet.

Of the other native buildings of the province little need be said. The stone revetment at Cuttack, a work of magnitude and indispensible utility, is probably of Mogul origin, built in imitation of a more ancient one, the remains of which are still to be seen. Fort Barabati has been described in speaking of the modern capital.

The ruins extant of the old palaces of the Rajas, at Cuttack, Choudwar, Jajpur, and Bhubaneswer, are mere shapeless masses of stone and mounds of earth, which it would be fruitless to attempt any detailed account of. The ancient fortress of Sarengerh, on the south bank of the Kajuri, opposite to Cuttack, is remarkable for the great distance to which its works may be traced, but no portion of it remains habitable; and a modern killah, of the Musselman time, occupies the site of the citadel and palace of the first of the Ganja Vansa Rajas.

The dilapidations of time, mouldering into oblivion and the dust, the proudest works of human power, forcibly remind us, that, as states and dynasties rise, change, and disappear, so we, and all we fondly call our own, are "going the way of all flesh." But let us remember—"God requireth that which is past." How ought the present then, to be devoted to those works of benevolence, piety, and zeal for the salvation of souls, the fruit and reward of which will remain when this vain world shall be no more. The Musselman and Marhatta misrule in Hindostan, has most providentially been subverted by the British power. India is given to Britain for her welfare. Orissa, one of her most sacred and interesting Provinces, now enjoys the increasing light of the Gospel. Colleges, schools, scriptures, tracts, preaching the gospel, &c., are scattering the clouds of darkness in almost every part of this region and shadow of death. It is "the morning light" of the sun of righteousness, which "shineth more and more unto the perfect day."

"See, knowledge, *slowly rising like the sun*
In early spring, upon the Lapland plain,
Gives forth *faint light*, but, lengthening days begun,
Its *growing rays do gather strength amain;*
And clouds spring up and interpose in vain.
The living principle asserts the sky
Driv'n back, or scatter'd wide in driving rain,
To furthest corners of the heavens they fly,
Shunning for aye the glare of day's all-lightening eye."

A BRIEF HISTORY OF

THE RISE AND PROGRESS

OF

THE GENERAL BAPTIST MISSION

IN ORISSA.

TEMPLE OF JUGGERNAUT, IN ORISSA, ON THE BAY OF BENGAL.

A BRIEF HISTORY,

ETC., ETC.

CHAP. I.

Rise of the Mission in Orissa.

Introductory observations—Sketch of the History of the General Baptist Denomination—Formation of the Foreign Mission—Embarkation and Voyage of the first Missionaries to India—Arrival at Serampore—Approbation of the British Government obtained to proceed to Orissa—Abundant supply of Scriptures and Tracts for distribution.

Hindostan presents a scene of deep interest to the politician, the philanthropist, and the christian. The rise and progress of the British empire in the east, is one of the most unprecedented events recorded in history. It has been observed, perhaps with rather too much asperity—"Notwithstanding the solemn declaration made by the Legislature in 1782, that schemes of conquest and extent of dominion in India, are measures repugnant to the wish, the honour, and the policy of the British nation; they have ever since been so eagerly and successfully pursued, that our dominions in the east, now embrace the whole of the Mogul empire, comprising a population of ninety millions."* And more recently, the intelligent Editor of the *Friend of India*, has observed to the same effect:—

* *East India Magazine*, Feb. 1833.

"When we recal to mind the reiterated charges which have been brought in Parliament against our Indian statesmen, for the extension of the empire within the Indus, and look upon the present course of affairs which is leading us into new scenes, *hundreds of miles* beyond *that river*, how feeble and short-sighted do all human councils appear. There is surely a power at work in all these changes, mightier than any human agency; and these grand movements which are apt to strike the mind with awe, belong to higher and nobler plans than any which have been dreamed of in the councils of India."*

The thoughtful and pious Christian, contemplating Orissa as the scene of missionary operations, may be reminded of the scripture—"a goodly heritage of the host of nations." What a host of nations does Hindostan present from the Brumapootra river to the Indus; and from the mouths of the Ganges to Cabul! And that Orissa should be, as by the special providence of God, and "the consent of the tribes of Israel" engaged in missionary labours, allotted to the General Baptists as "a half tribe of the Israel of God," may bring to pleasing recollection, the language of Moses concerning the destination of his people in Palestine; "When the Most High divided to the nations their inheritance, when He separated the sons of Adam he set the bounds of the people according to the number of the children of Israel."—Deu. 32, 8. Orissa, though comparatively a small principality, occupies a commanding position on the bay of Bengal, approaching Calcutta, the great metropolis of British power, and forming the connecting link between the Bengal and Madras Presidencies. The popularity of the "mighty Pagoda of Juggernaut," adds in the estimation of the Christian, the deepest interest to this scene of philanthropic labour, which contemplates the fulfilment of the scripture, "The idols He shall utterly abolish." "He will famish all the gods of the earth; and men shall worship him every one from his place, even all the idols of the heathen." At that time, even of the temple of Juggernaut, it will be verified, "The fortress of the high fort of thy walls shall he bring down, lay low, bring to the ground, even to the dust." Who that has perused the previous history of Orissa, but must cherish a lively interest in its civilization, and especially, its evangelization?

The Report of the Mission for 1821, commences with the following eloquent paragraph, highly descriptive of the moral state of

* *Friend of India*, 1839.

Orissa, at the time the first Missionaries were proceeding to that "region and shadow of death;" and of the inestimable boon they were honoured to bear to its teeming myriads. "Before the Son of God ascended from Bethany to heaven, he gave the most sublime, the most important, the most benevolent command that was ever delivered in this transitory world—*Go preach the Gospel to every creature.* When he uttered this divinely gracious precept, Britain lay shrouded in gloom more melancholy than the gloom of the grave, and more desolating than the hand of death. A night of darkness that had been deepening for ages, covered all the land. Death, spiritual death, reigned triumphant over our hapless ancestors. Not a gleam of light broke in upon the darkness, not a pulse of life was felt among the dead. The land was a golgotha, inhabited by immortal beings, but by immortal beings "all dead," possessed of souls formed for eternity, yet as ignorant of true good as the brutes that perish, and less happy than the brutes because polluted with vices that never polluted them. At length some unknown friends of ours heard in the Saviour's command a voice as it were saying, Go preach the Gospel in Britain. They came—and when will the blessings of that day terminate! The hoary druidical system of bloody superstition fell—the night of ages was dispersed, and the god of this world felt his British throne totter and moulder before the heralds of the Cross. What has been done for us it is our duty and happiness to do for others."

It may be interesting, in passing, to give a little information respecting the Denomination of Christians to whom the evangelization of Orissa is committed by divine Providence. Of them it is stated in the First Indian Report of the Society, printed at Cuttack,—

"The Missionaries labouring in Orissa whether from England or America, belong to that section of the Baptist church which in England is denominated "General Baptist." They are thus designated from holding as their distinguishing sentiment, that Christ has by his sufferings unto death made provision for the salvation of every man; while the other section of the Baptist church is designated "Particular Baptist" from holding the doctrine of particular redemption, or that Christ died only for the elect. These designations were far more appropriate fifty years ago than they now are; within this period both sections have approximated so closely to each other that the majority perhaps in either denomination have little to distinguish them but the name.

The spirit of Missions which was first kindled in the minds of the English Baptists by the labours of the apostolic Carey, soon spread its hallowing influence among the General Baptists. Indeed Dr. Carey was the pastor of a very ancient General Baptist church at Molton, Northamptonshire, and with his venerated colleagues, he ever looked with parental affection upon our infant Mission."

"The General Baptists of England, (says the Rev. A. Sutton,) were, during the 17th century,* an active, numerous body of Christians. They were orthodox in sentiment, and fervent in piety, but unhappily the doctrine of Socinianism crept into their churches, and while it ate out the vital spirit of Christianity, thinned their members, and spread a general torpor over the whole body. At length the indefatigable Dan Taylor, was raised up among them, and fanned the dying embers of piety into a flame. His spirit was grieved at the desolation of the churches; he wrote, and travelled, and preached and prayed in behalf of the pure doctrines of the gospel. He succeeded in many instances, in confirming the wavering in the fundamental truths of the Bible; he gathered around him a band of brethren of similar feelings with himself; they grew bold in defence of the faith once delivered to the saints; they opposed the deadening influence of Socinianism, and when they could do no more in reforming the body, they separated and formed themselves into a distinct society under the name of "*The New Connexion of General Baptists.*" This important measure was effected A. D. 1770, and from that time the New Connexion has gradually increased in numbers and influence, while the old General Baptists have continued to sink into comparative insignificance. The rise of the Particular Baptist Mission in 1792 spread a new influence through the churches; a higher tone of piety was excited; a more active principle of benevolence warmed the hearts of British Christians, and zeal for the salvation of the world was called into exercise, which had lain dormant through many preceding generations. The New Connexion of General Baptists partook of this revival of Primitive Christianity, though for some years they supposed themselves too few in number, and too limited in their resources to do any thing for missions, more than throw their mite into the treasury of existing societies. At length providence raised up the Rev. J. G. Pike to advocate the cause of missions among the General Baptists. His whole soul was called forth in behalf of the perishing nations of idolaters. He pleaded their cause with such affecting importunity, and such invincible ardour, that opposition was silenced; difficulties vanished; friends were encouraged; and the resolution to attempt to do something among the heathen was formed at the Annual Association of the New Connexion, in A. D. 1816.

In turning over the pages of civil history, we cannot help reflecting that the mightiest nations arose from small beginnings, and that some of the most famous heroes were once obscure and perhaps despised individuals. This remark is not intended to convey an idea that the humble memorial upon which we are now entering will yield to a more important history of mightier achievements performed by the little society to which it relates, (though in one view this will most assuredly be the case,) but it may induce a salutary application of the question "Who hath despised the day of small things?" and justify the attempt at preserving an accouut of the efforts of a body of Christians engaged in attacking one of the strongest holds of the prince of darkness; and which under Providence extracted the first stones from the foundation of that "mighty pagoda" which after ages are destined to see crumbling into dust. Juggernaut, *the great, the obscene, the bloody Juggernaut, must fall;* long, perhaps, will be the struggle and fierce the conflict, but he must fall; and the place which knows him now will know him no more for ever.

The Prophets and Apostles who foretold the triumphs of the gospel, and the blessings of Immanuel's reign, looked through many a bitter persecution, and beyond successive ages of pagan darkness. They saw in

---

* For an account of the Old and New Connexions of the General Baptist Denomination, see *Manasseh*, a Prize Essay, p. 33-41.

their prophetic vision the long night of antichrist, and the extended sway of the iron hearted man of Mecca; but we have passed those direful scenes; we anticipate no such obstructions to the spread of light and truth, we believe that the last struggle of expiring Idolatry has commenced, and that the first kindlings of the glorious day of universal bliss have already dawned to be obscured no more. Or if a passing cloud shall for a moment spread the gloom of night over our hopes and prospects, it will soon pass away, and the full orbed glories of the Sun of Righteousness, appear to diffuse eternal light, and life, and joy."*

The formation of the Mission, destined, it is humbly trusted, to undermine the Idolatry of Juggernaut, and to blot out its atrocities for ever, was an event of great importance in the church of Christ. "A thought (says Dr. Cox, in his *History of the Baptist Missionary Society,*) arises in the mind of an individual. There it works secretly for a time, till it irresistibly demands expression. Then it calls into exercise the sympathies of other minds, till, attaching itself to kindred elements around, it moulds into form, and stimulates into activity a series of efforts. These issue in the salvation of innumerable souls, and by the various combinations of christian benevolence, send down an ever augmenting influence to distant ages. Some of the greatest events, both of secular and ecclesiastical history, have been connected with circumstances apparently the most insignificant, or with men the most obscure and unpretending, that "the excellency of the power may be of God and not of man." The first publication of the Baptist Missionary Society commences with the observation;—"The origin of the Society will be found in the workings of our Brother Carey's mind, which has been directed to this object for the last nine or ten years, with very little intermission. His heart appears to have been set upon the conversion of the heathen, before he came to reside at Moulton in 1786."—As the Particular Baptist Mission originated with the venerable Carey, so the General Baptist Mission must be traced to the deep and anxious solicitude for the heathen of its Secretary, the Rev. J. G. Pike, of Derby, the author of so many valuable works on practical divinity. His name first appears in the Minutes of the General Baptist Association in 1809, as residing at Mr. Dan Taylor's, in London, or addressed at his residence. The following account of the rise of the Society, is extracted from "The Committee Book," and is in Mr. Pike's handwriting. "This Society arose in 1816. Some members of the New Connection of General Baptists had long felt a desire to see a Society for the propagation of the gospel among the heathen, established by the churches of the Connection. The

* Sutton's Narrative of the Mission to Orissa, 1833, *Intro.* p. 6-8.

writer of these lines has little acquaintance, from personal observation with what passed in the body previously to 1809, but thinks that he has seen a statement that a case respecting a Foreign Mission was sent from Castle Donington, to a Conference or Association before that time. If this were the case no visible effects appear to have followed. In 1809 an anonymous letter on the subject was read at the Association at Quorndon, Leicestershire. This letter appeared to excite some attention; Mr. Freeston spoke of it in terms of high commendation; and Mr. B. Pollard, observed that he could almost have sold the coat from his back for the missionary cause, or to that effect. This letter was printed in the General Baptist Repository, No. 17. In 1813, a question to the following effect was presented as from the Church at Friar Lane, Leicester, to the Conference at Derby,—"Ought not the General Baptists to exert themselves as much as they can, in establishing, though on ever so small a scale, a Mission of their own?" It is believed that the question was brought forward by the desire of an intimate acquaintance of the Minister; and in 1813 two letters appeared in the Repository on the importance of a Mission to the heathen. About 1812 the present Secretary of the Society applied to Mr. Fuller, the venerated Secretary of the Baptist Missionary Society, to know if their Society would employ as a Missionary a person who might be a member of a General Baptist Church. His answer amounted to a negative. In 1814 or 15, Mr. Fuller was again inquired of respecting the formation of an auxiliary Baptist Missionary Society, which should include both the bodies of the Baptist Denomination. It was thought this might be supported by the Churches of the former description, and being a mere auxiliary would not interfere with the management of the Baptist Missions. His answer to this proposition was decidedly unfavourable. It now remained for the friends of the heathen among the General Baptists, to see a little done among themselves for the support of the Missionary cause as carried on by others, or to make a fresh attempt to form a Missionary Society in their own Connection. In the early part of 1816, another letter* appeared in the Repository, calling for the establishment of such a Society. This letter appears to have had some effect. The subject was taken up by the Lincolnshire Conference. This letter appears to have been read at a Church meeting in Stoney Street, Nottingham, and a case from the Church was presented to a full Conference at Wimeswould, June 4, 1816, requesting the Con-

* It is most probable that Mr. Pike was the writer of these letters.

ference to take into consideration the formation of a Foreign Mission. After some discussion, which gave an unusual interest to the meeting, it was resolved that the subject appeared to be of such importance, that the Conference recommended it to the serious consideration of the next Association. It was determined that a copy of the resolution should be sent to every Church previously to the Association. The subject was accordingly taken up by the Association at Boston; and though the design met with some opposition, the result was favorable, and a resolution was passed recommending the friends of the measure to form a Society immediately."*

The writer was present at the discussion in the Association, and also his late valued colleague Mr. Bampton, and great was their satisfaction, in unison with the feelings of every friend of the infant Society, at its auspicious commencement. The Minutes of 1816 contain the Resolution which was unanimously adopted, that, "*We highly approve of a General Baptist Foreign Mission, and heartily recommend it to the Friends of this measure immediately to form themselves into a Society for the prosecution of this important object.*" This event took place at Boston, Lincolnshire, June 26, 1816. Mr. Pike, of Derby, was appointed Secretary, and Mr. R. Seals, of Nottingham, Treasurer. The names of forty brethren were nominated on the Committee for the ensuing year, "with power if needful to increase their number." An admirable Address, of which 5000 were printed, was prepared and circulated for the promotion of a missionary spirit. Two or three paragraphs cannot but deeply interest the reader.

"It is one of the glorious distinctions of our divine religion that it produces in the heart, which enjoys its saving power, a spirit of universal sympathy and benevolence. It will not let us live for ourselves alone, but teaches us to toil and live for others, as those who were before us in the church of Christ toiled and lived for us. Christianity teaches us to connect in our views eternity with time, and to behold in every human being a creature formed to live when sun and stars expire. It teaches us that such is the capacity of the soul for suffering or delight, that the whole mass of temporal happiness or misery, which a thousand nations could endure through ten thousand times ten thousand years, is but like a drop to the ocean, compared with the happiness or misery which every soul must enjoy or suffer in the range of eternity."

"Within a few years many Christians of different denominations have been exerting themselves to spread the knowledge of the holy name of Jesus; and, God be praised! they have not laboured in vain. We rejoice in their success, and would imitate their example. This has long

---

* See also the Baptist Jubilee Memorial, pp. 79-80.

been the desire of several among us who are the friends of missions. That desire spread further and wider, till it led to the formation of *a General Baptist Missionary Society;* whose object is the spread of the glorious Gospel of Christ among the heathen. The earliest business of this Society, it is conceived, must be the acquirement and diffusion of information on missionary subjects; the awakening the consciences of their fellow christians to aid its exertions; and the placing of themselves in a position to act when the providence of God shall call them into action: and it is for this infant institution that we solicit support. When its object is considered, can any decline supporting it with all the talents and all the power they possess? An eloquent friend of the heathen world has justly said, "The cause of Missions is one that will sanctify every church, every house, every bosom in which it has a friend. It is a cause stamped with the seal of heaven, dyed in the blood of Christ, and impressed with the characters of eternity. The command of Jesus gave it birth; the providence of God has watched its growth; the agonies of the cross INSURE its success; and the happiness of countless millions through eternal ages, is the end it has in view.

"The rapidity with which men are hastening to the judgment bar. A clergyman now employed by the Church Missionary Society in a public meeting, observed, "While Britain deliberates, the world is perishing. It has been calculated, that in every moment of time, the soul of one human being passes into eternity. How awakening this reflection! I am bound to call every human being my neighbour, my friend, and my brother. My Saviour has taught me to do so. A kindred soul to mine is at this moment departing—he is dying—he is dead! ere I can give utterance to the thought, another—and another—and another is no more. O could I call up the spirits of those who have departed this life, since the present assembly began its meeting. Could they tell you the scenes that in the last few moments have burst upon their view: some perhaps unfolding a tale that would harrow up the soul; others animating us by a ray of that joy, which eye hath not seen, nor ear heard, neither hath it entered into the heart of man to conceive; how gladly would I leave to them the pleading of this cause! but they are dead—*Still there are millions yet alive, and other generations yet unborn.*"

The first Report of the Society presented to the Annual Meeting in June 1817, contains some striking observations well worthy of preservation and mature consideration.—"The oak which forms the pride of the stately forest, and which bears unmoved the storms of revolving centuries, creeps through the first years of its existence a feeble unnoticed plant; while the gourd that has advanced to maturity in a night, has sunk to decay before the rays of one setting sun have shone upon it. The cloud that was repeatedly sought in vain, and which, when discovered, appeared small as a human hand, has afterward poured down its copious stores, and watered a nation with its fertilizing rains. If men do, the Lord doth not despise "*the day of small things.*"—A missionary Society, it should be considered, resembles the stream that tends to the ocean; at first a rivulet that may be measured by a span, but which, increasing as it flows, swells till the insignificant brook expands into a mighty river; and swelling still, before its course concludes, the river becomes almost a sea. Thus, brethren, has it been with other Missionary Societies; and let us hope that the little stream which last year sprung up at Boston, shall continue increasing as it flows, till some ages hence, when all who watched its rise are long forgotten, it shall, like a torrent, pour the waters of salvation through many a barren spot in the wide heathen wilderness."

The Rev. W. Ward, of Serampore, in his "*Farewell Letters,*" refering to the Society, observes—"Your Missionary Society may not be so extended as to excite great public attention; but a spirit of supplication may do more for you, than if your resources placed you at the head of all the Missionary Societies. I fear we do not perceive sufficiently, the immediate and inseparable connection between divine agency and success in these efforts for the conversion of blind and infatuated heathens.

"Prayer moves the hand that moves the world."*

The arrival of the Rev. W. Ward in England, in May 1819, was an event of great interest to the Society. In his first letter to the Secretary, he wrote—"I am glad to hear you are going to engage in missionary work. If you will send a missionary to Bengal, I am sure he will be hospitably received at Serampore, and a place of labour recommended. The exact spot would be better selected after his arrival. Any aid in the power of Serampore;—an asylum, advice, correspondence, &c., I am sure he may rely upon; and so far as a brotherly concern for his welfare goes, he would be one of us." In a subsequent letter he said—"I shall be very glad of the company to India of one of your Missionaries, and would assist him on the voyage in Bengalee." The Committee received this as an opening in Providence highly favorable to the Society. The *first* candidates for missionary labours, whose names deserve honourable record, were Messrs. Slater and Glover, who offered themselves in Sept. 1819. It was expected that Mr. Ward would return in the spring of 1820; and it was remarked that "the young men previously engaged were not judged sufficiently matured in experience and literature to be so soon employed." Mr. Ward's visit to America, Holland, &c., &c., delayed his return till May 1821. It is one of the mysteries of providence, that those who are most ready to engage in the cause of God, are sometimes not employed, "the purpose firm being equal to the deed;" and those who are most

* Ward's *Farewell Letters*, 1821, pp. 310-12.

diffident are pressed into the work. Mr. Slater, visited France to do good; and both he and his fellow student have long since rested from their labours, finishing their course in their native land. Mr. Slater died in Aug. 1822. Mr. Bampton, then minister at Yarmouth, in Norfolk, offered himself to the Committee, in a letter dated Jan. 11, 1820. A meeting was called, and "the offer unanimously accepted." Not long after, the writer, then minister at Norwich, though with great diffidence, wrote the Committee— "This afternoon I have solemnly devoted myself to the service of God among the heathen." The writer left Norwich in the April of that year, and continued at the Wisbeach Academy till a few weeks before the embarkation for India. Mr. Bampton also removed to Wisbeach, and subsequently studied medicine, surgery, &c., in London, which proved very useful to the Mission.

The Report of 1821, thus describes the ordination of the first Missionaries, at Loughborough and Wisbeach. These events were indeed, "a new thing in the land."

"On May 15th, the ordination of Mr. Bampton took place at Loughborough. The meeting was one of a highly interesting and solemn description. Crowds of friends to the best of causes flocked from the neighbouring churches, and some persons even from the distance of thirty or forty miles. The chapel filled to excess, was unable to receive all who sought admittance, and a number were thus deprived of the pleasure which those enjoyed who were happy enough to gain a place within its walls. The services were deeply impressive. Mr. Bampton with an unusual degree of firmness and with much propriety, replied to the questions proposed respecting his motives and principles. The congregation were then asked if they would pledge themselves to support the mission and pray for the missionaries, and requested if they gave that pledge, to express it by holding up their hands. Such a show of hands was instantly presented as has not been often seen. Never were so many raised at once before in our Connection; and hand and heart seemed to go together. Before this scene the mission had many friends, now it has many who in the house of God, and in his solemn presence, have pledged themselves to be its prayerful friends and constant supporters. Surely this vow will not be forgotten; the prayers of so many thus pledged to pray cannot be offered in vain. Mr. Smith offered an affectionate and earnest prayer, and Mr. Bampton was then set apart to the work by the imposition of the hands of the brethren. Mr. Pickering delivered a charge full of important advice. In the afternoon, Mr. Ward called on all present to regard their morning pledge, by addressing them from the apostolic request, "Brethren, pray for us, that the word of the Lord may have free course and be glorified." On the evening of this happy day, this day which may form a new era among our churches; a missionary prayer-meeting was held. Collections were made at all the opportunities in aid of the sacred missionary cause, and though made merely at the gates of the burying ground, the amount exceeded £70. The spirit that prompted these liberal donations was the spirit of christianity, which is not satisfied with professions, but with the professions of the lips connects the prayers of the heart and the bounty of hands.

On the Thursday following Mr. Peggs was set apart at Wisbeach. After an introductory discourse from Mr. Bissill, the ordination prayer was offered by Mr. Thomas Ewen, accompanied by the imposition of hands. Our esteemed friend who had been the Tutor of our beloved brother, afterwards delivered a very instructive and appropriate charge from Nehemiah's words, "I am doing a great work, and I cannot come down." The meeting was well attended—was a pleasing and solemn opportunity, and much tender solicitude for the comfort of the individuals engaging and for the success of the mission was apparent."

In the very judicious *Instructions to the Missionaries*, presented in a written form, the following directions were given in reference to their future scene of labour.—"We cannot with propriety decisively fix on your future station, but suggest one or other of the following,—Assam, the Punjab, Central Hindostan, viz., the Country in the neighbourhood of Aurungabad, or one of the great Eastern Islands which may be as yet unoccupied. The first of these may probably be found the most eligible, the last the least advisable. When you reach Serampore consult the Missionaries there on the eligibility of the above stations, or if none of these should seem suitable, on any other that may appear eligible. Value their advice and treat it with deference, yet you are to consider it as advice, and not as actual direction, but must endeavour to act as before God, seems most advisable to your own minds." How important the decision to be formed—surely the angel of the Lord went before the brethren, to seek out the lot of their inheritance, and to put them in possession of it.

The Missionaries embarked at Gravesend, on board the Abberton, May 28th, in company with Mr. Ward, Mrs. Marshman and her daughter and niece, Mr. and Mrs. Mack, Miss Cook (afterwards Mrs. Wilson,) so valuable a benefactress to the females of India, and two youths named Feris, born in India. Three or four days were spent at Madeira, and after an agreeable voyage the vessel arrived at Madras Sept. 24th. It is not requisite to detail the events of the voyage, it may suffice to say, that the society of Mr. Ward and Mrs. Marshman, and their kind assistance in Indian studies, were very valuable to the missionary band. The vessel was detained at Madras ten or twelve days, and the missionary party arrived at Serampore Nov. 15th. It was the weekly missionary breakfast and united prayer for the progress of the mission, and great was the pleasure with which the brethren and their wives were received by the missionaries Carey, Marshman, and Ward.

After mature and prayerful consideration, in accordance with the advice of the Serampore brethren, it was determined to make

Orissa the scene of the society's operations. This decision arose from the unsettled state of Assam, the distance of the Punjab, the preparation of an improved edition of the New Testament in the Oreah language, the contiguity of Orissa to Bengal, &c. It was requisite that application should be made to the British government at Calcutta, for permission to proceed to Orissa and settle in the country. A previous application for two missionaries was unsuccessful on account of the unsettled state of the country; but as peace was now restored, God gave his servants favour in the eyes of the Governor-General, the late Marquis of Hastings, and they were allowed to proceed to Cuttack the capital of Orissa. The writer remembers the pleasure which beamed in the countenance of Dr. Carey, when he first informed him of this important event. Did the Lord say of his people, as of the church of Philadelphia—"I know thy works; behold I have set before thee an open door and no man can shut it: for thou hast a little strength, and hast kept my word, and has not denied my name."

The missionaries in their Journal record,—"Jan. 22nd, 1822. Prayer-meeting for us at Serampore, as we were expected to go to Calcutta in the morning, and embark for Cuttack on board the Cyclops. Brethren Ward, Carey, and Marshman prayed very affectionately for us, and in the language of one of the hymns, showed,

> They wish'd us in His name,
> The most divine success.

We have been pleased with the respect and gratitude of our old Oreah Pundit. The Lord give him the knowledge of that gospel, which in his own language, he makes known to others. Our minds are affected at leaving our kind friends; but the God of our fathers who will be called "the God of the whole earth," will we trust be with us and help us."

The brethren were well supplied with good seed for the new field which they were about to cultivate. It is stated in the Report —"Previously to their departure from Calcutta, they were provided with a considerable quantity of tracts and copies of the Scriptures for distribution. From Serampore, they received a thousand gospels and epistles in Oreah, and five hundred tracts. From Mr. Pearce, of Calcutta, six hundred tracts, in different languages, furnished by the Calcutta Baptist Tract Society. From Mr. Thomason, the Secretary of the Calcutta Auxiliary Bible Society, between seventy and eighty copies of the Scriptures in English, Bengalee,

Persian, and Hindostanee ; and from Mr. Keith, from the Independent Tract Society, two thousand tracts in Bengalee, and in Bengalee and English. 'Thus,' Mr. Peggs observes, 'We go forth bearing precious seed : may we return, bringing our sheaves with us.'

"Agreeably with the wish of the missionaries, your Committee judged it proper to offer some remuneration to the kind friends whose liberality had provided them with these helps for immediate exertion, and voted a donation of £10. to the Independent brethren at Calcutta ; of £5. to the Baptist brethren in that city, and of £5. for the tracts furnished from the brethren at Serampore.—The Oreah gospels and epistles, and the copies of the Scriptures, were paid for either by the Calcutta Auxiliary Bible Society, or from the funds of that magnificent Institution, the British and Foreign Bible Society."

CHAP. II.

Establishment of the Mission in Orissa.

Arrival of the Missionaries in Orissa—Site of the Mission—Sketch of the extent and population, manners and customs of Orissa—View of the Idolatry of Juggernaut—Account of the Temple—establishment—festivals—pilgrimages—prostration under the cars—mortality—British connexion with Idolatry—Prevalence of Suttee—Churuck Poojah—Infanticide—human sacrifices—various austerities—neglect of the dying and the dead—moral and spiritual state of the people.

The Brethren being encouraged, by the appearance and movement of "the pillar and cloud" in the direction of Orissa, engaged a country vessel named the Cyclops for 200 rupees, to take them and their luggage. They gratefully record—"We have received much kindness from different friends in Calcutta, through whom our store of provisions for the voyage has been increased. Mr. J.

Carey sent us a ham from his breakfast table, which with another given us at Serampore, were very agreeable on the voyage. Mr. B. and I went on board the Abberton, and took our leave of the sailors with prayer. When we returned, we weighed anchor, and thus were separated from our friends and brethren in this city."—There accompanied them into Orissa, as 'a man of all work,' a native christian, named Abraham, born near Seringapatam, who had been baptized by Dr. Marshman, a few weeks previously. He could speak several languages, and proved a very valuable acquisition to the mission for a number of years. Near the mouth of the river on the coast of Orissa, the vessel struck upon a sand bank, but providentially sustained no serious injury; and on Feb. 7th, they state —"This morning on rising we found ourselves at anchor, about three miles from *Patamoondy*, the vessel not being able to proceed farther for want of water in the river." After much detention in disembarking their luggage, the distance to Cuttack the capital, about 50 miles, was travelled in native doolies constructed for the purpose, and they arrived Tuesday, Feb. 12th, 1822; a day ever to be remembered in the history of the Orissa Mission.

The pious christian often exclaims with the prophet—"O Lord, I know that the way of man is not in himself: it is not in man that walketh to direct his steps." Jer. 10. 23. This is evident in reference to the daily occurrences of life; how much more so in that which concerns the eternal welfare of families, communities, and nations! The missionaries were directed—"With respect to your station, we beg you to consider it, *a leading principle* in directing your decision, that it shall be one, *where the field for usefulness appears wide, and as yet unoccupied by others.* We wish you if practicable, to convey the gospel to some nation, for whom no man cares." Orissa fully realized these enlarged and benevolent views of christian philanthropy; and succeeding years have shown the special guidance of Providence, in leading the first missionaries into this untrodden, benighted, and idolatrous land. The approbation of the selection, gratitude to God for his direction in so important a step, and particularly for the adoption of Juggernaut as a station, are well expressed in the Report of 1824;—"It may be recollected by many, that when that distinguished friend of India, Buchanan, had witnessed the abominable Idolatries perpetrated at the temple of Juggernaut, he observed—'From an eminence on the pleasant bank of the Chilka Lake, where no human bones are seen, I had a view of the lofty tower of Juggernaut far remote; and while I viewed it, its abominations came to mind. Ruminating long on the wide and extended empire of Moloch in the heathen world, I cherished in my thoughts the design of some *Christian Institution,* which being fostered by Britain my christian country, might gradually undermine this baneful Idolatry, and put out the memory of it for ever.' When the members of this society first read these observations, little did they imagine, that ten years after the date of those remarks, a society would spring up among themselves, which should be so honoured, as to be allowed to fix the first Christian Missionary beside the infamous temple whose Idolatries Buchanan deplored."

The following extract from the speech of Col. Phipps, at a public meeting in London, in May 1829, evidently refers to the commencement of the Orissa Mission. The interest of a child for the salvation of the heathen is worthy of emulation.

"On my arrival at Madras, I expected to join a regiment returning to Bengal from the capture of Seringapatam; and, notwithstanding I was afterward ordered to proceed by sea, I will relate what occurred on its march. On entering the district of Cuttack, which at that period belonged to a Hindoo Prince, the troops found the inhabitants about to attend the great festival of the idol Juggernaut, whose celebrated temple lay in their route. Permission was asked by the Hindoo soldiers to stop and join in the religious rites. They were left in charge of two officers: one, an intimate Christian Friend, informed me, that no sooner had the soldiers joined the pilgrims, than the Brahmuns of the temple thought that a safe opportunity presented itself of gratifying their hatred of Christians: the officers were insulted, and their lives placed in jeopardy. No sooner did the soldiers, however, perceive what was doing, than they ran to their tents—got their arms—returned speedily—surrounded their officers—and told the priests that they had been desirous of joining peaceably in the worship of the idol; but felt indignant that those British officers, who had so recently led them to victory, should be molested; and declared that they would shed the last drop of their blood in their defence. The Brahmuns perceived that it would be prudent to pacify the soldiers: the religious ceremonies were resumed; and when the Sepoys were about to depart, they chose to mark their sense of the conduct of the Brahmuns, and to leave some memorial of their having visited the temple. To effect this, they went to a large pound, in which the priests had confined many poor pilgrims, in order that their rich friends or any charitable persons might redeem them; the pound was soon broken, and the pilgrims released. After this exploit, the soldiers continued their march to Bengal. The sovereign of the country having joined a league against the British government, a war ensued, which added this District to the British dominions: and the standard of England was planted near the temple of Juggernaut. In the course of my public duties, when on a visit to this place, I well remember, that one evening an officer returning home with his family on a large elephant, some Mahometans were observed celebrating their grand festival of the Mohurrum. The elephant was conducted close to the spot, in order that the ceremonies might be conveniently seen. A little girl, who was expected to take a lively interest in the pomp displayed, seemed rather absorbed in meditation; and the moment she got home, she earnestly intreated her mother to allow her to offer up a prayer to her heavenly Father, that he would have compassion on the deluded natives, remove the gross superstition and darkness in which they were involved, and teach them that there is no other name under heaven by which they can be saved, but that of the Lord Jesus! Such was the deep interest excited in the bosom of a little child for the spiritual welfare of the people! *Some months afterward, two Missionaries, at the hazard of their lives, came to Juggernaut; and the gospel has been faithfully preached ever since.* Thus the planting of the standard of England in the kingdom of Mysore, and the district of Cuttack, was followed, in the providence of God, by the lifting up the standard of the Cross!"

The ample information respecting Orissa contained in Mr. Sterling's valuable work, render any enlarged account of the extent and population, the manners and customs of the Province unnecessary. The following interesting extract from "*Sutton's Narrative of the Mission to Orissa*," may abundantly suffice.

"Ootkul K'hand or Orissa is supposed to be the ancient country of the Or, or Oreah tribe of Hindoos, and comprises an interesting and extensive portion of the Honourable Company's territory in India. It is situated between 19 and 23 degrees north latitude, and 84 to 88 degrees east longitude. But its boundaries have been so often enlarged and contracted in different periods of Orissian history, that at the present day it is difficult if not impossible to mark them with precision. The country of Orissa however as it is generally understood, consists of a long narrow strip of land extending from Midnapore in the north, to a few miles below Ganjam in the south, and from the shores of the bay of Bengal in the east to Singboom, Sumblepoor, and Sonepoor, &c., situated amongst the vast range of mountainous country in the west, comprising a tract of about 300 miles in length, and from 20 to 170 in breadth. The Orissa nation, however, has in different periods of its history, carried its arms and language to a much greater extent than is here described; and at the present day some traces of its former power are discoverable in the neighbouring countries of Bengal and Telingana.

"Orissa Proper may be considered as distinguished into three different regions.

"First, a low swampy tract of land extending along the sea shore from the Black Pagoda nearly up to the Hoogly river, about 100 miles in length and from five to twenty in breadth. The greatest part of this district is covered with impenetrable jungles through which numerous creeks and rivulets, abounding with ravenous and monstrous alligators, wind their way. The surface of the less jungly parts is covered with grass and reeds of an extraordinary length, which afford a fine retreat for the wild hogs, buffaloes, tigers and leopards that infest the country. Towards the Black Pagoda nothing but a wide barren sand is to be seen, excepting a strong kind of creeper bearing a gay purple flower, which with its exuberant arms enterlaces the ground in every direction, making walking over it very troublesome; occasionally tufts of tall thorny grass are to be seen, and here and there a stunted scrubby palm or cocoa-nut tree varies the otherwise barren and dull uniformity of the scene. During the year 1832 a most alarming inundation deluged this part of Orissa, and swept away 15,000 of its wretched inhabitants. A famine followed this awful visitation of Providence, and subsequently another tremendous storm, which have spread desolation and death over a great part of the district.

The second and most valuable part of Orissa includes the present District of Cuttack and part of the territory of the Raja of Moherbunge. Though this region is in general highly cultivated, and produces most of the grains and vegetables common in Bengal, its soil is certainly for the most part of a poor and unfruitful description, particularly near the hills. Such are the general characteristics of this part of Orissa: occasionally however, grateful and interesting exceptions are to be made, and the eye is delighted and the senses regaled with fruitful fields, agreeable perfumes, fine shady groves of trees, and pleasant rivers.

The third portion of Orissa is a long range of hilly country, extending from near Midnapore in the north to the river Godaveri in the south, a distance of nearly three hundred miles in length, and one hundred in breadth. This extensive and interesting region is parcelled out to nearly thirty petty Rajas who pay tribute to the Bengal government. These are again divided into a variety of estates or small zemindaries subordinate to the Raja's chiet zemindar. The population of that part of Orissa which is subject to the British sway may be estimated at about 1,200,000 of which number about 25,000 are Mussulmen. The inhabitants of the tributary states and mountain districts, are chiefly Hindoos, Chooars and Goands. It is exceedingly difficult to offer any statement as to their number. The Oreah language is spoken among the hills as far to the southward as Rajamundry. But the mountaineers speak a language, apparently, entirely distinct from it.

The Oriyas are pure Hindoos. Their Brahmuns are celebrated in the Pooranas as of a superior order, and are supposed to constitute one half of the population. The Mussulmans are chiefly descendants of the early conquerors of India. Some few are occasionally added to their number by conversions from among the Hindoos. The mountain tribes are supposed by some to be the aborigines of the country, who have been driven to their miserable retreat among the jungles and fastnesses of the mountains, by the present inhabitants of the plains. They differ essentially both in their language and appearance from their more civilized neighbours. Those toward the northern boundaries of the province, which the writer has seen, are of a dark slate colour, approaching the sooty black of the negro; but those in the neighbourhood of Ganjam are brown and much resemble some of the Mug tribes. It is not unlikely that the present campaign among the hill tribes will bring some interesting particulars to light respecting these unhappy people.*

The religion of the Oriyas is the same as that of Hindoos generally. The following brief sketch of their character contained in a letter to a friend, may not be unacceptable. No sooner is a woman pregnant than a regular round of religious ceremonies commences, for the future welfare of her offspring, which continues, if the child should be a boy and the head of a family, long after his death; I believe while any of his male progeny, to the most distant generations exist. Previously to the birth of a child, various ceremonies are observed, and at the birth many more, and again on the 5th, 7th, or 8th day, when a woman is considered out of danger. The children both boys and girls go naked till three or four years of

* This has been done in reference to the Khunds.

age, and, if they are not taught to read, require nothing but a little food. About the age of seven to twelve years their boys and girls are betrothed, and the marriage ceremony takes place as soon after as the circumstances or inclination of the parents will admit. Marriage is an important affair, and great care is taken to select a proper match as to family, rank, &c. Comfort and happiness are generally sacrificed for these, and the boy and girl are often married without having seen each other till the day when they are linked together! I need not say that this system is productive of incalculable wretchedness. They generally are very untractable and abuse their parents and one another in a way most shocking for civilized men to behold. Multitudes obtain no instruction at all. Girls are universally prohibited from learning to read, or from doing any thing in the way of mental improvement. They remain buried in their father's house till marriage, and after a girl has been united, without any choice as to her husband, for life, (often to a wretch who will never live with her,) she is shut up in the house of her lord. A woman of respectability seldom appears in the street, or if she should go out on any occasion, she is close muffled up, so that only her feet can be seen. She is not permitted to mention her husband by name, but calls him her lord, or the owner of the house, &c. She cooks her husband's food, waits on him while eating, and eats what he and the children leave. At night she shampoes him to sleep, (this is a sort of squeezing operation over all parts of the body.) Should she die before her husband, it is considered a blessing to her; should her husband die first, she is often expected to burn herself with his corpse.* Should she not burn, she either becomes a prostitute, or has her head close shaved, and becomes the slave of the family. Sometimes young widows marry again, but this seldom occurs. The women are very abusive to one another, and those of the lowest classes, which are seen abroad, quarrel and abuse one another upon every trifling occasion. I have seen them often stand a long distance from each other with their hands on their hips, and rage and storm till they almost burst with anger. Their language is of the most extraordinary opprobrious kind, such as I cannot pen; 'you strumpet, you wretch, you destroyer of your children, eat your son's head, you vile hussy, may your complete destruction take place, may your father and mother die, may you be childless, may you have no one left in your family to light a lamp,' are extremely common,

* This cruel rite has been abolished since the above account was written.

and even gentle wishes compared with many others which they use in their quarrels. Boys, about the time of marriage, or of being betrothed, or from eleven to twelve years of age, are clothed, that is have a cloth wrapper round their loins, which passing between the thighs, tucks up behind. This is the dress for life; generally they wear nothing else, that is the lower classes, excepting when they are cold, then they use another cloth which covers their head like the hood of a woman's cloak and wraps round their bodies. Some casts wear a kind of jacket of thin cotton, and others a loose cloth carelessly thrown over their shoulders like a shawl. They are fond of gold and silver ornaments, such as ear-rings, nose jewels for the women, and for both sexes anklets, bracelets, finger rings; some boys have silver chains or hoops for girdles to fasten their clothes to, and children often wear them for ornament. Women wear rings on the toes, and prostitutes often wear little bells round their ankels, which tinkle as they go. The men are fond of smearing themselves with sandal wood, mud, and powders of different kinds. They generally wear the mark of their debta on their foreheads. Women have a red spot between the eye-brows, blacken their eyelids, and the eyelids of their children with alcohol, or black powder.

Boys at about twelve years of age, if they are Brahmuns, are invested with the piota, and pass through a long round of ceremonies. The Brahmuns are the curse of Orissa. To these lords of creation all must submit; they call themselves the peculiar recipients of the divine essence, and claim in many cases divine honours. The poor soodra esteems it an act of merit to drink a cup of water in which a Brahmun has dipped his toe. He prostrates himself at his feet, seeks his blessing, dreads his curse, and in every situation and engagement of life from infancy to death, must seek to propitiate him, and contribute all he can collect to satisfy his voracious appetite. Nothing is to be done without propitiating the twice born.

The people generally are grave in their deportment, thrifty, and laborious; but they are, alas, very depraved in their morals, dishonest in their dealings, and unfaithful in their engagements. Their food consists principally of rice, pulse, fish, milk, spices, salts, fruits and vegetables. Some of them will eat flesh, especially deer flesh, goats, and that of the wild boar and buffaloe. There are many Byraggees and other religious mendicants in the country who live upon the people; these are usually base characters, practising the vilest crimes under the mask of peculiar sanctity; they

A NATIVE-HINDOO SCHOOL.

are generally naked, excepting about six inches of cloth, and have their hair long and sunburnt, sometimes lengthened by other hair, and their bodies smeared with ashes and dirt; they spend their time in gambling, eating, chewing opium, singing and sleeping."*

Mr. Sutton prepared an account of the Idol Juggernaut, the erection of the Temple, the scenes attending the Ruth Jattra or car festival, and the miseries consequent upon the accumulation of such masses of the population. This was published in *The Calcutta Christian Observer*, Oct. 1832, and cannot fail to be painfully interesting to the reader.

"Juguturunth, Jugurnath, or Jugunhath, (Lord of the world,) is the name of the most celebrated idol in India. He is said to be an incarnation of Vishnoo, or Daru Bruhma, literally "*wooden god*," but meaning god who has revealed himself in a body of wood. There are a great many images of this god, set up in different parts of India; but the one established at Pooree in Orissa is the principal, and by far the most venerated.

The origin of the idol is by the natives ascribed to Maha Raj Indradumana. This pious prince had been induced to set out from his own dominions in Hindoostan, upon a pilgrimage to a famous image of Nilu Madhuba, situated on the Nil Gri, or blue hills of Orissa; but just before he reached the spot the image suddenly disappeared from the sight of the people. The prince was inconsolable at being thwarted in his pious designs of adoring the sacred image, when behold Vishnoo appeared to him in a dream, and consoled him with a promise of soon re-appearing in a form which should be celebrated far and wide throughout the Kalee-joog. The prince, waited at Pooree for the advent of the new Abatar; at length, one propitious morn his attendant Brahmuns brought the welcome intelligence, that a most wonderful tree was making its way over the sea towards Swerga Dwar: and this could be no other than the new incarnation, as it was accompanied by the sacred insignia of Vishnoo, the *chockra*, *padma*, *concha*, and the *goda*. Indradumana, filled with joy, hastened to the spot, and *most devoutly embraced the sacred log!* A cloth of gold was then thrown over it, and immense sums distributed to the holy Brahmuns in attendance. The prince then by his pious supplications obtained the aid of Vishwakurma, the architect of the gods, who with one blow of his wonder-working axe formed the block into the *chatoor moorti*, or four-fold image.

* Sutton's Narrative, pp. 25-30.

A temple was then built, and the images set up with great pomp and expense. The gods and goddesses all came down to worship them; a number of rites and ceremonies were decreed, and from that time to this, Juggernaut has maintained his preeminence among the gods of India. Of the twelve annual festivals which are celebrated at Pooroosootama, the proper name of Pooree, the Ruth Juttra is by far the most important. The engraving which accompanies this volume furnishes an interesting representation of the commencement of this festival, and the remarks which follow are intended still further to explain or illustrate the principal objects presented to our view in the plate.

The buildings immediately over No. 1. is a *Muth* or Hindoo monastry, belonging to the Ramanuja sect of Voishnobs. Most of the buildings, which line the principal streets of Pooree, are establishments of a similar kind. These establishments tend greatly to keep up the celebrity of Juggernaut, as most of them are devoted to him, and interested in drawing pilgrims to his shrine. They are generally liberally endowed, and many of them are *very* rich. Within their cloisters, the most learned professors of Hindoo mythology are found, and to see and converse with them, must with the pundits of other countries be as much an object of desire as a sight of Juggernaut: indeed, it is difficult to account for the visits to Pooree, of many learned men who despise the popular idolatry, but on this ground. Disputation with pundits of other parts of India has ever been a favorite pursuit with Hindoos, and their history furnishes us with many accounts of the travels of their ancient sages for this purpose, as the sages Sunkara, Ramanuja, Choitun, &c., who are said to have disputed with and overcome the professors of every opposing sect.

It may be observed respecting the mahant or gooroo of the *Muth* in the plate, that when the late excellent Mr. Harington visited Pooree, just before he left India, the mahant called upon him. He is a venerable old man, with grey hairs, and on that occasion appeared leaning upon two of his favorite disciples. In reply to some questions respecting the connexion of government with Juggernaut, and the abolition of the pilgrim tax, he said, "that Juggernaut was never so popular as under the British protection; that his glory was now spread through the three worlds; and that it would be a pity for the Honourable Company to destroy all the holiness they had acquired by leaving him to himself!"

No. 2 in the plate directs our attention to the "mighty Pagod." Here "the Lord of the world," impiously so called, has for successive ages established his destructive sway. Here, from generation to generation, myriads of human beings have fallen victims to his impious domination, and whitened with their bones the horrid plain where he dwells. Hither, in obedience to the mandates of his priests, they have bent their wearied steps, and dropt and died unpitied and unknown. This far-famed temple is said to have been built in A. D. 1198, by Rajah Anunga Bhim Daib, under the superintendence of his minister Bajpoi, at a cost of from 40 to 50 lacs of rupees. The principal tower is supposed to be 184 feet high, and upwards of 28 feet wide within the walls. It is surrounded by a stone wall 20 feet high, and nearly 650 feet square. Within this inclosure are upwards of fifty smaller temples, devoted to the various gods of India. The walls of these temples, and especially of the great temple, are covered with the most filthy representations in durable and massive sculpture; and from fragments on the outer walls, it is probable they were once disgraced. These obscene figures and emblems are a very common appendage to the temples in Orissa; as may be seen at the Black Pagod, the temples at Jajipoor, and a new temple, now building, dedicated to Juggernaut, at Rhumba, on the side of the Chilka Lake. But they abound all over the Province; and in Pooree itself, it is easy to point out as much evidence of the above assertion as any man will feel disposed to contemplate.

The land within 10 miles, or according to some accounts 10 *koss*, of this temple is holy, and denominated the Shree Kshetra; and to die within its limits is considered a sure passport to eternal bliss. Upwards of 3,000 families of priests and other servants of the idol, are supported directly by this temple, while about 15,000 of the inhabitants of Pooree are supposed directly or indirectly to profit by it. Among other servants of the idol in this temple are 300 or 400 families of cooks, to prepare the idol's food, called muhaprasad, or "great favour;" and 120 dancing girls, prostitutes of course, to dance before the gods.

No. 3 may guide the eye to the principal gate of the temple, called Singha-dwara, or "the Lion gate." By this gateway the pilgrims enter when they go to worship the idol. There are three other entrances, one on each side of the square, but they are comparatively little frequented. At each of these gates is placed a number of *seapoys* or *burkandasses* belonging to the government, for the purpose of keeping off intruders and guarding the sacred idols. There is moreover a stone pavement, perhaps 16 feet wide, before the Singha-dwara, on which no polluted Christian, or Mussulman, or even a Hindoo of low caste, is permitted to set his foot.

No. 4 is placed beneath the beautiful column standing immediately opposite Singha-dwara. It is surmounted by an image of Aruna, or the dawn personified. This chaste specimen of Hindoo sculpture formerly occupied an appropriate place before the temple of the sun, or Black Pagoda. It was removed from thence, and placed where it now stands, by a wealthy inhabitant of Pooree.

Nos. 5, 6, and 7, point to the cars of Bullubhadra, Soobhudra, and Juggernaut. Bullubhudra, (No. 5) is called the Burra Thakoor or Great Lord, and in several minor particulars enjoys the pre-eminence, such as having rather the largest car, standing nearest the temple, being first brought out, &c. But he does not receive a tythe of the adoration, that is paid to Juggernaut. The face of Bullubhadra is painted *white*. Soobhudra, the sister of Juggernaut, has the smallest car. She is made without arms, and is painted a *yellow* colour. There is little notice taken of her by the majority of worshippers. Juggernaut is painted *black*, with a red mouth, and red and white circles for his eyes. He is the great object of attraction. Some of the pilgrims say, that he is more vindictive than Bullubhudra; hence their extra endeavours to propitiate him and secure his favour.

All the idols are made of the *Nimb* tree, and it is probable that the mysterious deposit within them is the Salgram. Some indeed have supposed that it is a bone of Krishnu, and others have fancied that it is a box of quicksilver. The images are as ugly and as monstrous in their appearance as any thing that can well be imagined. Their very distant approximation to the human figure does not extend below the bosom and all the rest is a mere huge block of timber Arms and feet they have probably none; but these appendages, made of gold, are supplied on state occasion.

All the images are profusely adorned with various kinds of ornaments, and their bodies are clothed with rich silks and shawls. These images are brought out of the temple on two occasions, viz. at the *Snan*, or bathing festival, and at the *Ruth Jattra*, or car festival. On the former occasion, they are placed on an elevated terrace to the east of the temple, within the sacred inclosure. Holy-water in brass lotas is brought in native pomp, with music playing, and the sacred canopy preceding it; and then poured over the idols, which has the effect of obliterating the lineaments of their misshapen countenances. While this ceremony is performing, many of the most zealous devotees rush forward, and with their hands rub off the paint from the images, to smear on their bodies, and thus of course rapidly hasten on the work of spoliation. When the uncouth blocks are sufficiently saturated with the holy-water, they are dressed up in the most captivating style. The crafty Brahmuns so manage to adjust the ornaments, that the face of the idols is almost hidden, and their faded beauty is scarcely perceived. Thus they remain till evening, receiving the adoration of the gaping multitude, while the Brahmuns pocket the offerings of many a kind, which the zeal of the worshippers prompts them to bestow.

After this day's exhibition, the gods, (for gods they are, though subjected to "all the ills which flesh is heir to,") are reported ill, until the Ruth Jattra; or in other words, they are kept secret, in order to be repainted, that they may appear with their freshest looks on that occasion. These cars are built new every year; and when the festival is over they become the property of the *pundas*, or priests of the idol, who break them up, and sell them for a considerable sum. The writer of these remarks paid five rupees for one wheel only of Juggernaut's car. Bullubbudra's car is 43 feet high, and has sixteen wheels. Juggernaut's car is 41 feet high, and has fourteen wheels. Soobhudra's car is 40 feet high, and has fourteen wheels. The upper parts of these cars are covered with green, blue, red, yellow, and other gay coloured cloths, hung in strips fantastically arranged, and adorned with various devices, formed with silver spangles, &c. The tower of each car is surmounted by a globe and flag, while from various parts of it, birds, monsters, and flags project, producing a picturesque effect. The platforms on which the idols sit enthroned are about ten or twelve feet from the ground. These are decorated with varied coloured shawls, and different figures of Hindoo mythology. Immense cables are manufactured, with which to drag the cars, and are fixed to the carriage part of the vehicles. As it has been observed respecting the wheels of the cars, they are extremely ponderous, and the rough spokes project from 1½ to two inches beyond the felloes, so that the poor wretches who may throw themselves under them are inevitably crushed to a horrid mass of flesh. Several such sacrifices have occurred to my knowledge within the last seven years; and on one occasion, particularly, I was coming up to Juggernaut's car, as it passed over the body of an up-country Brahmun. The entrails, blood, and brains, of this infatuated victim were spirted about in every direction!

On the second day of the new moon in Asar (June or July,) the Ruth Jattra commences. The cars are the previous day arranged in front of the Singha-dwara and purified for the reception of their holy burdens by various incantations and ceremonies. When the propitious hour arrives for the gods to take their annual ride, they are brought out of the temple—not with pomp and state, consistent with the divine honours they at other times receive—but as though they were the vilest dogs in creation; some drag them, others push them, with as little ceremony as can well be imagined, they are thus rocked along to the cars! Then oh! what desecration ensues, a rope, *yes, a rope is twisted round the neck of the great Juggernaut,* and what with some tugging above, and others shoving him below, he is constrained to ascend an inclined plain to his station on the car; then, however, as if to atone for the insult offered to his godship, the Brahmuns with the multitude prostrate themselves and worship him, while a shout, as of "the voice of many waters," shakes the earth, with "victory to Juggernaut our lord." The other idols are brought out in like manner. The Khoordra Rajah then sweeps the cars, and the purification process is completed, when suddenly a rush of some thousands of men, appointed to draw the car, who come jumping and shouting like so many wild infernals, announces, that the gods are about to commence their journey. They immediately seize the huge ropes, and range themselves in order; if peradventure any of them are found loitering by the way, a smart application of the ratan to their bare backs soon sends them to their posts. The scene now presents its most picturesque and animated appearance. The cars dressed in their gaudy colours, towering far above the vast wilderness of heads, have at a distance a very imposing air; while the loud sounds of idol music, the elephants of the gods and their worshippers stationed here and there, adorned with gay trappings, the vast numbers of devotees from the house tops and elevated verandahs of the adjacent houses, waving their *chowries,* and the various acts of adoration practised by the zealous worshippers accompanied by their loud acclamations, combine to give an air of state to the festival, and stamp its character as a worshipping assembly. Here and there a few Europeans are to be seen, some on their elephants, and others on horseback, witnessing the ceremonies. Some few are engaged in company with those who were once idolaters, but now Christians, in distributing the words of eternal life to the thousands of eager applicants, who are perishing for the lack of knowledge.

The tremendous shouts of men, and the hissing and the hooting of the women announce, that the cars are about to move. All seems infernal revelry, and involuntarily reminds one, that this is the triumph of hell over the fallen souls of man! Here satan seems to have carried his power to the utmost to insult the Majesty of heaven, and to laugh at the awful extent of his dominion over his deluded subjects. It is the very acme of his triumph. The object, which he has seduced the people to worship, is the ugliest and most senseless in creation; and the service, which under the name of divine worship, they pay to him, consists of the most lascivious gestures, and most obscene addresses. Buchanan in his Journals mentions these obscene songs and gestures, and the writer has heard and witnessed them many and many a time. Although it is a shame to speak of those things which are done by them, not in darkness but in the open front of day, and that too before upwards of 200,000 people, men, women, and children; yet a partial exposure of these abominable songs may perhaps be necessary to their everlasting suppression, as well as to give an idea of the moral degradation of the people, who can listen to them with such evident delight. In the repetition of these songs, the speaker steps forward to the extreme verge of the platform, and addresses the crowd in boisterous language; he has usually a long wand in his hand, with which he makes the action to accompany the words, so that his meaning is understood where his voice does not reach; and occasionally some half dozen of obscene Brahmuns fall pell mell upon each other close under the nose of the idol, and repeat the filthy pantomime."*

Gungadhor, the first brahmun in Orissa that received the gospel, assisted by another native, of the writer caste, prepared the following account, which may probably contain more truth than any yet offered to the public. The late Rev. W. Ward justly observed,—"to know what Hindooism is, a man must become a Hindoo." Here is the testimony of a Hindoo, enlightened by Christianity.

"In Orissa, having cut down the Nim-pita tree, they (the Brahmuns and workmen,) by manual labour form it into an image. Then they paint it into the resemblance of a (human) picture, with vermillion, yellow, black, white, and green colours. Thus making it with their hands, they anoint it with various kinds of perfumes and sandal-wood, and adorn it with flowers and leaves; after which, placing it in a stone temple, they serve and adore it.

* Sutton's Narrative, pp. 58-67.

"About 630 years ago, Anunga Bhim Daib, Raja of Orissa built the first temple, at an expense of from forty to fifty lacks of rupees. Then the Brahmuns with various *muntras* from the Veds consecrated the images. They made a representation of the lotus flower on the back of the three *moortis*, under which is an excavation with a door. Having brought from the Gangootree river, at the bottom of the Chitrakote mountain, three round stones (the Salgrama,) they designated them Sila Vishnoo. Then within the images they place them under the lotus, which they paint; they lock the door, and adorning the image with various coloured clothes, they worship it as Sila Vishnoo. From that time to this, they have cut down the *nim* tree, and made and worshipped this image fifty or one hundred times, or it may be oftener. But the old images, having been thrown out (in the temple yard,) from the operation of wind and rain became rotten. But the stone they call Sila Vishnoo, with great secrecy, no one seeing it, they take from the old wood and place in the new. They then falsely assert that he who effects this removal dies. The Raja sometimes begs the old block, and taking it a way, places in it the Salgram, and worships it.

"At this present time, in consequence of the power of the English extending through the numerous countries, many causes of alarm are suppressed. On this account the pundas spread themselves through different parts for the purpose of collecting pilgrims. Having arrived at the respective stations, they repair to people's houses, and compel them to eat Mahaprasad (Juggernaut's food,) and by much flattery, induce them to receive various kinds of cakes. Having furnished themselves with stripes of cloth, which have touched the sacred limbs of Juggernaut, they suspend them round their necks, saying, 'See you are highly favoured! sitting in your houses you have obtained these precious relics.' Then they say, 'Come, accompany me to my country. There God is revealed. There the goddess Lukshmee, Saruswuttee, Bimblee, and 10,000 others constantly serve him; moreover, the gods of heaven, earth, and hell, all the 330 millions of gods worship him. His glory is immense. All casts before him eat out of one vessel. In the month of Asar is the Goondicha Jattra. He himself comes out of the temple and sits on his car. He himself causes the car to move. In one day, he eats 70 poata, (about a thousand pounds weight!) but all that he eats of different kinds who can declare? Listen however to a truly wonderful fact. In the cook-house, they place seven cooking pots, one above the other, over one fire. The bottom pots are not cooked, but the top one is!" In this manner they tell a number of tales, and persuade the people to come. Having arrived, they direct them to the different houses saying, 'This is the holy land, here the fruit of your pious actions is enjoyed. Come, I will obtain for you an interview with Juggernaut. and cause you to bathe in the five holy places, viz. Indradummun tank, Lokenath do. Seeta-gunga do. Chokerteeth Sea, and Markunda tank, thus you will obtain salvation for seven generations of your ancestors: *but bear in mind how you will propitiate me.*' In this way they lead them to the temple, and give them a sight of Juggernaut. At that time many priests surround them, and stroking their heads, exclaim, 'Behold the visible god glorified! present him with an offering of 25 rupees; give us a present of ten rupees; come quickly, no delay.' In this way, by much talking, they wheedle them out of their money, and take all they can get. Others come begging to their lodgings. If they have no more money, these *pundas* coax them out of a promissory note, and make them engage to pay when they reach home. They also make a number of cakes, and bring for the pilgrims to eat. For that which is worth four annas they extract 12—for an anna's worth they take six annas. If they refuse to have them, they abuse them with filthy curses and speeches and say, 'You—where will you get such food as this!' Thus saying they cram it by main force into their mouths. Thus the *pundas* exceedingly oppress the people, and by a variety of cheating tricks get from them their wealth. Sometimes when the pilgrims enter the enclosure of the temple, they steal the ornaments from their noses and ears, and take away their clothes and money. If they resist, the *pundas* assemble and beat them till they make off, crying out, 'O father, O mother, I die, I die!' and thus they escape from the temple. Or if the *pundas* see a beautiful young woman, they allure her in the temple, and seduce her, let her go, telling her, 'This is a holy place, and I am a holy man. By having surrendered your person to me it is purified; the sins of a million births are destroyed; know that you have certainly enjoyed Juggernaut. God and his worshipper are inseperable.' On other occasions giving the pilgrims some potion to eat, they render them insensible, and rob them of their wealth. I have seen from five to ten boys watch near the gate for a single pilgrim; then laying hold of him, they beat him till he cries out, 'Mercy! mercy!' but no one coming to his assistance, he sinks down through much beating: then becoming insensible through fear, they rob him of his property and decamp."

It may be presumed that *the establishment at the temple of Juggernaut* must be very considerable. One of the head men stated to Col. Phipps, that the number consisted of 3000 families, including 400 families of cooks to prepare holy food. The following account was procured for the author, written on the leaf of a tree, by a native of Pooree.

1. "The *Moodeerut* as the Rajah of Koorda s representative with Juggurnaut, at all the festivals moves about the light, performs the daily service before him, and makes the offering of food.

2. There are three head *Pundas,* who having poured out clarified butter on the fire, and worshipped the sun and the divine regents of the gates, present the sacrificial articles from the kitchen, to the three gods at three of the daily offices, until the period of Juggernaut's retiring to rest.

3. There are three *Pushoo-palas,* who perform worship between the periods of the regular service; and ascending the throne of Juggernaut, clothe him in the three different dresses appropriated to the three services.

4. The *Bheet-baboo* guards the sacrificial food before it has been offered, prevents the crowd pressing on it, and should the smallest blemish be found in it, (such as an hair or an ant) he seizes and punishes the Pundas.

5. The *Tulubu Purehchas* guard Juggernaut when he retires to rest. In their absence the *Pushoo-palas* act in their stead.

6. The *Potee-muhapatra,* at twelve periodical festivals, make the proper offerings, aud move about the image of Soodha-buden; and at the great bathing festival, when Juggernaut moves out to the Neeladree beej, worship him during his progress, and during the fifteen succeeding days when *he is supposed to be ill, not having recovered from the effects of his bath !*

7. The *Patree-buroo* arranges the sacrificial articles, and calls the Pundas to worship.

8. The *Gora-buroo,* at the time of worship, places the water pot and presents the water to the officiating priest.

9. The *Khootiya* calls the *Phashoo-paluks* who are appointed *to wake Juggernaut,* and bring forward the vestments and necklaces with which he is to be invested.

10. The *Paneeya-mekab* presents the ornaments to Juggernaut to the *Pushoo-paluk,* and counts them as they come from Juggernaut's body; and likewise counts to the *Pureechas* any new ornaments offered by pilgrims.

11. The *Changra-mekab* carries the vestments of Juggernaut, and counts them out and puts them away.

12. The *Bhandar-mekab* counts out the ornaments when taken off from Juggernaut by the *Paneeya-mekab.* The vestments, presented by pilgrims, pass into their custody after they have been worn.

13. The *Suwar-buroo* sweeps the place, and places the sacrificial dishes before Juggernaut, presents odours to those who wake him and distributes flowers among the servants and worshippers.

14. The *Pureeksha-buroo* holds up a looking glass to Juggernaut during worship.

15. The *Ukhundu-mekab,* or lamp-lighter, places lights and removes the lamps,

16. The *Pureeyarees* watch at the gates and doors.

17, The *Dab-khat* brings out Juggernaut's bed!

18. The *Pureeyaree* of the southern gate cries out, 'the sacrificial food is coming.'

19. The *Pureeyarees* of the gate watch the food, and when Juggernaut moves out, carry with him the sweet smelling wood.

20. The *Jaya* and *Vijuya-Pureeyarees* allow no one to enter while Juggernaut is at his meals; and there are two watchmen at the door of the inner room where Juggernaut partakes of his food.

21. The *Khurgu-nayuk*, at the close of the daily offices, presents the paun to the officiating priests to be given to Juggeruaut; and on the occasion of the last daily office, offers it himself.

22. The *Khatsuya-mekab carries Juggernaut's bed to him at night for him to sleep on; and carries it back to its place in the morning.*

23. The *Mook-pakhul pureeyaree* presents *the water and the tooth-pick* to Juggernaut, and inspects every thing respecting the temple.

24. The *Suwar-Kota* prepares the cakes, and delivers them to the *Maha-Suwar*.

25. The *Maha-Suwar* brings the first service of cakes.

26. The *Gopal-bullubha* distributes it.

27. The *Bhatee-buroo* places food of a particular description before the Idol.

28. The *Rosh-payeed* lights the lamp in the kitchen, and expels the *suwars* when they become unclean; he accompanies the royal offering of food as far as the Juya and Vijuya gate.

29. The *Beeree-buha-suwar* takes the articles of paun from the *Sumurthas*, and delivers them to the *Suwars*.

30. The *Dhoa-pakhaliya* brahmun washes and cleanses the kitchen.

31. The *Unga-buha* brahmun removes the ashes from the cook-room, and throws them away.

32. The *Dita-suwaree* carries the image of Juggernaut when necessary, and prepares the image.

33. The *Datya* paints the image, and fastens the flags on his carriage.

34. The *Dwar-nayuk* is employed in opening and shutting the door.

35. The *Mahajkun* carries the image of Juya aud Vijuya, the two heavenly porters.

36. The *Beeman-buroo* carries the image of Juggernaut and fixes it in its place.

37. The *Moodolee-bhandur* guards the door, and puts the *chamura* into the hands of the distinguished pilgrims who desire to fan Juggernaut; and locking, guards the door of Juya and Vijuya, the two heavenly porters.

38. The *Chootar* holds the umbrella over the great god when he proceeds on a journey.

39. The *Turasee* holds before him the *turas* (a large fan) when he goes on a journey.

40. The *Meg-dumboora* proceeds with the *Meg dumboora* when he goes on a journey.

41. The *Moodra* holds the lamp when an offering of flowers is made to Juggernaut.

42. The *Paneeya-put* delivers the water pots to the *Buroo*, and washes them.

43. The *Keehuleea*, at all the stated festivals, during the service and during the offering of flowers, performs worship, and plays the *Kahulee*.

44. The *Ghuntooa* rings the bell during Juggernaut's meals, and when he goes on journeys!

45. The *Chumputee-tumukreeya,* at the time of *pusoowa* and during journeys, plays the tumuk.

46. The head *Punda* calls all the servitors to their duty, gives the golden sceptre to the *Pureecha,* and gives food to the Brahmuns of the *Mooktee mundupa.*

47. The *Ghutuwaree* prepares the sandal wood and gives it to the *mekaps;* and at one of the festivals, goes before the image with the incense.

48. The *Buree Deega* supplies the water for cooking; and removes the remains of food.

49. The *Sumundha* pounds peas of one kind, and grinds peas of another kind.

50. The *Gruhu-mekab* cleans the dishes after the principal meal.

51. The *Yogukuma* brings forward the articles of the principal meal.

52. The *Tomabutee* accompanies the principal evening meal with a lamp, and brings the pots and cooking utensils.

53. The *Chaulbacha* cleanses the rice and the peas.

54. The *Elek* carries the Chukru or discus of Vishnoo before the Idol when he moves out, and is a general superintendent.

55. The *Patrok,* having dismissed the attendants, cleans the temples, and *there* retires to rest.

56. The *Choonara* serves the image of Guroora (the bird god,) has charge of the great standard of the temple, and lifts the great lamp.

57. The *Khurga dhoaneeya* cleanses the space between the western part of the temple and the place called Jugunmohun.

58. The *Nagadhya washes Juggernaut's linen, and hangs it up to dry!*

59. The *Daree ganee* sings the songs which precede the anointing of Juggernaut with sandal wood.

60. The *Pooran-punda* reads the Pooranas in the gate of Juggernaut.

61. The *Beenkar* plays the *beena,* a musical instrument.

62. The *Tunubobuk* dances in the spot called Jugunmohun.

63. The *Sunkhooa* sounds the shell during the offices of worship.

64. The *Madolee* plays on the *madol,* a musical instrument, during worship.

65. The *Tooree-nayuk* plays on the *tooree* or trumpet.

66. The *Muhasetee* washes the linen of Juggernaut.

67. The *Paneepaee mahar* removes all filth from within the enclosure.

68. The *Hakeemeeshristar-buru-pureecha* is the great judge of all questions; he holds the golden cane."

A London Paper in 1841 contained the following additional information upon this subject. "From a return prepared for the House of Lords, we learn that there are about sixty officers to dress and ornament the idol of the temple of Juggernaut, and three hundred watchmen, day and night, who, if they allow any one to enter who is not admissible, and thereby defile the food for the idol, have to make good the food if they do not secure the offender. There are twenty keepers of the wardrobe of the idol, forty to ornament and perfume the idol, three "duts" to paint the eye brows, &c., of the idol different colours, and three servants to see that the several officers perform their several duties. There are, further, three hundred cooks, to prepare rice, &c., to make sweetmeats and the like; ten persons to take charge of the vessels with which the "pundahs" perform "poojah," and to hand them to the latter; ten to supply water whenever required; one to keep watch at the door *whilst the idol is asleep*, and to affix a seal on the door during the time. There is also a servant to witness the opening of the door "when the idol wakes," with the view of making sure that the seal on the door had not been broken during the slumbers of the idol; and there are further twenty keepers of the keys, and twenty keepers of the doors, to complete the list of officers to the temple of Juggernaut—there being, therefore, no fewer than 641 persons, whose sole duty it is to take charge of this celebrated Indian temple!"

At the temple of Juggernaut there are *thirteen festivals in the year*, which have been particularized. The most popular of them are, the *snan* or bathing festival, when the idol Juggernaut is exhibited on some part of the wall of the temple, and the water of the Ganges poured over it; and the *ruth* festival, when as previously described, the three idols, Juggernaut, Bulbudra his brother, and Soobudra his sister, are brought out of the temple, and taken in large cars to the extremity of the city. These monthly festivals cause a constant ingress of pilgrims to the city, and it has been observed "Juggernaut is the great resort of pilgrims from all parts of India; the number of which, according to a low calculation, is 1,200,000 persons annually." I think this estimate is too high, but the number of these "weary wanderers after rest" is very great, and may well excite the deepest sympathy of the Christian heart. Mr. Lacey gives the following particulars of the ruth Jattra of 1838, which may be considered 'a peep behind the scene.'

"I have gathered some information respecting the festival, some part of which I did not know before. The stupidity of the people is amazing. The Christian's faith gives existence to things future and unseen; the Hindoo's faith contradicts the senses. He sees a block of wood, but believes it a spirit; a temple of stone, but believes it gold; a car of wood, but believes it gold; sand, but believes it particles of diamonds! filthy biragees and brahmuns, but believes them holy and heavenly saints and gods; hears lying, unclean talk, cursing, blasphemy, sees adultery, theft, robbery, murder, but believes there is no sin in Pooree; sees disease, misery, or death, but believes that Pooree is Bhogkonta, where neither disease, misery, or death, comes; sees the car drawn by the strength of men, yet believes the god moves it himself! Juggernaut's temple is apart from his wife Lockshmee. She has a temple appropriated to herself and Surruswottee the daughter of Brumha. When he takes his ride in his car at the Ruth festival, the greatest care is taken lest she should hear of his going, otherwise she would prevent it; he steals away therefore unknown to his wife. After he has been gone about four days, she gets to hear that her husband is gone, and is in a terrible rage and all her establishment of priests and servants with her. This rage is vented by the lowest and most abusive epithets as, O that black-faced wretch! O that vile destroyer * * * * A wretch, but I will reckon with the debauched wretch! Lockshmee now orders preparations to be made for following her husband to beat him and bring him back. These preparations are set about with spirit by her priests and they frequently fight with Juggernaut's people if they meet them. When ready she is conveyed with flaming jealousy and wrath to the car of her husband, and there begins in the lowest manner to abuse him and curse him, and apply every possible epithet of obscenity to him, and all her priests unite in abusing him and his servants. She then proceeds to attack his car, and serious apprehension is entertained that injury will be done. Meanwhile Juggernaut confesses his crime, and says not a word in his own defence, and sends word to his enraged partner that he trusts that she will moderate her anger. This she rejects with indignation, and at length Juggernaut is driven to employ the mediation of Mahadab to settle the matter. Messengers are sent with all speed for two gods named Sowkasmer and Markundasmer. These mediators are brought in haste and state, and are introduced to the lord of the world; he is glad to see them, tells them his troubles with tears, and begs their interference. These undertake the task and proceed to the feet of the goddess. Here they unite their hands in humble posture, repeat hymns in her praise, speak of the penitence of her husband, remind her that the salvation of thousands of poor sinners depends on his going abroad, and finally promise that he shall soon return. They barely succeed however in restraining her violence, she consents to return to her temple, but vows vengeance on the guilty head of her husband, and that for herself she will never see his black face again. As she departs she throws handsful of sand, broken pots, &c. into Juggernaut's face, saying, O thou black-faced, who destroyedst the virtue of 16,000 gopees, who was kicked and cursed for thy vileness, can I expect to escape sorrow from thee? O thou black monkey-faced wretch who telledst thy wife was stolen in the jungle, and went about like a fool crying to this tree, and that monkey, "Saw you Seta, O saw you Seta!" O wretch, why should I think to escape sorrow! On her return she calls at the car of Juggernaut's sister, and abuses her freely, saying, O you * * * * * * what he has put ornaments on your arms, and a beautiful saree on your filthy body has he? O may fire be put into your face, you shame-faced wretch, who does not feel ashamed to elope with another woman's husband, and that her own brother, &c. Then she passes on to her temple. Thus things remain till Juggernaut returns to his temple, when, lo, the doors are closed against him. He sends to know the reason of this, and is informed that Lockshmee is highly offended and will not admit him. A great anxiety is now manifested by the poor lord of the world as to what is to be done; message after message is sent to no effect, he confesses, asks forgiveness, promises all she wishes, but all in vain; at last a happy thought occurs to one of his priests, that perhaps a present may appease the angry Lockshmee's mind. This scheme is immediately adopted, and ear-rings, nose-rings, armlets, anklets, beautiful sarees, &c., &c., are arranged on splendid salvers, and carried in procession to the feet of Lockshmee. When she sees all these nice fine things her anger becomes appeased, and she exhibits a half smile, and says to the messengers, O a black-faced wretch! a * * * * Well open the doors and let him come in! The doors are now thrown open, reconciliation proclaimed with acclamation, and the lord of the world enters his temple cheered by his devotees and worshippers, and even smiled upon by his angry wife!"

Pilgrims are sometimes seen *measuring their way to Juggernaut by constant prostrations.* The writer saw three cases of this kind.

When Dr. Buchanan visited Juggernaut's temple in June 1805, he observed—" I passed a devotee laying himself down at every step, measuring the road to Juggernaut by the *length of his body, as a penance* of merit to please his god." Mr. Lacey some years ago, furnished an affecting account of one of these wretched pilgrims that he beheld. " I had my attention arrested by a poor creature who was measuring his way to Juggernaut, by his own body, or rather by half its length : he never rose upon his feet, but only upon his knees, when on his knees he reached his hands forward, and then drew his body forward a little ; every time he made this advance, he beat his forehead against the ground three times, looking towards the temple, which was now in sight. When I got sufficiently near I called to him, but he did not appear to hear what I said, and continued on his way without paying the least attention. I succeeded in stopping him : a deep melancholy sat visible upon his countenance, his lips moving with prayer to his god, in a low grumbling tone of voice. When I had surveyed him a few moments he gave over repeating, and I began to converse with him as well as I was able. I first enquired how far he had come in that manner? he answered 750 miles ; how long have you been on the way? about eight months ; he appeared about twenty-one years of age, and was so emaciated by his austerities that his voice was nearly gone."

Immolations under the wheels of the Cars appear to have been of frequent occurrence. The Brethren unite their testimony in confirmation of this appalling fact. In July 1826, Mr. Lacey thus describes one of these horrid martyrdoms. "This afternoon I had an awful subject for my discourse, the body of a poor man crushed to pieces by the car of Juggernaut. The massy wheel had passed over his loins, and had nearly severed his upper from his lower parts; his bowels and blood had gushed out, and presented a sight too shocking to look upon. It was one of the most horrid spectacles I ever beheld; and while standing by it, I became quite ill with sickness, and every limb shivered with horror. The wheels of these cars are made for this work of death most effectually, as the spokes project three or four inches beyond the felloe. The poor wretch threw himself from the front of the car, and so became a voluntary sacrifice. He seemed a respectable man, apparently a Hindoostanee and a brahmin. I felt myself very much indisposed this evening, but could not lose this opportunity of witnessing against the system, which produced such effects: I felt my own mind in a serious frame, took my stand over the body, and spoke with some feeling of the nature of the Hindoo religion, and compared it with that of Christ;—and, perhaps, I never had a more serious congregation. Some hardened wretches said 'See, Sir, the glory of Juggernaut!' pointing to the mangled body. Concluded with recommending them to look to Jesus Christ for mercy and salvation, which Juggernaut could never give."

The Report of 1841 refers to the same fact. "Messrs. Lacey and Sutton, from Cuttack, with Stubbins and Wilkinson, from Berhampore, accompanied by several native brethren, attended the last car festival at Pooree. As this was the first Jattra since the abolition of the tax, it was confidently predicted that the attendance would be overwhelming, but so far from this being the case, there were fewer pilgrims from a distance than they ever remembered to have seen. Some Europeans calculated the whole attendance at the festival at thirty thousands, and none at more than fifty thousands; but on some former occasions the Missionaries have seen an assemblage of at least two hundred thousands. Though the concourse of pilgrims was so much smaller than formerly, the horrors of idolatry were not less apparent. One miserable pilgrim immolated himself under the wheels of Juggernaut's car. His brains were dashed out, and he instantly died. At another time during the festival, in consequence of a sudden rush of the frantic crowd, many persons were entangled in the ropes of the car. The car rolled over dozens. Six were taken up quite dead, several more insensible, who were sent to the hospital. This caused a perfect ecstacy of delight among Juggernaut's worshippers, because of the renown thus accruing to the festival of 1840.—Reiterated shouts of triumph and loud flourishes from their barbaric instruments of music were heard till midnight."

The *mortality attendant and consequent upon the pilgrimages* exceeds conception, and in its statements is almost beyond the bounds of credibility. "Idolatry," says Dr. Carey, "destroys more than the sword, yet in a way which is scarcely perceived. The number who die in their long pilgrimages, either through want or fatigue, or from dysentery and fever, is incredible." The Report of 1842, contains a very pathetic description how "their sorrows are multiplied that hasten after another god."—"A relation of the miseries and mortality of Juggernaut's pilgrims (says Mr. Lacey) I consider to be a business which I may not resume or dismiss, as a reader's feelings may dictate: it is a duty, an imperative duty. And once a year at least, that is on occasion of this wasting festival, so long as I am spared to attend it, I must let the world know, I must let the friends of humanity know, something of what is going on in that part where God's providence has placed me. On the former part of my journey while the light of the day enabled me to see them, I met with many dead; some of them were in the mud of the road which was nearly knee deep, others had crept under trees, or under the eaves or sheds of houses by the way side, and died there, some lay on the grass beside the road with their eyes picked out by ravens and crows, others again seemed to have died in the act of drinking water from the jeels or pools, or from the trench which runs parallel with the road, not being able to rise from their position. In the towns, and near the saries by which I passed, there was a large collection of corpses about which the dogs howled, and the vultures screamed. The circumstances of the pilgrims were most pitiable, and greatly productive of the fatal disease which was thinning their ranks. The incessant and heavy rain, had completely soddened their clothes to their skin. They lay by hundreds, in rows by the road side, and the pelting rain had battered their garments into the sand and mud of the ground. Weak and weary, and without proper food, they were fully prepared for an attack of the cholera, and they were presently carried off when attacked. When their companions arose to pursue their journey, how many they left who were never to rise any more! My wonder is, that considering the destitution and exposure of the people, they are not destroyed in much greater numbers. When the light of the morning returned, the same miserable and destructive scenes presented themselves to my view, till I arrived at my house."

Had this state of things been found in a part of the world before unknown to our countrymen, it would have been a subject of great surprise and pungent regret to the philanthropist and the christian; but the darkest shade in this picture is yet to be laid—the climax of the description of a people "sitting in darkness and the region and shadow of death," is yet to be told, and it is this—"Be astonished, O ye heavens, at this, and be horribly afraid, be ye very desolate, saith the Lord"—Britain, the mother of nations, the patroness of civilization, the liberator of the slave, the messenger of Christianity to the nations over whom her sceptre waves—has been found regulating and supporting, promoting and amassing wealth from the absurd and cruel Idolatry of Juggernaut's temple. Hamilton, in his valuable '*Description of Hindostan*," 2 vols. 4to., says,—"Possession was taken of the Town and Temple of Pooree by the British, Sep. 18, 1803—*the sacred will of the Idol, being first ascertained through the medium of the officiating Priest!*"—Is the historian in earnest, or in jest? Did our countrymen in arms, act so unworthy a part as to tamper with the superstition of the people, by condescending to ask at the shrine of the modern Baal, whether they should be peaceably admitted or not? *Proh dolor!* No British superintendence of the temple existed during the administration of the Marquis of Wellesley, whose enlightened mind firmly objected to any connexion with Juggernaut; but on his Lordship's return to England, a system was adopted in 1806 and 1809, for the regulation of the temple, making it a source of wealth to its professedly Christian Rulers, the details of which, to use the language of scripture, should cause "the ears of every one that heareth it to tingle."—This system, as Sterling shews, was a return to the mercenary and persecuting spirit of the Moguls, who gained possession of Orissa in the sixteenth century, and of their successors in power and oppression, the Mahrattas—unworthy leaders of the policy of enlightened Britain.

The following sketch of this system (though now happily abolished) shows the *entrenched power of Idolatry at Juggernaut's Temple, on the arrival of the Missionaries.* "The superintendence of the temple and its interior economy are vested in the Rajah of Khoorda. The Govenor General in Council posseses the power of removing the Rajah or any of his successors from this superintendence, on proof of misconduct. The superintendent of the temple is authorised to punish instances of neglect or misconduct by imposing small fines, or by removing the offender (if not one of the three head Purchas) from his office: *the amount of fines to be carried to the account of Government.* The three dewul Purchas are to be appointed by the Collector of Cuttack, subject to the confirmation of Government. In the event of orders being issued by the Rajah contrary to the recorded rules and institution of the temple, a representation is to be made to the Collector of the tax for the orders of the Governor General in Council, if it appear necessary. The third dewul Purcha shall give account to the Collector of the tax of *all offerings and presents made to the Idol.* The Collection of the tax is intrusted to an officer with the official designation of "The Collector of the Tax on Pilgrims," subject to the authority of the Collector of Cuttack; the general superindence of the collections, and the control of the officer in the performance of that duty, is vested in the Board of Revenue at Fort William. The avenues for the admission of pilgrims shall be confined to two Ghauts, Atturah Nullah on the north* and Ghaut Lokenauth on the south-west of the town of Juggernaut Pooree. The pilgrims liable to the tax shall be divided into four classes—*laul jattrees, nim lauls, bhurrungs, punj tirthees,* including the following persons of low cast who are not permitted to enter the temple.† The rate of tax payable by the different classes is as follows, viz. pilgrims of the first class from the north, passing the Atturah Nullah, pay a tax of *ten rupees;* from the south, passing Lokenaut, *six rupees.* Pilgrims of the second class from the north pay *five rupees*; from the south *three rupees.* Pilgrims of the third class, from either north or south, pay *two rupees.* Pilgrims of the fourth class, passing either Ghauts pay *two rupees.* A pilgrim of the first class is allowed free access to the temple for thirty days,

* We have authorised the disbursement of 10,206 rupees for the construction of a wall in the vicinity of Juggernaut's temple, in the district of Cuttack. The work was stated to be necessary for the purpose of preventing the pilgrims from forcing their way to the temple, and by those means evading payment of the established tax. Par. Papers, 1813. p. 20. Hamilton's Hind. Vol. ii. p. 55—57.

† These are kusbee, *prostitutes;* cullal, *liquor sellers;* machoowa, *fishermen;* numosooder, *boatmen;* ghooskee, *private bad women;* gazur, *labourers who carry burdens on their heads;* baugdee *fishers, labourers;* joogee, *weavers;* kahar bawry, *bearers;* raujbunsee, *different cast of boatmen;* chamar, *shoe makers;* dhomee, *washermen;* paun, *basket makers;* teor, *another cast of boatmen;* bhoinmalee, *makers of garlands, &c. for marriages;* haddee, *maters.* These sixteen casts are not suffered to enter the temple to worship Juggernaut.

constantly attended by a punda. He may be exempted from the attendance of these officers by *a further payment of ten rupees* to the Collector; and by surrendering his pass shall be allowed to remain in the town as long as he pleases. Pilgrims of the second class, at the Car Festival, are allowed access to the temple ten days; at other festivals seven days only. Pilgrims of the third class, at the Car Festival, are allowed five days; at other times but four; and must be attended by a punda. Pilgrims of the fourth class are *allowed to worship outside the temple* sixteen days. Pilgrims may enrol themselves in either of the first three classes on paying the prescribed tax. Printed certificates shall be procurable on the payment of the fixed tax, at the office of the Secretary to the Board of Revenue, the Collector of Cuttack and Ganjam, and at the two Ghauts. Form as follows:

"*A. B. inhabitant of ——— in the district of ———, having this day paid into this office the sum of sicca rupees, ——— is entitled to pass through the ——— Ghaut without further interruption, as a laul jattree to the cutchery of the Collector of the tax at Juggernaut. On producing this certificate to the said Collector, he is further entitled to receive a pass, and to have access to the temple thirty days.*"

Names, or designation of attendants.	*Amount of tax paid respectively.*	*Period for which to visit the temple.*

Forms No. 2, 3, and 4, differ only in the names of the class of pilgrims, the rate of tax, and the period of attendance at the temple. A pilgrim of the first class, desirous of visiting the temple with his family and attendants, not exceeding twenty persons, these must first pay the tax of the second or third class, and then they may stop as long as their master. The certificates shall be dated and attested by the *official seal*, the blank places filled up, &c. A pilgrim presenting the printed certificate is to be allowed to pass without interruption. The molestation of such an individual by the daroga at the Ghaut, shall be punished by a fine not exceeding his salary for three months, and dismissal from office. The duty of the Collector of Juggernaut is to superintend the conduct of the darogas. Pilgrims of the first, second, and third classes, having passed the Ghauts at Juggernaut, are to apply to the Collector for a *license of access to the temple*, in the following form:

"*A. B., inhabitant of ——— in the district of ———, is entitled to perform the customary ceremonies, under charge of ——— during ——— days, that is to say, from the ——— day of the month of ——— until the ——— day of the month of ———; and for that period you will afford to the holders hereof free access to the temple of Juggernaut. At the expiration of the period granted, you will return the license into the office of the Collector of tax.*"

The mischief of this unhallowed connexion of Britain with Idolatry, was further increased by the adoption of a *premium* to be paid by the wretched pilgrims to the *pilgrim hunters*, who had deluded and brought them. What infatuation in our countrymen! Hear the plea. The Collector of the Pilgrim Tax, in March 1806, wrote to the Governor-General at Calcutta—"As the pilgrims will never be well-treated by their conductors, unless they receive a present from their own hands, I beg leave to propose that the fees of the pundahs, &c., be *publicly fixed*, and collected by themselves, separate from the tax, as was formerly done under the Mahratta Govt." To this it was replied—"The Governor-General in Council approves of your proposition for permitting the pundahs to collect a fee of the pilgrims, exclusive of the tax; you will accordingly *fix the rate at which such fee should be levied, and publish the rates for general information at the temple, and in its vicinity*." Thus, a *bonus* was established upon the collection of pilgrims. Col. Phipps, who had been stationed at Juggernaut, informed the writer—"A purharee, in 1821, despatched 100 agents to entice pilgrims, and in the ensuing year, received the premium for 4000 pilgrims! He was busily employed in instructing 100 additional agents in all the mysteries of this singular trade, to send them into the Upper Provinces of India."—Could any line of policy have been more unchristian?

Harington's *Analysis of the Laws and Regulations of the East India Company*, vol. 3, p. 222, gives the following statement of

JUGGERNAUT.

	Rupees.
"Gross collection of Pilgrim Tax for 1815-16 (including seventy-two rupees mis. recepts)	53,725
Assessment of endowed lands	26,814
Sale of *holy food* *	5,488
	8)86,027
	£10,753

* "With the consent of the Purchas, I deputed an Aumeen to oversee and state the produce from the sale of holy food, the quantity and value of cloth presented for the purpose of being displayed on the wheel at the top of the temple, on which Government receives from the person presenting its full value as a fee, under the head of Dujja, exclusive of

	Rupees.
Deduct charges for establishment and contingencies	17,143
Expenses of Juggernaut's Temple	56,372
English cloth for three cars.	1,365
	74,880
Net collection	£11,147"

Dr. Buchanan, in his "Christian Researches," states, from official accounts, the annual expenses of the Idol Juggernaut, presented to the English Government, as follows:—

	Rupees.		£.
"Expenses of the table of the Idol..	36,116	or	4,514
Ditto of his dress or wearing apparel..	2,712	—	339
Ditto of the wages of his servants	10,057	—	1,373
Ditto of contingent expenses at the different seasons of pilgrimage	10,989	—	1,373
Ditto of his elephants and horses	3,030	—	378
Ditto of his ruth, or annual state carriage	6,713	—	839
Rupees	69,616		£8,792

"Thus (says *The Friend of India*, Oct. 1825,) *a regularity, a splendour, an attraction, are given to the worship of this Idol, and an impetus to the delusion it originates, which it never possessed under the former dynasty;* an impetus too, which, fatal as it is in its consequences to so many of our Hindoo fellow-subjects, is increasing with the gain it produces, which knows no bounds but the number of persons they are able to deceive from year to year; and these have no bounds but the inhabitants of Hindostan itself." Such was the state of things, at this high place of Idolatry,—its population increasing, its votaries triumphing in the favour and support of their Rulers, and the influence and glory of Juggernaut extending through the whole of Hindostan; when the Christian missionaries arrived in 1822, with the exhibition of gospel truth, to abash its nominally Christian Patrons, and with "the stone cut out of the mountain without hands, to smite the blasphemous Idol, till, like "the dust of the summer threshing-floor," the Idol and all its infamous atrocities, shall be found no more. Haste happy day!

It has been observed, "*If you would know the state of a people, look at the temple.*"—From thus reconnoitering the metropolis and citadel of the enemy, where, as Chamberlain said of Benares—

which, he has also to pay the fee of the Purchas and others, for their ministry during the ceremony." G. Webb, Collector of Tax, Dec. 1807. Par. Papers, 1813, p. 65.

"Satan sits enthroned," let us view the state of Orissa "in the length thereof, and in the breadth thereof;" and the necessity that existed for the introduction of Christianity, will be most evident. The Lord give "his word to have free course and be glorified," that, "his way may be known upon earth, his saving health among all people."

The state of a people is most clearly seen in their peculiar manners and customs. Those that relate to *caste*, the *degradation of the female sex*, the comparatively *stereotyped habits of the people*, &c., &c., have passed under review in the general history of the country; the customs which exhibit the nature and influence of Idolatry, naturally arrest the attention of the Christian philanthropist, viz., the *Suttee*, the *churuck Pooja*, *Infanticide*, *Human Sacrifices*, peculiar *Austerities*, the *neglect of the dying and the dead*, &c. No tongue can express, no pen depict, no heart conceive, the miseries of a people suffering from the sanguinary hydra of Hindoism. A brief description of these singular practices will demonstrate the value of Christian Missions.

The *Suttee*, or the burning and burying alive of the Hindoo widow, prevailed in Orissa, though not so extensively as in the adjacent Province of Bengal and other parts of India. In Dr. Carey's Bengalee Dictionary, the rite is thus described; "*Suttee*. From *sut*, good, chaste, pure, &c.; a woman who burns herself on her husband's funeral pile, being thought an irrefragable proof of her chastity." The Parliamentary Papers upon the Suttee, obtained through the late Sir T. F. Buxton, Bart., shew the number that perished in the different Presidencies.—"Total in ten years, (from 1815 to 1824,) 6632, give for the Cuttack division in 1821, 28—1822, 28—1823, 31—1824, 25." The author was present at a Suttee, at Cuttack, Aug. 19, 1824; but he prefers giving the account of one at the temple of Juggernaut, witnessed by his late colleague, Mr. Bampton. In Orissa, the woman was sometimes burnt in a pit; the author saw one of these pits at Juggernaut, but did not hear of the horrid deed till it had taken place, "so swift were their feet to shed blood."—What an appalling exhibition of the horrors of Idolatry, does the following relation contain. The account is dated, Juggernaut, July 7, 1824.

"The infatuated woman, whose death I witnessed, was the widow of a Brahmun who had died in the morning. The man's age seemed to have been about forty and the woman's thirty-five. The place where the Suttee took place was called Swurgu Dwar, which signifies the gate of heaven; and when I reached it I found the coolies employed in digging the hole, which was circular, about six feet deep, its diameter at bottom perhaps a little less than its depth, and at top twice as much. Soon after my arrival, about twelve persons came, each bringing a load of wood on his or her head; for several of them were women. I charged the labourers with being accessary to the crime about to be committed, and the general reply was, that they worked for money, and did this work as they did other work because they were paid for it. Carelessness or cheerfulness characterised all the Hindoos near or on the spot. The pit being finished, a quantity of water was mixed with cow-dung and sprinkled on the margin about one-third of the way down; two ropes were also well wetted with the same mixture. Inquiring the use of two bamboos which lay near, I was told they were *to stir the fire and turn about the bodies!* The bits of wood prepared for the occasion were between twelve or eighteen inches long, on an average five or six in circumference; a quantity of them were thrown into the pit, and a man at the bottom proceeded to set them up on their ends two or three thick round the sides; upon this he placed a second tier; and on the second, a third; he also covered the bottom perhaps five or six inches thick, so that the pit was now two-thirds lined with wood. Soon after all was finished, the dead man was brought on a rough bier, which I supposed might have been made in less than quarter of an hour. I soon saw the procession (if it may be called one), halting a few hundred yards before me: the crowd was kept off the woman by a square made of four pieces of wood, five or six feet long. The rabble were preceded by some of their rude music. Unwilling to see her burn herself, my worthy companions, Lieut. W. and T. B. Esq., tried several times to prevent the horrid deed, and I lent my feeble assistance, but all to no purpose. They halted twenty or thirty yards from the flaming pit, where the last effort was made, and, that failing, her infamous coadjutors gave her a lighted lamp, which I think she put into an earthen pot under her arm. In a little time all was confusion; and a scene, the most perfectly hellish that we ever saw, was presented; and a way was made for the woman to the pit, and its margin was left clear; she advanced to the edge facing her husband, and two or three times waved her right hand; she then hastily walked round the pit, and in one place I thought the flames caught her legs; having completed the circle, she again waved her hand as before, and then jumped into the fire * * * * * *

At this moment I believe the drums beat, and an infernal shout rent the air, but I can scarcely say I know—all was confusion. A dense smoke issued from the pit, entermixed at intervals with partial bursts of flame, occasioned by quantities of powdered resin thrown into the pit by handfuls. In a little time they allowed the fire to clear itself, and we then saw the wretched woman in the midst of it; I think her posture was that of sitting on her heels; she sometimes moved gently backward and forward, as if she bowed. The poor creature still kept an erect posture; but at length seemed partially to rise, and pitched forward with her head against the side of the pit, about two feet from her husband's left hand. The motion of her head in this position indicated pain, and she continued to live two or three minutes longer. The gentlemen then went home, but I stayed a little longer and saw the bodies taken out: for though the women are burnt in these pits, the bodies are taken out while distinguisable, and consumed in two different fires (at least that is the case here), and we are told it is done, that *the son may make sure of some fragments of both his parents to be thrown into the Ganges*. Now the ropes came into use; one was doubled and the middle thrown down to catch the man's chin, one or two bamboo levers were put under his head to raise it and get the rope round his neck; the rope was then twisted, in order to fasten it, and they began to draw, but they failed, for the rope slipped off. Another man then attempted to fasten the rope; he succeeded, and they drew up the body, with the exception, I think of the legs; but it was quiet dark, and nothing could be seen but by the light of the fire. They then tried

HINDOO SELF-TORTURE AT THE CHURUCK POOJA.

to raise the woman, but could not easily get the rope round her neck, so they put it on her arm, which projected in such a way as to favour their doing so; and, after twisting it well, they drew her nearly to the top of the pit: but they seemed afraid that they should lose her again if they trusted entirely to her arm, so she was held just below the edge of the pit till another man put the other rope under her chin, and she was then drawn quite up. Some of the people employed themselves in arranging the wood for the fires to consume the bodies, and I stayed perhaps ten minutes longer, finally leaving the bodies on the brink of the pit. Such are the facts, and I leave them to produce their proper effect."*

The *churuck Pooja* appears to have been as popular in Orissa as in Bengal. It is so called from *churuck*, a circle, the devotees being carried or whirled round in the air, suspended on a transverse beam, which turns on a pivot upon a substantial post in the ground; some are even carried on a hakery, or native carriage. It is a most disgusting and brutal exhibition. A friend in Calcutta, in March 1823, thus describes it:—"The places of the body which are pierced are, the back, the arms generally above the elbow, the sides, and the tongue. But the piercing is the least part of what is endured by the sufferers. The tongue being pierced, an iron rod is thrust through it, sometimes carried by the individual himself, and sometimes by one of the group of his attendants. One of these sufferers had the point of a bayonet fixed upon a musket through his tongue, and carried before him by the sepoy to whom it belonged, and thus he paraded the streets. Another had a live snake of five or six feet in length, the tail of which was thrust through the man's tongue, the head and part of the body remained twirling in frightful shapes above his head. A singular instance of audacity was seen this year: among the numerous groups there was a man having the iron through his tongue with the upper part fastened to the leg of a woman of ill fame, who was carried upon the shoulders of bearers in a chair precisely even with the man's head, and he dancing and frolicking below. Some are so determined to excel, that in order to insert a thicker rod, the tongue has been so far pierced as to leave merely a shred on each side, and it has happened that one side has given way, leaving the part of the tongue hanging on one side merely by a piece. The number of persons in Calcutta who thus torment themselves eaunot, it is supposed, be less than a thousand; in all probability it is much greater. Europeans are not likely to hear the tenth, or even a hundredth part of the evil that occurs from these practices. The natives are not sufficiently attached to each other to think the maiming or death of their countrymen of importance sufficient to induce them even to relate the fact,

* See Suttee's Cry to Britain, 1828, pp. 8-9.

unless it is elicited by some special circumstance, or inquiry should lead to the subject."

Infanticide was supposed to be almost confined to the Rajpoots of Western India, and it was not till within the last few years, that it was discovered to prevail to an awful extent among the Khunds of Goomsur, in Orissa. The following information is deeply affecting. The *Friend of India*, July 1841, stated—

"Meria Pooja or Human Sacrifice, takes place once a year, in one or other of the confederate Mootas in succession. The victims are stolen from the low country, or are brought from some other distant part, and sold to those Mootas where the sacrifices are performed. If children, they are kept until they attain a proper age. This cruel ceremony is thus performed. When the appointed day arrives, the Khunds assemble from all parts of the country, dressed in their finery, some with bear skins thrown over their shoulders, others with tails of peacocks flowing behind them, and the long winding feather of the jungle cock waving on their heads. Thus decked out, they dance, leap and rejoice, beating drums and playing on an instrument not unlike in sound to the Highland pipe. Soon after noon, the jani or presiding priest, with the aid of his assistants, fastens the unfortunate victim to a strong post which has been firmly fixed into the ground, and there standing erect, he suffers the cruel torture of having his flesh cut from his bones in small pieces, by the knives of the savage crowd who rush on him and contend with each other for a portion.

Great value is attached to the first morsel cut from the victim's body, for it is supposed to possess greater virtues, and a proportionate eagerness is evinced to obtain it; but considerable danger to the person of the operator attends the feat, for it happens also that *equal virtues are attributed to the flesh of the lucky holder of the first slice.* To guard against so disagreeable an appropriation a village will generally depute one of its number to endeavour to secure the much desired object, and they according arm him with a knife (mereri,) tie cloths round him, and holding on by the ends, at the appointed signal, rush *with three or four thousand others at the miserable sacrifice;* when, if their man should be successful in his aim, they exert their utmost efforts to drag him from the crowd. Should he escape unhurt, the whole turn their faces to their homes, for in order to secure its efficacy, they must deposit in their fields, *before the day has gone, the charm they have so cruelly won!* The intent of this human sacrifice is to propitiate Ceres.

In Guddapoor, another and equally cruel sacrifice frequently precedes the one already described. A trench, seven feet long, is dug, in which a human being is suspended alive by the neck and heels, fastened with ropes to stakes firmly fixed at each end of the excavation, so that to prevent strangulation, he is obliged to support himself with his hands over each side of the grave. The presiding priest, after going through some ceremonies in honor of the goddess Manekisiri, takes an axe and inflicts six cuts at equal distances from the back of the neck to the heels repeating the number one, two, &c., and at the seventh decapitates him—the body falls into the pit and is covered with earth, when the hellish orgies first described, are enacted. Women are sacrificed as well as men. Since the arrival of the troops in the Khund country, a female found her way into the Collector's camp at Pattingia, with fetters on her legs. She had escaped during the confusion of an attack on the Wulsa or hiding place of the people who had charge of her, by our men, and related that she had been *sold by her brother* to a mootikoo of one of the Pattingia Mootas,

INFANTICIDE AMONG THE KHUNDS IN GOOMSUR.

for the purpose of being sacrificed!! I need not say that she was instantly released, and that she adjured all further connexion with the people."

The form of Invocation to the Khund Goddess, forms an

INFERNAL HYMN.

Hail, mother, hail! hail goddess Bhobanee!
Lo, we present a sacrifice to thee,
Partake thereof, and let it pleasure give,
And, in return, let us thy grace receive.
With music's various sounds, on festive day
Lo! thee we worship, and thy rites obey.
Hail all ye gods who in the mountain dwell,
In the wild jungle or the lonely dell;
Come all, together come, with one accord,
And take the sacrifice we have prepared.
In all the fields, and all the plots we sow,
O let a rich and plenteous harvest grow;
O all ye gods and goddesses give ear,
And be propitious to our earnest prayer.
Behold a youth for sacrifice decreed,
Blooming with tender flesh, and flushed with blood;
No sire, no matron, says, This youth is mine,
His flesh, his blood, his life, his all, are thine;
Without the pale of sacred wedlock thrown,
We took and fed him for thy right alone.
Now lo! with rites from all pollution free,
We offer him, O Bhobanee, to thee:
Taste now this offering, satisfy thy heart,
And bid us joyful to our homes depart;
Taste now this offering, and propitious be,
And let us each, marks of thy favour see.

This extract was repeated from memory, by Abraham, a Khund boy, in the School at Cuttack, to Mr. Lacey, who translated it; he was then a great fat boy, and would soon have been sacrificed, had he not been rescued by the English Officers. He well remembers, and relates, how he was stolen from his mother. She was then a widow. They had laid down to sleep for the night, when the men entered the hut, and beating the mother and children, placed poor Abraham over their shoulders, blindfolded him, and carried him off. He is now sixteen years old and has been baptized."

One of the British Authorities, thus describes the scene represented in the engraving respecting Infanticide in Goomsur.—" They offer human sacrifices to their deities. The principal one is a peacock with three heads. From all I can learn, it would appear that the Chieftains of the different Districts take it by turns to offer a human sacrifice annually, to ensure prolific crops; but an offering is frequently made at other times, to avert or remove an evil. A spot being cleared in the immediate vicinity of the village, a girl, the most common sacrifice, is put to death by the blow of an axe. The body is then removed to the village; in the centre of which, a peacock carved in wood, with three heads, is placed on the top of a long pole, over which the blood of the victim is sprinkled. The body is then divided into as many parts as there are villages in the Mootab: each of these parts is again divided, so as to give a portion to each family; and these they again divide into the smallest possible pieces, which they bury in their houses or around their fields! The Molekoos frequently have a child, sometime children, purchased, or taken in their marauding exhibitions in the low country, to bring up for this express purpose: they treat them with kindness, perhaps for years, till they are required for an offering: the more full-grown and perfect, the better: a male, though less common, is prefered."*

Human sacrifices were found to exist, nor is this a subject of surprise, when it is known that they are formally enjoined in the Hindoo code of laws and religious ceremonies. Mr. Lacey wrote, in June 1827,—"A human sacrifice has lately been offered near Cuttack. *Human sacrifices are more frequent than is generally apprehended.* Every possible precaution is taken to keep them secret, so that few are heard of. In the present instance the sacrifice was a young child, a boy. His parents are of the soodra caste. He was either bought or stolen from them by the sacrificer. It seems probable, that the person who offered the sacrifice had made a vow to the goddess to offer a beautiful child in case of some favour granted. Hence, the boy chosen was of very respectable parents, about five years of age, and very handsome. How the ceremony was performed I do not know; but most likely by cutting off the head, as bodies and heads of human sacrifices have been found. And the goddess Kalee, of the Hindoos, is represented as being pleased with the flow of blood. I have witnessed the sacrifices of goats and buffaloes to Kalee, in Bengal, and this was the manner of sacrificing them. It is therefore most probable that the blood and head of the child, were carried immediately before the image and offered to her. The Brahmun, to conceal the murder, after offering the sacrifice, took the body of the victim, cut it into small pieces, and boiled it in a large earthen pot, in which it seems he intended to bury it. This was a most secure method, as the boiling disfigured the flesh, and no one here could suspect flesh being in a handy. It seems he was detected in boiling it. The *perpetrator* and the *idol* were brought before the magistrate of Cuttack, and a minute investigation ensued. The evidence appeared clear against the Brahmun. We, however, condemn no one without oaths! and, the murderer being a Brahmun, not one of the witnesses would swear against him, as it would have taken his life.

* See *Infanticide in India,* 1844, p. 22.

In this manner the murderer was quitted of all charges, though it appeared evident he was guilty of the crime."*

"Mr. N. told me (says Mr. Sutton,) that he feared *human sacrifices were frequent*. He mentioned that a little while ago, when the cholera raged here, that several of the people declared that Kalee had appeared to them, and said if they would sacrifice a man to her, she would stop it. He afterwards mentioned another circumstance, with which he appeared to be well acquainted. During the Ganjam fever, the servants of a Mr. M——, who was often in the habit of giving them money for their ceremonies, asked him for 500 rupees, which he gave them. But another servant, a Mussulman, who I suppose, was jealous of their obtaining so much, went to Mr. M. and told him they were about to offer a human sacrifice. He immediately called them back, and told them he thought they were about to attend to some *innocent* ceremonies, but he would be no party in murder; and of course made them return the money."†

Mr. Lacey records the following appalling fact in his journal:—"This morning Capt. C——, a very respectable officer of the Company's service, called on us and related the following awful instance of human sacrifice, which he discovered about a year ago, in the neighbourhood of his own station. On the occasion of a new Resident, one of the Company's tributary rajah's vowed to sacrifice twenty men to Kalee, if she would grant him a prosperous interview. He set out for the residency, and twenty men were seized, shaved, fasted, and anointed. He obtained a favourable interview, and as soon as he returned home, the twenty victims were beheaded, and their blood poured out before the image of Kalee. This account may be fully depended upon; Capt. C—— mentioned that human sacrifices are by no means uncommon in the part of India where he resides, which is in the Nagpore Residency. It is more than probable that human sacrifices exist under all tributary and independent rajahs."‡

Lawson, in his *Orient Harpings*, describes one of these deeds of darkness.§ The following are the concluding lines,—

"Not so
Died the pale boy this night, for he was led
Through the dark village to the place of death,
Where oft had died before him other boys.
Steady, inflexible, the Brahmuns walk

* Sutton's Narrative, pp. 288-9. † pp. 223-4.
‡ Gen. Bap. Repository, 1830, p. 312.—§ Vol. 1823, p. 103.

Behind, before, on either side, and calm
Chatter, and smoke, and smile. Some there are lean
And wrinkled, who betray that they are old:
With peevish self-conceit, they boast of skill
In learned books and righteous acts, and sputter
With toothless rage in pious controversy.
Others of broad and brawny limb, and step
Proud and majestic, toss the graceful poita;
And, unconcerned in matters of dispute,
Swagger with bloated face, and ogling eyes,
And muslin girded loins, and slip-shod heels
Triumphant. Younger ones are there, who pert
And slim, march in the infernal throng. No heart
In their brass bosoms throbs with shame, or fear,
Or pity. Never do they inwardly
Relent, or with reluctance plunge a soul
Into eternity.—They have arrived!
Eager they come! they urge the trembling youth!
Poor fellow! how he falters with the cold sweat
Bathing his forehead, and with speechless tongue
And chattering teeth. Of curious arch and turret
There stands the temple with its grinning queen,
Kalee, of bottomless darkness born, obscene.
There bends the neck of the poor quaking lad
A human sacrifice. The hatchet falls!
The crash alone is heard—the guggling blood
Is on the ground, the priests have done their work,
And coldly walk away; they find their home,
Nor feel one sting of guilt."

Various *austerities* are practised among the people, too justly descriptive of the system of Idolatry prevalent in India. At the temple of Juggernaut, persons may be seen having their heads covèred with earth, so that it would appear impossible to breathe, or sitting between two or three fires; or, (as the author has seen at Cuttack,) a man resting upon a piece of wood suspended from a tree, and not permitting himself to lie down for weeks; or with his arm elevated till it has stiffened. "While I was talking (says Mr. Sutton,) a byragge passed me with his left arm stiff, and his fingers rotted off."

The *Exposure of the dying and the dead*, strongly marks the character of the people.—"Pages (says Mrs. Lacey,) would not be sufficient to detail the miseries of the deluded worshippers of Juggernaut. The poor pilgrims were to be seen in every direction dead, and in the agonies of death; lying by fives, tens, and twenties. Mr. L. counted upwards of ninety in one place, and in another Mr. Bampton counted one hundred and forty. In the hospital at Juggernaut, I have seen thirty dead at once, and numbers in the agonies of death; and *even the living using the dead bodies for pillows!*"—Oh the miseries of this horrible superstition! Where the Suttee has slain its thousands, Pilgrimages have slain their tens of thousands! Myriads die in journeying to reputed holy places, unknown, unpitied, and unnoticed:—penury, famine, exposure, and sickness, lay numerous objects of superstition, at various stages of the destructive route, unnoticed and unburied, a prey to birds and beasts. The European who has visited Juggernaut at the great festival, may be forcibly reminded of the appalling description:—

"——He saw the lean dogs
Gorging and growling o'er carcase and limb,
They were too busy to bark at him.
From a pilgrim's skull they had stript the flesh
As ye peel a fig when the fruit is fresh;
And their white trunks crunsh'd o'er their whiter skull
As it slipt through their jaws when their edge grew dull;
As they lazily mumbled the bones of the dead
When they scarce could stir from the place where they fed;
So well had they broken a lingering fast
With those who had fallen for that repast."

It cannot be necessary to dwell upon the *moral and spiritual state* of such a people. This is most palpably evident in these harrowing details. Christianity, like an angel of mercy, enters a land thus filled "with mourning and lamentation and woe," and says, in the language of the apostle Paul to the jailer, "*Do thyself no harm. Believe on the Lord Jesus Christ, and thou shalt be saved, and thy house.*" I know not better how to close this chapter, than in the touching appeal of Mr. Sutton, when, as an eye witness, his heart was bleeding for the miseries of the Oreahs.

"Were the divine Saviour to travel through Orissa, as he did through Judea, it would doubtless be said of him, that *he had compassion on the multitudes because they fainted and were as sheep scattered abroad, having no shepherd.* It is strikingly the case with this poor people, for though apparently the most religious people on earth, yet in reality they have no one to guide them; they have no faith, nor confidence in any of their shasters; and as to all the consolations of even a false religion, they are eminently without God in the world, having no hope. One perhaps picks up a few sentences from the fragments of some old poem. Another gets hold of a few sage maxims from some celebrated gooroo. A third has sufficient strength of mind to see the futility of all the popular nostrums, and is constantly unhappy and unsettled till he settles down in infidelity respecting all religion. The majority go to the festivals, and receive the muntra from the gooroo, because others do so. But scarcely a man is to be found whose mind is at rest respecting even the hopes held out to him by his own system. So true is it, that—

"In vain would boasting reason find,
The way to happiness and God,
Her weak directions leave the mind,
Bewildered in a dubious road."

"Let the friends of the mission remember, that Orissa looks to them for all the knowledge of the way of life, that she can hope to receive for many years to come. Besides yours there is no eye to pity, no hand to save, not a soul cares for her idolatries, and perishing multitudes, but you: and will you cease to pity, will you cease to help, to pray, to feel for her deeply and constantly? Oh! no. I dare not think you will. It cannot, must not be. God has in his providence given us Orissa to cultivate, and I hope we shall cultivate it, and plant its jungles and its wildernesses with the rose of Sharon, till it shall flourish far and wide, and exhale a fragrance sweet and rich as the Paradise of God."*

CHAP. III.

HISTORY OF MISSIONARY OPERATIONS.

Rise and progress of the Mission at Cuttack—Pooree—Balasore—Midnapore—Berhampore—Ganjam—Calcutta—Christianpore—Kunditta—Choga—Pipley. Native Schools—Orphan Asylums or Boarding Schools—The English School—Circulation of the Scriptures and religious Books—Influence of the Press.

WE have seen that the destination of the Missionaries in Orissa was Cuttack, the capital, where they arrived February 12th, 1822. Cuttack is beautifully situated between the banks of the rivers Mahanuddy and the Katjoory, and contains a population of about

* Sutton's Narrative, p. 393.

fifty thousand souls. It has been the seat of power both of the Native Princes, the Mahomedans, and the Mahrattas, as it is now of the British. It may be painfully interesting to place upon record, the following description of the conquest of Orissa by the British, and particularly the taking of the Fort of Cuttack, extracted from "*Plummer's Journal*," a Sergeant in the 22nd regiment, whom the writer recently met with in Norwich. Alas! how great are the horrors of war. The Lord "cause war to cease to the ends of the earth."

"The expedition, which was 5500 strong, sailed from Bengal, Aug. 3rd, 1803, and landed at Ganjam the 25th. The army marched under the command of Col. Harcourt and Col. Clayton. We began our march for the capital, and advanced to Cuttack, where we took possession of the black Prince's palace. His soldiers had fled into a fort at Barabatti, and the next morning our army encamped in front of it. We began to build a battery in the front of the fort, which was completed in three days.

Oct. 14. At day-break we opened a fire upon the fort, but our guns made but little impression upon it, as the place was rendered strong by three walls one above another; between each there was a deep trench full of water. The only entrance into the fort was over a bridge secured by three strong gates. We had made an entrance through the first gate, where, if the enemy had had courage to sally out, we must all either have been drowned or put to the sword, which appeared to have been their plan. Our battery guns threw a ball through the upper part of the fort gate; but to prevent another occurrence of a similar nature, the Mahrattas had built a wall in front. I was ordered out with the storming party and one six-pounder. We began a smart fire upon the three-gun battery, and upon the enemy in the trenches. Our small gun threw a double-headed shot through the gate, but finding it would not give way, our officer put into the gun a blank cartridge, and brought the muzzle close; it blew open the small door; but the Mahrattas had dug a deep trench close to the threshold, that we might tumble in while entering, and that they might have an opportunity of cutting us to pieces. But the door blew open so suddenly, *it took off the legs of the man*, who was placed there with his drawn sword to defend it. *We entered through the gate, one by one, till the whole storming party were in!* The next object we had to encounter, was a gun loaded with grape shot, ready to fire in our faces: but, providentially, one of our party shot the man *with the lighted match in his hand*, just going to the piece; he fell, but while attempting to rise, a sergeant killed him with his pike, and brushed off the priming. One of our men was shot through the knee, and another through the heart! The enemy ran to shut the *third* gate, but before they could secure it, we forced an entrance. We then flew to the trenches and batteries, pulled down the flag, and hoisted in its place a soldier's jacket! Many of the enemy threw themselves into the trenches and were drowned; 400 were killed, and the rest threw down their arms. One poor woman was so frightened, that she jumped into a well, with her child in her arms; but we got them both out alive. Well might the poor creature be frightened, to see her husband killed by her side. The dead bodies were carried out of the fort in small carts, and laid in heaps by the river side, where there flesh was devoured by jackals and vultures!! It was terrible the first night to hear the groans and cries of the wounded men. How many were killed of our different regiments I never heard, but the two companies of the 22nd had two killed: the wounded all recovered, except one, who was disabled for service.

The fort is an exact square, with a very handsome temple in the middle, where the Mahrattas worshipped; it was not injured either by the shots or shells. The place was large enough to contain the whole army; a part stayed, and another division went to occupy the palace of the black Prince. Several of the officers were wounded, and one black lieutenant killed. We had no sooner buried our dead, than the jackals rooted up the earth, and dragged the bodies from the graves. About a thousand of the army pursued the black Prince, whose army lay near the banks of the river which ran past the fort: they followed him to the hills, but could not come up with him. Many of the men caught the hill fever, and returned, and were quartered in villages belonging to the Prince's dominions. One of the chiefs offered himself to the Commander as a Collector of taxes. He was frequently at the Colonel's house attended with great pomp; he was carried in a palankeen and a guard of his own running by his side with drawn swords and having pikes. He attended the Colonel to teach him the language of the country. He likewise waited upon Colonel Harcourt every day. There was a man who had frequently been in the Mahratta service, but had deserted it, and enlisted into a Regiment belonging to the Company's service. The black Collector, frequently gave the man money, and promised promotion if he would enter into his designs; and promised to inform him of his plan. He told him *two days* before the execution of the secret. He was to be a guide to the army of the black Prince, who would convey a letter by a servant to the other side of the river. The night of its execution was to be, when the *Officers had a ball where they were all to be murdered, and* 10,000 *men ready to rush into the Fort and put all the soldiers to the sword!* The man when he heard the whole plan developed, went and gave information of the conspirators. An ambush was laid to intercept the letters which succeeded. The black Collector was confronted with his own hand writing, which was found upon the messenger, but he flatly denied the whole. He was seized and confined in prison. Our army marched to *Pipley*, where the enemy were then lying who engaged us with great fury. We charged their guns and took them and made a great slaughter. The rest fled to a Fort on the hill, took some of the conspirators and hung them. We had many killed in the fray and almost every Officer wounded. We returned to the fort; and the principal conspirator was tried and executed."

The intelligent and pious Christian, cannot with propriety appear as the defender or apologist of war. He ever looks upon it as 'the act, the strange act,' of a mysterious Providence,

> From seeming evil, still educing good
> And better thence again—and better still
> In infinite progression.

Happy day, when all people shall 'beat their swords into plough-shares and their spears into pruning-hooks, when nation shall not lift up sword against nation, neither shall they learn war any more.'

CUTTACK.

The *first* sabbath at Cuttack, is thus described in a Journal of that period.—" A soldier of the 7th Regiment of Native Infantry, with his wife and several females coming, Bro. Bampton delivered an address, and our servant Abraham rendered it into Hindostanee.

He spoke afterwards from Col. iv. 3-6. A Mr. G., a Portuguese, whose two sisters have been baptized at Balasore, by Mr. Peter, attended. In the afternoon we partook of the Lord's Supper, the writer administered it. In the evening Bro. B. preached: the soldier brought his brother, who understands English. Now we see the day of small things, but who hath despised them?"—This was indeed the day of small things, but at *this time it shall be said*, "*What hath God wrought?*"

The Brethren purchased bungalows in the cantonments, at a moderate price, which proved comfortable habitations; and afforded accommodation for the public worship of God. At first most of the Europeans attended English preaching on the Lord's Day evening; but after a time, some little offence was taken at the faithful exhibition and application of gospel truth, and but few attended.

Cuttack being the capital of the province, employment was found in the Govt offices for a considerable number of Indo-British; these form the connecting link of the European and the Hindoo, and constitute throughout India, a very interesting and important sphere of labour to the missionary. Within a few days of the arrival of the missionaries, a native presented a petition for English books, ascertaining his ability to read, he was presented with a New Testament. The following was the petition—

"The bearer, Roykoanauth Loll, being to inform before your honor, that he is learning English. Therefore he begs to desire, if you will be good enough to favor him with any books by which he will be duly bound.

I am Sir,

Your most Obedient Servant.

Cuttack, Feb. 24th, 1822.

In the next month, reference is made to the commencement of an *English Sunday School*, after morning service. A few days afterwards it is stated—"In the evening we went with Mr. Baptist, a writer, to look at a spot for a Native School. We hope to promote education, as preparatory to the reception of the gospel."

On Lord's-day, May 5th, Mrs. Rennel and her sister, baptized at Balasore, united with the church. One of the Missionaries wrote on the occasion; "I feel encouraged that our number in church fellowship is now seven and looked forward with cheerful hope to the time when it would greatly increase."—"June 1. To day our *Oreah School* commenced. The schoolmaster preferred this day to Monday, that day been considered an unlucky day!" In the following month Mr. Charles made a present of a School-room which he had built. July 12th, it is stated—"We have been here *five* months to-day, and after much consideration, and, I fear, too much delay, this evening our servant Abraham, baptized in Calcutta, was introduced to his public work among the Natives."—The value of native help in the infancy of the Mission is self-evident; and hence the special providence that provided it, in the person and labours of our servant Abraham. It is stated of him—"From twelve years service, under two gentlemen of the army, he speaks Hindostanee almost like his native tongue. His action, tone, figure, and the attention he commands, have often caused surprise. We think it very likely to be useful to our mission, gradually to disengage him from service, that, supported by the Society at about eight or ten rupees per month, he may fully devote himself to the work among the heathen."

On October 1st of this year, the practice was commenced of the *monthly assembly of the school children*, at each others' bungalows, for examination and reward. Considerable difficulty was experienced in dissipating the fear of both parents and children; for rumours were in circulation that the children would be taken to Calcutta to make them Christians, or give them victuals, or in some way take away their caste. About fifty children were present at the first meeting, and several gospels were introduced into the schools.

In reference to the aspect of the Mission at this time, the Report quotes one of the brethren saying—"As it respects the state of the Mission, what can we say? Who can define the progress of the growth of seed, while buried in the clods of the valley? We have distributed tracts and scriptures, far and wide—have instructed a number of youthful minds in the schools established—have borne our humble testimony to the truth: how far this seed will thrive, it is not for us to say, *God giveth the increase.* You will not expect a fruitful field, a valuable estate, before we have been here one year. We rather suppose you to say—How thick did you find the woods? What quantity of ground have you cleared? What is the quality of the soil? How much have you under cultivation? Truly this is an uncultivated people, though capable of much cultivation. The Lord send forth labourers."

Vigorous efforts were early made to promote the instruction of the rising generation. From June 1822 to Dec. 1823, *fifteen* Native Schools were established, three of which were at a distance from Cuttack. They contained 305 boys and 63 girls. In Aug. 1823, a Fund was formed to promote Native Schools. It is observed in the closing paragraph—"The paper now contains *monthly subscriptions* to the amount of 35 rupees 8 annas, and may probably through the good hand of our God upon us, be enriched by some more subscriptions or donations from our wealthy neighbours. The means multiply; may the Lord give effect to them, to the glory of His name."

This hope was not extensively realized in reference to the Fund, but it was most delightfully exceeded, by the support afforded for the establishment of the *Cuttack English Charity School*, which commenced in Oct. 1823.

It may be interesting to families in Orissa, to give the names of the *first* Scholars. In the first Report it is stated—"Since the commencement of the Institution, twenty scholars have been admitted, whose names are, John, James, Charles and Charlotte Baptist, Henry Evans Kenny, William Mordick, Levi and Betsy Torrs, John and Lewis Emmanuel Xavier, Andrew Ransin, Maria and Mary Dermont, Neel Mahadab Halder, Gunga Naraign Chatoorga." This Institution was honoured with the patronage and support of the Civilians and Military Officers of the Station and different parts of the Province, and has doubtless proved a blessing to many youths, both Native, Indo-British, and English.

The first efforts to prepare books in the language, are noticed under date Nov. 1823. "Perhaps you will be expecting to hear that your Missionaries have begun to send something of their labours into the world. I have at last ventured to send to the press the elementary tables of the School Book Society from the Bengalee; a tract on Idolatry, wholly Scripture Extracts; a few select passages on *the Law and the Gospel, for a sheet, or a small Tract for Schools and first distribution;* and four Hymns from the Bengalee, for native worship. The Tables I expect will be printed in Calcutta; the other pieces at Serampore. The Oreah language has only the Scriptures and three or four Tracts in it; *how great must be the dearth of Christian knowledge!*"

The writer cannot forbear noticing the reference to the little Tract—"A few select passages on the Law and the Gospel," 4 pp. 18mo., as this Tract* proved the seed of the first fruits of Orissa unto God. This will appear in the subsequent history of the Mission. "You will be pleased to hear," says one of the brethren, "that while one of our dear partners is engaged in the English School, the other is attempting a translation of our venerable Bro.

* This Tract was sent to Serampore to be printed, Oct. 25th, 1823.

Dan Taylor's Catechism, which we should be happy to see introduced into our Schools."

The first baptism took place April 27th, 1822. The subject of it was Mr. F. Rennell, son of the eminent Engineer. His wife and her sister were pious persons, and his conversion and union with the infant church was hailed with great delight, as 'a token for good.'

The Missionaries soon began to feel the need of more help. They say—"We are almost lost in this place; and how much more as it respects the whole country. Pray for us—send others to our help—what are we for this Province?" Early applications were made to them to settle in different places. Under date, Jan. 22nd, 1823, they wrote—"*Balasore* on the Bay would be a good station, and we have been already invited thither." A few months after, Mr. Ward offered them the purchase, or even *gift* of the mission premises at *Midnapore*, the missionary at that station being about to remove. But these invitations could not with propriety be accepted. But help was soon experienced. Mr. C. Lacey, formerly a member of the church at Loughborough, Leicestershire, devoted himself to the missionary work. He was ordained at Loughborough, May 7th, 1823. The annual Report states—"The opportunity was one of the most solemn kind. Never probably did a more solemn service take place in the Baptist denomination. All the interest that had been felt two years before by the ordination of Mr. Bampton, and the presence of Mr. Ward, appeared again in action. The spacious chapel was crowded, if possible, still more excessively than even on that affecting occasion; and many after all, were unable to gain admission within its walls. Tears flowed from the eyes of hundreds of witnesses, which manifested the deep impression which they felt. The candidate for missionary labours passed through his trying part with much firmness and propriety, and gave in reply to the questions proposed, respecting his conversion and his design in engaging in public labours, answers of a very satisfactory nature. The same pledge to support and pray for the Missionaries as had been given on the former interesting opportunity, was repeated; and the uplifted hands of a multitude, declared that they would persevere in supporting with their property and their prayers, the great cause they have espoused."

While help was thus preparing, to "lengthen the cords and strengthen the stakes," of the little tent pitched at Cuttack, Mr. Bampton, after mature deliberation, removed from Cuttack to Pooree, in Sep. 1823. He had visited this 'high place' of Idolatry at the ruth Jattra, and in humble dependence upon the Lord, he determined to take his stand before this fortress of heathenism, which he never finally relinquished till death. Mr. and Mrs. Lacey arrived at Cuttack, Dec. 19th, and were a very valuable acquisition to the Mission. Mr. Peggs went to Patamoondy to meet his new friends, and on their journey home by water, which occupied several days, various opportunities were enjoyed of extending 'the savour of the knowledge of Christ.' Mr. Lacey's affability of temper proved of great importance in the acquisition of the language. He was at home every where, and with every body, and by this means soon made very great progress in the language. The advice of the venerable Dr. Carey to Mr. Lacey, before leaving Serampore, is too important to be omitted. Taking Mr. L. by the hand, he said—"My dear brother Lacey, though I cannot pray publicly for you, yet I have the same warm desires for you, and I give you my advice. Remember three things:—1. That it is your duty to preach the gospel to every creature. 2. Remember that God has declared that his word shall accomplish that for which it is sent. 3. That, when he pleases, he can as easily remove the present seemingly formidable obstacles, as we can move the smallest particle of dust. Be not discouraged, but look constantly to the great recompense of reward. Farewell, may the Lord bless you, and give you many souls in Orissa for your hire."

The year 1824 dawned upon the Brethren Peggs and Lacey, on a short tour of four days to establish some Native Schools in the adjacent villages. At Gungaswur, after dinner, Mr. Lacey, for a little amusement, and to shew contempt for idols, went up to a large tree as if ignorant of what was near him, laid hold of some of the little idols, and sat down upon them! He called his companion, and taking up one of them, placed it for his seat. The amazement of the stupid people was great. Inquiring of the cook what the people would say, he replied—"*That the Sahabs are great people, and fear nothing!*" The connection of the British Government with Idolatry was referred to by a Native in one of the villages, who inquired—*Why should the Company destroy Juggernaut; he is their chackar or servant?* Alas! for the evils of this unholy allianee.

After stopping some time at Cuttack, Mr. Lacey proceeded on a visit to Pooree; but settled at Cuttack, to assist Mr. Peggs, whose health began to give symptoms of decay. He proved a very agreeable and valuable colleague to the close of his missionary course in India. The first years of missionary labour are usually characterized by circumstances requiring 'the patience of the saints.' The early history of the Orissa Mission affords no exception to this general rule. But there must be ploughing and sowing, before 'the joy of harvest.' Reviewing the early years of the Mission, it is stated—"The first four years of the Mission in Orissa, saw the four original members strengthened by four others from England; encouraged by the addition of four others, baptized in different parts of India, and were favored to baptize four more." In this period no Native convert cheered the heart of the Missionaries, though some cases occurred which awakened their hopes.

The ordination of Mr. Sutton to the work of the Mission, took place at Derby, June 23rd, 1824. The Report of the Society stated—"At an early hour the chapel was crowded to excess. The ordination service was deeply impressive. Many were powerfully affected while the young Missionary detailed the progress of his conversion, and narrated the important change which took place in his state and feelings when he was brought from scenes of impiety, vice, and misery, to embrace the gospel, and to consecrate himself and his all to the service of God among the heathen.—Tears flowing from the eyes of hundreds testified the feelings of their hearts: the uplifted hands of perhaps a *thousand persons* offered the pledge given on former similar occasions, to pray for and support the mission. On the following evening, Mr. Sutton preached for the last time to his friends at Derby, and seven brethren engaged in prayer. The language of an eminent christian on another occasion, on this probably expressed the feelings of many; "*If I were so unhappy as not to be a Christian, I should now become one.*"

After an unusually long voyage, Mr. Sutton arrived at Calcutta in February, and at Cuttack March 11th, 1825, where he was hailed with delight by the brethren. Mrs. Sutton, who had greatly endeared herself to the friends of religion in Calcutta, Serampore, and Cuttack, was taken seriously ill, eight or nine days after the birth of her first-born; and being removed to Pooree for change of air, she continued in a state af partial derangement, and died May 15th, 1825. Death had previously invaded the Mission family twice, in the death of two of the author's children, and in a few days afterwards, in the removal of his third and only child. This was felt to be a very severe stroke, depriving the mission of one of its beloved agents.

Shortly after, the author, whose health had been declining for two years, was advised by the brethren at the Conference held at Juggernaut, to try the effect of a journey to Serampore, and if that was not attended with the desired result, to return to England. This appeared a very heavy stroke to the infant mission. The parting scene is thus described :—

July 15th, 1825. Last day at Cuttack.—Three years, five months, and three days, after arriving at my station, I was compelled to leave it from indisposition. But "my times are in thy hand." I kissed sister L. and gave poor Abraham one hand, while Lacey had the other, and hurried to the palque. Indulged reflections on leaving this place, so painfully interesting; thought of my departed children, schools, English and native preaching, labour, defects, fears, hopes, temptations, &c. and then commended all to God.

> "Some natural tears I dropt, then wiped them soon :
> The world was all before us—where to seek
> Our place of rest—and Providence our guide."

A few days previously, Mr. Sunder, the master of the English School, and Abraham the Native assistant, returned from a journey to Calcutta. It is observed; "Lord's-Day, July 10. Mr. Sunder and Abraham arrived to day; they are both married. Abraham has married the daughter of Solomon, a converted Jew at Serampore; Brother Yates married them at Chitpore. I feel very thankful for this Providence. The young men and their wives, Mr. Sunder's mother and brother, with Deena, have arrived safely, though much affliction and death were seen on the road." The two Sunders became useful characters in the mission, and served its interests for several years. The mother, brother, and wife, also joined the church. Thus we often see, that when one mercy is taken away, others are frequently given in its place.

The author may be permitted to occupy a short space relative to his farewell to India.—He arrived in Calcutta, the end of July, and spent three months and some days at Serampore, under the hospitable roof of his valued friend Dr. Marshman. Mrs. P. was brought to the verge of the grave by fever, but mercifully restored. No permanent improvement being experienced in his own health, a passage was engaged in the Fort William for England, and a final leave was taken of India, Nov. 9th. Dr. Carey's parting advice was—"*Commit thy way unto the Lord and he shall give thee the desire of thine heart.*" Dr. Marshman, on being asked for his, said—"*Look upwards.*" The homeward voyage was long, but upon the whole, agreeable. The visit to St. Helena was very interesting and refreshing. The complaint at the chest rendered preaching, conversation, and even vocal prayer, almost impracticable. The voyage terminated on Monday, May 1, 1826, by landing at Deal in Kent.

The Lord be praised for the special mercies of the past years. Mr. Sutton, in his Narrative, kindly referring to the author's labours for the Mission, adds;—"But our friend and brother still lives. The remembrance of him and his beloved partner, is cherished with affectionate esteem. May they long live to benefit mankind, whether in England or India, and at length obtain "an abundant entrance into the everlasting joy of their Lord."

The first Chapel at Cuttack built for the worship of God, was opened Nov. 6th, 1826. Previously divine service was held in the houses of the Missionaries. Of its dimensions it is said—"It is forty feet long and twenty-two wide, exclusive of the vestry, and is described as a neat respectable building. It stands on the ground on which an idol temple, dedicated to one of the most impure of the Hindoo idols, once stood. How changed the scenes that pass upon that spot of ground! Once it witnessed the abominable and untold impurities of Hindoo worship, now the voice of prayer is heard, the accents of praise rise there to the ear of the Eternal, the heart feels his love, and the aspiring soul exults in his salvation. Surely in the circumstances connected with this house, the friends of the Mission may behold an earnest and an emblem of that more glorious change, which shall one day be effected, and for which the efforts of this Society are, as far as Orissa is concerned, preparing the way:—the change that will be visible on that rapturous day, when the last idol shall be hurled from his seat, and the last idolator renouncing former abominations, shall bow in penitence at the Redeemer's feet. The day on which this meeting-house was opened, is represented as one to be remembered with gratitude. Messrs. Sutton and Lacey preached: a few more than usual were present; but the happy and enlivening influences of the Divine Spirit were more than usually enjoyed. Besides what was raised in the Province towards the expense of this erection, Mr. Sutton, when on a visit to Calcutta, collected 620 rupees. The Deputation of the London Missionary Society generously presented him with 100. Mr. P—— presented for the service of the chapel a handsome set of wall shades, worth at least 100 rupees."

In the latter part of the year 1826, "*the day dawned, and the day star*" appeared, the happy precursor of "*the sun of righteousness with healing in his beams.*" Mr. Sutton gratefully describes 'the sun the mountains touching, gilding now the spacious lawn.' "The God of grace and glory has declared, that his word shall not return unto him void, but shall accomplish that which he pleases. Of this truth, during the present year, the missionaries at Cuttack, were favoured with a peculiarly pleasing illustration. From an obscure village they were repeatedly visited by some inquirers of a hopeful description, whose attention was directed to Christianity by means of some tracts and portions of Scripture." He writes,—

October 10, 1826. The last three days have been the most interesting I have passed in India. On Saturday brother Lacey sent for me to come and see some people respecting whom we have, for a considerable time, been interested. It appears that about *eight or nine months* ago, they met with a tract containing the *Ten Commandments*, which arrested their attention: more especially the attention of an old man, who, like many others in India, is a gooroo, or spiritual guide, to a number of people who call him their religious father, and themselves his religious sons. Some of them came to Cuttack, made some interesting inquiries and obtained other tracts, a gospel, and a testament. During brother L's visit to Pooree, they made one or two calls, and soon after his return another, which increased our interest in them. Brother L. and myself determined on paying them a visit to see and converse with the old man, their gooroo. It appears that they had read the books with great attention, and to a surprising degree understood their meaning. A Brahmun in particular was well acquainted with them, and quoted in the course of our conversation many very striking and appropriate passages, such as "Not every one that saith unto me Lord, Lord," &c. and the different characters that should enter heaven; the necessity of a new heart, and others too numerous to write in detail. But the Ten Commandments to which they are wonderfully attached, which they make the standard of their moral conduct, and to which they refer incessantly, they all seem to have at their tongues' end. One principal object of their present visit was to ask our advice in an important affair. It appears that in addition to keeping the Sabbath, and assembling on that day to read the dhurma shasters, (which they learn from their favourite *Dos Agea*, or Ten Commandments,) the gooroo thought it their duty to spread the knowledge they had obtained, through other villages. Accordingly he sent some of his disciples for that purpose. But the Brahmuns in perfect consistency with what the friends of religion have always experienced, were filled with enmity; and assembling and incensing the villagers they loaded the disciples with abuse, and beat two of them unmercifully. They wanted our advice as to what course they had best pursue. We told them that such treatment they must certainly expect if they loved the Saviour, and chose the way of life; and that it was what the friends of Jesus had ever met with. We read to them the tenth and eleventh verses of the fifth chapter of Matthew, and other similar passages, and recommended patient suffering under their persecutions. In this they seemed to have anticipated our advice, and were quite willing to abide by it. But as we had already determined on visiting them and their holy father on Monday, we proposed a further consideration of the subject at that time.

On the next day, (Lord's-day,) eleven of their number came down to my house during our English service. After that was over, we had another long interesting conversation of several hours; when it was agreed that most of them should return, and one remain to accompany us in the morning. I accordingly went to brother L's to sleep, in order to be able to start early in the morning. Just as we were about to have our evening worship, three of them came in and joined us, one a messenger from the old man. It was exceedingly interesting to see them bow with their faces to the ground, and in that position join us in the worship of the blessed and glorious God, to whom all flesh shall assuredly come. We seemed transported back to the times of Abraham, and Isaac, and Jacob. After worship, two departed, and the messenger alone remained to be our guide.

In the morning, we were up about five; and after prayer for our heavenly Father's blessing, we set off. The place appeared to be about *nine or ten miles distant in a very retire situation*, which we reached about nine o'clock. On our arrival we found some course cloths spread on the ground, beneath a wide spreading tree, which was the spot prepared for our conference. Several of the disciples and villagers were assembled. The old gentleman soon made his appearance. He appeared to be about fifty years of age, rather below the middle stature, and inclining to corpulency. Round his waist he wore an iron chain, to which was attached a small piece of cloth, which passed between the legs and fastened or tucked up behind. Over his shoulders was thrown his capara or mantle, and his head was quite bare and shaved close. On approaching us, he saluted us by prostrating himself on the ground, and knocking the earth with his forehead. We of course did not let him remain long in that position, but raising him up, saluted him in European style, by a shake of the hand. He expressed himself much pleased at our visiting him, and after some preliminaries, we seated ourselves, tailor fashion, on the cloth. Our conversation, of course, soon turned upon religion. Although it appeared that the old man could not read, yet, we were frequently surprised at the correct scriptural knowledge he possessed on many subjects. The Brahmun, to whom I formerly alluded, it seems had read over to him attentively the books we had given them; and by the help of a strong mind and retentive memory, the old gentleman had acquired much information. Although we found that he was still in error on several important points of doctrine, yet the correctness of his ideas on others, and his peculiar method of conveying them, often drew forth tears, and smiles, and wonder, and gratitude. We spent the whole day with him, excepting about an hour, when the old gentleman went to eat; during which brother L. and myself ate a meal of rice and milk, and spent the remainder of the time in talking to the people, who, it seemed would not leave us for a moment. When the old man returned, we again seated ourselves on the cloth, and the disciples around us; the old gentleman's instructions, and generally his replies, were delivered in the form of parables or fables, which were often very striking. He frequently referred to the Dos Agea, or Ten Commandments, which were his standard. In referring to the death of Christ, he illustrated it by supposing the case of a criminal condemned to die, for whom another offers himself as a substitute. In speaking of the folly of the distinctions of caste, he pointed first to some clothes of a bearer in the place, which were spread out to dry. In another place to some clothes belonging to some other castes, and lastly to some maitre's clothes, and said they would be defiled if they touched each other; but pointing to the sun, said, *it dried them all!* His observations were generally introduced by 'Hear! hear! hear! children, attend.' Not thinking of returning that night, we did not bid the old gentleman farewell when we parted; but afterwards thinking it better to go home and come again another day, we followed him to his little hut, where we found the old man at prayer. We waited until he had finished, and then took an opportunity of looking into his house, but could see nothing in the shape of an idol. We then parted with mutual good wishes, and after some trouble in breaking away from the people, we reached home in safety. We have seen several of the disciples, at different times since, and have tried to give them more correct notions respecting the individuality of the soul, which seems almost, if not entirely unknown in Hindooism. * * *

"We paid another visit to the old Gooroo, but found it was an unfavourable time, as most of his disciples were absent on various occasions. We talked with the old gentleman five or six hours on religious subjects, and was better pleased with him than on our first visit. We proposed establishing a school in the village if he would superintend it. He seemed to approve of the plan, but it was not quite decided upon. He was to send the Brahmun about it. He proposed our building a small bungalow in the village, and paying occasional visits, for a month or so together. The plan is not a bad one, and will have our serious consideration."

Of what passed at the first interview of the Missionaries with these interesting inquirers, Mr. Lacey's journal furnishes some additional information. The old gooroo's remarks on the New Testament, are worthy of being long remembered.

"The gooroo said to his disciples, '*My children, there is truth, and great truth. This is the great truth. There are gifts of rice, of clothing, and of wisdom; this is wisdom, the highest gift: rice decays, clothing perishes, but wisdom never dies. Take this my children, and let this be your guide; all the silver and gold cannot purchase this.*' He said many more things that gave us pleasure; and would have eaten or done anything with us that would take his caste, but this we forbore at present. About four we left the place; he took a most affectionate leave of us, which created in us a love for him, and a regret at leaving him. Certainly he is a very hopeful person, and has much knowledge of the sacred Scriptures. We distributed books and tracts among the inhabitants, and came away rejoicing for this encouraging intimation. These people are already suffering persecution for Christ's sake. We rejoice, but with trembling, knowing the deception of the human heart; the many failures in like instances; and the many discouragements and obstacles to the profession of Christ by natives. We leave our cause in the hands of the Lord, with ardent desires, and fervent prayers. To the residence of this man, our way was through a rocky wilderness covered with jungle, with here and there a beautiful flower; a true picture of the moral wilderness in heathen lands. Among the millions of idolaters, there is here and there a disciple of Jesus; but when shall the wilderness become like the garden of the Lord—full of flowers, with here and there a weed!"*

On Dec. 24th, 1826, three persons were baptized in one of the rivers that skirts the city of Cuttack. One was the wife of Abraham, the others the mother and brother of Sunder the English Schoolmaster. The Report of 1827 refers to the marriage of Mr. Sutton with Mrs. Colman, widow of an American Missionary in Burmah.—"An important addition has been made, in the course of the year, to the number of the Society's female Missionaries in India, by the marriage of Mr. Sutton to Mrs. Colman. This lady is an American; she was the widow of an American Baptist Missionary to Burmah, whose labours soon terminated, by dying in Arracan. After his death, she continued her exertions to benefit the benighted natives of the east, by acting as the Superintendent of Female Schools in Bengal, under the direction of the Independent and Baptist Brethren. By those who knew her in Bengal, Mrs. Sutton was much esteemed; she is represented by Missionaries, who have come from India, as a truly estimable woman."

This year may be said to have closed auspiciously. The erection of the chapel—the diffusion of light among the followers of the old

* Sutton's Narrative, pp. 238-43.

gooroo—the addition of Mrs. Sutton to the missionary band—and the additions made by baptism, gave promise of abundant increase. Herein is that saying true—"One soweth and another reapeth," but "he that soweth and he that reapeth may rejoice together."

Of the inquirers among the disciples of the old Gooroo, Mr. Lacey states—"There is good reason to hope that their minds are seriously and well disposed towards the truth, and that eight, or ten, are more particular than the rest; these have repeatedly visited the Missionaries during the year for instruction, and their views as it respects Christianity, and their own idolatrous system, are exceedingly improved. They have diligently read the Scriptures, and other religious books; the majority of them have devoted the Lord's day to religious instruction; many of their heathenish customs and superstitions have been laid aside, and christian practises substituted: this is particularly applicable to the poor old gooroo himself, his beads are broken off, his chain is cast aside, and he sits clothed in good white raiment and in his right mind. They thought themselves a part of God; now, they acknowledge themselves sinners against God, liable to punishment: they offered idolatrous sacrifices, especially to fire, these have ceased; and "the stir they have made, and are continuing to make, is producing a very wide and strong impression on the part of the province they inhabit." Of these inquirers one of the most interesting is Gunga, the intelligent Brahmin mentioned in the Society's last Report. He, after upwards of *two* years deliberation, has requested baptism. The hopes of the brethren were alternately raised and depressed respecting him: his attachment to the gospel seemed sincere; but formidable obstacles lay in the way of his professing Christianity: to be the first that should break the chain of caste in the vicinity of Juggernaut needed resolution and christian fortitude. While his mind was exercised on the important subject of renouncing the superstitions of his fathers, his friends, and his country, various interesting circumstances contributed to encourage the hopes of the Missionaries."

The following letter from the old Gooroo, dated Cuttack, Nov. 1827, shews the dawn of Christian light. This man has certainly proved the precursor of gospel light in Orissa.*

A letter from Sundra das Bargee, to Christians in general.

"O ye favoured people, who are blessed with the Divine Spirit, ye have existed 1800 years, and what have ye done for this dark world?

---

* See the account of Dulol in Cox's History, vol. i. pp. 77-80.

I am a Hindoo Boistub, poor and destitute, but ask of you neither land nor elephants, nor horses, nor money, nor palanquees, nor doolies; but I ask, what can be done to teach the people to obey the laws of God? O holy people this I ask.

"*Pooree is the heaven of the Hindoos;* yet there the practises of mankind are, adultery, theft, lies, murder of the innocent, whoremongery, eating fish with maha presaud, disobedience and abuse of parents, defiling of mothers, defiling of sisters, defiling of daughters! *Such is the religion of Juggernaut!* For these crimes the people are visited with rheumatism, swellings of the legs, leprosy, scrofulas, grievous sores, and acute pains, blindness, lameness, and such like! Such are the servants of Juggernaut.

"And now holy people hear the names of the gods of this people—gods which the people, when they have eaten rise and worship—these are gold, silver, brass, cedar, stone, wood, trees, fire, water, &c., these be the names of their gods, and these be their servants. To serve these gods, they burden themselves with expensive ceremonies and costly rites; they afflict their bodies, and their souls with pilgrimages and many cruelties. The Brahmuns no longer observes the Vades, nor the devotees keep mercy. O ye Christian Rulers, ye feed the rich, the proud, and the great; while the poor and the destitute are dying in want! O good fathers; good children! good people! hear the cries of the poor, O good people!

"The thief is judged, the murderer is judged, the perjured is judged, and all the wicked are punished according to their crimes. A large army is kept in obedience to your orders; but why are not the people made to obey the laws of God? Ye are the seed of the good, ye keep God's word, cause the subject to keep it. The Mahrattas were robbers, but they relieved the distressed. Europeans are faithful rulers, but in their Government falsehood abounds. Children, Fathers! the fate of of all in the four quarters is in your hands! O good people! the subject has become wicked, having fallen into error, and in consequence get not food nor raiment.

"Rulers are the example of the people. O good people teach them God's commandments by your example. If ye will do this, then it will be well; if ye will not then ye are stones to them. What more shall I write? Do as ye will, still religion is true, religion is true, religion is true!"*

The indefatigable labours of Mr. Bampton in scattering the seed of the kingdom far and wide, were honored by the baptism of the first Hindoo convert. This important event took place at Berhampore, Dec. 25th, 1827. It is thus described—"Owing to the operations of various causes, the minds of Hindoos are generally weaker than the minds of Englishmen; but there are few, if any, English Christians who have been called to display so much Christian heroism as is displayed by a Hindoo who gives up his caste, especially if he be the first in the neigbourhood who receives the Gospel. And Erun's remaining fear, after again wishing to be baptized, showed itself in a proposal that I should tell the truth if asked whether he had eaten with me or not, but say nothing about

* Pilgrim Tax Pamphlet, p. 76.

it if I were not asked. But this I felt myself obliged to refuse, and I told him that if he determined to remain unbaptized, no sum of money, nor any consideration whatever, should ever induce me to publish his having eaten with me; but that if he was baptized I would certainly publicly declare that his caste was gone. For I told him, the *caste was an enemy to Jesus Christ, which none of his friends could spare; and stood like a stone wall across the road to prevent the progress of the Gospel.* This firm but fair and honest way of treating him, manifestly pleased him, and he soon expressed his determination to face every difficulty.

"*December 25th* was fixed for his baptism, and between three and four in the afternoon, to our no small satisfaction, he came to the tent, bringing with him a change of apparel; between four and five we proceeded to a tank called the Ramalingum tank, and on our arrival, including ourselves and servants, there were not present perhaps above ten persons; before we had finished there might be twenty. In an address I delivered, I briefly pointed out the way of salvation: said that Jesus Christ required, first faith and then baptism—that my friend Erun had forsaken Hindooism—that he *had given up his caste*—that he believed in Jesus Christ and wished thus to connect himself with his followers. Then I asked Erun if this was not the case, and he said it was. I had not given him notice of my intention to ask him any questions at the water; but I proceeded to say that I should request his answers to a few, which, with his replies, I shall subjoin,—

"Do you honour the Hindoo gods?'—'No.' 'What do you think of the Hindoo shastras?'—'They are all false.' 'Are you a sinner?'—'Yes.' 'Who saves sinners?'—'Jesus Christ.' What did Jesus Christ do to save sinners?'—'He died for them.' 'Who will be saved?'—'Those who rely on Jesus Christ.' 'Do you believe in Jesus Christ?'—'I do.' 'Do you wish to obey Jesus Christ?'—'I do.' 'Jesus Christ requires his followers to abstain from worldly business every Sunday, and devote the day to religious exercises: do you engage to comply with this requisition?'—'I do.' 'Do you wish to be baptised?'—'Yes.'

"We then prayed, and after prayer went into the water, when I said, *Peeta pootra dhurmatmar namorai amhhai toombokoo doobo dayee*; i. e. 'I baptize thee in the name of the Father, and of the Son, and of the Holy Ghost; and my friend thought that as he was addressed it would be right to reply, as he said Acha, i. e. 'Very good,' and I baptised him; and on coming out of the water much wished, that we had a host of Christian friends present to vent, in a song of praise, those feelings which the event could not fail to excite. After changing our clothes we returned to my tent, and Erun drank tea with us."

Of the state of Erun's mind under his subsequent trials, Mr. B. gives a pleasing account.

"When any new trouble arises, he seems to come regularly to my tent, and it is pleasing to observe, that he commonly goes away more cheerful than he came. I have exhibited to him the promises made to those who are persecuted for righteousness' sake, and they cheer him. One day soon after his baptism, I went to his house to see how things were going on; a number of people collected together, and I happened to say to Erun, 'If all these people forsake you, the Lord will not.' On which he turned to the people and said, 'If any of you had a son who ran about and lost his caste, when all his neighbours disregarded him, would you refuse to notice him and take him in?' to which they said, 'No.' 'Thus' 'if you all forsake me the Lord will not.' Sometimes he magnifies his profession and tells the people he is not a low caste, his caste he says is *God's caste*."

To the preceeding particulars respecting Erun, Mr. B. adds some other information, which while it may excite a smile at the new convert's simplicity, pleasingly shows how great, in his estimation, should be the power and efficacy of the Gospel.

"He is of course a child in knowledge, and has some wild fancies. He once thought of going to Pooree, and he thought that the Rajah, himself, and I, might all go into the temple, and if Juggeraaut refused to give us some proof of his divinity, we were I think to kick him, and show all the people that he was nothing! Again, he wanted a commission to go about the country and break all the idols. Another of his schemes was to go to England, and by means of an interpreter, to prevail on the Honourable Company to fill all the offices in this country with pious men; and on its being hinted that the Company wanted money, he seemed to think that a propensity of that kind might soon be cured, as money is of use for so short a time. It is, he says, *teen deenoro kotto*: i. e. a three day's word."

The Society's Report of 1827, contains reference to a new source of support, which has proved very productive—this was, the preparation of a *Missionary Bazaar*. These items are now interesting, viz., "By Miss Roberts, from sale of articles at Quorndon and Leicester Ordinations. By Mrs. Peggs, from sale at Derby in the Association week," &c. Thus, as in the erection of the tabernacle in the wilderness, a spirit of liberality was cherished, which has rendered great service to the good cause.

The first Oreah convert was a Brahmun, named Gunga Dhor. Erun is a Telinga. This very interesting event of his baptism took place March 23rd, 1828, a day long to be remembered. See the account in the Society's Report, 1829, pp. 11, 12.

In the early part of the year 1828, Mr. Cropper arrived in Orissa, to strengthen the Mission. He was ordained at Leicester, April 25th, 1827. "On this occasion Mr. Burditt prayed. A short but appropriate discourse was delivered by Mr. Payne. Mr. Derry proposed the questions, and received the young Missionary's replies. The ordination prayer was offered by Mr. Peggs; and a charge, grounded on 2 Tim. iv. 1, 2, was delivered by Mr. Pike. In the evening an animated discourse was delivered by Mr. Stevenson, of Loughborough. Both services were highly gratifying, and excited considerable interest and feeling. May the prayers offered, be answered in continued blessings on the sacred missionary cause through successive years." This interésting young man was indeed "a burning and shining light," and many were the tears shed at his early death, before the close of this year. The Rev. Mr. Brown, of Calcutta, said to Henry Martyn—"You burn like phosphorus, and you may as well burn in Persia as in India." Alas! that this promising young man should have so much imitated him in his consuming zeal, and early removal from the missionary field. His course was short, but it was not in vain in the conversion of souls, and in "preparing the way of the Lord," both in Britain and in India. The Report of the Society contains the following just encomium upon his character :—

"God often moves in a mysterious way: one of the mysteries of his providence has been this year seen at Cuttack, in the unexpected removal by death of *Mr. Cropper.* He had begun to travel through the villages of Orissa proclaiming the Gospel, and afforded fair indications of eminent usefulness. Not many weeks before his death a brother Missionary wrote,—"As far as I can judge, brother C—— promises to be eminent as a preacher in Oreah. I have observed his serious and affectionate addresses produce much effect on his hearers." Alas! the last of those affectionate addresses is finished. He, whose ways are not our ways, has called the labourer to his rest. How much the Missionaries felt at his removal is evident from their correspondence. Short as was his course, that brief course contributed materially to advance the interests of that kingdom that will endure for ever. As far as India is concerned

Mr. Bampton writes,—"With respect to our work it will perhaps appear eventually that our lamented brother Cropper, by turning our attention to one subject, has been of immense use; that subject is, *the expectation of success.*" In England his brief Ministry was, it is known, blessed to the conversion of many individuals. In his short life the value of early religion was impressively displayed. *He was a fervent Christian, a useful Minister, and a devoted Missionary; and all this before twenty-one years from the day of his birth had rolled away.* This Society was the favoured instrument in bringing him forward to public usefulness, as he had not preached a single sermon before his connection with the Society commenced."

But while one labourer was removed, the great Head of the Church soon raised up others. "In July, 1828, a Conference was held by the Missionaries at Pooree, and it was then part of their pleasing business to call forth other brethren to the work of the ministry. They determined, after mature consideration, that Mr. John Sunder, at that time the English Schoolmaster, at Cuttack, and one of the fruits of their labours, should be liberated from his employ, that he might devote himself to the Ministry of the Gospel. It was further agreed that he should spend some time with Mr. Sutton. He has accordingly left his former situation and proceeded to Balasore. These two young men are natives of Arracan, but have received an English education.

"Another interesting helper in the work of the Gospel is Gunga Dhor. His mind had long been exercised on the great truths of Christianity, and he became mighty in the Scriptures, even before his baptism. The brethren at the Conference at Pooree unanimously agreed to call him forth, and employ him as a native preacher in the service of the Society. Respecting his talents and spirit Mr. Lacey writes at different times:—"Gunga Dhor has been unanimously received on the funds of the Mission on a salary of *seven rupees* per month. The sum is trifling, and could some individual Church, or some rich friend take him as their labourer, and support him at this rate, they would perform a most important service to the cause of God, and free the Mission from the expense. Our Church at Cuttack proposed to support him, but we thought it would be better for him to feel responsible to us as the agents for the Society than to the Church here. His preaching is very simple and very affecting; principally consisting of a relation of the Saviour's death. He has a very superior mind, and with a little attention, will become a very efficient Minister of Christ; and his knowledge of the language, of the manners, religion and experience of the natives gives him a vast advantage. We not unreasonably look upon him with great hope, and we and all our friends have reason, great reason to bless our Master's name for raising us up such a convert. Guuga Dhor has not constantly laboured in Cuttack, but only as he stayed with us a few days before and after the administration of the Lord's supper. His sphere of labour has been around his own neighbourhood, and in his own village, where there are two large markets in the week. The Gospel has hence in this direction been widely proclaimed by him."

"A fourth individual, whom the brethren assembled at Conference esteemed gifted with suitable talents for promoting the great objects of the Mission, is Mr. Beddy. His conversion and baptism were announced in the last Report. Talents for the Ministry of the Gospel were soon apparent in him, and a zealous desire to promote its interests among his heathen servants and other pagans. Being in the service of Government, he was, soon after his baptism, ordered back to Calcutta. In the Conference at Pooree, the brethren considered what means could be adopted to facilitate his becoming a candidate for missionary labour, and decided, that he should be requested, if practicable, to obtain a four months' furlough, that he might spend three months clear with Mr. Bampton on probation; having particular reference to his progress in the language, and his missionary habits. The illness of Mr. Bampton frustrated part of this arrangement, and it was then decided that Mr. Beddy should study at Cuttack. One of the Missionaries writes,—"Brother B.—— is a superior Christian, and possesses superior abilities as an English preacher, and we hope his zeal for souls will enable him to apply these powers to Oreah labours."

The conversion and baptism of Ram Chundra, gave an interesting character to the year 1829. This important event is detailed in the Report of 1830. The following account of the Schools, both Hindoo and English, at this period, cannot fail to interest the reader. Mr. Lacey writes of the Schools at Cuttack. "Of these there are *seven*, containing upwards of 300 children. About 100 read the Scriptures—the History of Christ—Jewel Mine of Salvation—the conversation between Father and Son—the Essence of the Bible; and the Catechism. Many of these have committed all these tracts to memory, and, from time to time, repeat different parts of them. They have generally a very pleasing and correct knowledge of the doctrines and precepts of the Gospel, much more correct than the country-born Christian youth in India, and I think generally superior to the same class of youth in England. There are few important questions which they cannot answer. Another class of these children read the Conversations between Father and Son, and the Catechism, preparatory to being introduced to the first class; of these there are about eighty or ninety. The remainder are writers on the ground. There are a very few girls among the number, but they are small, and always leave school before they have obtained any good instruction. On a Lord's Day, *the larger boys are brought by their masters to the Mission bungalow, to our Oriya worship*, which, from the books they read, and the instruction they receive, they very well understand, and we have good reason to expect they will be profited. This plan also introduces a proper regard for the Lord's Day; instead of running about the streets and fields in play, they attend the worship of God. We have been obliged to discontinue the Bhulbudrapoor School for the attempt was hopeless, but have commenced another in Chowlia-gunge, with much better prospects of success. Mrs. L. also expects to commence a girl's school at another village near Cuttack; but we have had so many promises and failures of this kind, that it would not be well to speak of it yet. Mrs. L. has had the whole conduct of the Native Schools, except that I have assisted her in the accounts and payment of the masters' wages, and have sometimes gone with her to address and examine the children. We have occasional examinations of all the schools; the last was on the 4th, 5th, and 6th, of December, 1829; which was very numerous and encouraging. A number of rewards, in clothes and pice, were distributed among the poorest and most deserving children. Several of the elder boys have left the School for the purpose of obtaining employment, and others have been taken by us and placed with other masters, to prepare them to become teachers; which plan if we can succeed, will be a great advantage to our schools, as the class of men we are obliged now to employ, often leave their work to beg, whereas the other will not be able do so, being of a different class of people."

Respecting the *English School at Cuttack*, the Missionary at the Station furnishes some pleasing information. It appears in a state of progressive improvement, and when it shall receive the advantage of the Superintendence of an English master, is likely to become extensively useful. The following is the information to which reference is made:—

"This Institution has received the decided approbation of the English community at Cuttack; it is supported by the most influential and respectable residents. A boarding school, which provides for ten destitute children, has been added: these children are taught, fed, clothed, and lodged, entirely at the expense of charity. Mrs. Pigou clothes the children entirely herself, besides liberally subscribing to the school. Besides this improvement, a subscription has been made to build a new school and house for the Master; 1,100 rupees have been obtained, which, though it will not complete it, will do most of the work of the building, and we propose to raise the rest as hereafter noted. The building is as follows,—a house for the master, containing two principal rooms and two smaller ones, with a good veranda, all of pucka. A dining and sleeping room and school-room for the boarding girls, the whole *ninety* feet long by *fourteen* wide inside, and *thirteen* feet high, all of pucka. A school-room for the day-school, and a lodging room for the boarding boys, the same dimensions as the other side, and of the same materials. This will be a spacious and substantial building for the institution. It is now forward, and we shall have it ready for use about July, 1830. The school-master has been dismissed, and, indeed, no country-born person will do for the school, and till we get a master and mistress from England we have the school in our own hands. I take a general superintendence of it, and employ an assistant to do the greater part of the labour, they allow him twenty-five rupees per month; and the surplus to seventy rupees, will be devoted to finish the school-house. The funds of the school, in consequence of its increased expenditure, are not so large, but we have no reason to fear that it will not be supported. Mrs. L. conducts the girl's school, but it is very desirable that the Missionaries should be liberated from the school, as it takes more labour and time than is consistent with their more legitimate labours, and particularly as it keeps us out of the country."

To supply this defect, Mr. W. Brown was appointed to the work, which he fulfilled for a number of years; but ultimately settled at Balasore, in the service of the Government. He was designated to the work of the Mission, in Stoney-street Chapel, Nottingham, May 25th, 1830. "Various ministers engaged in the services of the day. The charge was delivered by Mr. Stevenson. Mr. Brown's peculiar department is to be the management of the English Benevolent Institution, at Cuttack, for educating, and in some instances boarding destitute Indo-British or Hindoo children; and his support is expected to be derived from funds raised in India." Mr. and Mrs. Brown, and their daughter, embarked for India in the Elphinstone, shortly after the ordination. They arrived in Calcutta, Nov. 14th, and were guests with Mr. Pearce till their departure for Orissa.

"The premises recently erected for the English School at Cuttack, have been secured to the Society, with the entire concurrence of the donors and subscribers. Much friendly feeling and liberality appear to have been manifested by the European residents to this Institution. When the buildings were completed a remaining debt appeared of 670 rupees. The report of the Institution, and a circular, were sent round, and on the first day between 300 and 400 rupees were subscribed; and the whole was expected to be procured without difficulty. Mr. Pigou, the pious judge at the Station, materially assisted the design, by employing convicts to labour in levelling the ground, and in various other ways. An expense of at least 500 rupees was thus saved. Mr. Lacey states, that this gentleman thus "finished off the grounds, and garden, &c., in a very complete manner." The whole imparts a character to the town. May the spread of the knowledge of the Saviour, and the glory of God, be subserved by it! I trust they will. The house is now ready for Mr. Brown. May he long occupy it happily and usefully! It lies well for the bazaar, the chapel, and for us."

The second Native Preacher raised up in Orissa, was Ram Chundra. It is stated in the Society's Report; "In May, 1830, the brethren finally concluded to receive Rama as a native preacher, indulging the hope that, if he continued steadfast, he would be very useful. He was then represented as preaching the Gospel clearly, with great affection and force, and as making Christ and his cross the essence of his discourses. He paid much attention to the inspired volume, and in his addresses to his countrymen frequently read a verse and then explained, applied, and enforced its doctrines, and in that way would hold a congregation together in the street for two hours daily. Before he was accepted as a native labourer, he spent a short time with Mr. Bampton, and the opinion of that lamented brother respecting him is highly satisfactory. Writing to Mr. Lacey, he remarked:—"I was glad to see him, and am much pleased with him. I think I never heard a native preacher that I liked so well; at Pooree, he does not show the slightest want of courage, and he preaches Christ. He has been in the habit of going into the bazaar, sometimes before I go, and he speaks so loud that I am really afraid of his hurting himself.

I think the good man is humble and intelligent, and I should wish him to know that I think well of him, but it may not be prudent to tell him, that I think so highly of him as I do."

In Oct. 1830, Mr. Lacey gives some pleasing information respecting our native brother, and in Sept. expresses his hope of sending Rama on short tours of six or eight days at a time, into the country, throughout the cooler season that was then approaching. "Down in Boro bazaar we met a large and interesting congregation. Rama preached well; as he has always done of late. He improves, and particularly in his application and invitation. The people, on our returning, were mad for books, and I readily and as I believe usefully, distributed all I had. Last evening Rama went to Telinga bazaar early, and when he had done there he joined me in Chowdry. I never heard him so eloquent. He almost astounded the people. He has not so much sarcasm as Gunga, but is more powerful and more clear. He used a very striking figure last night, which produced great effect; speaking of the righteous and the wicked he said, 'The servants of God, true Christians, are like beautiful trees by the river side; their leaves are young and green, their fruit tender and abundant, and their shade grateful. The wicked are like the skeletons of trees, on the rocky mountains in May, which have been burnt up by the devouring element, and their vicinity presents not a leaf.' The people felt much, and were eager to have books; gave away satisfactorily all I had."

In 1832 the annual Association of the General Baptist Churches was held at Boston, Lincolnshire, the Town in which the foreign Mission was formed. The retrospect is thus happily expressed by the Secretary.—"Sixteen years have elapsed since the day that witnessed the formation of the Society, within this house of prayer. Its first years were years of weakness, and compared with most kindred institutions, it is still weak; yet it was not formed in vain. Ten years ago, the Society's first Missionaries opened their heavenly commission in broken accents on the plains of Hindostan, and there Oreah converts have been gathered to the Saviour, and Hindoos now proclaim the unsearchable riches of Christ. The grand contest between light and darkness in one of the darkest regions of India, has thus commenced. Even in the land of the modern Moloch of the East, satan no longer maintains an unmolested empire. The first trophies of redeeming grace have been snatched from his power. The first fruits unto life eternal have been gathered into the garner of the Lord. Future years, and distant ages, will yield the copious harvest; and eternity will display the whole result."

The conversion of Krupa Sindoo, and the progress of the work generally, is thus recorded in the Report of the year.—"At Cuttack most of the baptisms of natives have taken place, though none of the converts were previously inhabitants of the town. During the past year several pleasing additions have been made by baptism to the little Christian band in Orissa. Some of the persons thus added to the flock of Christ are Europeans, or of European and Hindoo extraction. The greater number, however have been Hindoos. In April one interesting native convert was baptized. In June and July ordinance of baptism was administered thrice at Cuttack, and on each occasion two Hindoos were baptized. The circumstances under which some of the converts made the solemn profession of Religion have been peculiarly interesting. Krupa Sindoo had gradually renounced all his idolatrous practices, and continued to read the Scriptures and improve in scriptural knowledge, though backward to avow himself a Christian. At length he became so miserable that he could neither sleep nor eat. His friends wished to relieve the gloom of his mind, by taking him to an idolatrous festival. He felt this would add to his sorrows, and determined to confess the Saviour. "He told his wife and child that he should never be happy if he neglected to follow Jesus Christ; that he had given his life for him, and that he must obey his commandments. His wife for the first time consented that he should, and said she also was a sinner. He then went to all his relations and acquaintances, and informed them of his resolution, saying that he did not wish to leave them secretly, but that he was determined to leave them if they would not follow the truth with him. He also went to his landlord, and told him he need not fear for his rent, for that he should be paid, and he told two or three persons to whom he owed some two or three rupees, that he did not wish to go away secretly, lest they should say he intended to cheat them; that they should see that true religion would make him punctual in all his payments. Having thus fairly and openly declared his design, some persuaded, and some dissuaded, and some wondered at the man. A number came with him to the outside of his village, and there they parted. At that moment he renounced all that is dear to man on earth. His wife, sister, and children were among the number. Thus this man *after five years' struggle*, broke at length through his difficulties, to embrace the Gospel."

He went to Cuttack, and there, in the waters of the Mahanuddy, confessed the Son of God as his Lord and Saviour."

To alleviate in some degree, the trials of the converts, and to render them mutually helpers of each other, the foundation of a *Christian Village* was laid at this time in the vicinity of Cuttack.

Another plan adopted for the diffusion of the gospel, was the formation of *Country Bungalows and Circuits.*—Mr. Lacey wrote —"I have long been impressed with the conviction that circuits in the Country would be greatly advantageous to the spread of the Gospel light. Pursuant to this impression, we have erected a small Bungalow at Bhogerpoor, a place about eight miles north of Cuttack, surrounded with villages and markets to a great extent. Bhogerpoor is the neigbourhood from which most of our converts have come, and where great inquiry is abroad in regard to Christianity. We shall spend some time every year at this Bungalow, and besides that, shall visit it occasionally through the year. We intend also to erect a small place of worship, where we shall occasionally collect the native converts in the neighbourhood for divine worship, and thus afford means of comfort and improvement to them, as well as exhibit the ordinances of the Gospel before the mass of people; and as it is one of their first inquiries, 'How shall we worship God whom we cannot see?' it will be of use to them. We hope to enter into our new circuit house on the 3rd of January 1832. The place will cost about sixty rupees, but will last for forty years or more, with a little yearly repair."

The usefulness of the *English services of religion* is gratefully recorded at this time. The Secretary observes—"From the commencement of the Mission in Orissa, the Missionaries have laboured to promote religion among the European residents, nor have their labours been in vain; several individuals have been converted. Mr. Beddy, one of the first fruits of Mr. Sutton's ministry, who, soon after his baptism, removed to Calcutta, and joined the Lal bazaar church, has recently resigned his secular employments, and devoted himself to Missionary labours. He is engaged as a Baptist Missionary; was publicly set apart to the ministry and soon afterwards proceeded up the country. The following information, respecting the English services and the progress of religion, has been received ;—

"The English worship has been kept up twice every Lord's-Day, i. e. in the forenoon and in the evening. The attendance on the former occasion has generally been good, but on the latter scanty. Some good impressions have been made by these means on the minds of several European hearers; the piety of others has been nourished and strengthened; while a few have been we trust savingly converted, and have owned the Saviour in his own appointed way. From the English congregation two have been added to the church by baptism, and are now walking consistently with their profession, though they have been removed from Cuttack to Calcutta by their employers. Mr. S. who had been separated from the church for some time, has been restored to his place, and has evidently benefited by the discipline of the church exercise over him. We hope his spirit will be saved in the day of the Lord. His brother, who was formerly a member, has lately died. Good is moreover doing among our European neighbours with whom our chapel is now well and regularly attended. After a sermon from John xxi. 17. the other Sabbath, one of the officers wrote for a Bible. He has since called and purchased a hymn-book, the Guide and first volume of Sutton's Sermons, and we gave him Baxter's Saints' Rest. He looked over and took several religious tracts. Lieut. C. is decidedly pious, and sits down at the ordinance with us with Mr. Pingle, and thus we form one of the most pleasing appearances a christian can behold on earth. Our poor dark native brethren and sisters, ranged round the same table on the same seats with the civil and military officers of Government. You would be better able to judge of this, were you able to witness how the poor black natives are generally despised and avoided. Around our Lord's table, however, we find one level. Lieut. C. when spending the evening with us the other day observed, in the course of conversation, that he perceived lately a great improvement in the European residents, for, that wherever he went, they had something to say about religion.—The conversation and devoted life of a European, among these idolators, is a circumstance of great importance to the cause of religion in India. The regular and pretty general attendance of the civil and military servants of the Government, makes a very favourable impression on the native mind. They thereby discover that their Rulers, and professed Christians in general, at least acknowledge the obligations of religion. There are numbers who stand to witness our sacred exercises on the Lord's Day."

It is pleasing at this period of the Mission, to observe the preparation and circulation of useful books and tracts, before a press was established in the Province. It is well observed by Mr. Pike;—"When our great English Martyrologist refers to the wounds inflicted on the Papal system, by the invention of printing, he remarks, "I suppose that either the Pope must abolish printing, or he must seek a new world to reign over, for else, as this world standeth, "PRINTING WILL DOUBTLESS ABOLISH HIM." Subsequent ages have evidenced the truth of these remarks. The advocates of the Romish Antichrist, in the martyrologist's day, complained of the "pestilent little books," with which the Reformers were deluging benighted lands. The Missionaries in Orissa have been furnishing the brahmuns with similar causes of complaint, and printing appears to be one of the means by which the God of truth will abolish them. At the annual Conference held at Cuttack, several resolutions were adopted on the subject of tracts, and other publications. It may be more interesting to furnish the minutes of the Conference, than to present the details in another form.

"1st. Resolved, That brother Lacey print 300 copies of his tract, '*Am I a Chrstian?*' presented at a former Conference. This tract is an abridgment of '*Alleine's Alarm,*' translated from the Bengallee.

"2nd. That brother Sutton print 5000 copies of '*The True Refuge,*' a dialogue translated and improved from the Bengallee.

"3rd. That brother Sutton print 5000 copies of his revised edition of '*The Jewel Mine of Salvation.*'

"4th. That brother Sutton prepare a MSS. *Hymn-book in Oriya,* to be presented next Conference; and that he adopt as many plain metres as possible.

"5th. That brother Lacey print 3000 copies of the *First Catechism*, a second edition.

"6th. That brother Sutton print 2000 copies of the *Second Catechism.*

"7th. That if the School Book Society will print a second edition of brother Sutton's Oriya '*Easy Reading Lessons,*' we will take 500 copies at half-price.

"8th. That brother Sutton prepare and print 2,500 copies of *An abridgment of the Bible*; about forty pages, 12mo.

"9th. That an extra 2000 copies of '*Petumber Singh*' be printed."

Besides the publications referred to in the preceding Minutes, several others, from the pen of Mr. Sutton, have issued from the press, or are in a state of preparation. Some of these are expressly on the momentous subject of religion, and others are designed to promote that useful knowledge which, from its contrariety to the notions inculcated in the Hindoo shastras, cannot be diffused without preparing the way for the fall of Hindooism. The following may be mentioned,—

In English.

The History of the Hindoo Foundling Girl.—*The Family Chaplain, or Preachers' Substitute,* a volume of sermons designed to assist domestic worship in English families in India, that are so situated as not to enjoy the public means of grace. A considerable number of copies of this work have been subscribed for, at from six to eight rupees per volume; 200 copies have been sent by Mr. Sutton as a present to the society. It appears that he contemplated the publication of a second volume.

An *Oreah Grammar,* compiled by the request of Government, and of which the Honorable Company subscribed for 100 copies, at five rupees each. Of this Mr. Sutton remarks to a friend, "I have endeavoured to simplify the language as much as possible. That no improvement can be made I do not suppose; however, I did the best circumstances would allow." He further remarks that he hoped the Government subscription would about clear the expense, and that the Mission and the cause of humanity would receive sufficient benefit to justify the labour employed on the publication.

In Oreah.

Natural Philosophy and History; thirty-two pages, octavo. Printed by the Calcutta School Book Society.

A *Geography,* with maps; about sixty pages, octavo.

Neeta Cotta (or fables,) before the Committee of the School Book Society.

The *Durma Postock Sar;* second edition."

The return of Mrs. Bampton is referred to in the following terms, —"The widow of our much valued and laborious Bro. Bampton has returned to her native land after a voyage, on the whole agreeable, and about four months long. She has declined charging the Society with the expense of her passage home. This generous act would at any time have rendered the Society much indebted to her, for what in fact constitutes so considerable a donation to its funds; but in consequence of their depressed state, is peculiarly acceptable at this time." Some stringent observations are made on the decrease of the Society's funds, and "the friends of the Institution are entreated to weigh well the remark of Mr. Sutton, '*The only thing I fear for Orissa is, a decline of zeal and piety with reference to the cause at home.*' In a Committee Meeting held at this time, it was suggested that as Mr. John Goadby had offered himself for the work of the Mission, a special appeal should be made to the churches. See G. B. Repos. Jan. 1833. The Misses Barnes, of St. Ives, Hunts., gave £50, and various individuals and congregations responded to the call. The amount of this special subscription appears to have been about £280, besides the ordination collection; and the expense of outfit, passage, &c., about £300; so that the whole expense would be defrayed by the different contributions for that purpose."

In the Report of 1833, reference is made to the ordination of two Native converts as Evangelists. "This is such an event in connection with the progress of the Gospel in Orissa, as may excite the most pleasing emotions. The ordination of two Christian Natives of that country, to *the solemn work of Evangelists,* is doubtless, what that long benighted land has never before witnessed. Let us praise God for the first solemn service of this kind, that Orissa has witnessed; and rejoice in believing that it will be the precursor of thousands of such solemn services, that, through successive ages, will there take place, when we are gone to our eternal home; and when the idolatry of the dark land, into which we have been permitted to convey the light of life, shall have vanished like a dream, nor left a wreck behind."

FIRST NATIVE CHRISTIAN MARRIAGE.

Wherever the religion of the Lord Jesus Christ prevails its progress is marked by the blessings that follow in its train. Not only does the Gospel enrich the soul with peace and hope for an unseen world, but it becomes the source of numerous benefits in the present state. Its influence in reference to the connection of marriage is most important Only where Christianity prevails is woman placed upon her proper level; and only in such countries are the marriage tie and the mutual obligations and duties of the married state, appreciated aright. The past year has witnessed another step in the progress of the christian cause in Orissa, by presenting the pleasing spectacle of the first native christian marriage. The event is too interesting to be passed lightly over, and the details of it, as given by Mr. Lacey, must gratify the members and friends of the Society. He thus writes in November 1833:—

Mahadab and the daughter of Krupa Sindoo wish to be married, I have appointed the 20th as the day on which I marry them. This will not only be the first native christian marriage in Orissa, but most probably the first marriage of reason and affection. He is a widower of about 30, the girl is about 16 years of age.

This forenoon at half-past ten o'clock, I married Mahadab to Comela the daughter of Krupa Sindoo. Nearly the whole of the native christians were present, and the native school masters; besides a number of people from the town. Mahadab and Comela, sat forward before the table. They where dressed in clean white dresses which reached down to the floor. The native Christian females and their husbands sat around, dressed clean and white, and the scene was solemn and imposing; so much so, that the witnesses could scarcely write their names. This marriage is a dreadful smashing up of Hindooism. By it, it is discovered that Hindoos can be married who are of far different castes, and that without brahmuns, boistnobs, proctors, gifts, bades, or expensive festivals and noisy tom-toms for days or weeks together. An ordinary Hindoo cannot celebrate a marriage without involving himself in expense which often ruins him; but here is a marriage without any expense whatever! A certificate of the marriage was prepared, and after signature by the officiating missionary, the contracting parties, and the witnesses of the solemnity, was delivered before the congregation to the female. A duplicate was also prepared and signed in the same way, and recorded in a book belonging to the body of christians connected with us. The marriage form which was used, and which we have agreed to use among the natives, is, I consider impressive and scriptural.

After the parties were seated, they were asked in a tone sufficiently loud to be heard by the whole congregation, whether they desired to be united to each other in marriage? and they answered in the affirmative. Then Mr. Brown commenced with a few words of prayer in Oreah. When this was concluded, myself, and the man and woman stood up, and they repeated after me in an audible and distinct tone the following form. "We will love, and support, help, and comfort each other. We will dwell together, and henceforth we will have no separate riches, or possessions. If one of us be sick, or afflicted, or in any other difficulty, then, the other shall stay near, and according to ability shall help and comfort. For the purpose of committing adultery, we will go to none else; but until death we will never leave each other; and whatever God has commanded, according to that will we proceed. Into this covenant we enter."

They then sat down, and the following was read aloud, and the places in which the different passages are recorded pointed out.

"Concerning marriage, and the duties of husbands and wives, it is thus and thus recorded in the Holy Book.

"Before man had committed sin, when God made the order of man, then he gave this commandment, that leaving father and mother, a man shall cleave unto his wife; and they shall be one flesh." Gen. ii. 24.

"And our Lord Jesus Christ giving testimony to that word says, 'For this cause shall a man leave father and mother, and shall cleave to his wife; and they twain shall be one flesh. Wherefore they are no more twain but one flesh. What therefore God hath joined together let no man put asunder.' Mat. xix. 5, 6. Mark x. 7, 8, & 9. Again, by the inspiration of Paul, God says, 'Marriage is honourable in all, and the marriage bed undefiled; but whoremongers and adulterers God will punish."

(Then follow Rom. vii. 1-3. 1 Cor. vii. 1-3, 10, 11. 1. Cor. vii. 39. Ephes. v. 22-23. Col. iii. 18. 19. 1 Pet. iii. 1, 2, 7.)

After distinctly and slowly reading over these scriptures, the two persons stood up, and Mahadab in his right hand, taking the right hand of Comela, repeated deliberately after me to her.

"I Mahadab, taking thy hand in my hand, am thy husband. As God has commanded, so will I, to the utmost of my ability, preserve, and support, and comfort, and in a proper manner love thee; and until death I will not leave thee."

Then loosening their hold, she in like manner took Mahadab's right hand in hers, and after me, to him, repeated as follows:

"I Comela, take thy hand, and before these witnesses acknowledge myself thy wife, and as God has given commandment, so will I to the utmost of my ability, serve and help, and comfort, and in every proper way love thee; and till death will not leave thee."

In the afternoon the new married couple had their christian friends to dinner at the house of the bride, and we also went and eat a little rice with them; but of this part of the transaction Mr. Brown will give a more detailed account, and so I refrain from saying more about it."

Mr. Lacey communicated some interesting information respecting the old Gooroo, Sundra Das, and the manner in which he undesignedly promoted the diffusion of some measure of Gospel truth. "The old Gooroo is again contributing greatly, but undesignedly to the spread of the truth. Perhaps there never was a case nearer that which the Apostle mentions of some preaching Christ of envy and strife, than the old gooroo's. Phil. i. 15. He receives our Scriptures and tracts, compares them with the Hindoo books, commands the keeping of the ten commandments,—speaks of the instructions, miracles, and death of Christ; and many other things that are useful. He has no proper view of the gospel, and so cannot make it known further than by these means; nevertheless a degree of light gets abroad which soon exposes these designs of the old man, and makes his disciples wiser than their teacher; and when this discovery is made, they cannot remain attached to him, and are too much enlightened to turn again to their own books and old observances; and in consequence, those who really desire to find and follow the truth, turn their thoughts towards us. What shall we therefore say, to the conduct pursued by the old gooroo? Why, although we cannot commend his motives, yet with the Apostle we say, "Notwithstanding every way, whether in pretence or in truth, Christ is preached; and therein we do rejoice, yea, and will rejoice." Our English congregation remains low, though not so much so as some weeks past. If it shall be for the good of the cause of religion, and for the glory of God, I trust he will bring them back again, for it is distressing to have the preaching of the gospel closed, where such a number of persons reside; but if it will not, I hope God will prevent it. I hope I can truly say, unless these great ends can be answered, I have no desire to make a show in connection with the rich.

"Sundradas asked Ramara why we cut the corn he had sown and cultivated with so much care? (referring to the baptism of the two females,) to which Rama replied, that sometimes the master might set one servant to reap that corn which another servant had sown with much labour and anxiety; that we must not look so much to what we reap here, as to the approbation of our master at last; but really we had reaped that corn which he could not have reaped, but which had it been left to him, he would have suffered to spoil in the wilderness.

"The old man is very zealous in enforcing the *Ten Commandments* and the *Christian Scriptures*, and does much good: however his disciples grow wiser than their teacher, and pass beyond the line in which he would confine them; and then he involves himself in persecution. I am persuaded the old man knows the truth, but it is hard work, after all this reverence to take up the cross, and become an ordinary and despised Christian."

It was a subject of great thankfulness, that the year 1833 saw an addition to the number of the labourers in Orissa. "It is a matter of sincere congratulation (says the Secretary,) that this year a small addition has been made to the number of the Society's Missionaries.

Mr. John Goadby, the second son of the esteemed pastor of the Baptist Church, at Ashby-de-la-Zouch, has long had an earnest desire to devote himself to the work of Christ among the heathen. Three years or more ago, he offered himself as a candidate for missionary service. The circumstances of the Society then prevented any favourable attention being paid to his application. Soon afterwards he commenced regular studies in the Academy under Mr. Jarrom, of Wisbeach, but still his mind was directed, should a door ever be opened to him, to labour among the heathen. At length, in the providence of God, his way was made plain. He was solemnly set apart to the important work of the Mission, at Loughborough, on the 29th of May; when his Father with much feeling and force, addressed to him an important charge; and his worthy Tutor presented an ordination prayer, imploring numerous blessings on him, and the partner of his course. The day was one long to be remembered. It was apprehended that more persons were present, than at any ordination of any previous Missionary of the Society. Much holy feeling was excited. Many, by their uplifted hands, declared their determination to pray for, and support the Missionary. Mrs. Goadby's mind had long been directed to the same great object. In fact, so devoted were both of them to this object, that notwithstanding the sacrifice of country and friends, to which they are called, it appeared to them a cause of joy that the way was open for them to go, and in their spheres of operation to make known the Saviour's love. They proceed in the ship, Alexander, Captain Waugh.

"That this esteemed brother and his partner are thus proceeding to strengthen the Mission, is, under God, to be ascribed to the zeal and liberality of those friends, principally in a few churches, who, by an *extra subscription*, for the express purpose of defraying the expense of outfit and passage of another Missionary, have enabled the Committee, at this important crisis, to send them forth; and thus to strengthen the weakened hands, and encourage the hearts, of the brethren in Orissa, almost drooping for want of more aid. Let the subscribers to this object, reflect with pleasure, that divine goodness has thus permitted them to give to India two more Missionaries; and that India is indebted, under God, for this benefit, not to the Society generally, but to them, and them only, whose extra exertion and additional liberality, have sent these Missionaries forth." They arrived in Calcutta, Nov. 15th, the anniversary of the arrival of the first Missionaries in 1821.

The additions to the church this year, were of an encouraging character, particularly in the case of Pooroosootum, from Vizagapatam. It is thus narrated in the Report of the Society. "During the past year, several more Hindoos have been gathered into the Redeemer's fold, and have displayed their strong attachment to the Gospel by enduring sorrow and privations on its account. One of them is named Pooroosootum; and he appears to be the first fruits of the labours of the Missionaries of the London Society, who were stationed at *Vizagapatam*. This young Hindoo has furnished an interesting narrative of his own history. He appears to have been early initiated into the superstitions and idolatries of his countrymen; and was zealous in his regard to idols, idolatrous rites, and abominable practices. Yet while following these, he represents himself as desiring earnestly, "to know the source of true Religion." On one occasion he met with a tract, which had fallen into the hands of a boy. Pooroosootum obtained the tract, read it and laid it aside. Some time afterwards he obtained two other tracts; and at length a fourth, and this directed him to the Saviour. After passing through various scenes and trials he wished to avow himself a disciple of Christ; but the Missionaries were dead; and had died without witnessing any apparent success of their labours! Pooroosootum at length became acquainted with a pious officer, and he thought of sending him to Madras, a distance of not less than four hundred miles, to be baptized; but afterwards determined to send him to Cuttack, a distance of three hundred miles. *How awful is the state of a country, how deplorable the dearth of Missionaries in India, when a converted Hindoo could find, in no direction, a recognized Christian instructor, within less than three hundred miles of his own dwelling!* How pleasingly this interesting Hindoo was taught of God is evidenced from his own narrative! He gives the following description of his experience of the Saviour's care, previously to his becoming acquainted with his Christian Friends.

"The Lord Jesus Christ through infinite grace and mercy, made my soul to thrive and strengthen in faith and knowledge; and enabled his servant within me (the soul) to resist with firmness those friends of the devil, shame and anxiety about the mortal body, which had long caused me to struggle in sin; and had often thrown me into darkness and the most dreadful apprehension; and would have thrown me back for ever, had it not been for the help obtained of my gracious Saviour! He has freed me from the power of these two wicked enemies. Now as soon as my near relatives, as my brothers, mother, wife, several kinsmen and friends, as well as merchants who had from time to time lent me money, heard of my wonderful change, they began to afflict me. Some spoke ill of me; some execrated me; some calumniated me; some were enraged at me; some gnashed their teeth at me; some intended to imprison me; and others sought in various ways to injure me. Notwithstanding all this, the Lord Jesus Christ, on whom I repose my whole trust, and whom I followed as my heavenly Instructor, encouraged me with sufficient patience, to answer with reason, all the revilings of the persecutors; and to stand fearless, undejected, and unperplexed. And with firm purpose I avoided the society of such people as would perplex me; and for such mercy, I with wonder and delight praised the kindness of the blessed Saviour, who thus delivered me from my persecutors."

By letter he was introduced to Mr. Lacey, who furnishes an interesting account of his baptism, and offers some judicious remarks on his singular case.

"Lord's Day, October 6th, 1833, was fixed upon as the day for his baptism. The Circuit Judge readily granted us the use of the large tank, near the kutcheeree, which being in a central place, close to the large road, and near the bazar, was well suited for the administration of the sacred ordinance. We had a hymn, a prayer, and an address in the native language; and there were certainly not fewer than *a thousand persons present.* As soon as the previous service was over, the crowd involuntarily placed themselves on the grassy sloping banks of the fine tank, and the scene was most interesting. The multitude was silent, and the administrator and candidate descended the steps into the water, and the ordinance was administered. The sacred names were repeated, both in the English and native languages. The reasons for so public a place being fixed upon were, first, that a large company might be brought together and addressed; and then, that by seeing how baptism *was* administered, the people might be disabused of a number of ridiculous notions, which the interested have industriously propagated for the purpose of prejudicing the public against the ordinance.

"The same evening our new friend approached the Lord's table, and learned the meaning of that gracious institution. He has since that time up to this day, (when he starts off for his own country,) talked and walked so as to lead us to hope well of him. He is at present, humble, and diligent in reading the word of God, and zealous for its propagation amongst others. He appears to be the first fruits of the labours of our Independent Brethren on the coast; and on his first visit to Vizagapatam, when his intention was to profess the Saviour, Mr. Dawson, though very ill, was still alive. He speaks well of several others in his neighbourhood, and it is not unlikely that from henceforth, some important fruits will, in that direction, be gathered to the fold of the Lord Jesus.

"The case affords a fresh instance, that while we are mourning over our apparently fruitless labours, and *even dying without seeing one single individual turn to the Lord*, there are those, who are not only enquiring the way to Zion, but who have by means of some tract or gospel which we may have distributed, obtained a clear knowledge of the way of life, and are walking joyfully therein. And how cheering the persuasion, that after a life of labours in the Saviour's vineyard, we shall meet, perhaps many, whom we have been the unknown means of guiding into the way of life! How joyful the announcement will be! How delightful the interview! And how such a persuasion ought to stimulate us, still to pursue our object; leaving our 'work with the Lord,' either to be rewarded with visible fruit here, or only hereafter, as he shall see most fit, for he best knows what we can bear.

"We see also in this instance, the utility of Tract Societies; here is a young man, enlightened, convinced, and brought to trust and rejoice in the Saviour; and all effected through the instrumentality of religious tracts, without having once had an opportunity of conversing with a Christian! The distant consequences are still more important; for this young man will henceforth commence the preaching of the gospel to his fellow countrymen; and from the grace vouchsafed to him, and the sanctification of his naturally excellent abilities, he will demand great attention, and exert great influence: and so may, if he continue faithful, be a means of turning many to paths of holiness and life.

"He left Cuttack for his country, Oct. 21st, in company with Radhoo, whom I have dispatched with him for the two-fold purpose of accompanying him on his journey, of seeing his brothers who are well disposed towards Christianity, and also for the purpose of seeing several enquirers at Berhampore. He was rather sorrowful at leaving the society of the native Christians, among whom he has been very comfortable since his arrival. He is no ordinary addition to the Christian cause; and will be very useful among his Teloogoo countrymen, and very helpful to our friends of the London Society, on the coast."

The approach or arrival of one missionary, is often attended by the removal or death of another; and before Mr. Goadby arrived in, or even had embarked for India, Mr. Sutton, compelled by sickness, sailed from Calcutta, and arrived at Boston, in America, in May of this year.

The Society's Report of 1835, commences with an account of Mr. Sutton's return from England, to his missionary labours in America and India; and the ordination of the new missionary, Mr. John Brooks. "A few days after the last annual meeting, Mr. Brooks was solemnly ordained at Derby, as a Missionary. The day was one of very peculiar interest. A multitude of friends from neighbouring places, flocked into the town. The services were solemn and delightful in a high degree. Many tears were shed, while the young missionary narrated his religious history, and the circumstances that had led him to devote himself to labour for the perishing heathen. Fervent prayer was offered for him and his partner. Mr. Sutton delivered a deeply impressive charge. The evening service had also its peculiar interest. On that occasion Mr. Sutton bade farewell to multitudes that felt deeply the solemnities of the day, and a most numerous assembly united in singing a hymn, expressive of their hope that, 'when days and years are passed, they all should meet in heaven.' Since that time one year has nearly passed, and, already many that were present, have finished their earthly course. May it be the concern of all now on earth, that enjoyed attendance at those solemn services, to uphold the missionary cause, and love and serve the Saviour till he calls them to an unmerited, yet infinite reward."

It was found necessary this year, for Mr. and Mrs. Lacey to return home for a time, to recruit their health. Mrs. Lacey wrote to a friend—"Before this arrives, you will probably have heard that it is my intention to sail for England in January next. For several years I have been urged to this step by all who know what I have suffered in health, and the danger I have been in; till this, I never could prevail on myself to leave the field, but have at length concluded to do so, and I make no doubt but you will also approve of the step. I have been anxious as much as possible myself to pay the expenses I shall incur by my voyage, and am happy to inform you that I have two little girls to bring with me, which will enable me to pay sixteen hundred rupees of the passage money. I now begin to feel my approaching departure very much; the native Christians are weeping and dissuading me from leaving them almost every time I see them. The other evening I called at

Gunga Dhor's, to see his wife, and she wanted to know if I was going of a truth, I told her I was; and she burst into tears, saying, —I was her mother, her sister, her reprover, and old friend; what should she do? do not go, do not go, do not leave us; when I do wrong you come and reprove me, and bring me to a better mind, who will instruct us like you? I replied I was obliged to go for the sake of my little children, who doubtless would be left motherless if I stayed to have another illness in this climate, and their ends would be defeated by my death. That all my doctors said Go, flee for your life! all my friends said the same, and I believed it to be the will of God also; but that they must look to and listen to our other missionaries, and put their trust in God."

"Even now (says Mr. Goadby, referring to Mr. Lacey's departure,) we seem to be losing our strength. Lacey is returning to England, and Sutton is not returned; still the work will go on, the most efficient part of it cannot now so easily be stopped; our books are widely circulated, and we have every reason to believe much read; our Native preachers are the most efficient labourers in the field, and they are zealous and devoted to the work. European guidance and instruction they indeed want, and I have now sufficient of the language to make myself generally understood, though not enough to warrant me to attempt a public address."

Of the circulation of Tracts, it is stated—"During the year, about *twenty-eight thousand* tracts have been distributed. The American Tract Socieiy has voted a second grant of five hundred dollars to assist the Missionaries in the wide distribution of religious publications. The Religious Tract Society has continued its annual grant of paper for the printing of tracts. That grant this year is *forty-eight reams* of paper. In addition to this, the Committee of the Tract Society has voted *fifty pounds* towards the printing of the Pilgrim's Progress in the Oreah language, for the use of the native Christians. This work is now in hand, and Mr. Lacey hopes to be able to proceed with the translation, during his stay in England. This estimable work has, for almost two centuries, amused the young, and delighted and instructed the more mature, in its once persecuted author's native land. It has instructed many in other European countries; and now begins to speak in the languages of India, to guide the pilgrim in his way to God."

"In October, Cuttack was visited by a dreadful and destructive inundation. The waters of the Mahanuddy rose higher and higher, till at length, the lofty banks, that guard the city, were overflowed, and gave way, and the waters deluged the neighbouring country.

Many lives were lost. Beasts of various kinds, as elephants, cows, sheep, together with men, women, and trees washed from the hills, were seen floating down the torrent. The lives of the missionaries were graciously preserved, but much damage was done to the Society's premises. Mr. Brown states,—' The storms which are so frequent here, have unroofed the English School House, and left me almost in ruins. The great flood which happened in November inundated all the lower places of the district, including the town of Cuttack itself. Many thousands of poor people are, by this sad calamity, rendered houseless and destitute. The water rose *several feet in our yard*, and was for some days in the house. We took refuge with brother Goadby, till the waters subsided. The same flood which was so destructive in other places destroyed our chapel, which is now being rebuilt. We sent a circular to the Europeans, and they have generously enabled us to rebuild the chapel in an improved form. Thus, amidst judgments, the Lord remembers mercy. I trust the whole of the Mission property will be restored without any assistance from the missionary funds."

Of Cuttack in the year 1835, it is stated by the Secretary of the Society—" This city, being the first Station occupied by the Society, has of course continued a principal scene of the exertions of the brethren. Mr. and Mrs. Brooks arrived here, to reinforce the Mission, in a favourable state of health, on April 1st, 1835; and continue to be favored with that inestimable blessing. Mr. B. in his latest communication, states that both Mrs. B. and himself are well, that he had escaped fever, enjoys better health than he did in England, and hopes, by avoiding exposure, to enjoy many years in India. The evening after their arrival, they were introduced to the native brethren at Christianpore, among whom Gunga Dhor, though unable to utter a word that Mr. B. could understand, peculiarly interested him. Mr. Brooks appears to preach with considerable acceptance to the English congregation. The English congregation has much improved. It is observed, " Last Sabbath evening it was considerably better than usual; on the following Monday evening we had a large missionary prayer meeting, nearly as many as on the Sunday evening."

On April 12th, the English Chapel, having been nearly rebuilt, in consequence of the injuries it sustained from the desolating flood, of the preceding year, was re-opened. Mr. Brown preached in Oreah at four o'clock, and Mr. Goadby in English at seven. Both services were well attended. The place was rebuilt by subscriptions, kindly contributed in the neighbourhood. It is represented as a great improvement upon the last. Mr. Goadby remarks that it looks very well, and that there is not, he apprehends, much reason to fear dilapidation from a future flood, unless it were very violent indeed.

In the same month, a new native chapel was opened at Christianpore. Mr. Goadby states that it is a very neat commodious place. Mr. Brown remarks,—"This morning I preached for the first time in the new chapel at Christianpore; it was full, and we all seemed to enjoy the opportunity. The place was built entirely by the liberality of one gentleman, who has expended, within the last few months, *some hundreds of rupees upon our Mission.* The text was chosen for me, and one suitable to the peculiar circumstances in which the place was built. Luke vii. 5, 'He loveth our nation, and hath built us a synagogue,' which I applied to the particular occasion. This is a neat native chapel, and is beside a great ornament to the Christian village. I am to preach once on a week-night here, and once on the Lord's day in the other chapel. May these places be blessed to the conversion of many a benighted heathen."

The native preachers chiefly officiate in this chapel. One of them preaches at ten o'clock on the sabbath morning, and another at four o'clock; excepting on the Sabbaths when the Lord's supper is administered; one of the native preachers, also regularly preaches at Bhirapoor. At these places the congregations are good. It may be interesting to state that a piece of ground contiguous to Christianpore has been added to it. The old ground is stated to be about full. "This addition will be found highly useful The expense will be supplied here, and I hope this increasing Christian village will soon be doubled in size."

THE ENGLISH SCHOOL.

"This useful Institution has been proceeding during the last year, and the fruits have been seen in two young men having joined the Church. One is at present a scholar in the School and the other received his education here. The number of scholars on the books is not so large as last year, I have struck off the names of several who did not regularly attend; so that though the names on the books are less, the real attendance is better than last year. The engagements have been the same as in former years, embracing the usual branches of an English education, reading, writing, arithmetic, grammar, geography, and history. Their acquaintance with Scripture History and the general doctrines of the Christian Religion has been highly spoken of by persons competent to judge. Upon the whole our cause of thankfulness is great, that in this poor benighted country an Institution which has been so useful still continues to exist. A School *at Pooree* has been established, but this, though matter for rejoicing, has injured the subscriptions to this Institution. We have found excellent friends in the Collector and his Lady, who have frequently visited the school. Our examination passed off well, though as usual the attendance of the *great* was not large. The boys answered a multitude of questions apparently to the great satisfaction of those present. Many of the native Christian children attend the school, and besides English are learning to read and write their own language in the *Roman alphabet*, a system lately introduced and applied to all the Indian languages."

The year 1837 reported the return of Mr. Sutton and the arrival of Mr. and Mrs. Stubbins. It is gratefully observed—"The operations of the Society's Missionaries, and the sphere of their exertions, are now considerably more extensive, than they could be reported last year. An interesting addition has also been made to the number of the Society's Missionaries, by the return of Mr. and Mrs. Sutton to Cuttack, and the arrival of Mr. and Mrs. Stubbins in India. The week after the last annual meeting Mr. Stubbins was solemnly designated to his important work as a Missionary to India. The ordination service took place at Fleet, Lincolnshire, when an instructive charge to the young Missionary was delivered by Mr. Rogers, the estimable pastor of that Church. A few weeks afterwards he and his partner proceeded to India, in the Broxbournebury, Captain Chapman. In this fine vessel their accommodations were of the most agreeable description, and the kindness and attention of the excellent Captain of that ship, rendered their voyage peculiarly pleasant, which was also pleasant in every other respect. Mr. Stubbins by Captain Chapman's permission, had frequent opportunities of preaching on board, and also of endeavouring, by other methods, to promote the spiritual benefit of the sailors; and, previously to leaving the ship, Mrs. Stubbins collected *ten* pounds for the Mission. After having been ten weeks at sea, they reached the Cape of Good Hope where the ship touched. The passengers going for a few days on shore, the Missionaries took lodgings and pleasantly spent the short time they passed in Africa.

In the latter part of December, the Broxbournebury entered the river Hoogly. On the 4th of January, the Missionaries landed, and were kindly welcomed by Mr. Yates, and were then directed to the house of Mr. Thomas, the successor of Mr. Pearce, where they found lodgings, ready provided for them, and where they were treated with great affection and entertained most kindly."

On April 27, 1836, Mr. Sutton wrote to the Secretary representing his feelings on again beholding the wide wastes of spiritual desolation and death, presented in Hindostan, to the Christian's view.

"I wrote to you from Calcutta announcing our arrival in India, and giving an account of our Missionary party and voyage. The Brethren and Sisters destined for *Burmah*, *Siam*, and *China*, left us at Kedjeree, while we came up by the steam boat to Calcutta. It was an affecting parting with so many in whom I felt so deeply interested.

Our company now consisted of Mr. and Mrs. Day, destined for the Telingas, (their colleague Mr. Abbot, went on with the other party to fetch his intended wife from Burmah,) Mr. and Mrs. Noyes, and Mr. and Mrs. Phillips, myself, and Mrs. S. and Mary for Orissa, and Mrs. Tomlin for Calcutta. Never did I feel more the spiritual wretchedness and destitution of India than during this trip. The contrast between the blasting influence of Idolatry, and the blessed effects of the Gospel were probably more vividly impressed on my mind from my having just left the shores of a christian land. Oh it is grievous to contemplate the wide wastes of this benighted country, over which no Missionary's foot has ever trod, and where the joyful gospel sound has never been proclaimed. How did I long for one more opportunity of pleading with Christians in behalf of the wretched heathen! and how did I feel humbled and abased that I had allowed my golden opportunity to pass away with so poor an improvement! my feelings alas! too much resembled what they have ever been; regret and self abasement for the past, mingled with resolutions of more faithfulness and diligence for the future. How enviable the attainment, to have a conscience void of offence both toward God and towards men!

All the way from the sea to Calcutta, the banks of the Hooghly are crowded with villages, but not a single Missionary is there. Many a scheme did I revolve in my mind, for supplying these perishing multitudes with the bread of life; whether any one will prove fruitful time must reveal. We spent a fortnight in Calcutta, which was fully employed in making preparations for our journey, and future residence in Orissa. I preached four sermons, two in the Circular Road Chapel, one on board the Bethel, and one for Mr. Robinson, at Bow Bazaar. The first two I have since heard were not in vain. Two young men baptized last ordinance day, by Mr. Yates, both mentioned being benefited by my labours.

We at first proposed that the whole of our Missionary party should travel together over land, as far as Cuttack, but an opportunity having offered for brother and sister Day to go by sea, as far as Vizagapatam, they embraced it and are now waiting there for their colleague from Birma to join them. The rest of us acted upon our first agreement, and travelled over land to Balasore. Brother and sister Goadby were just settled here, and gave us a cordial welcome; as this was the case, and as brother and sister Phillips seemed to think favourable of Jellasore, a large village about thirty miles from Balasore, it was agreed to leave them with Brother and Sister G. to acquire the language, and otherwise fit themselves for this new station. This plan I ardently hope will be acted upon. After spending a few days with our friends at Balasore we prosecuted our journey to Cuttack: here we arrived in safety and health on Saturday evening 12*th March*, and were cheerfully entertained by Brother and Sister Brooks."

At this period it was stated—"The English congregation had increased. Several fresh Europeans attended. Several among them seemed hopefully serious, and Mr. Williams, the Judge at Cuttack, with his pious lady, appeared truly the friends of Religion. The latest reference to the state of the English congregation represents it as very serious and as numerous. Of one of the most solemn of Christian acts of worship, Mr. Sutton remarks,—

"Our assembly at the Lord's Supper presented a most interesting appearance; and cold must be the heart which is not affected at the sight. Our Chapel is almost filled with *Europeans*, *Americans*, *East Indians*, and *Hindoos*, who eat of the same bread and drink of the same cup. We are all one in Christ Jesus."

At another time he records the singular, but pleasing fact, that on a day when three Hindoos had been baptized, at a most refreshing opportunity at the Lord's table, they had in their company, communicants from *Mahratta*, *Bengal*, *Orissa*, and other parts of *Asia;* from *Portugal*, *France*, *America*, *England* and *Scotland*. Haste happy day when the nations to which these converts, uniting at one table at Cuttack, belonged, shall be all one in Christ Jesus!"

At a Committee Meeting in 1836, held at Loughborough, it was suggested, that *a Press* would be of great importance in Orissa. The suggestion was cordially adopted, and the annual Report stated, "To give more efficiency to the book and tract department of the Society's operations, the Committee have determined that a *printing press* shall be established at Cuttack, and placed under the immediate superintendence of Mr. Sutton. The Committee have accordingly determined that Mr. Sutton continue to reside at Cuttack, where, besides taking part in other departments of Missionary labour, he will take the especial supervision of the press; and it has also been arranged that Mr. Sutton and Mr. Lacey be joint pastors of the Church at Cuttack. This arrangement has been made with Mr. Lacey's cordial concurrence and approbation.

The Religious Tract Society has made its usual grant of paper for the printing of tracts: the grant is increased to ninety reams of paper, part of which the Missionaries are authorized to devote to the publication of *Baxter's Call to the Unconverted*. The American Tract Sociey, has announced to its supporters, that they considered it necessary for the year then passing, to appropriate the sum of one thousand dollars to thc Orissa Mission, and to that of their Baptist Friends, in the same district of India.

During Mr. and Mrs. Lacey's sojourn in their native land, they received the following letter, from the native brethren and sisters, whom they had left for a time, 'like sheep in the wilderness.'—But the great Shepherd, through the care of his under shepherds, preserved them from 'the lion and the bear.'

"Continually and for ever, may the grace and consolation of God our Father, and our Lord Jesus Christ, be with thee.

To our greatly beloved, our crown and our joy, even to Padree Lacey Sahib, and also to his Lady Sahib, do we address this epistle. All the christian brethren and sisters, who compose the Church of Christ in Cuttack, namely, Rama Chundra, Gunga Dhor, and Doitaree, with all the rest, send you much much love and christian salutation. On the following account have we written to thee: By the grace of God, at the present time, we are all well; and we desire to receive a letter, containing agreeable intelligence, from thee. Thou has shown unto us the great and glorious way of salvation. In the midst of darkness, by thy instructions we obtain to see a great light; thou hast been to us an example in the ways of holiness. The mercy which God intended before the world began, even that Gospel hast thou preached unto us. Affording us various help, and all kinds of excellent instructions, thou hast firmly settled and established our minds; and therefore by thy means, in the Lord Jesus Christ, we have obtained a new birth unto life. We are become of the household of God, and continually rejoice in the Lord Jesus Christ, offering praise to the Lord our God. Moreover, we enjoy the sweet hope of everlasting life; and therefore, O our greatly beloved, since the day thou didst depart from this place, and set out on thy journey to thine own country, taking with thee thy wife, and children, even from that day tears have not ceased to run down from our eyes for thee; for as a father and mother protect their children, so hast thou, with all knowledge, and understanding, and love of God, fed and nourished our precious souls. This instruction, even now, we daily digest in our minds. For thee we never cease to pray to God, that thou mayest obtain his grace; that as with thy wife and children thou didst leave this country, so thou mayest safely arrive in thine own, and there enjoy an affectionate meeting with all your brothers and sisters.

Give our affectionate christian salutation to all the Churches of Christ. May their prayers be to God on our behalf, for we are weak; then shall we be strong in the strength of the Lord. O may we remain steadfast in the good way even unto the end, and remain declaring the Gospel in this benighted land, till at length, in the day of the Lord, we shall all find grace from Him. That we obtain this grace, O pray for us. O, beloved brother, we heard of the affliction which happened unto you while you remained in Calcutta, namely, that you heard there how that thy father had gone to heaven: we were on that account much concerned for thee. Also we heard how that Boxoo stole some of thy property, being ungrateful, as well as how you had not money sufficient for your journey, and were greatly distressed. But most of all we heard of the affection which you manifested for us at the moment of your departure, even by your tears. We heard also that thy children, and thy lady Sahib, wept at the remembrance of us. All this we heard; and when the intelligence reached us, we gave ourselves up to grief, and were as though we should not again see pleasure. Goadby Sahib read to us the letter you sent from on board, which letter informed us of the illness of Willie baba, and we all united in prayer that God would recover him from sickness, and protect and save you all; nor shall we feel our minds at rest till we receive a letter from thee. In the cold season we went out with the missionary brethren to preach the Gospel, and we distributed many tracts. We have preached on the Lord's-day to the Native Christian congregation, and Mr. Brown has also done so. Mr. W.—— has greatly assisted the Church, being very kind and useful. In Christianpoor he has built a chapel for us, new, and of substantial materials. Here we have divine worship, while a large verandah in front serves for a school-room for the Native Christian children, where they obtain wisdom. He has morever opened a well in the new christian village, where our brother Hurree Paree lives; he allows our aged brahmunee sister something to eat; and has agreed to support Krupa Sindoo as a Native Christian preacher, as well as expresses himself generally very favourable towards all the brethren and sisters. From these intimations, we hope that his heart towards the Lord is well affected.

Since thy departure Sebo has been baptized, and now he and his family live in the house of Bamadab at Nokora. The rice you left has been sold, and the money deposited in the hands of Goadby Sahib. Padree Goadby went to Calcutta to seek for a wife, and from America there came a wife for him, and to her he was married, and returned in one month to Cuttack. Padree Brooks has arrived at Cuttack, and lives in the Bungalow belonging to Mr. Brown, where he is studying the Oriya under the pundit Bhagnutty-misser. We are all well. The chapel near the house of Gunga Dhor, which you know was destroyed by a flood, has been rebuilt and there is English worship therein. On Lord's-day, at four o'clock in the afternoon, we continue to have Oriya worship in this chapel, when Mr. Brown officiates. We have divine worship at Bhogerpoor, in the little chapel there; we preach by turns on every Lord's-day. Mahadab-das has not been restored to fellowship; his mind is not at present in a right state. *Gunga Dhor*, he who laid hold upon the river Gunga, and *Rama Chundra*, Ram, who is of the nature of brightness, and *Doitaree*, he who conquers demons, and *Krupa Sindoo*, he who is a sea of mercy, and *Bamadab*, he who is as a god of comfort, and *Rahadoo*, he who destroys Rahoo, and the *Bruddhee-bhoonee*, she who is the aged sister, and *Dahanee*, she who reduces to ashes, and *Komilee*, she who is softness, and *Hurreeparree*, he who is the saviour or deliverer, named Hurree, and *Treelochun*, he who is the three-eyed, and *Coranusowa*, he who bears mercy, and *Seba-purree*, he who understands Sebo, *and Boleram*, he who is the strength of Ram, and *Soobanee*, he who is the sweet worded, and *Sodanunda*, he who is the ever-joyful, and all the rest of the men, women, and children, are well. Truly some are occasionally indisposed in body, but get well again. All these brothers, sisters, and children, to thee, and to thy lady Sahib, once more much much affectionate salutation send. Also to the child Hannah, and to the child Willie, and to the child Charlie, all the above persons send kisses of love.

To all the brethren and sisters believing in Christ, of the churches in England, the brethren and sisters believing in Christ who are of the church in Cuttack, send their endless endless salutation. We are all in one mind, proceeding in the path of the Gospel, and are praying and labouring for the extension of the kingdom of God. The brother who came from Bisak-patna, (Pooroosootum,) and was baptized, has sent us a letter. He has had much inconvenience in travelling from place to place with his wife and children; but has been finally appointed to one of the mission stations on the Coromandel coast, along with Mr. Gordan, whom you saw at Madras. There he is preaching the Gospel. Bamadab and Krupa Sindoo have been chosen to preach the Gospel here; and the rest of the brethren are in the offices they held when you were here.

The charge which thou didst deliver to us, a written copy of which we received from thee, the same have I read, and in all things think of thee and long after thee. Please give my salutation to the other ministers of Christ there, and to my christian brothers and sisters. About many other things we intend to write to thee again in a short time. Favour us soon with an answer to this letter. Tell us where you are—the name of the town or city, and about thyself. We have some inquirers, who are obtaining instruction, and things are much as they were when you saw them. And now what more shall I write? all things here are known to thee. Pardon the liberty we have taken in writing to thee."

April 5th, 1835, *Cuttack.*

Appropriate reference is made to the new feature in missionary proceedings, occasioned by the consecration of Miss Kirkman to the good of her sex in India. It is stated—"The Committee received an application from Miss Kirkman, a young lady, who is anxious to consecrate herself to the promotion of the spiritual welfare of the female population of India. The peculiar departments of exertion, to which, it is conceived, she may devote her efforts, are female education, and the instruction of Hindoo women. The Committee *unanimously and with much pleasure* accepted Miss K's. offer of herself. Her estimable parents, in a spirit of consecration to the cause of Christ, like that of their beloved daughter, much as they feel the sacrifice, cheerfully resign her; and with a similar devotedness to the Redeemer's glory, *engage to allow her annually such a sum as will be sufficient for her support.* Surely the friends of the mission will pray, that His favour, whose presence fills the heart with nobler joy than even the society of the most affectionate and pious child, may rest abundantly upon them; and that they may rejoice in the confidence, that whether in this uncertain world they meet again or not, the interval, at the longest, will be but short before they meet in heaven; and there feel that every sacrifice they could ever make, was infinitely more than merited by Him who bought them with his blood. May they part in the spirit of that eminent Christian, who leaving, for a scene of danger and death, the beloved wife of his bosom, calmly said, 'We have an eternity to spend together.'"

The Report of 1838, announced the return to India of Mr. and Mrs. Lacey, accompanied by Miss Kirkman to Orissa. It is stated —"Amidst the numerous population of this first station of the Society's labours, the glad tidings of redeeming love have continued to be proclaimed, and some additions have been made to the Saviour's flock. During the past year, Mr. and Mrs. Lacey have returned to their former station, accompanied by their devoted young friend Miss Kirkman. The farewell services connected with the departure of these friends from England, took place at Leicester, August 22nd, 1837; and early in September they left England for

India, in the Royal Saxon, Captain Renner. During the voyage, they had many opportunities for public and social worship, the Captain encouraging Mr. Lacey to conduct divine service.

"As the Commanders of some East India ships are so unfavourable to religious worship, it should be known that Captain Renner manifested a very different spirit. He always endeavoured to make way for divine service; the men were generally present; but when they could not be spared from the management of the ship, the Captain and others attended; and besides Lord's day morning worship, lectures on Lord's day evening and on Wednesday evening were delivered by his request. Among the sailors, books and tracts were distributed; and hope was entertained that salutary religious impressions were made upon the minds of several individuals during the voyage.

"They reached Calcutta in January; they received a kind welcome, and were entertained at the house of Mr. Hughes, Ballegunge. During their stay in Calcutta, Mr. Lacey had frequent opportunities of addressing numbers of Oreas on the great truths of the gospel. So many of the natives of Orissa resort to Calcutta, that he found himself every where surrounded by persons who could understand him. By many he was recognised as 'the Cuttack Padree Sahib, who preaches against Juggernaut, and exhorts the people to worship Jesus Christ,' and felt it not unpleasant to be thus recognised.

"On the 19th of February, Mr. Lacey and his companions embarked for Tumlook, and thence proceeded to Midnapore. While there, for a few days, Mr. Lacey preached to large and *attentive* crowds in the Bazaar. Thence they proceeded to Balasore, and Cuttack. Of their arrival at the latter place, Mr. Lacey states,—'About eight o'clock in the morning of the *first of March*, the bearers set us down at the school-house, where brother and sister Sutton are located, and thus our long journey ended. We were glad to see our old friends and fellow labourers, and joined sincerely and fervently in thanksgiving to our kind heavenly Preserver, that he had so long preserved us by land and by sea, and had at length brought us together again, where many of our best days have been spent, and much interesting labour bestowed. As we passed through the town, the people ran to express their pleasure to see us again, and throughout the day numbers of persons arrived, to say how glad they were to see us again in Cuttack. Komile and Danee were here, when we arrived, and were much affected, when we again spoke to them; and the native Christians one by one dropped in to pay us a visit. I need not say there was a mutual pleasure from once more seeing each other. Brother Stubbins postponed his departure till our arrival; he is now gone to Berhampore, where, judging from the place and the labourer, there is every prospect of his usefulness. I found the native church better than I anticipated, the *number of the members has considerably increased.* The native Christian children's boarding school, forms now an interesting feature of the Mission in Cuttack. The first sabbath after my arrival was of great interest. I preached in the morning in Oreah, with much liberty and pleasure, in the chapel in Christianpore. Almost all the Christian community was present, and the chapel was well filled. In the afternoon I administered the Lord's Supper to the Church, composed of Natives, Indo-British, and English, in Oreah and English. O what a pleasing sight! a large chapel full! At night preached again in English, chapel full. *We must have a new and larger chapel, and are setting about it.* We thank God and take courage. I am much engaged in the Bazaar and at Mellas."

The return of Mr. and Mrs. Goadby to their native land, is referred to, and the expected ordination of Mr. Wilkinson to the great work in Orissa.

The blessed cause of the Redeemer gained ground in the following year. The first Tract printed at the Cuttack Press, was hastily composed for the Ruth Jattra of 1838, and was entitled—"*The wonderful advantages of a Pilgrimage to Juggernaut.*" The evils of this pilgrimage are there detailed. Many of these Tracts have been circulated.

Of the manner in which church business is conducted, one of the brethren gives an interesting statement, in furnishing an account of a church meeting. "This evening we had one of the most interesting Church Meetings I ever attended. The members were almost all native. Of Europeans there were only ourselves, Captain Bamfield, and Mr. Palfreyman. After singing and prayer in Oreah and English, an application for re-admission was dismissed on account of the individual having been discovered to make too free a use of gunga, so much so as to become intoxicated. A candidate's name also was struck off the list. The names of *eight* candidates were then read over. Some were fresh ones. Their cases were considered, and their experience, profession, and conversation canvassed with much prudence and christian feeling. Four were received, Mr. Harris, schoolmaster, Komilee, the wife of Mahadab, Rosikaront, and Harree, the wife of Boliakonta. The baptism to take place next Lord's day; the natives to be baptized in the open air, where heathen natives can come to see and hear, and the European in the chapel after the evening sermon." The baptismal services took place as appointed: Mr. Harris was baptized in the chapel, and the Hindoo converts in the open air, when, it was supposed, about eight hundred spectators were present.

The enlargement of the chapel is particularly referred to at this time. "The chapel at Cuttack has been enlarged to more than double its former size. Its present dimensions are fifty feet long by thirty wide, with a verandah ten feet wide on the sides and front. This enlargement was rendered necessary by the increase of Europeans at the station; by the additions made to the native church, and by the increase almost every month of the native congregation. This rendered the former chapel inconveniently small, especially on those sabbaths when the Lord's supper was administered. Mr. Sutton collected for the object about seven hundred rupees, which he transferred to the hands of Mr. Lacey, who had much of the superintendence of the work. A circular was sent to the Christian residents in Cuttack and the vicinity, which soon raised about five hundred rupees more. To this, subsequent additions were made, and the whole expense, amounting to *one thousand four hundred and twenty rupees*, has been defrayed. Above an acre has been added to the chapel ground. A tank has been opened in the centre of this ground, for use on baptismal occasions. This tank is about one hundred feet wide. With the soil taken from the tank, the ground in the old chapel yard has been improved, and the whole of the ground enclosed with an embankment, to prevent the ingress of the flood in the rainy season. The whole of the ground which has been enclosed, is planted round with cocoa-nut trees of five years growth, which add much to the appearance of the place, and will hereafter add to the usefulness of the addition. The cocoa-nut plant being the exclusive perquisite of the sacerdotal class, and being usually planted around the temples of the land, their appearance around this christian sanctuary produces a favourable impression on the natives.

The chapel was re-opened on Lord's day, August 19th. Mr. Sutton preached in the morning, from 1 Cor. iii. 9. In the afternoon the native congregation assembled at four o'clock, and Mr. Lacey preached on Isa. liii. 11. A goodly company of natives, all clean and orderly, were present, and many were in tears. Mr. Lacey preached again at seven in the evening, from Isa. liv. 2, 3.

The attendance was good, the attention serious, and the whole a day of mnch holy pleasure.

After relating these events Mr. Lacey remarks,—"It is just twelve years since the chapel was first opened. I laid the foundation stone in May 1826, and on November 5th of that year delivered the first sermon. Brother Sutton was at Cuttack at the time, and assisted, and we have been spared through twelve eventful years, in an Indian climate, and are now permitted together to re-open the Chapel after an enlargement to more than twice its former size. This is what is seldom seen in India. We were then without a single native convert, and yesterday the coldest heart must have been warmed, to have beheld our native christian congregation."

The ordination of Mr. Wilkinson, is mentioned at the close of the Report. "The ordination took place at Wisbeach, Cambridgeshire, August 1st, 1838. The services of the day were of an interesting and solemn nature. Mr. Wilkinson's account of his religious history, excited much deep feeling throughout a crowded and numerous congregation. His conversion from sin and infidelity was connected with circumstances of a singular kind, and strikingly displayed the power of divine grace. An introductory discourse was delivered by Mr. J. B. Pike, then of Boston. The ordination prayer was offered by Mr. Jones of March, and was very solemn and appropriate. The questions to the young Missionary were proposed by his warm friend Mr. Peggs, of Bourn, and a short charge was addressed to him by the Secretary of the Society. During the solemn services of this important day, the presence of the Lord was enjoyed. On the morning of the day, Mr. Wilkinson was united in marriage to Miss Desborough, a valuable young friend, much esteemed and beloved in the church at Wisbeach, to to which, like her partner, she belonged. They were to have sailed for India in a few days, but various delays took place, so that they did not finally leave their native land till late in September. They then sailed in the Moira, Captain R. M. Carthy. Another Baptist Missionary and his wife went in the same ship. They touched at the Cape, and from thence Mr. Wilkinson addressed a letter to the Secretary.

The Socicty was, this year, much indebted to a kind friend, the late Miss Barnes, of St. Ives, Hunts, for two bequests, one for *a thousand pounds*, to be paid without needless delay. The other for *four hundred and fifty pounds* at the decease of an individual, who is to receive the interest during her life. Miss Barnes had long been a warm friend to the Society. She has left the larger legacy for the expressed purpose of sending out additional Missionaries. The subject has been laid before the Committee at a recent meeting, when the following resolution was adopted, "The Committee pledge themselves to appropriate the money left by Miss Barnes, to the purposes specified in her will, on the receipt of it."

Mrs. Wilkinson has given an interesting account of their first interview with the Native Ministers, which took place at Cuttack, March 30th, 1839, where the brethren were assembled for their Annual Conference.

"The native preachers soon heard of our arrival, and came to see us. They had assembled in an adjoining room. Brother Lacey led us to them. All were seated on the floor, but they instantly arose, and presented a noble army on the Lord's side. I was truly delighted to see their intelligent faces, and hear their solicitude for the best interests of their countrymen. Gunga, in his figurative manner of speaking, asked Mr. Wilkinson "*If any other Missionaries were hanging to his tail?*" We said, "Why are you so anxious that others should come?" He gave three reasons,—

First.—Because there was a great sinking in the well of ignorance, and more ropes were wanted to pull the people out.

Second.—Many were drowning in the sea of sin, and more ships must be sent to rescue them.

Third.—He desired that many more Christians should follow the example of Christ, who left heaven that he might do good to men."

The year, whose proceedings are thus in part detailed, proved on the whole an important and encouraging year. For the measure of success that has been enjoyed, much gratitude and praise are due to God. This is the view taken by our estimable brother, Sutton, who observes, "On the whole we consider the year to have been one of general prosperity, and which in many views calls for our fervent thankfulness to the Author of every good and perfect gift. Let us labour on, taking fresh courage from the past, and present success; and animated by the hope, "that when we have fought the good fight, kept the faith, and finished the course, there is a crown, in reserve, which the Lord the righteous Judge, shall give us at that day."

In reference to the future, Mr. Stubbins takes a very encouraging view. He writes, "*My conviction is, that Orissa is whitening to the harvest, and we want only men to gather in the precious and immortal grain.*" Thus encouraged by mercies received, and by hopes excited, the Society is bound to use every effort to send other labourers into the harvest."

An anonymous donation of £60. was, a few months ago, sent to the Secretary, to assist in sending out Missionaries. A considerable part of Miss Barnes's legacy, for the same object, has also been paid to the Treasurer; and John Wright, Esq. of Birmingham, with singular liberality, offered to the Committee, to defray one third of the expense of the outfit and passage of four Missionaries.

The statistics of the church at Cuttack in 1840, is stated—"Since the year 1828 when the first Hindoo was baptized the record of baptisms is—Europeans and East Indians 53; Hindoos 95. To the above are to be added nominal Christians and Enquirers 196.—The Report of 1845 states—"The number in connection with the Society's stations, that are freed from the shackles of Hindooism, cannot now be much, if any, below one thousand; for according to statistics furnished by your senior Missionary, the number at Cuttack, and the locations more especially connected with the station amounts to 816. Of this number there are at Cuttack 409. Christianpore 89. Laceycie 34. The Asylum 92. Societypore 39. Khunditta 39. Choga 44. Bhogerpore 15. Indo-British 55. It is not pretended that all these are really christians, but many of them are such, and the rest, including children, are delivered from the chains of Hindoo superstition and idolatry, and are brought under christian instruction. This is not a trifling measure of success, though small compared with what is needed."

The year 1841, saw the mission considerably assisted by the ordination of Mr. and Mrs. Grant, the appointment of Mr W. Brooks as a Printer, and of Miss Derry as assistant to Mrs. Stubbins, (formerly Miss Kirkman.)—"These brethren with their wives and Miss Derry, sailed for Calcutta, June 17th, in the Pekin, Captain Laing. The service in which Mr. Grant was set apart to this great work, and in which all this interesting party were reminded of their duties, and commended to the divine blessing, took place at Nottingham on Tuesday the first of June. The day was one of much sacred pleasure. Numbers displayed a lively interest for the object, to which this band of young disciples of the Saviour were devoting themselves. Mr. Grant in his answers to the usual questions, manifested much intense concern to be employed as a Missionary labourer, declaring that he would prefer being a Missionary to the highest earthly dignity, and that his desire was in India to live, in India to die, and in India to be buried. The Committee have determined that his station shall be fixed by the next Orissa Conference. Mr. Brooks is placed as a Missionary Printer upon the same footing as a Missionary in every respect. In the first instance he goes to take the superintendence, and whole management of the mechanical part of the Printing Establishment; but as he has manifested talents for preaching, it is deemed most probable that he will by degrees, engage in other Missionary labours. Miss Derry goes out to assist Mrs. Stubbins in promoting female education, and instructing Hindoo women. The expense of her outfit and passage has been defrayed by the Ladies' Society for advancing education in the East. The managers of this Society have manifested the interest they take in Mrs. Stubbin's labours, and their satisfaction with her efforts, by a grant of twenty pounds to assist her schools."

The year 1842 terminated *the first twenty years of the Society's actual labours in Orissa.* Mr. Pike in his own peculiar style, describes the position of the Society, and his views are happily confirmed by Mr. Lacey.—"When your Society was just struggling into life, it was remarked, that a Missionary Society resembles a stream tending to the ocean: at first a rivulet, that may be measured by a span, but which, increasing as it flows, swells till the insignificant brook expands into a river, and swelling still, before its course concludes, the river becomes a sea. A hope was then expressed that this then little stream might, in some distant age, long after those, who saw it rise, were forgotten,—pour the waters of salvation, through many a barren spot, in the wide heathen wilderness. The events of the past twenty years furnish evidence that this hope was not presumptuous. You may look forward to a time when thousands of christian churches, as so many centres of light and love, shall bestud that portion of India, which falls to the lot of your Society. Then the land will have its temples, but they will all be temples of Jehovah. It will have its songs and its offerings, but its songs will be the sweet hymns of Zion, and its offerings millions of renewed and consecrated hearts. It will have its pilgrims, but they will all be pilgrims to the city of the living God. Prophecy predicts these triumphs, the zeal of the Lord of hosts will accomplish them; and their commencement is found in your humble yet expanding efforts. Your little rivulet has already swelled to a brook. On this fact one of your brethren in India has remarked;—"Twenty years have now elapsed since our brethren and sisters, Bampton and Peggs, with one native christian attendant, Abraham, trod their unfriended way to this place. The darkness of Idolatry was then universal and unbroken; and compared with what then existed, in relation to the good cause, our present circumstances must induce the exclamation, '*What hath God wrought?*' It is the Lord's doing, and is wondrous in our eyes! From this spot, where five souls formed the little christian band, the cause has spread from the centre to the uttermost *north and south of the land;* nor overlooking intermediate places, and more local settlements. At Berhampore, we have three European and two native labourers, with a native christian church of more than *twenty members:* and the Gospel is being made known throughout a wide and populous district. At Ganjam, sixteen miles north of Berhampore, we have two European and three native labourers, with a church of *ten or twelve members;* and through a wide field the empire of Idolatry is being invaded by the light of divine truth. At Balasore, there are two American and one native labourer, with a church of some *twelve or fourteen christians.* At Jellasore, a few miles north of Balasore, there are two American and two native labourers; all actively employed in circulating that knowledge which in its progress subjects all mankind to the love and service of God. At Midnapoor, although no results have appeared, yet books have been put in circulation, and to some degree the tidings of mercy have been made known. And now, at Calcutta, amidst a population of more than a million souls, we have four European and two native labourers; with a church of *sixteen or eighteen members,* seeking the eternal salvation of some forty thousand of the sons of Orissa, who have wandered there in search of the bread which perisheth. While at Cuttack, from whence these branches have generally shot forth, we have six European and four native labourers, with a church of *one hundred and twenty two members;* and three minor stations, where native preachers are labouring for the edification of the native christians placed under their care, and for the instruction of the multitudes of heathens all around them. And the movement of all these Stations, (except Midnapoor, now for a time vacated,) is onward. The preaching of the Gospel, is awakening enquiry, the tracts are distributing knowledge, and the numerous schools are instructing the young, while our Press is pouring forth a tide of instruction to be let into a thousand channels to fertilize the whole land. Upon the whole, there is reason to say, "*The Lord has done great things for us, whereof we are glad.*"

The efforts of the Missionaries to diffuse the Gospel in Cuttack, and its vicinity, have continued through the past year, and have not been in vain. *Sixteen* have been added to the church by baptism, fourteen of them Hindoos, and the other two Indoo-britons. Mr. Lacey states, that the year has been marked by no circumstances of *unusual* interest in the progress of the sacred cause, but it has offered no reason for discouragement. He justly observes, that in India the progress of christian light is like the dawn of a morning, darkened by dense and universal fogs. On such a morning the light struggles long with the darkness, but its progress though imperceptible, is certainly, and finally triumphant. Thus the dawn of a bright and blessed day has broken upon the benighted Oreas; and that dawn has advanced during the past year.

On the first Lord's day in December, five candidates were baptized, four of them young persons. The other was a widow of an enquirer from Choga, who died while he was seeking instruction. She assists in cooking for the girl's department of the School, and is very steady and consistent. On the day of baptism the chapel was crowded. Mr. Lacey preached and baptized, and afterwards administered the Lord's supper. He observes, it was a happy, "a very happy opportunity, a day long to be remembered."

On the first Sabbath in February, a Telinga convert belonging to the sixth *Madras Native Infantry*, was baptized, being the eighth baptized from that regiment during its sojourn at Cuttack. "They are now," the Missionary writes, "called to China, but they value the word of God, and can use it with great ease, and I hope and think they will be able to go forward in the good path."

Of Missionary Students and Native Ministers, it is stated—"The last Report announced that *Somnath*, *Damudar*, and *Sebo Naik*, had been placed under Mr. Sutton's care, as students for the ministry; the two former were boarders, and the latter being married was a daily attendant. They thus continued till a special Conference in October, when it was agreed that they should be received as assistant preachers, Damudar to accompany Mr. Sutton to Calcutta; and Sebo to go to Berhampore, and assist Mr. Stubbins; and Somnath to remain at Cuttack. Mr. Lacey referring to them observes, "We have added three to the number of our native preachers, who are all men of more than ordinary promise."

Mr. Sutton referring to them and to the period of their continuance under his care writes, "It was a short experiment, but long enough amidst all the imperfections attending it, to show its importance, and what results may be expected from a proper and thorough system of training. These young preachers bid fair to make useful men, and fully justify our selection of them to the office they sustain. Still it were to be wished, the two youngest could have had a year or two of close study of several subjects, immediately bearing on their work." He adds,—"Khumboo has not been received as a student yet, but I have still hopes of him. The next most promising class on our premises, are four of the youths recently converted, but they are still so very young, that nothing can be said of them as preachers for several years, though I am determined on commencing a course of preparatory studies with them, so soon as I can find a master. My pundit that I employed in teaching them Sanscrit, is retained by Brother Lacey, and I have not yet been able to find another. At present, therefore, I can only report on the past, and say but little as to what may be done during the current year. I hope however, to lose no opportunity of promoting this important branch of our work, so far as I can do it, or secure co-operation in it. May the Lord raise up and send forth during the present year, a class of Damodurs, and Somnaths, and Seeboos."

The subject of cultivating native talent, and of training up suitable converts as native ministers, has been frequently referred to, in letters from the Secretary, especially in correspondence addressed to Mr. Sutton. In a recent communication he expressed his strong feelings upon this subject, and made a proposal to which the Committee have most cheerfully acceded.

"I suppose I may do something in the matter of Government translations; and this, in connexion with my probable return to Cuttack, leads me to make a proposal to which I beg your kind attention. I find that it is vain for me to expect to do much, (excepting on the Sabbath), beyond my daily labours in translating and correcting the press, and taking the general oversight of our educational department; and that the little time I can spare from writing, may be most advantageously employed in endeavouring to train up a class of young men as native preachers. Now we can have little hope of permanently and extensively benefiting Orissa, without raising up an efficient native ministry; but to do this involves considerable expense, both for their education and support. My question therefore, is, Will the Committee sanction me in endeavouring to increase and improve this department, and in devoting to it any funds that I may realize by my labours in translating and printing, beyond what is necessary for my own support? or, if we should be unexpectedly prosperous, beyond that of the support of Brother William Brooks also? Teachers of some kind must be employed in this department, and if we should prosper so as to get any thing of a class, it will be well worth a considerable portion of the time of the best qualified man the Committee can send. We want no display either in our establishment or our men, but the means of raising up a body of hardy efficient labourers, who need not to be ashamed, rightly dividing the word of life. I cannot expect to do more perhaps than get such a branch of our Mission into operation, and lay the foundation for its continuance; but to do this is worth living for, and I should feel that it is an object worth all the time and labour I can spare, and happy should I be to commence it, and then hand it over to some Brother better qualified by talents and grace, to carry it on to perfection. Most Christians may by a little extra exertion and self-denial, do something more than they would otherwise in behalf of a favourite object. We, I suppose, are no exception to this general law; it rests with the Committee to supply the necessary stimulus to exertion."

At the Conference the following arrangement for the labours of native ministers was made for the coming year.—*Calcutta*, Gunga Dhor, Seebo Sahoo, and Damudar.—*Cuttack*, Rama Chundra, Ramadab, and Somnath—*Midnapore*, No application.—*Khunditta*, Luckindas and Doitaree, in succession—*Pipley*, Doitaree and Luckindas, in succession.—*Ganjam*, Balage.—*Berhampore*, Pooroosootum aud Sebo Naik.—*Ballasore and Jellasore*, Bickharee. In case of Gunga not going to Calcutta, Bamadab takes his place.

The Society was this year much indebted to the Religious Tract Society, for the grant of 200 reams of paper, part of which was to be appropriated to the publication of Barth's Church History, and two volumes of Tracts for the use of the Native preachers and others. The Bible Translation Society made a grant of £150, and the American and Foreign Bible Society, the handsome grant of 1300 dollars, or £265. 18s. 2d. Of this sum 300 dollars were directed to be given in copies of the Scriptures, to the American Brethren at Balasore and Jellasore.

The Report for 1844, gave a favourable view of the parent Church at Cuttack.—"At this first station, christian truth has continued to exert and extend its influence. Several converts have been added to the church though not so many as in some preceding years. The long-tried Missionaries have on the whole been favoured with a large measure of health. Mr. Lacey in his annual Report records the divine goodness in having permitted him to spend another year in India in the enjoyment of almost uninterrupted health. He remarks:—"I have felt much less of that lassitude and weakness which are so natural to this climate in the past year, than in any former years of my Indian existence, and have consequently been able to spend most of those months among the people, during which the weather admits of our being out with safety. I have not felt it to be either unpleasant or injurious to be out in the sun all day long, in communication with the people, or in going to and returning from their places of resort. I have, I believe, no greater desire than that my time, my health, and my life should all be devoted to the cause of God; and I hope as He has hitherto, so also, in time to come He will enable me, every year of my remaining existence, to do something for the spread of His knowledge, and the promotion of His glory. I feel that as the past portion of my life recedes and mingles with the ages that are past, never more to be available for serving God or benefiting man; the small portion that may remain is infinitely important; and the more so as my capabilities henceforth for doing good will not increase but decrease."

"Our personal labours (says Mr. Sutton) are carried on in a narrow space, but I would hope are destined to have a wider influence. For myself I have been "nailed to the wood" pretty closely all the year. The past year like all the years which have preceded it, has had its lights and its shadows, its sorrows and its joys. The conditions of our warfare are present toil and future rest—present sorrow and future joy—present expectation, and oft disappointment, but future realization and fulness of delight. He who now "*goeth forth weeping bearing precious seed, shall doubtless come again with rejoicing, bearing his sheaves with him.*"

The church contained 140 members, of which eleven had been added during the year. Amidst the defects of which their pastor complains, the fact that family worship prevails among these dear people is an interesting evidence of the reality of their religion and a token for good. Mr. Lacey observes that the means for improving in christian knowledge, which the possession of the Scriptures and other religious books furnishes are *daily* used, and he adds, "Their family worship has generally been attended to with regularity, and on a morning visit I have sometimes found—*every house in the village engaged at their devotions. The head of the family sings a hymn, reads and prays.*"

The following is the arrangement for the labours of the Native Ministers :—

"*Calcutta*, Bikharee.
Balasore, Seeboo Naik.
Khunditta, Somnath and Parasua, on trial.
Choga, Bamadab and Doitaree, if restored to his office.
Jellasore, (belonging to our Society,) Rama, junior,
Berhampore and Ganjam, Balagee and Denabunder.
Cuttack, Gunga, Rama Chundra, and Damadur, in part.
New Station, Sebo, and Damudar partly.
Pippley, No supply."

In the Report of 1845 it is stated—"At the conference at Cuttack it was agreed that the Hindoo brethren, Seboo Sahoo, Sebo Naik, Balagee, Damudar, and Somnath, should be ordained to their work as native evangelists. To this number Denabunder was afterwards added. Most of these brethren had satisfactorily passed a probation of three or four years as assistant preachers. At the same time it was agreed to receive Prasa Rout as an assistant preacher.

Several English friends have forwarded presents to the native ministers, which have not only administered to their comfort, but been received with gratitude as expressions of christian union and love. Friends at Nottingham took a leading part in this labour of love, and very pious and interesting letters have been received from their Hindoo friends; several of which have been published in the *Repository*. One of the Hindoo brethren writing to a lady at Nottingham, observes,—"The articles which, on account of the grace of Jesus Christ, you sent to me and my wife as tokens of your regard to us, we have duly received.—For these tokens of your love, what return can I make? When I look upon the articles, be assured I will not forget your kindness. The warm clothing has been a great comfort to me. In the cold season when we were travelling about with our dear pastors, it protected me from the cold and rain, and thus aided me much in attending to the Lord's work. Though we may never see each other in this world, through the grace of our Lord Jesus Christ, I hope to meet you in heaven."

It appears evidently desirable that manifestations of love, like that to which these lines refer, should from time to time be repeated by christians in England to their brethren and sisters in India.

Of Mr. Buckley's ordination to the work of a Missionary it is stated—"In imitation of Apostolic example as recorded in Acts xiii. 2, 3, he was solemnly set apart to this work by prayer and the imposition of hands on May 29th. The service took place in the new and spacious chapel at Derby. On no occasion, it is believed, not even when the Society's first Missionary was ordained, did a greater number of friends, attached to the sacred cause assemble. The service was solemn and impressive, and when the congregation were requested, if they would pray for and support the Missionary, to express this, by standing up, nearly the whole assembly instantly arose. Let all who then, before the Lord, expressed their determination to support his cause, remember that the vows of God are upon them. That day week, your devoted brother commenced his voyage, by going on board the Wellesley, Captain Toller, which with the divine permission, is to land him at Vizagapatam, thus diminishing his travelling by land, and lessening his voyage several hundred miles."—The voyage was very favourable. He writes from Madras, Sep. 10th, 1844, "I have had a remarkably propitious voyage; it is with one exception the quickest ever made. We lost sight of dear Old England shores June 14th, and 78 days after, August 31st, we anchored in Madras roads." The voyage and journey to Vizagapatam and Berhampore, were attended with many mercies. May this beloved brother long prove a great blessing to India.

The Society's Report of 1845, gratefully records the return of Mr. Stubbins and also the ordination of Brethren Miller and Bailey. "The home proceedings of the Society, during the year, have demanded an unusual degree of attention and exertion. The number of missionary services attended by different brethren, and especially by the brethren Stubbins and Hudson, has been very considerable. The calls on the Committee have been more frequent, than in most preceding years, and it is trusted that they have not laboured in vain, in endeavouring to carry out the resolutions announced in former Reports, of sending Missionaries to China, and considerably increasing the number in India. The result of their efforts on the former subject is before you. And towards the accomplishment of the resolution of sending *five* additional missionaries to India, some pleasing progress has been made. The attention of the Committee having been directed to Mr. William Miller and Mr. William Bailey, as candidates for missionary service, their applications were considered, and after much enquiry and deliberation, the Committee determined on accepting them as candidates for the important office, and of placing them, on probation, under the care of the estimable Tutor of the academical institution at Leicester. The improvement they made under his tuition was so encouraging, and his report and that of other friends, as to their spirit, deportment, diligence, and mental ability, so satisfactory, that the Committee, at a subseqnent meeting, cheerfully accepted them for the great work to which they wished to devote their lives. To that work they have since been solemnly set apart. The designation services of Mr. William Bailey were held in Broad-street, Nottingham, where a most crowded and deeply interested audience attended. The ordination of Mr. William Miller took place at Heptonstall Slack, where, as at Nottingham, much holy interest and sacred feeling were experienced. Soon after these interesting and momentous days, the farewell services of Mr. Stubbins were held at Leicester. These were solemn and impressive in no ordinary degree, and will not be soon forgotten. Multitudes of friends from neighbouring towns and villages crowded the house of God. Intense feeling pervaded the breasts of many who went that day to receive and bid farewell, in the case of numbers a last farewell! to their beloved and devoted missionary brother and sister. Hundreds then again pledged themselves to pray for, and support their missionary friends, and many prayers were offered, which it is hoped will be recorded in heaven, and answered through future years. All these brethren, with Mrs. Stubbins and Miss Collins, who is sent out to assist Mrs. Sutton, sailed in the *Wellesley*, Captain Toller. In their way to Portsmouth they passed a few days in London, where they experienced the kindness and hospitality of some of the London friends. At Portsmouth they were welcomed with equal cordiality, and experienced a most hospitable reception at the hotel of Mr. Totterdell, who had previously welcomed and treated with equal kindness your missionaries for China. Letters have been received from some of your friends since they went on board. Mr. Stubbins observes, "I believe we are all devoutly thankful that we are on our way to India—

> "I would not change my blest estate
> For all the world calls good or great,"

is I believe the feeling of all our hearts. I have spoken strongly at many of our meetings, but never too strongly, never stronger than I would wish to do on a dying bed. My only regret has been that I could not more fully depict the state of those to whom, blessed be Jesus! we are carrying the gospel. I should like to be at the meetings next week, but I had rather be where I am." Influenced by such feelings, your brethren and sisters go to the burning plains of distant India. Surely you will think of them, pray for them, and support them!"

In reference to the progress of religion at Cuttack, it is observed —"At this first station, it is trusted that the word of truth has made some advancement. The number of the real and nominal christians at this station has been already mentioned, as *about five hundred,* including the young persons in the Asylum. The number in communion at Cuttack itself, is stated to be *one hundred and thirty-seven,*—but this evidently does not include those members that are connected with the six christian locations in the neighbourhood, for the whole number of members is stated to be one hundred and eighty-nine, though the number at each of these places is not distinctly named. During the year 1844, fourteen were added to the church by baptism, and four by restoration; while two were separated from it by exclusion, and one by death. Various information is given respecting events that have transpired, the labours pursued, and the effects resulting from them."

At an experience meeting, Ram Chundra spoke of 'the delightful contrast that was exhibited between what he then witnessed of the progress of the gospel, and the gloomy scenes of his early pilgrimage.'

"I bless God for what my eyes have seen and my ears have heard; things which I never believed I should see, yea, of which I always despaired. When the first brother Gunga became a christian, and Krupa followed, and next by the grace of God, I was brought in, how few and feeble we were. Of knowledge we had very little, of right conceptions how few. We met with our instructors and tried to profit, but all our services were in so small a way! All around seemed dark; there were none but ourselves to speak to; none to bid us God speed. Whenever we past the door of those we knew, they pointed and said, che! che! fie! fie! I used to have a thousand fears whether I was right. Sometimes I wondered what was before us, how our families would be preserved, where I should get a wife for my son, and to whom I should give my daughter! No others seemed to come forward and I despaired of them coming. If I went to a distance I used to have a thousand fears. Satan disturbed my peace by suggesting, your wife is dead, your house is burned, some misfortune has befallen your children; while every where, from every body, we met with opposition. But God has been better to us than all these apprehensions. *Here I can meet with two or three hundred brethren and sisters, a thing I could not have believed would ever be.* We can read and pray and tell of our experience, and help each other.

The gospel has brought down our pride and levelled our distinctions; and we can marry our children without difficulty and as we please. I see our young folks growing up to succeed us old ones. Yea, I have heard our children* preach to me the gospel, and seen them go forth with us to the work. Again, then, I bless God for what my eyes have seen, and my ears have heard."

The writer fears that this sketch of the history of the Mission, in reference to Cuttack, may be thought too full and disproportionate; but it is hoped, its intimate connexion with every movement of the cause of Christ in Orissa, will render this record of *the mother church* valuable for reference and example to her sons and daughters for generations to come. May "the little one become a thousand, and the small one a strong nation. The Lord hasten it in his time."

POOREE, OR JUGGERNAUT.

This celebrated seat of Hindooism in Orissa, is the second missionary Station of the Society. An invitation had been given by the Serampore Brethren to settle at Midnapore, but this great high place of Idolatry, appeared more central and important. As the English Government might disapprove of a Station so near the Temple of Juggernaut, the Brethren consulted their valued Friends at Serampore. They replied under date August 18th, 1823.

Very dear brethren,—After giving your case every degree of attention in our power, we are of opinion that one of you is warranted to remove to any other place in Cuttack,† or even near it, without any new application to government. Indeed, we think such a step in reality more pleasing to them, to do it without them than with any fresh application. Our ideas are, (although we may be mistaken,) that while an application is necessary at the first entrance into a country, the less they are troubled afterwards the better they are pleased. *Permission* is at all times *authorizing* to a certain degree, and this relative to missionary efforts seems like an attempt on the part of government to change the religion of their native subjects; every apparent advance towards which they wish to avoid, even while they may in reality wish it effected, on the ground of humanity alone. Hence as you have their permission to reside in Cuttack, we think you need not apply for any minute permission as to the part of Cuttack you may choose; or whether you may occupy, jointly or separately. The land is before you; arise and possess it in the name of its Maker and Lord. Pooree we think a good station."

Mr. Bampton first visited this city, during the Ruth Jattra, July 1823, a full account of which is given in the Report of the following year. He thus described his removal from Cuttack to his new scene of labour. "Mrs. B. and myself left Cuttack in a

* Younger members coming forward to engage as preachers.

† That is, the District so called.

boat, Sept. 17th, and arrived here in about twenty-three hours. We should have waited till the rains were over, but the river from Cuttack to Pooree unexpectedly becoming navigable, we thought it best to take the opportunity; I should however be more careful about removing in the rains again, for many of our things got very wet, and it has cost us much care and labour to prevent books and other articles being much injured. Our bungalow stands on the barren sand, about a furlong from the sea, and twenty minutes' ride from Juggernaut's temple; it contains six rooms, and we can see the temple from five of them; a hill of sand twenty or thirty yards from the house, partially hides the pagoda, but ascending that, we have a view of it. I shall not now attempt a description of the temple; unless it could be put to a better use, we should triumph in its downfall. The people, however, are by no means willing that it should be dilapidated. A wealthy native has just given fifty thousand rupees towards repairing and perhaps beautifying it: and no wonder, for it is the residence of his god."

In a later communication, he writes:—"During the first few weeks I went about the town to make myself acquainted with it, and daily, or nearly so, gave away some books; numbers took the books very readily, though I had reason to conclude that some were shrewd enough to regard them as so many stones thrown at the great idol. Thus, comparatively inactive, I was not very comfortable, and began to open my mouth quite as soon as my judgment would admit of it; and I now talk a little to them every evening. Besides the resident population, the town is important as a place of great resort. We had many pilgrims here a few weeks ago, at the Kartiku festival. Besides going out in the evenings as usual, I was amongst them several hours in the day time for three successive days; I went in a palanquin, and kept as much in the shade as I could, but was obliged to stay at home the next three or four days. In the present state of things, European Missionaries are indispensable; but we are poor creatures in the torrid zone. There are in Pooree, several tanks or pools, in which the pilgrims bathe, and they are thought very sacred; one of them, called Sagtee Gunga, is said to have a subteranean communication with the Ganges. They also bathe in the sea, at a place (perhaps a mile from my house,) called Swurgo Dwaro, literally translated, heaven gate. When I was going out this morning, I was told there was an assembly at that place; so taking thirty or forty pamphlets and tracts, I repaired thither, and soon disposed of them; the assembly was so numerous, that I wished I had had many more. I generally hear every one read a few words before I give a book, and where there is a crowd, this is not only necessary for its most obvious reason, but also to preserve order, which, on two or three occasions, has been so far interrupted as to render it difficult for me to prevent the people's taking the books away from me by force."

Of the labours of 1824, the Report of the Society stated, "At Juggernaut, Mr. Bampton continues to labour with an assiduity worthy of the cause in which he is embarked. His station is in many respects peculiarly important, yet peculiarly painful. Cut off almost from christian intercourse, banished even from European society—surrounded only by idolators, who are mad upon their idols—beholding sand plains strewed with human bones, and the lofty tower of the horrid temple in which Satan seems to entrench his power; this, circumstance from day to day, from month to month, from year to year, the Missionary has peculiar need for confidence in heaven, and exercising that confidence; even at Juggernaut, our brother declares he expects great things. His labours, like those of his brethren, were for some months interrupted by an alarming illness, which brought him apparently to the brink of the grave. At this critical period the medical knowledge which he acquired previous to leaving England, appears to have been of considerable advantage; with a firmness which few would have displayed, he bled himself repeatedly, till he had extracted from his veins nearly five pints of blood, and thus checked the progress of a fever, which otherwise would probably have terminated fatally, before medical assistance could have been procured. On two occasions his knowledge of medicine appears to have been the means used for preserving the life of the Native assistant, Abraham. In about two months from the period when his illness commenced, Mr. Bampton was sufficiently recovered to resume his labours, and appears to devote himself with unabating fervour to his work. His labours among the Natives are abundant—his perseverance in pursuing those modes which may qualify him for extensive usefulness, appears great."

Not content with the sphere of his immediate vicinity, from a letter recently received, it is learnt that he was about to undertake a journey that would occupy a fortnight, into another part of the benighted regions around him. The Natives manifest, in many cases, the utmost eagerness for tracts and the scriptures; in fact, so much eagerness, that the distribution of those little messengers of mercy becomes a task of considerable difficulty, yet their distribution at Juggernaut is peculiarly important, as thence they will be carried to the remotest regions of India. At this station various difficulties obstruct the progress of education, yet two schools have been established. A biragee who had received a grant of land from the high priest of Juggernaut, has actually given a part of that land for the erection of a school-room. There heathen children will be taught those sacred scriptures, which are adapted to benefit men in every age and clime, and of which a converted African once said—These are the weapons that will conquer Africa—they have conquered me.

Mr. Bampton speaks of a greater degree of attention, as paid by the Hindoos, to the sacred instruction he delivers. At another time, he mentions an inquirer coming from a distance, to acquire some knowledge of the new religion. To those painful feelings which spring from disappointed hopes, Missionaries must be subject, and he has experienced these. Amidst labours and trials, privations and difficulties, he, and Mrs. Bampton persevere; and while he feels the weakness of human efforts, he leans on the Almighty, and expresses his confidence of final triumph."—In this year, a most horrible Suttee was reported, of which, our brother was an eye witness. It occurs in a former part of this history.

Though exposed to insult and contempt, Mr. B. was, through divine grace, enabled to pursue with unabated zeal, his benevolent labours. He wrote in 1825—"If the violent partizans of Juggernaut imagine, that either clamour or bitter reproach will deter me from preaching the Gospel among them, they have formed a false estimate of my character; or else I have formed a false estimate of it myself. Though I have sometimes thought whether it were wise to attack the strongest holds first: if, however, the result be a failure, it may resemble a blow at the heart. I am in the hand of God, and if he say, *go hence*, I must go; but I hope the poor Hindoos will find a friend, and the Idols an enemy, wherever my lot is cast. On the whole, I never was so happy in the ministry before, and I never was so much given up to it. Except a newspaper, I read nothing that is not closely connected with my work; and though this people oppose, opposition strengthens the spirit that contends with it; and the Lord being my helper I shall doubtless be a match for them: and the time may come when they will find me out a little more. I do not wonder at a spirit of opposition shewing itself, for besides what Abraham does, the people have what English preachers would call four or six short sermons every day, in different parts of the holy city; so that, as my pundit once said, they have nothing but Yesoo Kreest, Yesoo Kreest, Yesoo Kreest."

In 1825, a poor wretched woman was rescued from the burning pit, in which, at Juggernaut, the Suttee was accustomed to be immolated. This was an event of considerable importance, contributing to the suppression of the practice, which a few years after crowned the labours of the friends of India. A description of the scene by Mr. Sutton, is given in the Society's Report for 1826, pp. 12, 13.

This year was peculiarly affecting to the indefatigable missionary at the station, by the affliction and death of Mrs. Sutton, who had been in the country so short a time. The following extract of a letter from the author, will briefly record here this mysterious event. "I accompanied brother and sister Sutton to Pooree, April 28th, and continued there till May 12th, endeavouring to bear my part of the affliction that lay upon us through the continued delirium of our dear sister. I took my leave of her with forebodings that I should see her no more in this world, and events soon ratified the truth of them; O what a heavy cloud was now passing over us! On the 13th I arrived early at Cuttack, and before 12 o'clock that morning, saw my third sweet babe expire, aged five months and nineteen days. How mysterious are these dispensations to us, but "He erreth not in council." The next morning early, the Collector lent us his palanqueen carriage, and we conveyed the dear remains to the depository of the dead. Three years that day our first child was born; thus in three years, three dear children have been born and buried at Cuttack, but "He doth all things well." On the day following, Lord's day, 15th, our dear sister Sutton was removed—her imprisoned spirit escaped from its chains of mortality, insanity, and affliction, and bowed before the eternal throne.—Help Lord, and let not the heathen say, Why are the Padres so afflicted, if their religion be true, and God love them? Dear brother Sutton will inform you fully of these painful circumstances. Thus purified, may we bear much fruit."

Though Pooree, (says the Secretary of the Society,) is considered Mr. Bampton's station, yet he by no means confines himself to it, but travels about spreading the tidings of the gospel, during several months of the year. In the early part of 1826, he finished an excursion of *three months*, during which he had left Mrs. Bampton at Pooree. In some later journeys he has been accompanied by Mrs. Bampton. Of his views on the subject of such excursions to make known the gospel, and of his assiduity to become increasingly qualified for the great work he has so labouriously pursued, some information from one of his journals must be gratifying.—

"Some people talk of staying and cultivating a small spot well, and so on: for my part, I think that a town containing thirty or forty thousand is nothing like large enough for any one healthy active Missionary. And I think travelling a great deal the plainer path of duty; the difficulties of it are the greatest hinderance.

"*Aug.* 23*rd.*—Ganjam. I arrived here with Mrs. B. yesterday, having spent six days on the road. Previously to leaving Pooree I had filled three sheets of paper with objections to Hindooism, under the following heads:—Idolatry is contary to the shastras. It is contrary to reason. A number of actions connected with Hindooism are ridiculous. Many of the Hindoo religious sentiments and practices are very grossly wicked. Many others are chargeable with having a very wicked tendency. The examples of the gods have a tendency to encourage sin. The shastras have also a wicked tendency. The shastras contradict one another. Hindooism exposes its adherents to much pain and expense when they have been guilty of any faults. There is much in it, which renders it probable that it was invented by brahmins for their own advantage. The first of these heads contains ten sections. The second, five. The third, four. The fourth, five. The fifth, four. The sixth, fifteen. The seventh, thirteen. The eighth, three. The ninth, eight or ten particulars; and the tenth, forty-five. Perhaps several of these heads will be enlarged, and I have more matter which wants arranging. I commonly carry my notes with me, when I go among the people, and read them, sometimes among my very perverse hearers at Pooree, with considerable advantage. Besides them, I carry with me five sheets of notes on evangelical subjects. I walked the greater part of the way hither, and Mrs. B. rode my horse. I hope to be out a good deal, and think that there is nothing either very reasonable or scriptural in my wife spending a deal of time alone at Pooree, while I am wandering alone about the country. Peter and some others of the Apostles led about their wives, and I am at present favorable to modern Missionaries doing the same. During our journey we slept three nights in places built for the accommodation of travellers. Their exterior looks better than most buildings in the country, but their interior is not half so desirable as those of an English barn; but they were the best lodgings we could get, for being the rainy season, I dare not trust to my tent."

Thus several months in the year were employed by Mr. and Mrs. Bampton, in travelling through the distant parts of the country to publish the glorious gospel. These journeys must necessarily have been connected with much fatigue; but the seed sown will assuredly bring forth much fruit.

In 1829, the first reference is made to the illness of the invaluable missionary at Juggernaut. It is stated—"One of the trials experienced by the Society has been the severe illness of the indefatigable brother, who was stationed at this emporium of idolatry. This illness being long continued, has prevented, in a great degree, his exertions during the past year. Probably those exertions have been too great for his frame, notwithstanding his constitution appeared so peculiarly adapted to India. On one occasion his journal contains the following statement,—'I was walking, chiefly barefoot, and preaching *nine hours and three quarters*, only stopping a few minutes to eat some biscuits I had with me. I am almost always barefoot, partly because it makes me more like the majority of the people; partly because it adds to my hardihood, and partly because it is very convenient. One is stopped by no sort of roads; and if one is at any time up to the ancles in mud, one is probably soon after up to the knees in water, out of which I come clean and comfortable, whilst in an English dress all this would be miserable."

Reference is here made to the adoption, to a considerable extent, of the native dress, for the advantage of travelling and conciliating the people. No one doubted the sincerity and the magnanimity of Mr. Bampton in this proceeding; but the writer's convictions, in unison with other brethren, are unfavourable to such a line of conduct. When Capt. Minchin, his neighbour, first met him in this dress, he had to assure him that he was *compos mentis*. Such explanations to various individuals and classes of society, must be any thing but desirable or useful. Indeed it is not improbable, that his health was seriously undermined by this step. His labours however were enough in a few years to have worn down the best constitution.

We have seen that on Dec. 27th, 1827, he was honoured to baptize the first Hindoo convert. This important event occurred at Berhampore. By the itinerant labours of Mr. B. the land was "searched out,"—and both Ganjam and Berhampore have become interesting stations. A trip to the sand heads was found useful, and in Sep. or Oct. 1828, he returned by sea to Pooree, his health for a time improving. During part of this year, Mr. Sutton devoted his labours to Pooree, and met with less opposition than formerly.

At the great festival in 1830, the Missionaries could not do so much as in some former years; some exertions, however, were made by preaching and the destribution of Religions Tracts to pilgrims on their way, to diffuse the Gospel. At this festival an impressive illustration was furnished of the inefficiency of mere human science for effecting the destruction of idolatry. Many wealthy, learned, and respectable Bengalees were present, who had been educated in the colleges and institutions of European literature in Calcutta and its vicinity; yet these learned heathens, notwithstanding their acquaintance with European science and their cultivation from European manners and customs, could adore the detestable wooden idol, with as much apparent devotion as the most ignorant idolater. A friend remarks, "I had many opportunities of witnessing this fact, for scarcely a day passed but I had a dispute in English, with one or more learned Bengalees on the subject of Idol worship."

It is with pungent feelings of regret, that the death of dear Bampton is recorded. "The severe illness of the estimable Missionary who laboured here, has terminated in his removal to a better world. He died in peace, Dec. 17, and his mortal remains rest, till the resurrection of the just, near the temple of that modern Moloch, whose infernal rites he laboured to destroy. He has fallen in the sacred warfare, but doubtless the confidence he indulged in the anticipation of such an event, will hereafter be realized; that strong-hold of superstition itself will fall: and in some future age, when that temple has lost its votaries, Oreah Christians may gaze on its deserted ruins, or stand on the spot that covers the dust of Charlotte Sutton and William Bampton, and thank God that they loved not their lives unto death; but went forth to India, bearing that precious seed, from which will spring the copious harvest of many following years."

In the Report of 1832, the notice of this station is very brief. It is stated—"At Pooree Mr. Sutton spent a considerable part of the past year. Gunga Dhor assisted him during a part of that time, and after leaving, spoke encouragingly of a few people there. Mr. Lacey says there has been good done to some of the Pooree people, but as usual opposition has run high. In March, Mr. Sutton remarks,—"Our daily work in the bazaar has not been neglected. The congregations have been usually less than at Balasore, but they have behaved pretty well for Pooree people.

The people are awfully sunk in sensuality, infidelity, and sin. Were it not for the pilgrim hunters, I apprehend the numbers who come would be very small. The opposition in the way of obscene abuse, runs very high, and has probably deterred one or two from making a public profession. Oh the abominable expressions shouted out against Gunga and me this evening! It would frighten half England to hear them. Still I have no doubt it produces a favourable effect. All reasonable persons see that abuse is not argument, and that we do not deserve this treatment."

Of the following year it is said—"At this high place of the abominations of idolatry, efforts to diffuse Gospel light have been continued during a considerable part of the year. In 1832 the brethren remaining in the province assembled here, and held their annual Conference, at which a variety of business of importance and interest in connection with the cause of religion was transacted The senior missionaries engaged in public labours, and were assisted by several of the native brethren, who at times addressed to great numbers the message of heavenly mercy. Rama Chundra on one occasion was supposed to have as many as 7000 hearers, and was engaged in preaching the Gospel or in disputation with its opponents most of the day: yet opposition here continues violent. For at this place not only human depravity and satanic rule support idolatry, but the same principle which led Demetrius and his coadjutors to excite the madness of the mob at Ephesus, influences the pundas and brahmins at Juggernaut. "Ye know," said Demetrius, "that by this craft we have our wealth. This our craft is in danger to be set at nought." Just thus at Juggernaut all the worldly interests of a most abandoned, impure, and depraved people, are connected with the support of their demoralizing idolatry.

Pooree had been for some time the scene of Mr. Sutton's labours, but illness obliged him to vacate this station. He visited Calcutta in the latter end of 1832, where he was attacked with fever, and in accordance with the advice of his medical advisers, sought renewed health and usefulness in a voyage to America and England. From this time this station has not been regularly occupied, but has been the scene of occasional exertion. At the great car festival, the Brethren generally, with the Native evangelists, improved the opportunity afforded by the immense concourse of pilgrims, of disseminating far and wide the good seed of the kingdom, the fruit of which they have gathered in various parts of the great field.

In a letter after the festival of 1833, one of the Missionaries wrote,—"The evil of the unnatural connexion of the Government with temples and the system of worship, is more and more apparent, and more and more operative. *The support and protection of Government is the great bulwark of Juggernaut's strength, and the all prevailing plea for his divinity.* An attempt has been made to remove the odious union, by a pious, good man the Secretary of the Board of revenue, but the opinion and advice of interested persons have been asked, and at present seem to prevail. The advice, &c. you may suppose was not the abolition of the tax, and was supported by various specious arguments: yet surely the time will not be long, ere the tax will be abolished and the people left to support their own idols. When this shall be the case Juggernaut will fall; but the measure will be received as a boon by the people, and none will complain but the interested Pundahs and Biragees." Two months after making these remarks the writer had the pleasure of stating,—"September 16. Orders have been received from the Court of Directors to do away with the tax upon all holy places! From hence does Juggernaut's fall commence and he will rise no more."

Great was the triumph of Christian principle over a system of wicked, worldly policy, when it was determined that Britain should no longer postitute her power in the East to support the abominable idolatries of Hindostan. Let this event be regarded by the Members of this Society, with unfeigned delight; and while they praise Him, under whose blessing every desirable event is accomplished, let them be thankful, that their institution has contributed in part to accomplish a good so great, as the dissolution of British connection with Indian idolatry." But it was not until April 1840, that the pilgrim tax was repealed, and this good work was marred by an annual "Government Donation of 60,000 rupees to the Temple."

Of the year 1836, the Secretary states—"As usual this detested seat of the Moloch of India has been the scene of exertion, though no one of the Society's Missionaries has recently *resided* here. In July Mr. Sutton, accompained by his *American* brother Noyes, visited Pooree, to embrace the opportunity for diffusing divine knowledge, afforded by the confluence of pilgrims at the ruth jattra. The festival was unusually late, and, in consequence, a much thinner attendance, than Mr. S. had ever previously witnessed; but it was, as heretofore, a most heart-sickening sight. Death triumphed before the close of the festival; and himself and fellow labourer were glad to hasten from the scene of blasphemy and cruelty. They distributed a considerable number of tracts to the pilgrims, especially as they were leaving the town to bend their steps homewards. Mr. S. remarks, "My companion was much affected by the scenes he witnessed; for myself I could not help contrasting this vast worshipping assembly with the holy convocations, I attended in Exeter Hall, and in New York. O how did I wish they could be seen in contrast by the Christian world. *A glance at the festival of Juggernaut, one would think would be enough to rouse the Church, and especially to send home the attendants on our religious anniversaries, watering their path with precious tears of gratitude for the blessings of the Gospel.*"

At a special Meeting of several of the brethren this year it was determined, that Pooree should be visited at its various festivals by the neighbouring Missionaries; and that the bungalow formerly belonging to Mr. Bampton, and subsequently to Mr. Sutton, should be retained and repaired for their accommodation, at such times. This arrangement was approved at the Cuttack conference in 1837; and has since been sanctioned by the Committee. The propriety and importance of this arrangement are evident, when it is considered, how numerous are the idolatrous festivals at this horrid place; how vast the crowds that assemble at some of these festivals; and how desirable it is that the Missionaries should attend at such times, to circulate religious truth; and to have the opportunity of meeting with those weary wanderers after rest, that are occasionally found among the crowds that are attracted to Pooree, by the fame of Juggernaut."

At the great festival in 1838, no less than *seven* brethren were employed in diffusing gospel light among the myriads of benighted pilgrims. The brethren thus engaged were Lacey and Stubbins, Gunga Dhor, Ram Chundra, Pooroosootum, Bamadab and Bikharee. About 200,000 pilgrims were computed to be present at the festival. One of the Pundas of Juggernaut, exclaimed,—"If the hopes of the worshippers of Juggernaut be all a delusion and we are all deceivers, why does the Company levy a tax and support the Idols in all this glory?"—*Proh dolor!*

In the Report 1842, it is stated—"At this high place of Hindoo idolatry, the labours of your brethren have resembled those of former years. The brethren Sutton and Lacey, with Bamadab, Rama Chundra and Seboo Naik, attended the last great festival, which presented scenes of the most appalling misery. It being the third year of the famine in the district, so much scarcity of food existed, that the Magistrate at Pooree sent notice to various parts of India, warning the people of the danger, to which they would expose themselves, by undertaking the pilgrimage. This is supposed to have lessened the attendance at the festival, which, notwithstanding, is stated to have amounted to at least two hundred thousands. Mr. Sutton states, that as he approached Pooree, there was no crowd at the gates, as in former years, the tax office being removed; but he was surprised at the number of dead and and dying lying about in all directions. He observed, "Never did the place appear to me so disgustingly wicked, and miserable. The filth every where was abominable; the atmosphere was loaded with the effluvia, every spot seemed redolent of cholera, while the multitude of cadaverous countenances, and extenuated framework of human bodies, seemed a perpetual comment on the text, "Their sorrows shall be multiplied who hasten after another god."—I was glad to leave Pooree again. It never looked to me so much like the habitation of devils, and the abode of every unclean and hateful thing. I did not see the idols nor the temples this year excepting from a distance, my work lying in a different direction. I found the roads excessively muddy; nevertheless the people laid themselves down to sleep in the muddy places, by hundreds and perhaps thousands, all the way to Cuttack. While the day-light lasted on my journey I saw many dead by the road side, and many more of the living, or rather dying, who ere the morning dawned, would be added to their number."

In 1825 the Society adopted measures to remove British connection with Idolatry in India. "A Petition founded on a draft was brought forward by the Secretary to be presented to the House of Commons and the East India Directors, against British support of Hindoo Idolatry, and a copy of the petition to be forwarded to the Secretaries of the other Missionary Societies." This vitally important object has been steadily prosecuted to the present time, and with considerable success. In reference to Pooree, in 1843 it is observed; "Of the labours of the brethren at this high place of idolatrous resort, the information received this year, is much scantier than usual. Petitions have been adopted from the Committee to the two Houses of Parliament, against the unholy connection between the British Government in India and the idolatry of that superstitious land. And memorials on the same subject, have been forwarded to the Court of East India Proprietors, and to the President of the Board of Control. The first of these memorials was presented by Mr. Poynder, who however postponed a motion on the subject till September, in consequence of Sir Robert Peel having stated, in the House of Commons, that a dispatch upon the question at issue, had already been sent to India. The memorial to the President of the Board of Control, was presented to the Earl of Ripon, by Wm. Evans, Esq., Member for North Derbyshire, and Mr. Peggs. His Lordship read the memorial carefully, and expressed his interest in the proper settlement of the question, to which he engaged to pay attention."

The Report of 1845 refers to the visit of the Brethren to Pooree, and fully details, "the sorrows of those who seek after another God." It is added; "The public prints have announced that the efforts of Christians to dissolve the wicked connexion between the Indian government and the temple of the Moloch of the East, have been at length successful. It is stated that the British government have renounced all connexion with the Temple, have withdrawn their money, and surrendered the temple lands to the votaries of the idol. This is another triumph of christian principles over a system of wicked worldly policy."

BALASORE.

This is the third station occupied by the Society. *In the first Report of the Orissa Baptist Mission*, printed at Cuttack, reference is made to the occupation of it by different Missionaries.—"In 1814, Mr. Peters, an East Indian, under the patronage of the Serampore brethren, commenced missionary labours at this station, but it was not occupied by the Orissa Missionaries till 1825. Early in January, Mr. and Mrs. Sutton visited this place on a missionary tour, and eventually decided on making it our third station. At that period, and for many years previously, nearly all traces of Mr. Peters labours had disappeared, and the whole town had undergone an entire change. The five factories of the Danish, Dutch, French, Portuguese, and English, had mouldered into ruins, and the walls of an old Catholic Chapel alone remained to testify that it had ever been visited by the professed ministers of Christ. Mr. and Mrs. Sutton continued to labour at Balasore until the death of Mr. Bampton, when the weak state of the mission obliged them to leave a field that seemed "white unto the harvest," in order to be near their solitary colleague at Cuttack. The station was subsequently occupied by Mr. and Mrs. Goadby, and after their return to England, in 1838, it was made over to the American Missionaries."

The Report of 1828 announced the formation of this station. "The Society has now the satisfaction of possessing a third missionary station in Orissa. This is at the populous town of Balasore; and was established by Mr. and Mrs. Sutton, who removed thither in the early part of the year 1827. Of this station letters of Mr. Sutton furnish some interesting information. "Balasore, in point of size, is the first town in Orissa Proper, and contains about 10,000 people. It is surrounded by an infinity of little hamlets; the whole neighbourhood is covered with numerous little villages, which send forth an immence population, and which give it the character of the most populous part of the province. The town is situated about 170 miles from Calcutta, 100 from Cuttack, and 150 from Pooree. It has been in its day one of the most important of the European settlements, before the way was opened to Calcutta. At this day may be seen the remains of the British, French, Danish, Dutch, and Portuguese Factories; and many of the inhabitants remember the flags of these five nations all flying at the same time. Very little now remains of all the glory and authority of the last four, besides the tombs of their adventurers. There are indeed two very high triangular pillars, with the word 'Copenhagen Factory;' and the ruins of a Catholic Chapel. The Danes also have about an acre of ground and a few trifling buildings; just enough to give them authority to hoist the Danish ensign on Sunday morning. I have seen nothing particular belonging to the French; and the general trade of the place is now nearly annihilated. The inhabitants of the town are a mixt community of Oriyas, Bengalees, Mussulmen, and a few low Portuguese. One of the principal inconveniences which I at present experience from the distribution of the people, is the want of a focus or meeting place, where the people are to be met with in large numbers, similar to the principal bazaars at Cuttack or the vicinity of Juggernaut's temple at Pooree. I have not as yet discovered any temple or object of worship remarkable for either its size or popularity, though there is a great variety of objects which share the veneration of the people—Juggernaut, Krishnoo, Mahadaive in different forms: Doorga Punchunun, (five faces), and Ade Mata (first mother), seem the most popular. My acquaintance however is as yet but superficial. The general character of the people, however, seems to proclaim them exceedingly depraved. The lasciviousness of their character seems to be more glaring than in other places."

Besides direct missionary efforts, Mr. Sutton preached to a small congregation of European and Indo-British that assembled at the house of a military officer, Col. D'Aguilar; which led to the publication of his *Family Chaplain*, in two volumes, a work which has been extensively and usefully circulated in India. Mr. Bampton died at Pooree, Dec. 17th, 1830, and a few weeks after, Mr. Sutton removed to that station. He left Balasore with regret, and missionary operations were thus suspended for some time. That town with its vicinity, was the scene of a dreadful inundation, by which, according to the Magistrates' reports, upwards of 20,000 persons perished! Mr. Sutton's house was swept away. At the annual Conference, to the enquiry, "Can Balasore be occupied?" the missionaries were compelled to say, "We regret, that with our present strength, it cannot."

Mr. John Goadby removed to Balasore in Jan. 1836. It is stated in the Report—"But for long and severe affliction he would have removed thither at an earlier period. Since his settlement in India, he has experienced a large portion of affliction. Having lost his estimable partner, he some time afterwards married an American lady, who went out from the Western American Missionary Society in company with Mr. and Mrs. Brooks. In August last, Mrs. Goadby was taken seriously ill and was confined to her bed nearly three months; during which time, of course, she demanded a large share of her husband's attention. Previously to her illness commencing, disease was insidiously attacking his constitution, and scarcely had she left her bed before he was obliged to call in medical aid. He suffered much for several months, but in February last, stated that his general health had greatly improved and was better than previous to his illness.

At this time Mr. Goadby contemplated fixing in a populous neighbourhood entirely away from European example. He reremarked,—"I have begun to entertain very serious thoughts of going from Cuttack, to some thickly populated neighbourhood, and commencing a station away from European example. This appears to promise more success, and that will be an abundant compensation for the increase of privations and difficulties. The only serious objection is distance from medical aid, but God is able and willing to preserve us as well in the wild, as in the cultivated spot. And I am happy to say I shall not meet with any opposition from Mrs. G. indeed it is what she wishes as well as my own desire. It is worth all the vexation attendant upon travelling in this country, to be far away from Europeans, surrounded by jungle, to feel that though there be no loved object near us, no friend with whom we can take sweet counsel, God is with us; our union to Him seems closer, our intimacy with Him increases, and He becomes our friend and companion. These have often been my feelings, and I doubt not the feelings of many others engaged in the same good work."

Soon after the time when these remarks were penned Mr. and Mrs. Goadby experienced their long afflictions, after which it appears they determined on fixing at Balasore. For this step the following among other reasons are assigned. "Balasore is a populous neigbourhood and the key to Orissa, as important a station quite as Cuttack. All pilgrims from Bengal and upper Hindostan must pass it to Pooree; and of all the pilgrims, who visit that Moloch of the East, nearly ninety nine hundreths come from those parts." Gunga Dhor, with his family and another Christian convert, accompany Mr Goadby to Balasore, and thus will form a little Church there. This other native brother is likely to be employed in Mission work, according to his ability. Mr. G. referring to him and to his own plans, remarks,—"I have some thoughts of stationing him at the ghat or ferry over which all travellers entering Orissa must pass, to distribute tracts, &c. to them; it is about two miles from Balasore, and I should visit him frequently. Respecting Schools I cannot decide anything yet, but hope that in addition to the native one we shall be able to raise an English School, if we do, I intend it shall not be liable to be in any way chargeable to the Society. At present the Gentlemen are all absent from the station, therefore I cannot make a beginning in any thing of this kind. I shall begin an English service as soon as I am able to preach, which I hope will not be long. Mrs. G. is extremely anxious to obtain a native female school but this requires time. You are aware that there was many years ago a Christian church here, there are no remains of it now."

In 1838 reference is made to the station being again destitute. —"This station has been a second time deprived of a resident Missionary. For some years it formed the scene of Mr. Sutton's labours. After his removal had taken place, the station was, for a time, unoccupied. At length Mr. Goadby removed to this place, and, though he suffered much from illness, hopes were entertained that he would be able to persevere in his important labours. These hopes, however, have been disappointed. The ill health of himself and Mrs. Goadby rendered it absolutely necessary for him to leave Balasore, which was thus, again, deprived of the services of a resident Missionary. While there he was assisted by the native minister Gunga Dhor, who, besides frequent preaching, visited the Schools, that were established, and examined the children. Some pleasing appearances were presented during Mr. Goadby's residence at Balasore. When for about two months he seldom went to the Bazaar, and Gunga not frequently, the people flocked to his house, and would sit in the verandah, *sixty* or *eighty* daily, from two or three o'clock till evening. They came from different parts of the county, and hundreds of them carried home the word of life, while many fervent prayers were offered that it might make them wise unto salvation.

In the cold season, before the time of his leaving India, Mr. Goadby made several missionary journeys, but at length was altogether laid aside by illness. In visiting various villages, he felt much encouraged by the attention of the people. In the beginning of December he crossed the river, and visited ten or twelve other villages, and spoke in most of them. He then went to Seragun, and after spending ten happy, and he trusted useful days there, removed to Buddruck, where he continued till sickness drove him home. In that district he spent nearly a month, went round the whole neighbourhood, and had many pleasing and many painful opportunities with the people. During the latter ten or twelve days of his stay there, Doitaree and Bambadab were with him and laboured well. Thus the good seed of the word was scattered far and wide. Three men offered themselves as candidates for baptism, but none of them were received; there being reason to apprehend that they were not truly converts to Christ." This interesting station, after the return of Mr. Goadby to England, was occupied by the American branch of the Mission.

BERHAMPORE.

This Town, though not permanently occupied for some years, early enjoyed the visits of Messrs. Bampton, Sutton, Goadby, Lacey, Brown and Stubbins, and much good seed was sown which has rewarded the toil of the labourers. Mr. Bampton often visited this Town and its vicinity.

Mr. Sutton thus describes his visit Dec. 1825, Christmas-day and Sabbath. "I arose to go into the Bazaar according to my promise; but the natives gave me no opportunity. Early in the morning they came in flocks, of all ages and pursuits, from the proud byraggee Brahmun, to the little child, Oriyas and Telingas, to hear about the new doctrine and get a book. I never had such a day in my life; as soon as one group left, another came, so that I was perpetually engaged from morning till night, to different sets, in preaching and giving away books. Indeed I talked till I could talk no more, and was obliged to steal away in my palanquin for a little ride and relief. On Monday morning many more came for books before I left. I think altogether, I may say the whole city came together to hear me. Mr. N. was highly delighted with the feeling which had been excited, and was very sanguine of good being done. Before leaving I examined the language, with Mr. N's learned man, and had my own ideas of it confirmed; namely, that it was the same language which is spoken at Pooree, with a different pronunciation of two or three letters. I was informed that the language was spoken *nearly* 100 *miles beyond Berhampore*. Mr. N. then walked with me and pointed out a piece of ground where, if I should come and labour in the place, he would build a school-room; and at my suggestion, he engaged to make it large enough for a place of worship on sabbath days. At ten o'clock I took my leave of these kind friends, with the conviction that, if my brethren approved it, I ought to return as soon as possible and commence my labours. Berhampore is nearly seventy miles from Pooree, and is the last station in the Northern Circars under the Madras presidency. It is in a very high situation, surrounded with hills, inhabited by a wild race of Oriyas, under six or seven independent rajas. The population is less than at Pooree or Cuttack; but the villages near it are numerous and populous. The inhabitants, of which three fourths are Oriyas, and one fourth Telingas, are not so tenacious of their caste as in other places; and many features in their character seem favourable for Missionary labour."

In the early part of 1826, Mr. Sutton paid a second visit to Berhampore. In November he was out on a missionary excursion for nearly three weeks, accompamied by Mrs. Sutton, and Gunga Dhor, then a hopeful inquirer. In this journey he made known the truth in a number of villages, and proceeded as far as *Kontiloo*, or *Cooloo*, which he apprehended would be an important station.

In December 1834, Mr. Goadby visited this town, and baptized the wife of Mr. Cadogan. He preached in the mess bungalow, and nearly all the Europeans of the station were present—the text on the occasion was, "*The redemption of the soul is precious.*" The opportunity is thus described—"All paid very great attention, and seemed pleased with the opportunity. At half-past four, baptized

Mrs. Cadogan, in a large tank, and afterwards administered the Lord's Supper; only six communicants, Gunga, Bamadab, Erun, John Cadogan, his wife, and myself; a refreshing opportunity." Mr. Goadby spoke very favourably of Berhampore as a station.

In the annual Report of 1837, it is stated—" This town, situated about 360 miles from Calcutta, was several times the scene of the occasional labours of Messrs. Bampton and Sutton. Mr. Brown has spent some time there. It appears that, independent of the Cuttack people, a small church of ten members was formed. Of these, one is Irish, two English, one Scottish, two Indo-British, and four Hindoos. Erun is one of these, and though aged, as lively and active as a young man.

A place for native worship has been opened. It was formerly a small heathen temple. Where idols once were worshipped, the word of salvation has been proclaimed. It was obtained after many disappointments, and difficulties, and in the midst of a populous part of Berhampore. Many of the heathen were drawn together by curiosity, at the time of their deserted temple being opened, as the first place for Christian worship, in their idolatrous town. But few Europeans reside at Berhampore. The spirit of kindness, and in some cases of affection, displayed by some of them, is said to be truly delightful.

It is a reason for satisfaction and for gratitude to God, that Berhampore has become a regular station of the Society, and that the appearances are pleasing and promising, yet it should be remembered that the field is there so wide, that an English Missionary and one native Brother, or even more can do bnt little. Mr. Brown observes, that the field of the Missionary at Berhampore, extends over a space, perhaps as large as all England; at any rate large enough for twenty Missionaries. One Christian marriage has taken place at Berhampore,—Debaka, the daughter of Doitaree, was married by Mr. Brown to Bhikaree the son of Bhugaban."

Mr. Stubbins and Miss Kirkman were united in marriage at Cuttack, Jan. 23rd, 1840, and soon after left for Berhampore, where they found Mr. and Mrs. Wilkinson and the Native Christians well and happy. In February Mr. Stubbins wrote—"I think the disposition to hear, and trust in many cases, to regard the Gospel, is not at all abated, but rather increased. We now scarcely know what it is to be interrupted, though our congregations were never larger. It is almost as common as Idolatry in India, for the people publicly to acknowledge while we are preaching, that idolatry in all its forms is sin. Though some of the Brahmins oppose

Christianity, it is very evident to all present, that their motives in doing so are merely sinister, consequently they are not much regarded. Pooroosootum said the other night, "I have seen many different places, and preached the gospel in many different parts, but in none have I seen such general interest as in the neighbourhood of Berhampore."

Mrs. Stubbins' report of the Orphan Asylum at this time was very pleasing. "My present charge at Berhampore consists of nineteen girls; this number includes Pooroosootum's daughter, and the child of an enquirer. They live on the same compound and enjoy advantages equal with the other children. Three children have lately come to us in consequence of the famine which is beginning to be felt severely. One was half starved, having for several days subsisted upon a few handsful of kunda, (the husks of rice) which she had begged in a neighbouring village. The other two are from a village about eight miles from Berhampore. Having spent a day there when on a missionary tour, the poor children followed us to another village. On being discovered two days afterwards, they said they had nothing to eat at home, and wished to go with us. Their mother proved to be a widow with four children, and said she found it impossible to support them in the present scarce season. The eldest is about ten years old, and her sister about five; they appear quick children and are prepossessing in their appearance. After the eldest had been with us a few days her mother came, and as a pretext to gain a little money said she would take her daughter away. The child wept much, said she would not go, and then hid herself; as her mother's object was not reaily to remove her, she at last quietly gave up the contest. Three of the girls are members of our churches. The third, who requested baptism just before leaving Berhampore, was baptized at Cuttack. I trust that though young in years, they are really interested in a Saviour's love. May they be preserved faithful unto death, and shine as lights in a dark place."

This station, which has become a very interesting one, has suffered several trials in the removal of Mr. Stubbins, on account of ill health, and the death of the young Missionary Mr. Grant, which unexpected and solemn event, occurred Feb. 18th, 1843. When Mr. Stubbins left,—"there were twenty members who were growing in grace and meetening for the church above." Mr. Sutton took a journey thither in consequence of the trials of the station. His report of his journey is very interesting.

"It is, I believe about eleven years since my last visit to Berhampore, but the scenery appeared to me as familiar as though it were but so many days. But how many eyes that eleven years ago gazed on the beautiful Chilka or wandered over the vast mountain range, are closed in death! As I sailed slowly up the lake, I thought of my early associates, and every now and then involuntarily exclaimed, O that Bampton were with us now! But there is something like murmuring in this. What we know not now we shall know hereafter. "My Father's hand prepares the cup, and what he wills, is best." I reached Berhampore about twelve on Saturday, and Mr. Wilkinson about two o'clock. Found our friends as well as I could expect, our sister Derry still wearing her English roses, but sister Wilkinson had assumed the Indian lily. Poor sister Grant was very much cast down. The day however glided swiftly away, and much of the night in talk of auld lang syne, and the next day was the sabbath.

At eleven o'clock I preached to an interesting little gathering in the Chapel in English, but a few steps from where the old barrack room, my former preaching place, stood. In the afternoon, the Oorea flock assembled, and brother Wilkinson and myself united in administering the Lord's supper, and again in the evening I preached in English. Seventeen years ago I preached, what I was told, the first sermon ever preached at Berhampore, from "*Behold I bring you glad tidings*," &c. From that time to the present the word of life has been more or less preached in it. Some of the preachers are far, far away—some of those who heard and received it are, we trust, in heaven, and some on their way thither, and a few still remain to form a little church. O that it were larger. Yet still, though our progress here has been slow, it is matter for thankfulness that there has been progress. Here is a chapel now, there was none then; here is a little church, there was none then; here is a school, there was none then; above all here is a resident Brother, there was none then; and so, though oft have changes taken place, it has been for many years.—Berhampore however is a striking illustration of Christ's church militant. It may not improperly be likened to a spring in a desert, at which the weary pilgrim may delight to halt and refresh himself, but where he has no intention of taking up his abode. Thus at different periods the number is not small of those who have been refreshed here. Some indeed have drank to thirst no more. Some are with joy drawing waters from the wells of salvation, a few press around the brink, and some alas have forsaken the fountain of living waters and have hewed out to them cisterns, broken cisterns that can hold no water. Yet who would wish this fountain closed, who that looks around him upon the myriads that must drink or die, does not pray that the blessed Holy Spirit may speak by our Brother who shall be stationed here, " Ho! every one that thirsteth come ye to the waters!"

The Report of 1844 speaks favourably of the progress of the cause of Christ in this part of Orissa. " This station having been deprived of its own missionary, has during the year received much attention from Mr. and Mrs. Wilkinson, who principally reside here. Some circumstances of a pleasing, and others of a painful nature, have marked the progress of the year. The principal circumstances of the latter kind, is the fall of two individuals, who have been excluded—one of these is Pooroosootum. But considering that the element in which the Hindoo lives is impurity, that their gods, their shasters, their religious festivals, and most sacred worship, are distinguished by lewdness; that it is the atmosphere in which they 'live, and move, and have their being,' it is not surprising that such cases should occur. It is a matter of thankfulness that they have not been more frequent.

" The chapel that had been prepared at Berhampore, having been seriously damaged, Mr. Wilkinson has been engaged in the erection of another, near to the Schools. An eligible site was purchased for one hundred and five rupees. In April he mentions that the erection of the chapel was proceeding, and that the building of new school-rooms was nearly completed. Three young persons instructed in the asylum were married in February or March, two of them to young men that had been instructed in the school at Ganjam. One of them named Dootee, the daughter of Bamadab, was married to Juggernaut, a member of the church, employed as a schoolmaster, and likely it is thought to become a preacher. She was for several years in the Cuttack School, whence she was removed to Berhampore. Mrs. Wilkinson pronounces her a very worthy young woman, says that her conduct in the school had been most exemplary, and adds, We hope they will be happy and adorn their profession."

In reference to these marriages, Mr. Wilkinson adds,—" The day of the marriage was one of great enjoyment to all the native Christians, all seemed to strive to make it as much unlike a Hindoo marriage as possible. Captain Macpherson made the girls a present on their wedding day of ten Rupees each, this was given for the purpose of making a feast, but all who wished to join in partaking of it thought it would be better that the dinner should be paid for by subscription and the ten Rupees be used to build houses for the new married people; it is a very unusual matter, if a native does not involve himself in debt for many years; our plan not only avoided this but turned to a useful account, the money which was intended for the feast, at the same time it added to the harmony and pleasure of the whole party." To this Mrs. Wilkinson adds, that Captain M. not only made the presents mentioned to their young friends, on this occasion, but promised similar sums for six others.

A circumstance very encouraging to the missionaries at Berhampore, has been the interest taken in their work by a young officer. He was educated at one of the English Universities, but is stated to be in principle, a Baptist. He appears to possess considerable ability for the acquisition of languages, having made himself master of three Oriental languages in less than four years, and made such progress in Oorea, in six months, as to write and compose with ease in that language. Occasionally he has conducted worship with the children, when the missionary has been absent. He has translated several little books for the school and delivered addresses to the scholars. He makes great sacrifices, it is stated, to serve the cause of God and the mission. Ought not the friends of the mission to pray that one promising so fair for usefulness, where eternal interests are concerned, may be rendered willing to sacrifice his worldly prospects, and to devote himself wholly to advancing the cause of Immanuel ?"

Mr. Buckley, whose favorable voyage to India has been noticed, safely reached Berhampore, Feb. 20th, 1844, the vessel landing him at Vizagapatam, distant 150 miles. Mr. Wilkinson and another European friend met him there, and accompanied him to the station. On October 9th, 1844, Mr. Buckley and Miss Derry, who had been so usefully employed in the Native schools, were united in marriage in the new chapel at Berhampore. May these dear young friends long prove a blessing to this part of India. It is pleasing to observe the occasional visits of missionaries leading to the permanent occupation of missionary stations, and the diffusion of the gospel around them to teeming myriads of Idolaters.

The Report of 1845 states—"During the year the Missionaries from Ganjam have resided and laboured here. Mrs. Wilkinson observes, 'This year we have to record the goodness of the Lord in restoring our health, and enabling us to attend to our various duties with interest and delight.' To these sources of satisfaction a new one was added, by the arrival of their former companion and friend, Mr. Buckley. He reached Berhampore on the 24th of September, a day that he declares he shall ever deem one of the bright and sunny days of his life. His first sabbath there was a day of holy enjoyment. "On Aug. 11th the new chapel was opened. Mr. Wilkinson states that it was to them all a most delightful sabbath. Not many strangers were present, yet the congregation presented an unusually interesting appearance. Worship had previously been conducted in a private room, which was so crowded that several usually sat outside; and on this account, before the chapel was opened, their number appeared much smaller than it really was. He preached in Oorea morning and afternoon. The subscriptions exceeded their expectations. The influence of christianity on a people, in their unconverted state eminent for selfishness, was strikingly manifested by several of the native Christians contributing each ONE MONTH'S INCOME towards the erection. This, though the sum was not large, manifested much liberality of mind."

Denabunder and Balagee have been ordained. Mr. Buckley thus describes the service. "Friday, Dec. 13th, was a high day at Berhampore. Two of our native brethren, who, as we trust, were inwardly moved by the Holy Ghost to take upon themselves the office of the Ministry, and who in some good measure have proved their fitness for it, were solemnly set apart to the holy and blessed work of preaching the gospel. Rama Chundra read the Scriptures and prayed in a very comprehensive and appropriate manner. Bro. Wilkinson followed with some introductory remarks explanatory of the work of the day, and shewing the propriety of a public designation to ministerial work; he referred at the close, with much feeling to the labours and trials of Bampton—to the baptism of Erun, who was present, and to what Bampton's feelings would probably have been, if he could have witnessed the scene presented that day. He proceeded to ask the two brethren as to their conversion—call to the ministry, and the doctrines they intended to preach. The first question elicited statements, pleasingly illustrating the manner in which the "marvellous light" of divine truth obtains its first entrance into the dark mind of an idolator; the other answers were satisfactory; the last was very concise, wisely so in this case. It was in substance, that the Bible contained all truth, and what they found there, that they would make known. Bro. Lacey offered the ordination prayer; many important blessings were supplicated for our native brethren, and supplicated with much fervency. Rama Chundra, Bro. Lacey, Wilkinson, and myself, united in the imposition of hands. Thus ended the morning service. Erun said, at the close, O, if Bampton (whom he still thinks of with much affection) had lived to see that day, how rejoiced he would have been. We assembled again in the evening, when Seboo Naik read the hymns, Somnath prayed, and Bro. Lacey delivered a charge containing much important instruction, from "I charge thee therefore, before God and the Lord Jesus Christ, who shall judge the quick and the dead, at his appearing and his kingdom; preach the word; be instant in season and out of season;" some judicious remarks were addressed at the close to the wives of the native brethren, who may do much to help or hinder their husbands in the work of the Lord. Doubtless the Son of God beheld what was done with complacency, for it was to publish His glory—make known His gospel, and enlarge the boundaries of His kingdom, that these dear friend were set apart. My mind was much impressed during this day with the immense importance of native agency. I rejoice that God has blessed our Mission so much in this respect, and trust that there are indications of others rising up that will be useful."

MIDNAPORE.

This station is situated at the northern extremity of Orissa, and contains a mixed population of Bengalees and Oreahs. During the occupancy of Balasore by Mr. Sutton, he made one or two lengthened visits to this place; and several brethren in their journeys to and from Calcutta, have occasionally preached there, both in English and Ooreah; but it was not till the year 1836, that Mr. and Mrs. Brooks removed from Cuttack and occupied it as a regular missionary station. Its distance from Calcutta is about seventy miles. Mr. Brooks gives the following information about the station.

"This is a very large and populous city, containing upwards of fifty or sixty thousand inhabitants, principally Bengalees. There is a considerable number of Oreah people in Midnapore, but they live chiefly in small bazaars, and are generally of low caste. There are nearly fifty European residents, civilian and military, besides a considerable number of East Indians, of Portuguese origin.

"The climate of Midnapore is very dry and healthy, but excessively hot, partly owing to the extensive beds of ironstone, which extend on all sides for several miles. Its elevated situation (standing higher than almost any other part of Bengal,) contributes much to the healthiness of the place, though of course this subjects it to greater degrees of heat and cold. The thunder and lightning storms here are very dreadful. Soon after my arrival the officers of the 24th N. I. engaged a large room for Divine service, which would have been continued, had not the owner's circumstances rendered it necessary for him to let the whole of his house at a higher rent. Service is now held in Mr. Pennington's house, which was immediately offered for that purpose. The congregations have been very good and encouraging. Colonel Simpson and his lady have been most exemplary in their attendance, scarcely ever absent. The time of service is Sunday evening, the Church service and a sermon being read in the morning by the Collector of the station. There are several Portuguese living in the neighbourhood, who of course are Catholics, but generally attend our worship."

The chapel at this station is a neat building, fifty feet in length by twenty-five in breadth, with a verandah ten feet wide on each side. Its cost was 1500 rupees, which the Missionary collected and paid. He also raised some money towards the erection of a commodious English school-room, and if possible a school-house attached. In the Report of 1840, it is observed—

"Since my coming to Midnapore, I have confined myself chiefly to the numerous bazaars in the city, rather than travel a great distance to villages. Generally I have attended bazaars from three to six days in the week, as the weather or state of mind allowed. I have been to several villages, but they contain so few people that we can obtain a much larger congregation in the bazaar, chiefly of persons from the country; and the villages of any consequence being situated from eight to twelve miles from Midnapore, there would be no possibility of visiting them in the best part of the day, viz. the evening. I wish to keep in mind what is the main work for which I am sent to India, and am, though slowly, endeavouring to carry into effect the wishes of the Society, as well as to fulfil my engagements on the day of my ordination; and above all my solemn dedication of body, soul, and spirit, to the great head of the Church."

"As regards English Services, I have but one on the Lord's-day Evening. I had two, one morning and evening, previous to the very hot weather, and intend to commence with two services again, as soon as the weather permits. On the Thursday evening we have a Bible class, one of the most interesting meetings I ever attended. Several Officers of the Corps attended, and others that I think highly of. Before I leave this subject, I must say the English Services do not in the least interfere with Native labour, as they are invariably held at a time when it is impossible to hold service in the open air. The chapel being at a great distance from the Native population, a congregation could not be obtained for Native Service. Besides I prefer open air, and see no possibility of obtaining a Native congregation in the chapel until more are induced to attend from principle. I do not despair of seeing good done in Midnapore, should the Almighty spare my life."

In December 1841, Mr. Brooks, with the concurrent advice of the Orissa Missionaries and the Committee in England, removed from Midnapore to co-operate with Mr. Sutton in the new station recently formed at Calcutta, through the Christian munificence of Mr. Alexander of that city. Mr. Brooks thus describes this important step :—

"An important measure was recommended to be taken by the last Conference, in reference to the extension of the Orissa Mission. Previous to the Conference held at Cuttack, I wrote a letter, asking advice of the Missionary brethren as to whether or not I should proceed to Calcutta as Bro. Sutton's colleague in this new enterprise. I was recommended to do so, and am now settling myself in Calcutta. You will expect me to give my reasons for wishing to leave an important and now deserted sphere of labour. One chief reason was, I have been almost isolated from the other Missionary brethren since my residence in India, and heartily wished to be brought closer to them both in labour and affection. Another reason was, the very discouraging prospects in Midnapore, so far at least as the conversion of the heathen may be considered. None seem willing to take up the cross, though hundreds upon hundreds have visited me, received the Scriptures, and heard the glorious Gospel of the blessed God. I hope some are halting between two opinions, but nothing seems to decide the matter with them. When the number of years I have spent there, is taken into consideration, with little or no positive success, perhaps a remove might be deemed necessary. Nothing would give me greater happiness than to see one more fitted than perhaps I am to labour *alone*, entering that field and reaping a rich harvest. I wish to draw the attention of the Committee especially to Midnapore and its neighbourhood. Another reason which led me to wish to leave Midnapore for a season, was the necessity which appeared to me, that Mrs. Brooks should have a little change. She has never been from home since our entering Midnapore, and on many accounts it was desirable she should have a change of scene. There was no other Missionary who could with so little inconvenience, occupy Calcutta, as myself. I shall for the present, have charge of Native Preachers and Preaching, I sincerely hope with greater prospect of success than heretofore. I might urge other reasons, but the chief object I have in view, at least if I can trust my own heart, is a hope of being more useful as a Preacher of the gospel, a Missionary to the Heathen."

Mr. Stubbins being compelled by ill-health to leave Berhampore, the southern extremity of Orissa, visited this station in the opposite part of it, hoping that it might be beneficial to him. This hope was disappointed. But under its influence, he took up his abode and laboured to diffuse the blessings of the gospel. Of his labours and prospects he thus wrote:—

"We started for Midnapore, where we arrived on Nov. 5th, 1842, and were hospitably entertained by a gentleman in the station, till we were able to secure a house. The gloomy and depressed state of our minds on our arrival, will be more readily conceived than expressed. Among the tens of thousands of Idolaters, not one Christian could be found—not one to welcome us or greet us with a smile—not one to gladden our hearts by asking the way of life, (of course I refer to the Hindoo population). We felt like a person cast upon a wild barren rock, without any thing to please or interest. After we had been here about a week, we were joined by our dear native brother Langham Das and his wife, from Balasore. He had no sooner arrived than we commenced in good earnest in the bazaars, &c. and the people were not long before they commenced in as good earnest with us; for they soon "became as cheerful in their minds as a bear robbed of her whelps in the field," and about as furious. However in spite of all their vociferations of Huri Bol, Huri Bol, &c. &c. with handfuls of dust, gravel and the like, we have been able to visit them almost every day, (Sundays excepted) and to exhibit to large congregations the word of life. When I remember that on my arrival at Berhampore I had to witness similar scenes, and experience similar treatment, I feel encouraged to hope this storm will blow over, and that our sky here will yet become clearer. But whether this should be the case or not, our duty is to preach the Word—to be instant in season and out of season—to sow beside all waters—and the Lord helping us, neither the opposition nor rage and fury of men or devils, shall prevent us.

O for grace to instruct with meekness them that oppose themselves —to endure hardness as good soldiers!

"On Jan. 14th, I baptized three people here, two of them accompanied us from Berhampore. Their minds have long been impressed with the truths of Christianity, and have long since abandoned all regard for Idols, but I did not feel sufficiently satisfied with their experience to admit them to baptism; but lately their whole conduct has been so unexceptionable, and the statements of their experience together with their anxiety for the means of grace and religious ordinances, have been so fully in accordance with the spirit of the gospel, that I could no longer refuse them admission into the Church of Christ. The other candidate was an East Indian. She seems to have been under serious impressions for some time, and had a desire to be baptized, (her parents were Baptists,) but it was not till she came into the station ill, and had been frequently visited by myself and Mrs. Stubbins, that she was enabled fully to lay hold upon the hope set before her. After she recovered, she desired before she returned to her residence, about forty miles distant, to be baptized. I trust we may say with confidence of them all, they are brands plucked out of the burning. O that in this fearful, benighted, and depraved place, our divine Redeemer would get unto himself a great name—that he would breathe upon these dry bones the breath of life, and here establish his own kingdom."

Mr. Stubbins was unable to occupy this populous place, but was compelled to return home to recruit his health. The station has been recently adopted by the American brethren.

GANJAM.

The first Report of the Orissa Mission printed in India, contains the following account of this Town. "This was once a very important and populous European settlement, but in consequence of the growing prosperity of Calcutta, and subsequently of a destructive visitation of providence, called the Ganjam fever, but which was in all probability the plague introduced by the shipping from Arabia, it has been for many years nearly forsaken by Europeans, while the Native population is much reduced. The splendid but desolate European residences still attest the former importance of the place, while its now healthy climate, its salubrious breezes, its geograpical position, and commodious harbour, invite a reoccupancy by Government, of this once valuable port. It is still however a large town; and situated as it is between the Berhampore and Pooree districts, forms an important as well as a convenient station for a missionary. After nearly two years' testing of the place, Mr. and Mrs. Wilkinson have come to the decision that it is their duty to accord with the wishes of the Missionary Committee in occupying this place, and in which decision our conference concurs." This town had been occasionally visited by Messrs. Bampton, Sutton, Stubbins, &c., before its occupancy by Mr. Wilkinson. It is another proof of the utility of exploring a land to ascertain the most eligible sites for more permanent missionary labour.

In the Society's Report of 1841, Ganjam is first mentioned as a regular station. It is stated—"Besides labouring at Ganjam, Mr. and Mrs. Wilkinson have been out on several missionary tours, in which they have visited numerous places to convey to them the gospel of salvation. An Orphan Asylum has been formed at Ganjam. It began with one poor destitute child. This number had increased to eighteen. As Mrs. Stubbins has an asylum at Berhampore for girls, it was judged best to let that at Ganjam be especially for boys in the first instance. It is remarked, 'our great concern is their spiritual welfare,' but while attentive to this, they were desirous of communicating to them habits of industry. A christian schoolmaster, who had been converted under the ministry of Mr. Stubbins, was obtained. Mrs. W. adds,—"We have a number of excellent elementary books in the language, amongst which, are '*Watts*' and *Pinnock's Catechisms*.' In reading, we have '*Henry and his Bearer*,' '*Pilgrim's Progress*,' (Bunyan's,) '*Rise and Progress of Religion*,' &c. &c., besides a variety of tracts. At present we do not contemplate teaching English, as this, unless it be a thorough English education, does not really benefit the children. We are anxious to make them industrious and worthy members of the community, and to this end, would like they should learn such trades as are here most useful, as carpenters, weavers, &c. Mrs. Stubbins' girls are industriously employed spinning cotton, and when some of our boys can weave, the children of the two stations will be able to make clothes for themselves. The native loom is the simplest imaginable. And weaving after their manner, is such very slow work that a man here is not able to do one-sixth part of what a boy can do at home with a hand-loom: should any friends of the Indian youth be disposed to make our school a useful and most acceptable present, I beg to say that nothing could be more thankfully received than a good weaver's loom, that is, all the parts of one except the wood, which is very cheap here, and can easily be supplied, also three or four shuttles. We should be delighted to find that our expected brethren had brought this out for us. I might add that our school children cook for themselves; it is done by the elder boys alternately. We are very pleased with the progress that some of them have made in their learning. I trust, before another year has passed, I may be able to speak with some degree of certainty respecting the piety of some of these dear children. Several appear well disposed."

The first fruits of the gospel in this new field of labour were early gathered. It is stated "At Ganjam, as elsewhere, the Missionaries have had their discouragements, but Mr. Wilkinson observes that when they were almost ready to despair, several enquirers may their appearance, of whom they had heard nothing previously, and one of them soon applied for baptism. This convert, who may be regarded as the first fruits of the mission at Ganjam, is a respectable man of the writer caste, who has been employed for *eighteen years*, as tutor to the sons of Brahmins. He was brought to read the new Testament, and, at first, tried to convince Mr. Wilkinson that there was a little difference between the Word of God and the Hindoo shasters. He soon however abandoned this opinion, and declared that such truth and holiness were no where to be found but in the Bible. He had frequent conversation with the missionary and the native ministers. At length he removed the signs of idolatry from his forehead, and forsook the temple he had long frequented every morning and evening. This conduct aroused the suspicion of his neighbours, who, at first, disputed with him, and then commenced a series of petty persecutions. They refused to allow him to have any water from the public well, and made his home so uncomfortable that he at length went to the Missionary, and said, "He could no longer live among the brahmins, but must leave his wife and home, and live with Christians, if he could only have a place as good as a horse." He was asked, why he wished to leave his home? and answered, 'Tigers and sheep cannot live in the same place. When I was a heathen it was my custom to sit in my house, and read the shasters, when many would come around me to listen, and join in the singing; but last night as I was reading the word of God, many came not to hear, but to insult me, and I was so pelted with mud and stones that I was glad to make my escape.' A place was found for him. For a while his wife and children lived with his brother, and a party of her female relations visited her to mourn with her for the loss of her husband, and they recommended her not to think of enduring such disgrace, but to drown herself. Not long after this, his baptism took place. That solemn service was then, probably, administered in Ganjam for the first time, since the ascending Saviour gave the great commission. On this account that baptismal day must be in Ganjam a memorable day, and will be contemplated with pleasure, in distant years, by christians, that are yet unborn."

Mr. Sutton, in a recent journey, gratefully observed—"At Ganjam where we have been accustomed to halt, yea, in *the very house* we passed our solitary interval between one stage and another, we have now a missionary brother and a little church, and a cluster of school boys. I should judge from my imperfect observation of things, that the prospect of raising a native church at Ganjam is quite as encouraging as at Berhampore."

Referring to some recent conversions, the Annual Report states: "By these pleasing, though not large additions, to the little flock of Christ, at Ganjam, your Missionaries have been privileged to gather fruit to life eternal; fruit that, doubtless, will be gathered there much more extensively, as years and ages roll onward, and the period of millenial day approaches. Mrs. Wilkinson, in the letter containing the account of Moni Ma, states that there were then several enquirers, three of whom were very hopeful. One of them, a sister to the young man last baptized, had in a short time learned to read the word of truth, and was a quick intelligent girl. Her early years having been passed without any restraint, when she first came under their care she was at times troublesome, but they had for some time had the satisfaction of seeing a pleasing change in all her manners.

A neighbouring Rajah had paid a visit to the Missionaries at Ganjam. He was attended by his retinue, and during his stay large companies of the people, sometimes thirty or forty together, frequently went to converse on religious subjects. He received a new Testament, and seemed interested in the accounts Mr. Wilkinson gave him of the state of manners and religion in England. Mrs. Wilkinson's sewing work attracted his attention, and when informed what English ladies could do, and what kind of education they received, he appeared astonished, and said if any of their females were such, "they would be esteemed perfect goddesses." But alas! woman there is dreadfully degraded and debased. Mrs. Wilkinson's statements furnished frequent illustrations of this truth. On one occasion, when she was conversing with some Hindoo women, Mr. Wilkinson passed at a little distance. The woman said, "Dare you remain, now your husband is left? Did he give you leave to come?" 'These remarks,' she observes, 'shew the servile subjection in which the poor women are held.'

The more recent information refers to Mr. Wilkinson's indisposition; but his health appears to have improved in answer to the prayer of his friends. It is stated of the station generally:—"Ganjam has latterly appeared less healthful than it was supposed to be, and fears began to be entertained that it would be necessary to withdraw the native ministers from the station. Bamadab was stationed there with Balage, and was obliged to leave; death entered one of their families. The sickness to which they were exposed gave an opportunity for an interesting display of christian sympathy, in the little band of Hindoo christians. Mrs. Wilkinson states, "Conversing the other evening with the native preacher's wife respecting her recovery, I was much pleased to find that she referred all to the goodness and mercy of God; and to learn from her, that when the complaint seemed not subdued by the use of ordinary means, the brethren met for *special prayer* on her account," and with much feeling she added, "The good Lord was pleased to hear our prayers for I have not had fever since that day—how greatly it delights us to see these dear people going to the proper source of all health and blessings." Those who are familiar with the history of the sainted bands, of Puritans and Nonconformists, that form the glory of Britain, will remember that they frequently set apart seasons for such special prayer, for suffering friends, and attributed, as Baxter does, much success to such intercessions. It is pleasing to behold Hindoos in the infancy of their piety, adopting the practice, that English christians loved in the best days of theirs, but which has been less frequently followed in later years. To the preceding statement Mrs. Wilkinson adds some information and mentions their loss of a kind friend by shipwreck.

"There has lately been so much sickness at Ganjam that many of the natives have become alarmed and have left the place. The other two Europeans who reside there, have also been obliged to leave, they are here, but are both recommended by the medical officer to go to England. About nine months since our friend Mr. Adams was afflicted with dysentry, which obliged him to leave Ganjam for the purpose of visiting his native land; but, we are grieved to add, the vessel, in which he sailed for Madras was lost: from our intimate knowledge of his character, and from the progress of his religious feelings while at Ganjam, we have no doubt but his end was peace, though what were the feelings when encountering the last enemy, or where "*he sighed his soul away*" is not known to us; not one was left to tell the tale; he was accompanied by a Missionary, Mr. Smith of the London Missionary Society."

Amidst these various trials, your estimable sister states, that they had much which demanded gratitude. Their minds were kept in perfect peace, being stayed upon God, nor could they call in question his wisdom and love; nor were they without some encouragement as to the progress of the work of God. In February one convert was baptized. Mr. Wilkinson mentions that another candidate from this place had been recently baptized. She is a relative of Denabunder, the first convert, and had been an enquirer more than two years. There were then two other candidates for communion from Ganjam, who had been enquirers for some time.

Mr. Wilkinson mentions another very interesting fact in connection with Ganjam. He states that there were three young men, who were members of the Church, whom he deemed it desirable to bring forward for the ministry. He had been thinking of employing them in studies for this purpose. Tama, one of them, had been with the Missionaries ever since they were in the country. Another, named Juggernath, was a schoolmaster in the neighbourhood. Joysing, the third, was with a pious officer, assisting him in the study of the Oorea and the Khund languages. He judged it desirable that they should continue in that district as they would thus keep up their knowledge of the Teligoo language which there adds to the usefulness of the native preachers, and he apprehended that their instruction would furnish interesting employment for himself, and Mr. Buckley to whose arrival he was looking forward. In this same letter he states that Mrs. W. and himself were thankful their health is so much better than it was last year.

Mrs. Wilkinson's Report of the *Ganjam Orphan Asylum* contains some pleasing information. Some Khund boys rescued from the murderer's knife have been added to it, in whom the Missionaries find more to interest and encourage them than in the children from the plain country.

CALCUTTA.

In this great metropolis of British power and influence in the East, it was ascertained that from twenty-five to thirty thousand

Oreahs were living, for whose religious instruction no adequate means existed. This state of things attracted the attention of a pious and benevolent Gentleman, J. W. Alexander, Esq., who opened a correspondence with the Orissa Missionaries upon the subject of extending their labours to the myriads of Oreahs in Calcutta. Upon this important subject the Secretary of the Society observed—"In the latter part of 1841, Mr. Alexander, a gentleman of eminent liberality, resident in Calcutta, encouraged Mr. Sutton to attempt the formation of a station in that city, with the especial design of conveying the gospel to many thousands of the natives of Orissa dwelling there. To effect this object he offered if his life were spared, to guarantee for three years, about £480 a year to meet the expenditure. An offer so noble and Christianlike could not but command attention. Mr. Sutton visited Calcutta, and after mature deliberation judged it advisable to remove thither. A special Conference was held at Cuttack, in October, when the brethren recommended his complying with Mr. Alexander's liberal proposals, and agreed to the removal of the printing office. In reference to his removal, the brethren considering the time it would occupy, and the preparations to be made for the accommodation of the establishment, during the cold season, recommended that it should take place as soon as arrangements could be made. The minutes of the Conference add, 'In reference to the above important measures, the brethren, and especially Bro. Lacey (who was present at a discussion in the home Committee, relating to a former proposal for Bro. Sutton to remove to Calcutta,) feel a full conviction, that they are acting in accordance with the views and wishes of our Brethren and friends in England, and have therefore proceeded with confidence in the business.'

Mr. Sutton accordingly removed to Calcutta, with several of the native christians, and was joined there by Mr. John Brooks, from Midnapore. Previously, however, to any proceedings of this kind, he had forwarded much information upon the case, that the subject might be brought before the Committee. They discussed the subject, and though they perceived various advantages in a Calcutta station, and could not but admire the generous offer of Mr. Alexander, yet they objected to Mr. Sutton's removal. On one important point in Mr. Sutton's account of the case, misconception existed in the Committee, and this had great influence on their decision. They however judged it desirable as far as could be, to embrace Mr. Alexander's most liberal offer, and judged that Mr. John Brooks might remove from Midnapore; accordingly they determined on his removal, if agreeable to Mr. Alexander, and resolved that one or more of the native preachers should accompany him. This resolution with the reasons for its adoption, was forthwith forwarded to India. Soon after another letter on the subject was received from Mr. Sutton, giving additional information on the business, and entirely removing the misconception on the one important point, not so clearly explained in the former letter. The Committee again met, and, after mature deliberation, agreed to sanction Mr. Sutton's removal to Calcutta; but particularly wished that *it should be made subservient to the training up of native preachers*, who, it was supposed, might enjoy educational advantages in Calcutta, while under Mr. Sutton's general care and direction, that they could not so fully at Cuttack. On this subject particular stress was laid, but, as will be seen, this hope was fallacious.

As it was desirable for Mr. Sutton to avail himself of the cold season for removing, the delay, that would have been occasioned, by waiting till he could hear from England, might have occasioned great inconvenience; he therefore removed to that city. He observes, "We felt the fullest conviction, that we were acting in accordance with the wishes of our home Committee, or we should never have consented to abandon our interesting labours, our home, and many advantages for the toil and anxieties and discomforts we saw before us. So confident were we all, that we thought it worse than needless to lose the best season for their journey, in order to write for a reply from home. In all this it seems we were wrong." Mr. Brooks also removed, and this, as it will be observed, met with the entire approbation of the Committee, and was according to their vote, though it took place before he could gain information of the resolution they had adopted.

The Report of 1843 contains some interesting information. A few extracts will gratify the pious reader. "In this city, the metropolis of British India, Mr. John Brooks is labouring, and has been assisted by Bikharee and another native preacher. The expense of this station is not at present defrayed by the Society, but is met by the funds furnished by, or through, that liberal friend of the heathen, J. Alexander, Esq. Some communications by no means devoid of interest, have recently been received from Mr. Brooks. He states that the *Oreah population* in and near Calcutta, amounts to from *twenty-five to thirty thousand*, and observes that the hope of conveying the blessings of the gospel of peace, at least to some of these benighted multitudes, had borne him up amidst discouragements and trials. His own health had been generally good. Mrs. Brooks had been attacked with the fatal cholera, but after being brought very near the grave, was mercifully restored. He and the native brethren have preached in various bazaars, and other public places; their congregations varying from twenty persons to two hundred or more, and varying as much in the manner in which they received the heavenly message: sometimes violent opposition has been manifested, at others, silent and respectful attention.

"In January Mr. Brooks visited the bathing festival at Saugur, so infamous for infant murders. The bathers were chiefly widows, many of them young. Others were old, emaciated, and scarcely able to support themselves; and mournful was it to behold these so near the grave, clapping their hands, and attempting to dance to the honor of their idol. Some were shivering in their wet clothes, worn in penance, or because they had no change of raiment. Numbers of hypocritical, whining beggars were calling out to different parties, to remember their forefathers, not to forget the departed, but to make offerings for the dead. This part of the idolatrous scene strikingly harmonizes with scenes beheld at popish funerals in Ireland, where offerings for the dead are solicited, and the voice of the priest is heard exclaiming '*Who will give for the soul of the faithful departed?*' and when contributions slacken, '*Will nobody give more for the soul of the faithful departed?*'

Other sickening scenes of idolatry and sin were beheld. A number of Bengallee and Oreah books were distributed. On the whole the missionary's impression was that the fame of this place of idolatrous resort is declining, "and that Saugur in a very short time will lose its sacredness in the estimation of the people of India."

Mr. Brooks has met with an interesting field of Oorea labour at *Gloucester Mills*, by water, twenty-one miles from Calcutta. Here upwards of *two thousand Ooreas* are employed in spinning cotton. At this place he was well received. He met with several that had received tracts at *Trebini*, about fifty miles distance, some months before. Several could repeat Christian Tracts from memory almost from the beginning to end; and here was evidenced the advantage of extensively distributing religious publications. At his first visit to this place, he distributed a great number more of books, Gospels, and tracts. He and his fellow labourers had a congregation near their boat all day, with whom one or another was incessantly employed in preaching the truth, as it is in Jesus. The people were glad to hear their own language spoken. Mr. Brooks proposed that himself or the native preachers should frequently visit this place. Subsequently he adds, that he had been to Gloucester Mills, to make arrangement with the overseer for a school and place of worship. The overseer was very kind, and willing to further the efforts in behalf of the gospel. The people connected with the mills, are not allowed to work on the Lord's day, which gives a good opportunity for Oreah service on that day. The missionary adds, 'There are several in a very encouraging state of mind, and I have hope that something will arise out of an attempt to introduce the gospel among them, which will cause our hearts to rejoice.'

In Calcutta, a school was established by Mr. Brooks, for Oreah boys. Also at their own request, a reading class for adults both male and female. There are in it, three women and about twelve men. On Lord's day afternoon he has worship in his own house, and a 'pretty good attendance.' Four persons had applied for baptism. It is stated that one is an encouraging young man, and that the other three are very steady; the missionary adds, 'I hope soon to receive them into the fellowship of the church of Christ.' On the prospects of the station generally, Mr. Brooks states that he thinks there is not in Orissa a more encouraging field of present labour, than that which he now occupies in the metropolis of India; but he observes, 'One thing is certain, I require help, nor can I possibly do what is necessary to be done."

The Report of 1843 (says the Secretary,) announced that Mr. John Brooks was labouring in Calcutta, under the sanction and at the expence of J. W. Alexander, Esq., having ceased, on his removal to that city, to draw any support from the Society's funds. Since the information contained in the last Report, no communication whatever has reached the Committee from Mr. Brooks, nor has he sent any intimations of his future plans. A few months ago, the Committee received a letter from that very liberal friend of India, Mr. Alexander. This letter announced that if the Calcutta station were continued, an arrangement must be made to defray its expence from the Society's funds, as Mr. Alexander's engagement to support it for three years, would terminate before the close of the present year. Considering the great liberality that that gentleman had manifested, the case was felt to involve difficulty and perplexity. After serious deliberation the Committee judged it needful to adopt in substance the following resolution: "That we consider Orissa as the more immediate field of our mission in India, and, being anxious to strengthen the mission there, feel that it would expose to considerable difficulty, to take the responsibility of the station in Calcutta: the difficulty is further increased, because no one of the Brethren in Orissa can possibly be spared for Calcutta. A further obstacle arises from the consideration, that we do not understand the effect of Mr. Brooks' labours in Calcutta to have been such, as to give much promise of success. From him we have heard almost nothing, and we have understood that before Mr. Alexander left India, Mr. B. had not satisfied him, that he would prove an effective missionary to the Oreahs in Calcutta. Under these circumstances, while we admire Mr. Alexander's liberality, cordially thank him for past aid, and trust that, in a better world, his Lord will acknowledge with approbation, the desire that was in his heart, we do not see our way clear to continue the Calcutta station under the care of Mr. Brooks." After a copy of this resolution had been forwarded to Mr Alexander, a letter was received from him containing one from Mr. Brooks to himself in which Mr. B. wrote, "I should be glad to know whether it is your intention to carry on the Mission in Calcutta beyond the time understood. I do not think the General Baptist Society has any intention of maintaining a Mission here, and if it is to be relinquished finally, I should suggest the sooner the better." Mr. Alexander, referring to the Committee's resolution, expressed his persuasion that their determination would be even strengthened by the information he then sent, and added, "Such being the case the sooner it is carried into effect the better. Some seed has I trust been sown which the Lord of the harvest will in his own due time bring to perfection. The most promising part of the field has been the manufactory at Fort Glo'ster." Two of the native ministers were employed among the Oreahs in Calcutta, but it was not a field of exertion that was pleasant to them—one of them died there, and of Damudar the other, Mr. Sutton, under date of April 17, 1844, writes, that he had just returned from Calcutta and required nursing both for body and mind, and that he certainly ought not to return to that city." Mr. Brooks returned to England in the early part of 1845. See the testimonals respecting him in the G. B. Repository of the same year, pp. 317. He afterwards settled at Manchester.

CHRISTIAN VILLAGES.

It is a pleasing stage of progress in a Mission where the converts can "come out from among the ungodly and be separate," and like Israel of old "dwell alone and not be reckoned among the nations" of Idolaters around. The Report of the Society for 1832 gratefully refers to this event. The first Village to which reference is made, is

CHRISTIANPORE.

To alleviate in some degree, the trials of the converts, and to render them mutually helpers of each other, the foundation of a Christian village has been laid in the vicinity of Cuttack. The annual statement furnishes the following pleasing information on this subject:—"Another plan which we have adopted at Cuttack, is the settling of the native converts together. Hitherto they have been scattered any where, where they could get a place to reside in, and have, on that account, been unable to render each other any assistance, and have not been recognised by the people. I have purchased a piece of land, near the military bazaar, sufficiently large to form a tolerable sized village, and the native Christians are to build their houses in a uniform manner on this ground. The houses will form two rows outwards, leaving a space for a road down the centre, and there will be a chapel provided for their worship. The advantages of this plan will be, that the brethren will be nearer each other; and, as they are outcasts, and none will assist them, they will be able to render mutual help; and they will form a visible body of the people, and their place of residence will be known. It will moreover be very convenient for their assembling for worship. They have already named the place Christianpore, i. e. the place of Christians. Ramara's house stands now at the head of this piece of ground."

The Report of 1845 referring to this station says,—"Of the school at Christianpore, Mr. Lacey states that about twenty-five children, partly heathen, were receiving instruction in the rudiments of the native language, and in the elements of Christianity, and that a school had been commenced at Odyapoor, chiefly for the benefit of the native children."

CHOGA.

Mr. Lacey thus describes the vocation of the native Christians at this place, about eight miles from Cuttack.—"At Choga I have taken a piece of ground containing ten acres, for the purpose of locating the native christians. This land forms a mountain in the midst of a large rice plain, of many thousand acres. The crops are always sure in Choga, and this hill is just separated from the heathen villages around. Our friend Mr. Hough, has erected a small house, which serves for a residence, and a chapel, and the kind donation of J. Miller Esq. which you sent me, as well as another from W. Brown, Esq. of Balasore, will assist in settling a christian village in this place. On our late visit we discovered the retreat of the divinity of the mountain, fixed under the shade of a large mangoe tree. It is a form of Doorga, and she was surrounded with inferior deities, elephants, camels, horses, sacred stones, and other appendages of Doorga. The image was too heavy to be removed, but her numerous attendants were soon dispersed. Our children soon mounted on the horses and elephants, and the school boys some of whom were with us broke others, and brought some to Cuttack. This Doorga has in this mountain, been the patroness of neighbouring thieves. Her glory is now ended, and the jungle is being cleared to make way for the habitations of christians. Thus may all the idols be famished, and the dark places of the earth, the abodes of ignorance and crime, become full of light and righteousness.

I have paid a visit to Choga, and last Lord's-day we had a baptism. The object of my visit to Choga was to visit the native Christians, to see some enquirers, and to settle the locations of a christian colony there. I found two enquirers, one of whom is very hopeful. He is a poor man, though of a good caste, and was formerly not only a devoted idolater but exceedingly superstitious. About seven years ago while on a journey to Patamoondy with Mr. Goadby, the latter happened to touch a piece of lighted stick with which the man was boiling his rice, whereby he gave great offence. The poor man esteemed his meal as contaminated, and threw it to the dogs, and took himself away from Mr. Goadby's neighbourhood, lest he himself should contract the like defilement. While at Cuttack I had many conversations with him, but his stubborn ignorance preserved his heart from all impression, and his understanding from all light. He has lately been located at Choga, has been in constant communication with the christian natives there, moreover God has visited him with a long affliction. The latter he interprets as a warning to him, and with tears in his eyes, he confessed to me the alteration which had taken place in his views; the long and stubborn resistance which he had made to the gospel, and that now he would resist no longer. His wife is as wild as an antelope, and withal abundantly ceremonial. To me she was unapproachable, and Mrs. Lacey had much ado to obtain an audience with her. She told her she knew she was a sinner, that she knew Jesus Christ was the only Saviour, that she knew her husband would become a disciple of Christ, that she believed in Christ also, but could not bear to think of losing caste, and becoming unclean."

In 1844 some very pleasing circumstances are mentioned connected with Choga. "At this place a native christian village has been established. Reference was made in the last Report to proceedings intended to effect this desirable object. Mr. Lacey now states that the christians have removed from the heathen village, where they formerly lived, and have located themselves on the ground he had procured from the Rajah of Autghur. Here they form a christian village, have a small chapel in which they attend the means of christian instruction and worship every Lord's-day; and now a school is being provided for the instruction of their children. About sixty have renounced idolatry at Choga. They have named their village Odyapoor, or the village of rising. "I hope," writes the Missionary, "the light of the celestial sun will rise and shine upon this place." The idol formerly worshipped on this hill has been cast out and its residence pulled up and burned. Messrs. Sutton and Lacey assisted by the school children obtained levers and raised it out of the earth from which it was said to have sprung, and cast it into the open plain, where it lay neglected, till some of its former votaries from another village took up their god and carried it away. Mr. Lacey has visited Choga several times, and furnished various pleasing statements respecting the progress that Christianity is making. In Dec. 1843 he writes:—"Yesterday I visited Choga, and am encouraged, not to say delighted with my visit. Just before I set off Rama returned from his weekly visit to that place, and mentioned several persons who appeared seriously disposed, and to those I found several more; there are in fact about ten individuals more or less well disposed towards christianity, and some of them appear not far from the kingdom of heaven. One man who has for years known much of the gospel was some time since heavily afflicted, and he looked upon his affliction as a visitation from God to punish his disobedience; he resolved if God would spare him, to attend to the concerns of his soul. God has spared him, and raised him up from affliction and now he wishes to serve God. Another man, who has for years been lingering on the verge of Christianity, and of whom I think I have written to you in past years, appears resolved *now* to decide. His wife has left him in consequence of his determination, and is irrecoverably lost. Besides these, there are two or three heathen who are earnestly enquiring after the truth, and several nominal christians who appear very serious; upon the whole Choga, or, as we have called it Odyapoor, (the city of rising) is in an encouraging and improving state. One of our native friends there named Purasua, is a very active and well informed man, and has much talent for imparting instruction."

Five or six weeks later he remarks, that several of the nominal Christians at Choga appeared deeply concerned about their eternal salvation and confessed their sinfulness with many tears; while they expressed a confidence in Christ, so as to give good hope that they are not strangers to his grace. Several heathen also are much concerned for their salvation, and are struggling between the loss of caste and credit on earth and a profession of Christ. Some of these have gone too far to retract. At a later period he announces that several at Choga were enquirers. One man had come forward, broken his sacred necklace, and renounced caste, his wife appeared in a still more encouraging state than himself, and had urged him forward. Others appeared on the point of coming out to the Christian party. One has recently put on Christ by baptism. In February the wife of one of the Choga Christians was baptised. It is stated that she appears to be a quiet and sincere christian, and had long seemed to possess good feeling before she appeared the subject of converting grace."

KHUNDITTA, *or* BEECHER-NAUGUR.

In 1840 reference is made to the formation of this station. —"This is another new and important station; for which the Committee have agreed to send out a Missionary, as soon as can be. The last Report related the baptism of Seeboo and two other converts in this place; to these, others have since been added. Hitherto they have formed a branch of the church at Cuttack, though the distance between the places is considerable, being about forty miles. Doubtless after the station shall be more regularly occupied, they will form a distinct church. Seboo and Luckindas, two of the native ministers, are stationed here. The Committee of an auxiliary missionary fund at Cuttack, have determined to appropriate a liberal sum for the erection of a bungalow, a Chapel, and a native preacher's house. The bungalow has been completed at a cost of about one hundred and fifty rupees, and the chapel and preacher's house were in progress. George Beecher, Esq. late of Cuttack, who has been a warm friend to the mission for several years, has given *twenty acres of good land for the location of a christian village.* Several other friends have assisted to provide cottages for the converts. The native chapel is erecting in the centre of the settlement. The prospects at Khunditta are stated to remain very encouraging: the christians are respected and the truth is making a wide and deep impression on the surrounding population. Mr. Lacey has visited the district several times during the year, and for about eight months divine worship has been conducted on the Lord's-day by Doitaree, who was for a time stationed there. Several converts have been baptized.

Mr. Sutton mentions that of the last natives baptized, three were from Khunditta, making six, in that new field, to which a further addition has been subsequently made.—At this place, Sebo-saho and Lockhundas, have been received as preachers, nor have their labours been in vain. Mr. Lacey has furnished an account of the settlement. The ground given by Mr. Beecher, which forms the site of the settlement, is eastward of the great Juggernaut road. The land is fertile, but has some drawbacks in consequence of being infested with monkeys from a neighbouring jungle, and from its nearness to the Juggernaut road, being liable to the petty plunderings of the idol's pilgrims. About eight professedly christian families appear to be located on the spot. Four of these families have each two acres of land allotted to them, a quantity, it is stated, equal to the maintenance of six or seven persons, and as much as one man can well cultivate. On Lord's-day, Nov. 1, Mr. Lacey opened the small village chapel. He states,—"I preached in the chapel, which has been erected in the midst of the village. My congregation was but small, but combined much interest. There were present all the christians, nominal and real, amounting to about thirty-two or thirty-three souls, and a number of heathens sitting and standing around the door. My text was selected from Acts v. 20. The people paid good attention, and appeared impressed. In the afternoon Bamadab preached from "Blessed are they that mourn, for they shall be comforted." In the evening for the first time in this place, we had the Lord's-supper. I spoke to the Christians about remembering Christ, his love, his sufferings, and especially the object of the latter; and pointed out the effect such remembrance should produce on the affections and the character. The opportunity was solemn, and useful. This morning some enquirers arrived to whom something was said, and they were invited to stay and attend worship. Also early this morning,

Narabaree walked over to his village and brought away his wife. He effected his object without molestation."

A very pleasing instance is related of success crowning the labours of the native brethren.—"One day about the middle of November, as Sebo-saho and Lockundas were preaching to the passing pilgrims on the large road at Khunditta, a person named Kessari Naik, going to his field to reap his rice crop, stood with a number of others, to hear what was being said. The preachers were reading and explaining *one by one the ten commandments*, and showing how all men had broken them and were consequently, exposed to the wrath of God. As they proceeded the mind of Kessari Naik was powerfully arrested, and he found the truth applying itself to his conscience; he felt himself a guilty sinner, and became greatly distressed. After the native preachers had laid open the guilty state of man, they adverted to the remedy for sin, the death of Jesus Christ, as an atonement, and exhorted sinners to withdraw their trust from idols, and believe in the only Saviour. Kessari Naik felt that this intelligence inspired him with hope, and he thought in his mind, *Who then have I but Christ! in him I will put my trust: he shall be my Saviour.* Instead of proceeding to his field that day, he returned to his house, and entered on a more deliberate consideration of the resolution he had taken. He examined the claims of his own books. In this examination some of the instances of monstrous fiction recorded in the shastras occurred to his remembrance. When Urjoon, thought he, balanced the whole earth for nine days upon the end of his bow, where did Urjoon stand? He soon became entirely convinced of the falsehood of those records, and at once renounced them for ever. His people soon perceived the anxiety of his mind, and he explained his feelings and determination to them, especially to his wife and children. They entreated and threatened, but to no purpose, and after about four months spent in such exercises as above; he tied up a little rice and salt in his cloth, and set out for Cuttack, where he requested to be baptized, and where he now stands a hopeful candidate for christian fellowship." He has since been baptised.

An American missionary travelling in Orissa, stopped at this *oasis* in the moral desert. He administered the Lord's-supper, and fifteen sat down to that holy feast. He says,—"No sooner had they received intelligence that a Padre had arrived, than they came running to me with great glee, and spent the evening with me in religious conversation and prayer. After this, as I intended to start early the next morning, I visited their houses by lamp light:

found all in the neatest order, not even a straw on their floors or in their door yards; and their little gardens exhibited a taste which does not exist with 'the heathen.' This brief but gratifying testimony to the effects of the gospel at one of your minor stations, it may be remembered comes from a stranger, and was sent not to England but to America.

Mr. Lacey's testimony when he visited the station while on his way to Buddruck, is not less favorable than that of the American traveller. "This morning we moved into Khunditta, our little christian settlement. Found some of the native christians sick, to whom I administered medicine. They were all very glad to see us, as I am sure we were to see them; and it is very refreshing amidst the wild wilderness of idolatry, to come upon a little christian garden planted with the trees of righteousness—amidst the darkness of Hindooism, to enter upon a little spot filled with christian light and principle. Our people here are growing in the confidence of the heathen around them, and the little colony is doing well. The twenty acres of land which, when the christians entered upon it, was one third waste, is now all under cultivation; the large ant-hills have disappeared, the patches of jungle have been rooted up, and fertility smiles all around the little spot. The people have corn in their houses, have added cows, bullocks, and hackeries to their little stock, and the whole place abounds with marks of prosperity." Of their spiritual condition he elsewhere adds, "The little native christian band have maintained their christian profession, and have generally increased in knowledge and piety, and in the respect of the heathen around them."

Mr. Lacey's recent account of Khunditta is, that the native christians are "consistent, respected, and in their temporal circumstances thriving." This place has been repeatedly mentioned as an important sphere for the location of a missionary. It should be remembered as an interesting field of labour, and prayer should ascend to the Lord of the harvest to send forth labourers into his harvest.

PIPLEY.

In the Report of 1840, this Town is mentioned as a native station. It is said—"At the last Conference in Orissa, it was determined to occupy this place as a regular though subordinate station. Pipley is situated on the Juggernaut road, about half way between Cuttack and Pooree, and is near the ancient city of Bhobaneswar, so celebrated for its numerous temples. The neighbourhood is populous; several markets and mellas, or superstitious festivals, are held in the vicinity, and the place is excellently situated for meeting with pilgrims on their way to or from Pooree. Rougburdass had a house and ground at Pipley, which he offered to make over to the missionaries for a native preacher. Doitaree has accordingly been appointed to labour there for the present year."

At the Conference in 1842, Doitaree and Luckindas, in succession were appointed to labour at this place. Lying on the great north road from Cuttack to Juggernaut, it has doubtless been frequently visited. Much seed has been sown, and in 'due season we shall reap, if we faint not."

The Report of 1840 makes the following reference to these places, describing them as *colonies*. What a delightful thought, that these villages may grow into colonies, and colonies into towns, and towns into cities; fulfilling the promise to the ancient church, "Thou shalt break forth on the right hand and on the left; and thy seed shall inherit the Gentiles, and make the desolate cities to be inhabited." Of the locations of native christians, Mr. Lacey says—"Of these interesting and important institutions, I have to note more than at any former period in the history of the Orissa mission. They form the criterion of its outward enlargement and prosperity. Christian natives must form themselves into colonies and separate communities. They have no possessions when they embrace the gospel, and they are not permitted to mix with the population of the country. Our four colonies are *Christianpoor*, *Khunditta*, *Bhogerpoor*, and *Choga*. The latter is in the territory of the Athgur Raja. In Christianpoor there are eighteen families, in Khunditta four, in Bhogerpoor five, and in Choga one; besides these, at all these places there are families of inquirers; and other christian families are either separately located, or are living upon our compounds. Choga is five, Bhogerpoor is eight, and Khunditta is forty miles from Cuttack. Choga is the village whence Bamadab, Hurree-pare, Kinapore, and Treelochun came, more than six years ago. Christian light has been at work ever since. Prosua has since been baptized from Choga, we have three inquirers now at Cuttack from the same place, and hear of many more upon whose minds the light of truth is breaking. Prosua has obtained permission to retain his house and farm there, and as he is permitted to do so, others will have the same privilege. Bhogerpoor remains without alteration. We hope the time is not very far off, when our christian colonies will be able to be recognized as separate churches, and support their own native ministers."

In the Report of 1844, Mr. Lacey says, "The increase of nominal christians, or of such as have joined the christian community, but have not been baptized, has been greater in proportion than the number added by baptism. The natives are held to idolatry by their caste, and their social relationships. When therefore they see their way clear to prosecute their employment, so as to live in the world among christians, they, or many of them, are very willing to renounce idolatry and nominally to profess Christ, and attend the means of christian worship. Several families have joined the christian communities in the past year. They have located themselves among the christians and form a part of their body, and their children have been taken into the school. Eight couples have been married during the year, and have either commenced a separate household, or have gone to their friends into houses already prepared for them.

"In this way our native christians will soon form a numerous body of people in this land, without the prejudices of caste or idolatry. The habits induced even by a nominal profession of christianity, are greatly conducive to increase, and will soon in this country extensively multiply the christian natives. They are very much more hopeful to labour among than the darkened and prejudiced heathen, and their increase therefore is a real accession to the good cause. On this account I have felt, and do still feel very anxious to encourage the location of such people in separate villages, and this encouragement I think should not be confined to such as are converted, but to any and all who will forsake their idolatry, lose their caste, and attend means for christian instruction. The whole of the nominal christian natives attend the means of christian worship, and have laid aside every idolatrous practice."

It is a very gratifying fact that *seven Christian locations*, or small villages of professed christians, are already formed, containing in the whole fifty-four households. They are as follows:

Christianpore, seventeen households.
Laceycie, six and about four more to commence.
Societypore, six.
Khunditta, eight.
Bhogerpore, three besides six or eight who have detached dwellings.
Choga, six.
Odyapoor, eight."

An interesting account of these places is given by the same pen, under date March 1844. He writes—

"I wish I could give you an account of

Our Locality at Cuttack.

Conceive then, first, a hill about eighty yards in circumference, and about eight feet above the surrounding level, standing in the middle of five acres of ground, belonging to the Cuttack cantonments. On this hill, which is named 'The Mount,' stands a moderate sized pucka-house, one story high, surrounded by a verandah, and fronted by a portico. This is our residence. To the eastward of my house, and at one hundred yards distance, is the printing office and school premises, on a piece of ground about four acres. Here Mr. and Mrs. Brooks reside; and here Bro. Sutton has built him a house. The old school-house is now occupied by the press, and the school abolished. On these premises are locations for about eighty boys and girls, under the care and instruction of brother and sister Sutton. The devotion of sister Sutton to these children is beyond all praise, and she has been rewarded by many of the children becoming pious. Several couples have been baptized, married, and have set up their household in life. Connected with these schools, and on the same premises, I must *now* mention that there is

A neat little Chapel

erected. This Chapel was opened for divine service, with the children, only yesterday. Brother Lacey preached in Oriya from Leviticus xxvi. 11., "And I will place my tabernacle among you." Returning to our own house, twenty or thirty yards to the west of us, is the little native Christian village called

Society-poor,

Having at present in it five or six families. These are fast increasing. Again, to the south east of us, distance about 300 yards, and joining the Press compound, is another Christian village, which has been denominated

Lacey-cie.

Here there are already four families located; and, two days ago, I portioned out land for three young men, who want to be married, and build themselves houses here. Here also increase is proceeding. Half a-mile east of us, brings us to our oldest Christian village,

Christianpoor.

This comprises about two acres, and has long since been filled. Increase is here rapidly going on, and some of the branches have been obliged to migrate to other places. In Christianpoor stands a house, which serves the double purpose of chapel and school room. Mrs. Lacey has a school here, containing Christian and heathen children. They are in number about twenty-five—they read the scriptures, Christian poems, and catechisms. Turning from the road which leads to Christianpoor, and directing our steps southerly, after walking about 150 yards, we come to the residence of Gunga Dhor, our senior Christian, senior native preacher, and the first native I baptized. On the ground now occupied by his house once stood a temple of Hoonuman. I purchased the god's house over his head, and then pulled it down upon him, and for several days the divine monkey was exposed to the piercing rays of an Indian sun ; but such was his power of endurance, that he never, no, not once cried out, or manifested any signs of uneasiness! The owner at length carried off the godship in a cart, but that owner afterwards becoming a Christian, he was brought again to Cuttack, and with other divinities and divine things, was delivered up to me. He stood for some time at my door, and my little boy John, and my little girl Harriet, one day got a hammer, and by way of amusing themselves, knocked off the arms, and ears, and nose, of the unfortunate Hoonuman! But even, then, he manifested no signs of pain or uneasiness, and the natives said as they say of Juggernaut, that he was a god of "great patience." Gunga Dhor, you are aware, proceeds from this place to proclaim the Gospel every day, in the streets and bazaars of Cuttack. Ten yards beyond Gunga's house stands our chapel. It also is erected on the site of an ancient temple of Mahadab, or Sebo ; and in the chapel compound are located two other families of native Christians. Five miles due north from our residence, and visible from "the Mount," is the village of

Oodya-poor,

The village of rising, or, what we commonly call Choga. It is a Christian village, and has about twelve families located in it. The village is situated in the middle of a large rice-plain, and stands on a hill, a prominent object in all views to all around. We have had many converts from Choga, but some have become preachers, and are at work in their stations, and others are usefully employed at the press, schools, &c. North-west from

Cuttack, on the large Juggernaut road, and forty miles distant is a village named

Khunditta.

Near this village a piece of ground has been given to me, by Mr. Beecher, a friend to our mission, for the purpose of locating native Christians. Here are eight native Christian families, and they are fast on the increase. We have at this village a small chapel, a bungalow, and a house, for the native preacher. A native preacher is stationed here, and looks after the Christians, as well as peregrinates about in the thickly populated neighbourhood. I should have mentioned Bhogerpoor but I have mentioned till my paper is full and I must cease. Lying on our south, and commencing 200 yards from my door, is the city of Cuttack, populated by 50,000 inhabitants."

NATIVE SCHOOLS.

We have seen that the first native school commenced at Cuttack, in May 1822. The establishment and superintendence of these schools formed a very useful employment in the infancy of the mission—preparing the way for the dissemination of the gospel, and the cultivation of their own abilities for its promulgation. In the Report of 1828, the missionary at Cuttack wrote of the Schools in that populous city—"We have seven schools at Cuttack, which contain 233 children; of these, sixty-six read the New Testament, commit the History of Christ to memory, and repeat other religious tracts and poems: these also learn to write on the tall pottra. The greater part of these sixty-six boys have obtained as good a knowledge of the sacred Scriptures as children in England of their privileges and circumstances; and particularly are they informed of the way of salvation by the atonement of Jesus Christ. We are, on the whole, much encouraged with their general information, industry, and improvement. Of the above number, thirty-six are learning a catechism and writing; and the remainder, except ten boys, are writers of the lowest classes. They have all succeeded in committing some Christian poetry to memory, which may be useful to them in future life."

In 1840, "a native heathen school was established, under the tuition of a *christian master*, and the progress it has made is decidedly pleasing." Less attention appears to have been given recently to native Schools, from a deep impression that the great work

CHRISTIAN-ORPHAN GIRLS.

of a Missionary is the preaching of the gospel. Several schools are supported at Cuttack, but the establishment of Orphan Asylums have been found the most efficient means for the instruction and conversion of the rising generation.

ORPHAN ASYLUMS.

These valuable Institutions commenced in Feb. 1829. Mrs. Lacey writes from Cuttack;—"On Feb. 2nd, we commenced a *Boarding School*, for the indigent Christian children of the station. We have placed twelve boys and girls with the master already, and others are making application for admission. These children are very destitute indeed, generally fatherless. Their friends have no care whether they be able or not to obtain their bread respectably, and they are equally careless about their eternal welfare; so that the condition from which they are taken is wretched indeed in all respects. By being placed in the school they will not only be taught the importance of religion, but have the means of obtaining a living put in their power. The board of these children will be of considerable expence monthly; but our excellent Judge and his lady, whom we may truly call fellow helpers in the Lord, exert themselves to the utmost in behalf of the school. They subscribe largely themselves and obtain subscriptions from others, with whom we could not succeed. Mr. and Mrs. Pigou subscribe £16 yearly to the school, besides finding money for beds and clothing for the children. They also visit the school once a fortnight, and give rewards to the children according to their diligence. We have made it a rule, that the children attend our chapel morning and evening on the Lord's-day, and it is very pleasing to see the boys and girls arranged in rows on each side the pulpit; it reminds us of the Sunday Schools in England; surely these children will rise up a better generation than their parents."

At *Berhampore* similar Institutions are formed. The Secretary observes.—"A condensed view of the progress of these benevolent Institutions, furnishes a powerful claim for their support. They were commenced May 3rd, 1836, with ten or eleven children of both sexes. Since that time upwards of one hundred children, including eighteen for a time sent from Berhampore, have found a refuge in them, for a longer or shorter period. Some have completed the system of education their kind friends could afford them, and are now entering on the active duties of life. One that belonged to Mr. Sutton's senior class is now the native preacher at Balasore; one his employed by Mr. S. in is study, as a copyist; six are in the printing office, preparing, it is remarked, "to use the mighty press in enlightening their country!" Four of the girls have been married to native christians. Several received in a state of extreme exhaustion or disease, have died, and thirty males and thirty-six females, still remain in the different asylums. Within two years eleven of the native pupils and five from the English department, including the master and his wife, have been baptized, and of course united to the church. To this may be added, three or four more baptized by Mr. Stubbins. From the different Schools at Cuttack three have been baptized during the year, viz. Ghunu Shyan, a son of Doitaree, the native preacher, from the English School department, Khumba from the boys' asylum, and Moola from the girls'. Two candidates, Boishnub, a former pupil in the boys' department, and Dooke, now in the girls', have long applied for baptism."

The Report of 1844 contains very interesting information. "At Christianpore and Odyapore there are day schools, the former having about thirty scholars, the latter about twenty. In these schools the children have been partly those of Christian parents and partly of heathen. No native books are allowed. The scholars read the Scriptures and other Christian books. At Christianpore the master's salary is three rupees eight annas per month; the other master has one rupee per month less. The Cuttack asylums maintain their importance as benevolent Institutions, eminently adapted to benefit the rising generation. The whole number of scholars during the year has been *fifty boys* and *forty-seven girls.* Many of the earlier scholars have become men and women. The girls especially, it is observed, go off fast to take charge of their own homes; and so quickly rolls on human life in India, that many who were pupils in the asylum a few years ago, are now heads of families, and their children are springing up in rapidly increasing numbers. None from the female Asylum have been baptized during the year. Indeed most of the elder scholars are members of the church. From the male Asylum five youths have professed Christ in baptism. Seven of the eldest are employed in the printing and binding offices, and three others are learning other employments. One interesting youth has finished his short course. He was a candidate for baptism, and died the very evening on which he was accepted for Christian communion. Mr. Sutton saw him, and gives an interesting and encouraging account of his last interview with him. His name was Senjama."

Of the Girls' Asylum, Mrs. Sutton states, "The number of scholars reported as having attended in whole or in part during last year, 1843-4, was of boys fifty, and of girls forty-seven. This year the record gives, boys sixty, and girls forty-six, making a total of one hundred and six. Several however it will be seen were but for a very short time in the school."

These Schools have been liberally supported.—Mr. Sutton thus refers to the success of his appeal under date July 1844. "Last July I published a brief account of the first seven years of our orphan asylum in the *Calcutta Christian Observer*, and in a post-script gave a hint that assistance towards building a chapel for the use of the Institution, would be acceptable. Our first contribution was from Mr. Alexander, our generous Calcutta friend, 100 rupees; Col. Eckford, who was baptized at Cuttack, fifty rupees; J. W. Skipworth,—now a pious magistrate, but when I was at Balasore a wild young man who, with three others, use to turn their hounds loose to hunt close at our door nearly every Sabbath, (three out of the four, I have heard, have become changed men.)—100 rupees. Anonymous 100 rupees; Capt. H. Lyall (perfect stranger), 50 rupees; George Thompson, Esq., sent to me from Delhi with a little commission; I saw Mr. Thompson in the United States of America, twenty rupees. James Alexander, twenty-five rupees; Mr. Robert Trotter, says he saw that Mr. Skipworth had given and therefore he sends 100 rupees; Captains Martyn, Townshend, and Mac Cleghan, from the banks of the Indus, 50 rupees. A reply to my note thanking these gentlemen brought another which led me to copy these subscriptions; the note being short I copy it. Enclosed was a draft for fifty rupees.

"My dear Sir,—I had the pleasure of receiving a very nice letter from you enclosing one to Col. Eckford, which I forwarded to Sheh-jehan-poor. The Lord has been very bountiful to me, and I would humbly present the enclosed for his service, and place it at your disposal. Let us return thanks for his goodness".

I apprehend the gentleman and his brother officers, who united in sending the first contributions, have passed through the dreadful Affghan campaign. Col. Eckford was shut up with the illustrious garrison at Jellahabad, there also was Dr. Marshman's youngest daughter's husband, the gallant captain Havelock, a pious man. Col. E. was very busy in his attempts to do good. Mrs. E. in a note lately received speaks of his collecting a large company of officers and men, and reading my sermons to them, (forgive this personality) and goes on to say, "I doubt not at the last great day, when we shall see clearly all the way the Lord has led us, we shall then bless him for sending my dear husband to Jellahabad." He was then in daily attendance upon the sick soldiers in the various hospitals, and I rejoice to say many heard him gladly. One man, who died, wrote to his wife in the provinces to tell her, if she was every near the 6th regiment, to go to it and tell the good colonel "what joy and peace he had been the means of imparting to him." The poor man died soon after leaving Jellahabad.

You will forgive me quoting these letters, notwithstanding personal allusions, as they seem to show something of the liberal spirit of christianity in India; for all these donations were voluntary, and most of them from perfect strangers; while the quotation referring to Col. Eckford will, without I hope trespassing too far upon private communications, show how widely christian influence may be spread, and that even amidst the most appalling wickedness (for such was the Affghan war) there may be an under current for good."

THE ENGLISH SCHOOL.

This school commenced October 1823, and has doubtless been a blessing to many. In the Annual Report of the Society for 1828, Mr. Lacey states—"The English Charity School has this year continued under the care of the Missionary at Cuttack. The number of Christian children is about as last year: the native children have increased. Three have finished their education; two have retired to their homes; and one has obtained a situation as English writer in the Commissioner's office at Cuttack. All these have left the school with some good degree of religious knowledge, and have taken with them that word which is able to make them wise unto salvation. The prospects of the school are, however, not pleasing, for the income is a good deal below the expenditure, and the little fund in hand is nearly exhausted. We hope some friends will be raised up to support so useful and promising a cause but the prejudices which prevail over the minds of Europeans in India against every thing connected with Missionaries, has done our school much injury.

"I have made an effort for fresh subscribers, and have succeeded in getting three: the Rev. D. Garide at thirty rupees per quarter; Dr. Brandee, Pooree, at ten rupees per quarter; and Thos. Garide,

Esq., Madras, at twenty rupees per quarter; as well as a few donations, the principal one from the Hon. J. H. Harrington, 160 rupees: however, I much question whether we shall now keep on, as we must have a school-room soon; but we will leave this for the present, and see how we stand, if spared another year: we may have new friends springing up by that time. How well it would be if we could have an English Teacher: he might be a great help to our mission, and would bring forward the children much better. If our Society could select a pious young man who would devote himself, as Penney does, to the work, and send him out, allowing him some forty or fifty rupees per month, which, with the present salary of eighty, would be sufficient, they would render a most efficient help to the mission and the school. The passage money is the greatest difficulty. You can mature your thoughts on this subject, and so act accordingly. I believe the gentlemen would have no objection to such a measure, though I have never mentioned it to them.

"The progress of the children, particularly the Bengalee children, has been encouraging in all the branches of learning taught in the school. We held the annual examination of the school on the first of March, in our chapel. It was attended by Thomas Pakenham, Esq., Acting Commissioner; Dr. Stiven, Civil Surgeon; and Mr. C———, who, I believe, was then Acting Secretary to the Commissioner. The boys exhibited some very neat specimens of their hand-writing, also their account books, which gave great satisfaction both as to proficiency, correctness, and neatness. They also were desired to work sums before the Commissioners, and although a good deal disconcerted before the above-named persons, they managed exceedingly well, particularly James Sunder. After this, they repeated some moral pieces of poetry, which was the least acceptable part of the performance; for although they understood well the drift of the pieces, their pronunciation was defective, particularly that of the native children. It is extremely difficult to get a native to pronounce English well. Poor lads, they were extremely desirous to pronounce well, and had endeavoured to prepare themselves for the occasion, but the presence of the gentlemen quite disconcerted them. This evening they declined and compared some pronouns, adjectives, and substantives, and conjugated verbs in different moods and tenses, and parsed, repeating at large the syntactical rules. Upon the whole, the examination gave great satisfaction, and evinced a good deal of improvement. The gentlemen present assured me they were much pleased, and hoped succeeding years would bear equal testimony to the improvement of the institution. The lower classes read, exhibited their copy-books, spelled, &c. The examination lasted for three hours and a half, and would have been longer had I not curtailed the lessons; the gentlemen expressed their desire to be at liberty as soon as possible. Mr. C. promised a donation of 100 sicca rupees for the school, and expressed his best wishes for the welfare of the institution in future. He seemed surprised that we had been able to accomplish so much as he thought it; but he was little aware of the pain we ourselves feel that we have done no more. Perhaps it is well that it is so.

"Hearing of a vacancy in the Commissioner's cutcherry, I recommended Hurree Chund Bhose to Mr. Pakenham, who placed him in it at a salary of twenty rupees per month. I hope this young man, through the instruction obtained in the school, has become acquainted with better feelings than the Hindoo system imparts."

In 1841 this Institution was merged into a larger Government School. Mr. Sutton states,—"I would first advert to the now defunct English School, defunct so far as relates to our Mission. About two years since the Bengal troops were withdrawn from the province, and their place supplied from the Madras presidency. Up to this period, since the time of my taking charge of the School, the contributions had met the expenditure, but our Madras friends, partly from being accustomed to less liberal contributions than their predecessors, and partly from feeling themselves to be but temporary occupants of the station, reduced their subscriptions to a very low scale. Still as there were two regiments, we managed by close economy to meet the expences; but on the removal of one regiment to Midnapore, and some of our best friends in the other to England and distant parts of India, there was a sudden fall almost to nothing. While this process of pecuniary reduction was going on, conversions in connexion with the schools in different parts of India, so alarmed the wealthy natives, that they chose to be at the expence of employing private teachers, rather than send their children to a mission school.

To these causes operating within, there were others without, especially the determination to remove the Government school from Pooree to Cuttack. This last determination turned the scale. The Government school promised to give a better education than we could do, and upon a scale of expenditure to which we could make no approach, and would moreover absorb the funds upon which we had hitherto depended. Even the abolition of the pilgrim tax affected us, for on its abolition, the funds from which five boarders had been supported were withheld to keep up the pilgrim hospital. Under these circumstances Messrs. Lacey and Sutton proposed to make over the School to Government, on condition, that the managing Committee on the part of the subscribers should relinquish all right and interest in the school premises in favour of the Society. To this they agreed, and the premises are now the property of the Society. Thus after running its useful course for seventeen years, distributing the stream of knowledge through many parts of this desert province, the stream has swollen to a river, whose waters if less limpid, will yet form a vaster body swelling on we trust with increasing power, and bearing on their bosom the ark of knowledge through the length and the breadth of the land."

Circulation of the Scriptures and religious Books.

The necessity of such exertions is shewn in the Report of 1827, furnished by the author, on his return from India. "To shew the necessity of this department of missionary labour, it may be interesting to the friends of the Mission to know the whole number of printed Books and Tracts in the Oreah language in 1822. It appears to have been as follows;—1. The Oreah Bible, by Dr. Carey, in five vols. 8vo. 2. A Vocabulary, Oreah and English, by a Native. 3. A poem of 100 pages on the Christian religion, written by a Bengalee Christian. 4. A Tract on the stopping of Juggernaut's car at Serampore, by Mr. Ward, written to prevent a human sacrifice that the car might proceed. 5. A Tract upon the folly of the worship of Juggernaut. 6. Scripture Extracts. (one leaf). A copy or two of another Tract has been found in Orissa. Behold, dear brethren *the whole of a Christian Oreah Library* on the arrival of your Missionaries in Orissa. In addition to several pieces, in different degrees of preparation for the press, the following have been printed at Serampore and Calcutta:—1. Elementary Tables of the Oreah language. Printed at the expence of the School Book Society, Calcutta. 2. On the Law and Gospel. (Scripture Extracts). 3. Half-a-dozen Hymns, from the Bengalee. 4. The Word of God concerning Idolatry. Scripture language relative to its nature, absurdity, wickedness, &c. 5. A Catechism from one in Bengalee. 6. A Word for Christianity, (one leaf). Thousands printed. 7. Death and Resurrection of Jesus Christ. 8. Serampore Copy-Books, partly printed." To this list may be added, 9. A Harmony of the Gospel in verse."

We have seen that Mr. Lacey took out a Press with him on his return to India in 1837. Mr. Lacey states that on the arrival of the Press, several persons called to look at it, and appeared to view it as *half a miracle.* Mr. Sutton soon announced that one press was insufficient for their work. In consequence of these additional facilities, the Missionaries carry on their operations in the printing department, on a more extensive scale. Previously to the arrival of the printing press, Mr. Sutton, who has the care of the publishing department, felt increasingly the extreme inconvenience of being placed three hundred miles from the place where the Society's publications were printed, and expressed an opinion that it would be needful for him to remove nearer to the press, or to have that brought nearer to him. Unless this were done, he stated, that the work of revising the scriptures would occupy a long life, and even then be very imperfectly performed. The establishment of the printing office, has, of course, removed the inconvenience complained of.

The Report of 1845 contains a very interesting account of the labours of the press. The Secretary observes—" In this department of labour the past year has witnessed important progress. Mr. Sutton, as has been mentioned, has been enabled to complete his new version of the Old Testament. This has been carried through the press at the expense of the British and Foreign Bible Society. For his personal labours as translator, Mr. Sutton has received 5,000 rupees, which he has carried to the credit of the Society, thus displaying most honorably his disinterested zeal for the Mission, of which he is so faithful and efficient an instrument.

The Committee of the Calcutta Auxiliary Bible Society thus refers to this work :—" Your Committee are happy in being able to announce the completion of the new version of the Old Testament into the Oriya language, which the Rev. A. Sutton, of Cuttack, has been preparing for the Society. The edition, which consists of 2,000 copies of the entire Old Testament, in three volumes, besides 3,000 copies each of Genesis, the Psalter, and Proverbs, has been printed at the mission press at Cuttack, under the immediate superintendence of Mr. Sutton ; 1,000 copies of Isaiah, in a separate form, have also been struck off while the work was passing through the press. It is pleasing to observe the steady progress of the work of God in this country ; every year adds something to the great cause; and your Committee look, with thankful feelings, to every additional version issued. In the present instance, where missionaries have been labouring for a number of years, and where already Christian congregations have been gathered from among the multitude, it is especially a matter of gratitude to be able to supply those faithful labourers, and the people whom they have been the instruments of bringing under instruction and training, with the Oracles of God. To Mr. Sutton, who, by his indefatigable labours for the last four years, has, almost single handed, accomplished this important work, the especial thanks of your Committee are due."

Mr. Sutton furnishes the following report respecting the publications of the year:—" Since the completion of the Old Testament Scriptures, I have been at Calcutta and presented my accounts for printing, &c., which I expect will be paid at the next committee meeting of the Bible Society. In the mean time they have paid me the last instalment of 2,000 rupees for my personal labour as translator, making the sum of 5,000 rupees, which I have carried to the credit of the General Baptist Missionary Society. I trust it will not be deemed unbecoming in me, here to record my humble thankfulness to Him, who has been to me so much better than my fears or deserts, and permitted me to accomplish an undertaking of so responsible and important a character. May it still further please Him, that neither the imperfections of the work, nor the sinfulness of the workman, shall be permitted to operate against this translation of the Holy Bible being rendered an extensive blessing.

"The Sanscrit and Oriya Vocabulary for the Government schools, announced in the last Report as having commenced, has, during the year, been finished, printed, and paid for.

'The Oriya and English Grammar, with idiomatical exercises, &c., intended to furnish a compendious and easy introduction to the language, and especially designed for missionary students and candidates, has also been completed, and a hundred copies have been taken by Government, which will cover the expence of preparation.

"The third volume of Tracts, entitled 'controversial series,' intended as a 'Guide for enquirers,' containing 244 pages, has also been finished, and a number of copies of this, as also of the two preceding volumes, have been put in circulation. One other volume of miscellaneous tracts yet remains to complete the series.

"Our Hymn book in Oriya, has been completed, and is now in constant use at our different stations. It contains three hundred and ten hymns by various authors, chiefly native metres, and an appendix for children of a hundred and forty hymns and poems, some original and the rest taken from Watts, Doddridge, &c. This appendix has been translated into Bengalee, and has been printed for general use at the Serampore press.

"Two or three tracts have been revised for new editions, and added to our stock for distribution. Our tracts on 'Drunkenness' and 'being in debt,' have been adopted by our Calcutta brethren and are published in Calcutta by the Tract Society. The introductory part of a little treatise on 'Remedies for Bodily Diseases,' pointing out the disease and remedy of the soul, has been drawn up by me and accepted by the Calcutta Tract Society, but has not yet made its appearance. I anticipate much good from the distribution of such a work, both among native christians and heathens. In publishing a book of this kind among a people who suffer so much from ignorance of the most common remedies, I trust we are following in his steps, who went about doing good. At the same time, it may be hoped that under circumstances of bodily affliction, some will be willing to attend to the things which belong to the welfare of the soul.

"We are going on with the printing of revised editions of the New Testament, but hitherto our progress has been but slow. While I write, the proof embracing the last chapter of Mark is lying before me. If spared to complete this edition, with the folio edition of fifty copies for the pulpit, I deem it probable that my labours in biblical translation will be pretty well concluded, at least my long cherished plan will be accomplished. But a report calls for history, not prophecy.

"I may however add in concluding this brief statement, that I have been at times during the year, engaged in the compilation of a work similar to the Tract Society's 'Companion to the Bible,' with a 'Summary of Scripture truth.' I hope to finish this during the current year, for the use of our preachers and students.

"In connexion with this department of labour, it may be stated that Government have concluded to establish a number of vernacular schools in the Province, and there will probably be a call upon us to assist in furnishing books.* The call has in fact been made upon me for some time, but I have hesitated about compliance with it while I had so many other engagements on hand. Indeed I had cherished the hope of being liberated somewhat from the desk, and having the opportunity of doing more in the direct preaching of the gospel. My way however seems hedged up for the present."

* "While writing this paper the Government order for the translation of a book of 200 pages has reached me."

The following testimony from the *Englishman* Newspaper, may show the estimation in which some of the important publications of your valued brother are held in India. The unknown author remarks,—" A very useful Dictionary also, of the Oriya language, in three volumes, has proceeded from the Cuttack mission Press, which both in the literary and typographical departments reflects the very highest credit on the ability and perseverance of the gentleman, to whose exertions every individual in the District, native or European, is debtor."

Of the amount of printing done during the year, Mr. Brooks sends the following abstract:—

	Pages	Copies.	Total No. of Pages.
SCRIPTURES.			
Third vol. Bible, (Psalms to Malachi,) 8vo.	508	2,000	1,016,000
Gospel by Matthew, 12mo.	100	5,000	500,000
TRACTS.			
Oriya Prose Tracts, vol. 3, 12mo.	228	3,000	684,000
Christ's Invitation	12	10,000	120,000
The Gate Thrown Open	12	5,000	60,000
Jewel Mine of Salvation, royal 32mo.	24	10,000	240.000
Instruction to Religions Inquirers, 12mo.	20	5,000	100,000
Brief View of the Christian Religion; 12mo.	20	5,000	100,000
God is a Spirit, 12mo.	8	5,000	40,000
Address from Hindoo Christians to their Heathen Brethren	12	10,000	120,000
SCHOOL BOOKS, &c.			
Poetical Dialogues for Children, royal 32mo.	8	250	2,000
Oriya Hymn Book. (second edition, enlarged,)	252	1,000	252,000
Government Regulations, (13,) 8vo.	36	300	10,800
Introductory Lessons and Idiomatical Exercises, (Oriya and English,) 12mo.	256	250	64,000
Vocabulary of Sanscrit Terms, 12mo.	226	400	90,000
Barth's Church History, 12mo.	236	500	168,000
Total....	2,058	62,500	3,566,800

WORKS IN HAND.

New Testament, (2nd edition,) and separate Gospels.
Oriya Geography, (Rev. J. Phillips'.)
Amara Kosha, Sanscrit.
Reprints of Tracts, &c. &c."

Usefulness of Religious Tracts.

The Report of 1839 states—" The *first tract* printed at the Cuttack Press was hastily composed for the Jattra in 1838, and was entitled "*The wonderful advantages of a Pilgrimage to Juggernaut.*" The evils of that pilgrimage are there detailed. Many of these tracts were circulated.

"One pleasing proof that the tracts circulated at this horrible place are not circulated in vain, has recently occurred. Referring to it, Mr. Lacey writes,—'Yesterday a very interesting enquirer, or rather convert, arrived. He is from Nuaga Siloe. He received his first information on Christianity from me at Pooree, on occasion of a Ruth Festival, and took a book. He make no progress from this for some time, and though he could read, he could not comprehend the book. Afterwards he received a tract from Rama in the Telinga Bazaar, Cuttack—he read and understood it. Then he met with Gunga, in Chowdry Bazaar, and questioned him and received much information. His views of his own religion and on scripture truths are very correct. He has no hope of pardon and salvation except through Christ crucified for his sins. About baptism he knew nothing till he arrived here yesterday. He is a widower, and has a son about twelve years of age. He seems determined not to burden any one, and though a man of reading, he this morning engaged as a common coolie about some work in Christianpore. O for money to purchase some pieces of land now at liberty all around us. Our native converts are anxious to get their bread, are ashamed of asking help from us, but we know not how to help and assist them.'"*

"Last week (says Mr. Lacey) the following cheering incident came to my knowledge. A person of Kasenpoor, a small village four miles from Cuttack, about six years ago heard the gospel, and had conversation on the way of salvation it reveals. He went away and I saw him no more. He dwelt with his brothers, and attended his calling as usual, but remembered what he had heard, and read the books which were given him. By these means he lost his regard for idols, and placed his trust on the Saviour. About a year ago he was taken ill, and his recovery appeared doubtful. As he grew worse his mind clung to the Lord Jesus, and in vain his brothers offered him the mysteries of idolatry. He became anxious to see me and the native christians, that he might talk on religion, and profess Christ, but his relations strenuously opposed his desires. His resolution however increased, and apprehending he would by some means become contaminated and involve them in loss of caste;

---

* This object was realized through the liberality of some friends in England and India.

they stinted him in his food, and thereby increased his weakness so much that he soon expired. His mind continued firm, and at the last hour he persisted in his trust in Jesus Christ, and refused all their idolatrous rites. Thus he died, partly half murdered and wasted by disease, but placing his trust in him who has compassion on the weak, and who can see those who put their trust in him though they may not be known to his people. This information was owing to a conversation apparently accidental with a neighbour of the man's brothers, who compliment themselves on having cleverly escaped family disgrace. How many such instances there undoubtedly are, though we hear not of them, and they ought to encourage all whose hearts are set on the missionary cause, and whose hands are employed to support it. In eternity, we shall meet unknown thousands to whom we have been the means of conveying the word of salvation.

"I cannot say exactly the number of tracts distributed by all the Brethren this year 1835. I have distributed in all about *ten thousand,* principally in those parts of the Cuttack district not lately visited by other Missionaries. Several instances of their great usefulness have appeared. To mention no other, a man now a member of our Church some years ago received a tract. He read it till literally worn to tatters. He at length left his wife and village, and came to Cuttack to enquire of us the way; assigning as a reason the wonderful things written in the paper. We did not like his manner, a trifling circumstance increased our prejudice against him, and so we dismissed him. But he would not leave us. To whom, said he, should I go, my own people are in sin, and their minds, dark, you have the way? I will work and do any thing you wish me, but I will not leave you. At length convinced of his sincerity, we received him into the Church."

The Report of 1844 contains the following encouraging instance of the usefulness of a religious tract. "One instance of usefulness has just been brought to my knowledge by the person who derived the benefit. A certain man of his acquaintance, who lived about eight miles from Cuttack received a tract named the Jewel Mine of Salvation, but could not read it. This little book he sent to our friend, desiring him to read it. He soon applied himself to read and comprehend the tract. It was in easy poetical measure, and he presently understood all it contained. The tract made a beneficial and powerful impression on his mind. The first thing that attracted his attention was the unity of the design, and uniform oneness of the book in comparison with his own shastras. The more he read, the more his judgment opened, and the greater his approbation became; till, to use his own very descriptive language, his own shastras looked like a tangled and intricate jungle which it is impossible to penetrate, and like a cow pasture, which in this country is intersected by a thousand paths, neither resulting from or conducting to one place, but after circuitous windings terminating in nothing. The receiver of this tract sought and obtained others, till he finally became a consistant disciple of Christ, and is now baptized and become a christian preacher."*

Influence of the Press.

Of the establishment and influence of the Press, *The Friend of India* observed,—"We have received a copy of a tract printed at Cuttack, at a press which the Missionaries have this year established at that station. It is printed in the Oriya character, and for neatness of execution is not exceeded by any other similar brochure which has issued from the metropolitan press in Calcutta. It does no little credit to those, to whose feelings of public spirit and christian benevolence, the district is now indebted for an efficient press. *The establishment of a press in any province is an important era in its history.* It is delightful, thus to contemplate the rapid increase of the means of intellectual and religious improvement, through means of this mighty engine in the various and even remote provinces of this empire. We now witness the establishment of presses, at the opposite extremities of the Bengal Presidency through the spirited exertions of Missionaries; but for whose labours those provinces might long have remained destitute of them. Looking down to the southermost of the provinces, we find a press set up in the country of Orissa.

"We rejoice that a press has been established in that country capable of executing any work in the Oriya language and character. The extent to which the language is used has only been discovered of late. We find that it is spoken and written through an extent of country *three hundred miles* in length from the sea, to *one hundred miles* in length west of Sumbhulpore, and more than *two hundred miles* in breadth from Midnapore where it melts into Bengalee, to Ganjam where it meets the Teloogoo. It was indispensable therefore to the completeness of missionary operation to that kingdom, that means should be provided on the spot for

* See G. B. Repository, 1831, pp. 467, and 1832, pp. 436.

multiplying books in a language so extensively used. But why should the benefits of this local press be confined to missionary operations? Why should not Government avail itself of the means of communication with the people which have thus been provided, by publishing its own acts and notifications through the same channel? We know that a strong disposition exists in the highest quarter to provincialize the public service in Orissa. It is the wish of Government, that those who are appointed to this province should apply themselves earnestly to the acquisition of the vernacular tongue, and should move in a circle of promotion within the Province itself. In this arrangement there is much wisdom. Indeed since the principle has been adopted, that the people can be more efficiently governed through their own language than through a foreign medium, it has been necessary to consider the civil officers in Orissa as in a measure individualized from the rest of the service; this is a great step towards the improvement of the Province. But to render it efficient, it is necessary to follow it up by the translation of all orders which the people are required to understand and act on into their own language, and by a liberal use of the press which has now been established in the Province."

CHAP. IV.

The American Branch of the Orissa Mission.

Rise of the American Mission in Orissa—Labours and Success of the Missionaries at Sumbulpore, Balasore, Jellessore, Midnapore, &c.

Dr. Cox in his valuable "*History of the Baptist Missionary Society* from 1792 to 1842," has the following beautiful observations on the rise of the Society from a very small beginning. "At the Kettering meeting, Oct. 2, 1792, the society was formally incorporated; and the first subscription, made on the spot, amounted to £13. 2s. 6d. This sum though really small, was comparatively large; for it was the contribution of a few poor, but enlightened servants of Jesus Christ. It was such as to free it from all charge of ostentation in the motive, and yet such as to evince the faith and self-sacrifice of those who had laid it on the altar of God. The warring world was at the time expending millions in sanguinary conflict, which exhausted nations and terminated in death and desolation; these men were contributing to enhance the happiness of the earth, and promote the glory of the Redeemer. "What" said the objectors of the time, "is thirteen pounds the mighty sum with which it is proposed to undertake so vast a scheme?" "And were these the men and the means," have said opponents since, of fifty years of reiterated scorn, "with which the conversion of the world was to be attempted?" Precisely so, we reply; for means are accepted of God, when they are proportionate to possessions, and blessed with success, when they are employed in faith."

It has been well remarked,—"We are *really* what we are *relatively*;" and the importance of the mission whose history is here narrated, must be estimated by this rule. The first persecutors of Christianity "*doubted whereunto this would grow*;" and the early friends of missions could not have conceived the mighty influence they wielded for the benefit of their own country and of the distant nations of the earth. When this mission was contemplated, little was known of the brethren of similar views in religion, residing in America; nor was it probably expected, that any resources for the promotion of its great objects in the east, would arise from that country. At a Committee Meeting in Aug. 1821, it was resolved —"That the Secretary write a letter, accompanied by a few Reports, to the American General Baptists." It may be presumed, that this tended to prepare the minds of our distant brethren for co-operation in the great work. It must be considered a very interesting circumstance, that the claims of India should have been laid before myriads in America by an invalid Missionary; and valuable aid contributed to the dissemination of the gospel in Orissa. These efforts are worthy of distinct and honourable mention; and may fully occupy the following chapter.

In January 1833, Mr. and Mrs. Sutton, embarked at Calcutta for the United States. This step was considered requisite on account of the state of his health. In a letter dated Jan. 7th, he says,—"To morrow I expect we shall embark for America, by the ship Fenelon. My own health is much better than it was, and under this consideration, I have felt great reluctance in leaving India; but then I am perpetually receiving fresh intimation of a relapse, which obliges me to concur in the opinions of the Doctors, that there is no prospect of a permanent recovery without taking a long sea voyage. I do hope that you will be enabled to obtain three or four well-qualified young men, to return with me to India within the next eighteen months ; and that our American brethren will send as many. O let the cry from the dying millions of Hindoos be heard and felt: *Come over and help us.* I once heard of one of our ministers being terribly afraid lest one of several sons should become a missionary. I hope this feeling will never wither our hopes again. Domestic union and comfort are too dearly purchased at the price of the blood of souls, and the Saviour's favor!" How far these pious and enlarged views were realized, it will be interesting to state.

On the voyage from Calcutta to America, Mr. Sutton, aided by his amiable and beloved amanuensis, prepared the MS. of a very interesting volume, entitled—"A Narrative of the Mission to Orissa, the site of the Temple of Juggernaut; supported by the New Connexion of General Baptists in England." Of this work, 3000 copies were published at Boston in America, and has doubtless extensively promoted the missionary spirit, in that section of the church of Christ for which it was principally intended. The character and design of this work will appear by the following brief advertisement, dated *Ship Fenelon*, April 20, 1833.

"When the compiler of this Narrative first turned his attention to the work, he had not sufficiently considered the delicate situation in which he was about to place himself, by narrating the progress of a Mission with which he stood so closely connected. But as he advanced he felt this difficulty so sensibly, that many times he had nearly resolved to abandon his task. When, however, he reflected upon the weak state in which he left the Orissa mission, and the sweet hope that his American brethren would render some assistance was present to his mind, he was again induced to prosecute his work. The praise or censure of mankind, so far as respects himself only, he feels to be of little consequence, provided the cause which he has espoused is not injured; but should the Narrative of this Mission have the effect of eliciting the prayers of God's people in its behalf, or of adding to its means of benefiting the immortal myriads of Orsssa, he will have accomplished his design.

On the ground of authorship the compiler begs to state explicitly, that he lays claim to nothing. His task has been to arrange such materials as he could obtain from printed documents or private memorandums ; these he has connected, sometimes by remarks of his own, and not unfrequently by the remarks of others which have been so blended with his own observations, that it was difficult to mark them with precision. He hoped to accomplish his humble labours more carefully, but his floating study was so thronged with passengers, and rendered so incommodious by the variety of business transacted in it, that very little opportunity for literary pursuits was afforded him. Indeed, he could not have accomplished his task, but for the willing services of Mrs. S. as his amanuensis. But too much has perhaps already been said respecting this Narrative. May the Lord of the vineyard condescend to employ it as a means of benefiting his cause; and to him, as is most due, shall be the praise."

The work has been reprinted in Scotland, and the Narrative is introduced by a well-written and powerful Essay, on the subject of missions to the heathen, by a Scotch minister. In a review of it in the *General Baptist Repository*, 1835, it is said—"The work is well-written; the publication may be considered very cheap; and it ought to have a place in every church and congregation, in every school and family connected with the interesting Christian Mission in Orissa."

Mr. Sutton's visit to America was well received, and the following letter was addressed to the Committee in England.

"North Parsonsfield, State of Maine, Oct 14th, 1833.

To the Rev. J. G. Pike, Secretary of the Committee, of the G. B. Foreign Missionary Society.

Dear Brother,

We have had the satisfaction of receiving a visit from Brother A. Sutton, your Missionary in Orissa; whose coming has been greatly blessed to the awakening of the spirit of Missions amongst us. We have heretofore done nothing in this cause; but many of our brethren are now disposed to do what they can; and we think if brother Sutton could labour with us, a few months longer, he might render essential services to the cause in which he is engaged.

HOSEA QUINSBY."

The Committee approved of the proposal and passed the following resolution—"That in compliance with this request, Mr. Sutton be recommended on leaving England, to revisit America, and to endeavour there to put the missionary cause on a permanent footing, by the formation of Associations, &c; not extending his labours beyond twelve months, without a further vote of the Committee."

It was stated by Mr. Sutton that in 1832, there were in America "400 Free Will Baptist Churches, 300 Ministers, 16,000 Communicants, and a population of 150,000 souls." In 1846 the Connexion consisted of "1193 churches, 107 Yearly Meetings, 801 ordained Preachers, 233 licensed Preachers, Communicants 58,174." *(Free Will Baptist Register,* 1846, p. 70.) Among so numerous a people, it may be hoped that much aid will be rendered to the evangelization of India.

The Report of the Society for 1835, gives information of Mr. Sutton's labours in America. It is stated—" Early in August, Mr. Sutton and Mr. and Mrs. Brooks sailed for the United States. They arrived there towards the end of September. It was soon determined that Mr. and Mrs. Brooks should take an early opportunity of proceeding to India. During their continuance in America, they enjoyed many christian privileges, and experienced much christian kindness. Early in November they left the United States. Three Missionaries from American Societies, with their wives and a single lady, were appointed to sail in the same vessel in which a passage for our friends was engaged. Previously to their going on board, a united meeting of the friends connected with these different Missionaries, was held. On this occasion Mr. Sutton gave an address, which afterwards appeared in several of the American religious newspapers. They sailed from Boston, November 4th, and had every prospect of a pleasant voyage, in consequence of having much christian society on board.

Mr. Sutton soon after his arrival in the United States, recommenced his assiduous labours, to promote a missionary spirit in that body of American Baptists among whom he had been introduced. To promote this object, he accepted for *one year*, the office of Corresponding Secretary to their newly formed Missionary Society. In this office he has been actively engaged, in visiting different churches, making collections for the Mission Fund, and diffusing information. Thus employed he has travelled over some large sections of the Union. Still however, his attention and that of Mrs. Sutton have been directed towards their Indian home. Their hearts have been in India. The Missionary Society, that Mr. Sutton has been instrumental in forming, has had several applications from young men desirous of being employed as Missionaries. Mr. Noyes, one of these, has been accepted, and is expected with his wife, to sail with Mr. Sutton. It was also hoped, that at least one other Missionary would accompany them, though no decision had been formed upon the other offers for missionary service that were before the Committee."

The Report of 1836, narrates the departure of Mr. Sutton and his new colleagues for Orissa. " Mr. Sutton was successful in exciting a considerable degree of missionary spirit, in some districts of the United States. In September last he left that country, on his return to India. A considerable number of Missionaries sailed in the same vessel. Of these Mr. and Mrs. Noyes, and Mr. and Mrs. Phillips, were going out to be fellow labourers with our brethren in Orissa. The Missionary Society, which sends them forth, appears to possess an honour, which does not belong to the American Baptist Missionary Society. Its friends and supporters are the enemies of Slavery; and are not like many of the supporters of that, and other American Missionary Societies, raising thousands of dollars annually to send the Gospel to Birma and India, while they are mad upon supporting that cruel and murderous system, which by law, dooms millions of Africans, not only to the temporal horrors of Slavery, but to live and to die in a state of heathenish ignorance. Mr. Sutton appears to have been highly esteemed by many professors of religion in the United States. As far as this was the esteem of the truly pious in a land of Slavery this was desirable. But no consistent christian could desire the esteem of persons who are in reality robbers of mankind, and by the word of God described as "menstealers," who themselves trample underfoot or support others in trampling upon, all the rules of immutable justice; and who rob the negro of his liberty, of his children, of his privileges, of his opportunites of acquiring divine knowledge, and, in many instances, of his life. If such persons profess to be Christians, or Baptists, with them, consistent English Christians can neither desire nor hold communion. Information has just arrived of the safe arrival of Mr. and Mrs. Sutton in India. Of their departure from the Uuited States; of the views and feelings with which they contemplated resuming their Indian labours, and of their arrival at Calcutta Mr. Sutton thus writes.

"Ours is the largest party of clerical Missionaries that ever sailed from America, and this circumstance added to the celebrity which some of our party have acquired in America, excited considerable attention. On the Sabbath Evening we had our farewell services in Dr. Sharp's spacious Meeting House. It was crammed in every part long before the services commenced, and many hundreds went away, unable to get a hearing. We expected to sail the next day, but received notice of our detention till Tuesday, in time to announce a prayer-meeting at Mr. Stow's (Dr. Baldwin's) meeting-house on Monday evening. This proved a still more interesting scene.

"I do not know that I have anything particular in the way of incident to record. You will see that goodness and mercy still follow us, and that we are constantly meeting with fresh reasons why we should unreservedly devote ourselves to Him, who died for us and who rose again. The prospect of resuming our labours in India looks very pleasant to us. It is indeed a drawback on our pleasure, that our Brother and Sister Lacey will not be there to welcome us. Yet still it seems a privilege, to look forward to a few more years of labours and sorrows in that benighted land. We know now what we have to expect, but yet beyond the trials and discouragements of the present generation of Missionaries, we see a delightful succession of seasons of enlarged prosperity; churches upon churches rising up to glad the land; thousands and millions of happy converts travelling on to glory; and idolatry with all its guilt, and all its wretchedness, passing away into everlasting forgetfulness. O it is an honor to labour and die in this divine enterprize! Our most ardent wish is to live worthy of it. We know that we shall soon fall in it, but we resolve by God's grace to sell our lives as dearly as possible: to do Satan all the injury, and the cause of Jesus all the good, we possibly can, before we quit the field.

"We safely arrived in Calcutta, Feb. 6th, 1835. We once more were welcomed by our beloved friends in this great city. We are all well. I have heard from Cuttack and Balasore. The Goadbys have been ill, but they are pretty well again. We hope to see them in eight or ten days."

Mr. Sutton received a grant of one thousand dollars from the American Bible Society, and grants of three thousand three hundred from the American Tract Society.

The character of these brethren is very strongly drawn in the succeeding Report of the English Society, which describes the commencement of their labours in Orissa. "It is known to many of the members of this Society, that Mr. Sutton was instrumental in establishing a Foreign Missionary Society, among a numerous body of American Baptists, that from their views of the general provision which is made by the Saviour's death for human salvation, were denominated free-will Baptists, a name by which they are generally designated. They are a body of Baptists, with which you may cheerfully co-operate, for they are the enemies of the system which renders America, in a great degree, a land of tyrants and of slaves. They have no triennial Convention at which those who hold not slaves themselves trim to those who hold them; and treat as dear brethren in Christ, men who live violating the most golden precepts of the Saviour, and robbing injured Africans of their dearest rights. They are not a community partly made up of men-stealers and men-sellers, and partly of those who tolerate and palliate the oppressing and thieving propensity of others, who are very good christians, except that they are thieves; and thieves not merely of a little cash, but of the daily labours and of every civil right their injured victims might possess. Your American brethren are not Baptists of this description. Their accredited organ, the *Morning Star*, is a decidedly abolition paper. It pleads the cause of the negro, and exposes the cruelty, the murder, and the lewdness of the system, which allows no marriage tie—which sells young women for prostitution—which rears human beings for sale, as in your land of real liberty cattle are reared; and which tortures and works to death multitudes of men and women far more estimable than their iron-hearted, and in many instances, hypocritical oppressors. For those persons can be nothing else who boast of liberty and cling to slavery; who talk of religion, while they trample underfoot the grandest and most equitable precepts given by the God of love. So well known are your American friends to be abolitionists, that the State Legislature of New Hampshire recently rejected a bill for the incorporation, according to American usage, of their Home Missionary Society, because there were so many abolitionists among them. As Mr. S. was instrumental in establishing a Missionary Society among them, they have now become your fellow-labourers in India. Their first two missionaries, Messrs. Noyes and Phillips, with their wives, proceeded to India with Mr. Sutton. Mr. Phillips for a time resided with Mr. Goadby at Balasore, and proposed to commence a new station at Jellasore, about thirty miles from the former town. Mr. Noyes, for a few months, acted as master of the English School at Cuttack. Mr. Sutton, referring to these Missionaries, remarks, "Our friends the Noyes are promising labourers —we have spent a very happy twelvemonth with them, and part with great regret. The Phillips' have been but a little time with us, we hope however they will be very useful."

From a recent number of the Morning Star, we learn, that a meeting was held at Cuttack, to consider the propriety of the American brethren entering upon a new field of labour. At this meeting Mr. Sutton presided; and it is stated that "the most perfect harmony and unanimity of views and feelings prevailed among the Missionaries. The place selected for the field of their labours is Sumbulpore, far in the midst of a great population entirely heathen, there being only one european settler within one hundred miles of their location." Sumbulpore is described as a very interesting and important station. Some of the tracts issued by your Missionaries, a few years ago, reached that neighbourhood, and appeared to excite, in some minds, considerable alteration. The Executive Committee of the American Society have found it necessary to appoint an agent to travel among their churches, to raise subscriptions, form associations, establish monthly concerts for prayer, &c. A brother named Mack, has been appointed as their first travelling agent.

SUMBULPORE.

"Sumbulpore is a large city pleasantly situated on the east bank of the Mahanuddy, about two hundred and fifty miles from Cuttack. It is on the government mail road between Calcutta and Bombay, which with the present method of shortening communication between Bombay and England, renders it an important and promising station. As it regards the population of this place, like the most of Hindoo towns and cities any thing like an exact census is unknown, but I should suppose it could not fall short of *thirty thousand*. The inhabitants are usually more dark than in Cuttack and their features more spare.—They are very timid, but unaccommodating and ungrateful. The bands of caste I have understood are not so strong as in Cuttack. The high caste brahmuns eat flesh of almost any kind, and do any kind of respectable labour. The females of respectable families are not kept very close, but it is common for them to stand and listen to our conversation, and sometimes ask questions. There are more temples than I have seen in any place except Pooree, and the people are strangely prejudiced in favour of their idols. Sumbulpore is the capital of a fine country, governed by a Rajah, who, though under a small tribute to the English government, exercises almost unlimited power in his dominions. All land is considered his property and at his disposal; hence he frequently takes the land of one man and gives it to another. It is not probable that the English government would interfere in case of the greatest anarchy, providing their mail, which runs through the country, should not be obstructed. The desirableness of conciliating the favour of a prince, having such unlimited sway, is readily seen; and though at first, we did not on his account apprehend much danger in forming our stations, yet it seems that the Rajah's suspicion has been made to rest upon us. Being himself a devoted follower of Juggernaut, he is much concerned lest we should change the custom of the times, in detracting from the honour of his god. When we walk out we are generally watched by his emissaries, who often come near and quesion us in regard to our plans. They show us some respect, because we wear the fearful white face, but his repeatedly refusing us some small favours shows plainly that he wishes us out of his country. —Without his favour we see no way to get along, since without his command we cannot get men to build us houses, or even a single article of provision from the market."

On their removal thither, Mr. Sutton accompanied them for a considerable part of their journey; they then pursued their way and travelled through, and fixed themselves in a district, which is not British territory, though the Rajah is tributary to the British government. They experienced considerable inconvenience from being thus situated. In fact the difficulties to which they were exposed, may render more conspicuous the wisdom and goodness of God, in subjecting the greater part of Hindostan to Great Britain.

Notwithstanding their difficulties they commenced their labours of love, and experienced more of the Rajah's favour than they expected. Your brethren sent the native Evangelist Doitaree, to their assistance. From recent accounts however, it appears that they have been so tried with affliction, as to have removed from Sumbulpore, and it would seem without the intention of returning. Mrs. Phillips one of the little band, has finished her short course. Mr. and Mrs. Noyes have both been dangerously ill, and for change of air visited Cuttack, where their health improved. After they left Sumbulpore, Mr. Phillips had an attack of illness. From the latest information it appears that they were then at Balasore. At Sumbulpore, there was but one European, within one hundred miles of their abode. Some of the information they gave respecting that part of India, and their situation there, must excite the interest and sympathy of those who love the gospel.

The Rev. E. Mack, the travelling agent of the Society, represents the exertions of Mr. Sutton, when in the United States, as having been productive of very considerable good.

"We regard the past correspondence with your Connection, and the actual help which you have as instruments of divine Providence afforded us, to be of incalculable value to us; rather might I say, to the interests of our Redeemer's kingdom, as the interests of that kingdom are connected with our Denomination. The assistance rendered us by the visits of Mr. Sutton, will never, we hope, cease to be remembered and appreciated;—appreciated to some degree at least, for it must remain for the day of judgment and eternity, to develope the vast amount of good effected through this instrumentality in all its fulness. Our Mission must still continue dependant on yours to a great extent. You must continue to be a father in the gospel, unto us, at least in respect to our India Mission. The establishment of your India Printing Press especially, will afford you increased facility for laying us under obligations yet greater and more numerous. Indeed by recent letters from our Missionaries, we are informed of the reception by them, of some hundreds of Testaments of Mr. Sutton's translation, and some hundreds of tracts—and yet further your Mission had furnished them with a native preacher of a character, such as justified the expectation of much assistance from him, in the labours of their Mission."

From the brethren at this station, the writer received the following letter, which shews the circumstances of missionaries in the beginning of their labours.

"Sumbulpore, Aug. 18, 1837.

Beloved Brother Peggs,

With much pleasure I received yours by the hand of brother Stubbins, and should have replied long ago, had not my time been completely taken up with the building. Probably you are aware brother Phillips and myself have taken up our residence at this place, and we think it, in many respects, a promising field for missionary exertions. But there is one advantage we had fondly anticipated, we are extremely sorry to say we have not realized. We thought, at such a distance from Juggernaut, the people would, in a great measure, be unacquainted with the manner in which the government supported idolatry; but alas, even in this dark corner, we have it thrown in our teeth. This vice is twin brother to American Slavery; and it is hard to tell which is the worse—the manner in which the English Government betrays its unwary subjects into the hands of the cruel pundas, or the manner in which America holds her 2,700,000 subjects in the most abject and cruel bondage.

But, dear Sir, enlightened as our countries are, they are the kingdoms of the world. The policy of our rulers is entirely averse to that of him, whose kingdom is not of this world, and, like our divine Redeemer, we must testify that their works are evil. Let us, therefore, while we mourn over the present sad state of things, fix our eye on the day-star of prophecy, till the Sun of Righteousness shall arise, when it shall be lost in his resplendent blaze. Then shall Christ reign king of nations. We must now pray and labour, for this is not to be accomplished all at once. I bid your books God speed; may the truths therein prove effectual to the conversion of Christendom from Idolatry.

You will wish to hear a word of our prospects:—In company with Doitaree we daily visit the bazaar, and the people usually hear with attention, and often come to our house to converse and to get books. I am sensible many are already convinced as to the genuineness of our religion, and were it not for their strong worldly attachments would become Christians. As we have had much fine weather this rainy season, we have had several short excursions in the country; and at such times our hearts have been peculiarly refreshed, from the good attention which the villagers paid to the word. We intended to commence boarding-schools immediately. We have already four children which we have adopted as our own, and expect to take more. Brother P. has the same number. Our interest is the same with your Missionaries; our sentiments are one; our cause is one, and we are one. O may nothing ever take place to disturb our union.

Remember me to all my Christian brethren in your Society. Tell your friends to write to me, and I will be punctual in replying, though my epistles may sometimes be short. When you can make it convenient please send us your pamphlets and papers. Yours, &c.

E. NOYES."

The propriety of the occupancy of the station is strongly urged by Mr. Sutton. "This station is situated in the centre of the hill district of Orissa, in the direct route from Calcutta, via Midnapore and Bombay. It is a large and populous town, stated by Mr. Babington to be nearly as large as Cuttack, while there are many large towns and villages at an easy distance from it. It was occupied for a short time by our American brethren, but scarcely had they completed their habitations, when death and disease broke up the Mission and drove them to Balasore. During the residence of Messrs. Noyes and Phillips at Sumbulpore, the importance of the station grew daily more apparent, and the prospect of extensive usefulness was very cheering. They had enquirers visit them from the neighbourhood of Ruttenpoor, upwards of one hundred miles so the north-west, who speak the Oriya language, and who asserted that it was commonly spoken in their neighbourhood; while the wide fields of Gundwana and the Khund districts on the west, with, the whole Cole country on the east, strongly invite the Missionary of the Cross. At present, however, we can only hope and pray that God will raise up the men who are able and willing to enter upon this field, and connect our stations on the plains with those on the hills."

BALASORE.

This station we have seen had been successively occupied by the Brethren Peters, Sutton and Goadby. After the return of the latter to England, in 1838, it was made over to the American Brethren. The Report of the Orissa Mission, printed at Cuttack, 1841, contains a full account of the Missionaries' operations. Mr. Noyes states—" Upon our arrival we found no native christians, nor any visible traces of our predecessors labours, though the almost unparalleled antipathy of the people to the Gospel appeared to evince that they were not strangers to its doctrines. We make this remark not to undervalue those labours, but to explain why we have to report so little success. At first we could seldom get a hearing in the bazaar, but the people soon changed their method of attack and strove by silent contempt, and occasional sneers and curses, to do what they were unable to perform by raising tumults. Their unusually intemperate habits, such as using ardent spirits, opium, and other intoxicating drugs, appear to render Balasore less hopeful than many other stations.

" The place is important. Its proximity to Calcutta, both by land and water, its populous vicinity and good country roads, are advantages. The population of the zillah, from Jellasore on the north to Budruck on the south, a distance of seventy-five miles, is said to consist of half a million. On the west are the countries of several Rajas, some of which are very populous. Since our residence at B. we have made several excursions into these countries for the purpose of preaching the gospel and distributing books. We found the Oriya language spoken by the people, excepting the Santals and Bhomyas, races who though interspersed with the Oriyas, have a language and religion peculiar to themselves. In 1839 a chapel for English and Oriya worship was erected, the expense of which was defrayed by the liberal donations of European friends. This year two natives were baptized. One was a man from Budruck, of the Khundait caste, who is now a preacher of the gospel.

" At the commencement of 1840, Mr. Phillips and his wife removed to Jellasore, about thirty miles north, and formed a second station, since which time I have laboured alone at Balasore.

"*Bazar preaching and distribution of Books.* With few exceptions Prasaram and myself have visited the bazar daily, for the purpose of preaching and distributing books. The people usually hear with good attention. It is indeed seldom the case, that we are prevented from proceeding with our discourses with all that composure we enjoy in the chapel. Within two years a change has taken place in the manners of the people. The reason I suppose is, that we have so long been unmoved by their noise, that they despaired of putting us down in this way. We have had many interesting discussions, and met with many promising hearers; but I must not pass over the case of one man, with whom I formed a most agreeable acquaintance more than a year since. While travelling through the country I came to his village, about 10 miles from Balasore, when he sent for me to come and pray in his house. I did so, and an acquaintance commenced, which I trust will yet become more sacred. He accompanied me to Balasore, and would have broken caste, had he not been prevented by his family connections. For several months, I had heard nothing from him, when one evening, I saw him in the crowd to which we had been preaching. He told me he had been in the constant habit of reading our books, and wished to live a christian life, asking me if he could not bcome a christian without breaking caste. I of course replied that he could not, at which he appeared seriously affected. I gave him a copy of the New Testament which he promised to read attentively. I might refer to several similar cases of persons who are almost persuaded to become christians. I cannot give the number of gospels and tracts distributed, but it is certain that thousands have been scattered throughout the Zillah and the Mohar Bunge. That they are read, the inquiries and objections of the people clearly evince.

"*Enquirers.* I could refer to more than 20 who would have been willing to break caste and profess christianity the past year, but as it was evident they had sinister motives, they met with no encouragement. There are two, a man and his wife, who have for the last year lived on my compound, who have at times manifested some sincerity. In addition to these, I have had frequent visits from some of the most respectable classes, who have desired books, and wished to converse upon religious subjects.

"*Changes in the Church.* During the past year five native members have been dismissed to Jellasore, three have been added by baptism, and one excluded. Our present number of members is eight. We were joined by the Rev. O. R. Bachelor and wife and Miss Cummings in September.

"*Candidates for Baptism.* We have at present three candidates for baptism, who have been waiting some time for an opportunity to be baptised. These are children from our Boarding School. The case of one, a girl about 15 years old, deserves notice. For a long time she had manifested deep conviction for sin, when one day she came into my study, and with tears, said she had often wished to open her mind to me, but fear prevented her; but now as God had forgiven her sins and given her a hope of eternal life, she could no longer keep silent. Indeed I never saw greater evidence of a work of grace than she manifested.

Boarding School. We have about 30 boarding children, 20 girls and 10 boys, who live on our compound, and are taught by a native christian, also seven children of native christians. Of these I have a class of eight who have made good proficiency in the Oryia gospels, Geography, History, Arithmetic, &c. I spend an hour or two with them daily, and have reason to believe that these children form no small part of the hope of our mission. The girls are taught to cook, clean their houses and spin, and spend from three to four hours a day with Mrs. Noyes, who teaches them to sew, &c.

"If the gospel is a system that must be learned, it is evident that those who commence in childhood have a great advantage over such, as come under its influence at an advanced period of life. They may be unaffected by innumerable disadvantages that must follow the converted heathen to the grave. Though the whole expense of food, clothes, &c. for each child, has not exceeded two rupees per month, yet we have not been able to meet this expense the past year without incurring debt, as our society was not aware of the rapid increase and consequent greater demands for our school.

"*State of native schools.* There was about 30 Oriya schools in Balasore, each containing from 15 to 30 boys. I have of late spent much time visiting and examining most of them. Saying nothing of the impure books, it is evident their system of education is very deficient. The situation of a schoolmaster is far from being respectable, hence no well informed native will engage in the profession. The books read, though calculated to engage the memory, contain nothing to call into action, and strengthen the rational faculties. This appears to be one reason why the people so lightly esteem our books, which are generally argumentative. Their taste is formed from early childhood, for narrative, stories, fables, &c.

"*Need of help.* Though we are in the habit of itinerating as circumstances will admit, yet we are far from being able to answer the demands of a million of souls. There are several large towns in this Zillah, where it is highly desirable to establish missions. We have often sent urgent appeals to our society, and to some extent have been gratified; but alas! labourers are few, and means insignificant for the accomplishment of so great a work as lies before us. Several European friends have liberally contributed towards the support of our Boarding school and native preacher, for which they have our gratefnl thanks, and we pray that the blessing of many ready to perish may rest upon them. Any additional donations from friends in India will be thankfully received and duly acknowledged.

"*Present state of the Church.* Baptised Europeans two, East Indian one, Natives seven, excluded two, present number eight."

Recent communications indicate the steady progress of the cause at this station. A baptism of two interesting individuals is reported in the Morning Star, Jan. 4, 1846, published in America.

JELLASORE.

The Indian Report of 1841, contains Mr. Phillips' account of this station. He says—"It is one year this month since I removed to this place, and commenced my missionary work here, though a part of the previous cold season had been spent in travelling and preaching in the neighbourhood.

"Jellasore is a pleasant country town situated on the east side of the Subunreeka river, 46 miles from Midnapore and 33 from Balasore, the nearest European station to it. It is about fourteen miles inland from the Bay. Including Patna and Lukanath, two villages situate on either side of it, the population is estimated at about 6000 inhabitants. The Oriya language is spoken as purely here as at Cuttack or Pooree. Immediately on becoming settled, regular meetings of worship were commenced. These are attended by the native christians, school children, and some of our servants, with occasional visitors from the heathen. My usual practice has been to preach a familiar discourse on some practical subject on the Sabbath school lesson, which the elder children have learned during the previous week. Evening meetings for prayer and religious conversation have been held twice a week, with pleasure and I trust profit to all concerned. In these meetings all the native brethren take a part.

"On the 7th of last month, with the assistance of my esteemed brother and colleague Mr. Bachelor, we were organized into a church, there being six native members. Three of these were originally from the church at Cuttack, and one, a native preacher, is soon to leave. One of the others is our eldest school-boy, who was baptised and received into the church at Balasore in October 1839. The two remaining ones have been baptised the past year, one formerly a brahmun was baptised in October last; the other a Talee (oilman,) in February. These are both young men, and appear studious. The former is very amiable, posseses some talent, and bids fair to become useful.

"During the year, preaching in the bazar and at the country markets, (of which there are not less than twelve within reach of home, and most of them held twice a week) has been attended to so far as other important duties would allow; with what success the future must determine. We have often had our hopes very much raised, but about as often disappointed, as it regards real conversions. Still we have good reason to believe the truth is gaining ground.

"Since the commencement of the last cold season, about 12,000 tracts, 1000 single gospels, about 40 New Testaments, and numerous other portions of the sacred word have been distributed among eager applicants. Most of them have been given at the different markets visited, and thus must have been scattered very extensively over the country. Oh, may the precious word thus sent forth prove the savour of life unto life to many undying souls. A few of these tracts and scriptures were in the Bengalee language, and generously furnished by the kindness of our Baptist brethren in Calcutta. The greater part however were in the Oriya language, and kindly supplied from Cuttack. The judgment and propriety manifest in the selection and compilation of these publications, and the neatness and taste displayed in their execution, prove the ability of the Cuttack press to supply the demand for books of this kind in the language.

"*Native Boarding School.* A year ago we had twelve children in school; the number has since increased to twenty-six, besides six who have died and three who have run away. The progress of the children in their studies has been such as to afford much encouragement. Thirteen are able to read in the New Testament, and a number of the oldest have advanced very well in a variety of elementary studies. As before remarked, one of the boys is a member of the church. One of the girls is now a candidate for baptism. The manual labour system is adopted as far as we have the means.

"My sheet is about full, but I cannot close without a word respecting the *Santals*, whose villages Mr. Bachelor and I visited on the opposite side of the river a few weeks since. Beside visiting a number of their villages, we attended an annual donu which happened to take place at the time. There were about six hundred people assembled, both men and women. In the centre of a circle were placed a number of small images, &c., around which the females marched with a slow step, and outside of them the men formed a ring, and moved on with great glee. They were equipped with swords, clubs, &c., and a variety of feathers about their heads, and some of them carried horses' tails in their hands. A liquor made of rice, which made all very merry, was served out in cups made of leaves. The perspiration ran freely, and mingling with the dust on their bodies looked like muddy water. These are a very simple and peculiarly interesting people. Many of their customs reminded us of the North American Indians. May they soon be blest with a knowledge of the glorious gospel. A missionary situated at Patna would have very ready access to their villages. O may we soon have the happiness of welcoming a Brother here, who will gladly devote all his energies to labour for their salvation. At present they have no written language, and we could only speak to them through the medium of Oriya, of which many of them can speak a little. They certainly must be far less shackled with idolatry and superstition than their Oriya neighbours. May "*the day spring from on high*" soon rise upon them!"

The supporters of the American missionaries in Orissa are free from the plague spot of Slavery, which Wesley designated—"The execrable sum of all human misery." The English Report of 1840 and 41 contain some tremendous charges against this national sin of America, and highly commends our brethren for washing their hands from its guilt. The Rev. J. G. Pike, states,—

"Though acting under the direction of a distant Society, the American brethren in Orissa, as to their object, are but one with your Missionaries. No reference would here be made to them, if they were connected with those American Baptists, who support the atrocious and infamous system of American Slavery. Nothing can be more inconsistent than for persons, who support a system of perpetual robbery, and slow but extensive murder, to profess anxiety to diffuse the heavenly system of Christianity. No taunts, with which the missionaries of such professors could be met in India, would be too severe. The priests of Goomsur, when shedding the blood of human victims to their gloomy goddess, might exclaim, "We offer a few victims to Kalee, you offer myriads to your idol!—Covetousness—the love of dishonest gain. We fertilize our fields with pieces of human flesh, you fertilize yours with the sweat and agonies of many victims destroyed for one that we slay." The Thugs, those robbers and murderers by profession and descent, might exclaim, "We murder hundreds that we rob, and when detected suffer death for doing so. You murder by lingering cruelty thousands, that you have robbed all their days, and yet boast yourselves freemen and christians, and profess to send teachers to us." Even the prostitutes of Juggernaut's temple might upbraid such missionaries. "You denounce the lewdness of our land, and the prostitution of a few hundreds at our temples in honour of our gods, but you maintain a system of lewdness not less atrocious and far more extensive. We devote ourselves willingly to the life we lead; you breed human beings for sale, deny to hundreds of thousands of your female population, the ties of marriage, and rob them of their honour, and then vaunt your love of freedom and christianity. Away with such teachers sent from such people; India needs them not." Every Missionary, sent from America by pro-slavery men, deserves to be met with such rebukes as these; and were the American Missionaries in Orissa sent by such professors, no reference would be made to them. Were that the case it would dishonour and pollute this page to acknowledge them as fellow labourers, but they are men of a different class, and sent by men, who advocate the abolition of the wicked system, which fixes such a stigma on various bodies falsely called christian churches. This being the case, we acknowledge them as brethren and fellow labourers in the Lord.

"At Balasore, their first station, they have a native church consisting of seven members. A few months back they baptized an intelligent and respectable man from Buddruck. He subsequently remove to Balasore, with his wife and family, and appeared encouraging. They have also baptized the wife of Bikhari, a daughter of Doitaree, the native preacher. They were when Mr. Sutton wrote, daily expecting a reinforcement from the United States. An extract from the Report sent from Balasore, by Mr. Phillips, to the last Conference at Cuttack, narrates their progress.

"It has been my practice during the hot and rainy seasons to visit almost daily one of the bazaars, or some village or market in the neighbourhood, for the purpose of teaching the way of eternal life to my heathen brethren, and distributing among them tracts and portions of the Sacred Scriptures.

"During the present season, I have been able to itinerate more than in any previous year, since being in the country. As the cold weather set in early, I commenced a tent life by the middle of October, and continued it but with little interruption till the 11th Jan. when other duties required my attention at home. I have no exact account of the number of villages visited, but during the time I attended more than twenty country markets, where the word of God was preached and tracts and Scriptures distributed. Many of these places were unknown to missionary efforts before the present year; but if life and health are spared me, I hope to visit them again and again, and to enlarge my circuits as I may be able.

"On the first of May, I commenced a small Boarding school, consisting of the four native children which had been given me at Sumbulpore. Since then we have received into the school six other poor destitute children, but three of them have either run away or been bribed away after remaining a time. Our number is seven, three boys and four girls. The proficiency made by those longest in the school is truly gratifying. The eldest boy, an interesting lad about twelve years old, has given evidence of decided piety, and been baptized, and received into the church the past year. A day School was commenced at the same time on my compound, in which two masters were employed. The average number of daily attendants was forty, and the proficiency made was quite pleasing.

"In accordance with the views of brother Noyes and myself, in relation to the propriety of occupying separate stations, and of making Patna our next, I have made arrangement for removing there for the purpose of commencing a new station. At this place my work will be entirely among the natives. This circumstance renders an efficient native preacher a great desideratum. Should you not be able to spare Gunga Dhor, I trust you will do the best you are able to send another efficient native brother."

In the following year reference is made to the return of Mr Noyes, through ill health, but hopes were entertained that his return would be for "the furtherance of the gospel." The American brethren at Balasore and Jellasore, persevere in their honourable efforts to diffuse the light of truth, nor have those efforts been in vain. Several Hindoos have become converts to the Gospel. They have had some striking and highly pleasing instances of conversion. That they are in heart one with your brethren, may be inferred from the fact that in this arrangement of native ministers for the current year, it was agreed to send one these brethren to assist them. They have experienced a trial in the return through ill health of Mr. Noyes to the United States, though probably he may there be instrumental in exciting so much missionary spirit, as shall cause his return to be for the furtherance of the Gospel.

Some interesting facts respecting the *usefulness of religious books, and tracts,* have been given by the Brethren, which may well encourage "to sow in hope." "All who are acquainted with the history of this mission are aware, that the religious publications issued have been, in the hand of the Eternal Spirit, one of the principal means for enlightening many benighted minds, and subduing many hearts to Christ. The distribution of this sacred seed has been extensively carried on, from year to year. Mr. Lacey, when giving a report of the Cuttack Station, writes, "The distribution of religious publications has been attended to on every occasion of our preaching the Gospel, aud though I cannot speak with certainty about the number of tracts which has been put into circulation, yet I do not think fewer than *thirty thousand* have been given away. Our books have been readily received, and many we know have been read. The festivals and markets have been our best opportunities for distributing tracts—then the rush to get them has been overwhelming. Several instances of good arising from this means have come to my knowledge during the year."

One pleasing instance of this kind is the following :—"Down near the sea coast, nearly *ninety miles from Pooree,* Mr. Phillips, an American Missionary, discovered a number of people, who appeared far advanced in christian knowledge. Soon after this discovery Mr. Phillips dispatched a native preacher to see them. He went, and returned with a very pleasing report of the knowledge and proficiency of the people, and bore a request from three of them, for baptism. On further inquiry Mr. Phillips learned that *twelve* or *thirteen* years before, these people had received some tracts at Pooree, in the midst of the noise and bustle of the Car Festival." After referring to this narrative, Mr. Lacey remarks,—"How plainly we read in such instances the divine precept, 'In the morning sow thy seed, and in the evening withhold not thy hand, for thou knowest not which shall prosper, whether this or that.' How often have I, with our native brother, been pelted with cow-dung and sand, followed with the abusive vociferations of the infatuated multitude; almost speechless with hoarseness, and sore with the crowding of the people, retired from the town of Pooree wearied and discouraged, and ready to conclude that these people are accursed of God! But while we have been thus discouraged, the precious seed we have sown in tumult and persecution has been quietly carried away, and has taken root and brought forth the fruits of eternal salvation.'

Encouraging as is the preceding fact, another, very similar but still more interesting, has been narrated by Mr. Noyes, whose ill health compelled him to revisit his native land. The fact is evidently connected with the labours of the brethren at Pooree, though the narration has not been received from them, but from the United States, where it was published in a recent Report of the Freewill Baptist Missionary Society. Mr. Noyes writes,—

"One day as I was sitting in my house, Lokanath was introduced to me by one of the native Christians, as an enquirer after salvation. The following conversation took place between him and myself:—Well, my brother, from whence have you come? 'About one hundred and forty kos'—two hundred and fifty miles. For what purpose have you come all this distance? 'Sir, I heard you could tell me about the invisible God, and the means of finding him.' But your people all worship idols, so how has it happened that you should think about the invisible God? 'O Sir, will you hear my message?—Three years ago I went to see Juggernaut, and as I was returning, I saw a European, who with three or four Hindoos, was teaching the people from a book. I came near them, and they put three small tracts into my hand. These books I took to my village, where they were read openly. We found that they were about one true, invisible God, and one Jesus Christ, who was said to be his Son, and the Saviour of sinners. Thus things went on. The books were daily read in the centre of the village, till some of us began to conclude, that if the books were true, *then the religion of this country must be false.* At this, many were displeased, and said, they were the books of the Englishman, and that by reading them, we should become outcasts. Only eight of us remained firm, and as we met with much persecution, we commenced the habit of retiring once or twice a week to the jungle, where we read the books, and supplicated the invisible God. We also gave up the worship of idols, and broke all the badges of idolatry. *Thus passed nearly three years;* when we began to conclude that we needed some one to teach us the new religion. Now, my comrades said to me, you are the oldest, and we will send you in search of a Teacher. You shall go to him and become a Christian, and then return and tell us, and where you go, we will go, and what you do, that we will do. So saying, *they all took an oath by the book of the invisible God,* which they held in their hands, and I immediately took my departure. I knew that there was a Padre Sahib at Berhampore, but as I had many relatives and acquaintances there, I was afraid of their resentment. So I came on to Cuttack, where I arrived late in the

A BRAHMIN AND HIS WIFE, AT THEIR DEVOTIONS.

evening, and left early the next morning, the people telling me there was a Padre Sahib at Balasore. [It appears that in his short stay at Cuttack, he did not hear of the missionaries and native Christians there.] Thus hearing, I came immediately to this place, and enquired for your house, which I at length found—and now sir, *I wish to hear the word of the Lord, by which I and my comrades may be saved.*" After remaining some weeks at this station, and affording satisfactory evidence of piety he was baptized by brother Noyes, and departed for his country, to communicate the results of his journey to his associates in seeking for the kingdom of heaven.

One of the publications of the English Tract Society in 1844 contains this statement,—"Mr. Phillips, stationed at Jellasore, has communicated the following facts:—Upwards of thirteen years ago, a man from the eastern corner of the province travelled upwards of 200 miles to Pooree to attend the car festival. He then obtained a tract and carried it back to his village, where the perusal of it introduced light into a mind hitherto dark as midnight. He continued to read it till his convictions induced him to abandon idolatry, and follow the teachings of the tract. Whether he obtained any other tract or further information I know not, but he continued to walk in the way of truth, so far as he had been able to discover it, till he died, which was a year or two since. His younger brother then, amidst the loud lamentations of his aged mother, adopted the same course, and has recently found his way to Jellasore, where he avows his intention to become a Christian, and gives this account of his brother. This, we are happy to believe, is only one among many similar instances of the influence of these silent messengers of mercy.

"In an interesting revival of religion in our native boarding schools, several of the boys referred to our tracts and books as first inducing serious impressions. Little Henry and his Bearer was mentioned by one or two, but upon inquiry of Solomon (our dear Khund boy) what first impressed his mind, he replied it was the Call to Unconverted Sinners, (in Oriya of course,) and especially the words, "Turn or die." He afterwards became a candidate for baptism, and we hoped to add him to the visible church, but he was, with two other dear boys suddenly cut down by the cholera. We grieve not for him, however, as for those of whom we have no hope. But shall I thus dismiss the record of our poor boy? May not some eye glance on this brief notice, to whom the words which first impressed his mind are as applicable as to the poor barbarous Khund? Yes, ye young, ye gay, ye refined, ye amiable, whether in America or England, you must "turn or die." Oh may these words prove to be one of the arrows of the Holy Ghost, piercing your heart, and leading you to turn and live!"

The following interesting letter from Gunga Dhor to Christians in America, will be read with deep attention. In a letter to an American friend, Mr. Sutton observes: "The duplicate of your letter of June 5th, reached me a few days ago. Gunga Dhor was with me when it arrived; so I explained the purport of it to him. His eyes filled with tears at the mention of *the liberality of Christians in America for people whom they have never seen.* He is a man of exquisite sensibility and generous sentiments. I immediately proposed to him to write a short letter to your Society, to which he readily assented; and the next day handed me the accompanying, (written in the Oriya language,) to which I have annexed a literal translation.

TRANSLATION OF GUNGA DHOR'S LETTER.

April 3th, 1838, Pooree, Orissa.

"To the Friends of the Lord Jesus Christ, rendered benevolent through his love, delivered from sin, and by the power of the Holy Spirit reconciled to God, even to you, the holy people dwelling in America, Ghunga Dhor Suring, a Christian, sends this congratulatory epistle.

"O my fellow-heirs of everlasting life, a short time since my soul was enveloped by the gloom of sin, and through violating God's law, I was deserving of perdition; but God having mercy upon my country, sent missionary brethren to preach the Gospel of his Son. They circulated many tracts, and in consequence I obtained one or two. By continuing to peruse them I discovered the wickedness of my heart, became acquainted with Christ, and learned to know that God is a Spirit, dwelling in heaven and separate from matter. What I worshiped, even created things and men—all these forsaking, and believing in the name of Christ, I was baptized. According to my ability I now preach the gospel; and should God bestow the blessing of the Holy Spirit, then will my countrymen yield good fruit. As I have obtained a knowledge of the Scriptures, so will they; and from those shasters from which I have turned, they also will turn. For I plainly perceive that the books of my native land are false; there is no truth in them.

But alas! there are none to teach the true wisdom, or bestow the true shaster. They wander like forlorn sheep. O my beloved brethren in eternal life, if you pray for my countrymen, if you are concerned for the salvation of their souls, then I entreat your aid, according to your ability, in behalf of my brethren and sisters. The sacred book, which like a sun is able to irradiate their hearts and minds, which is able to convert them to everlasting life in heaven, which can save from the fear of death and from the torments of hell, and deliver from the evils of sin and the temptation of Satan—even that holy book bestow, and we may distribute it and scatter it like seed. As the wealthy in India in this time of famine, are bestowing their thousands of rupees to save men's bodies, so, or even in a superior degree, bestow your aid for the salvation of men's souls. Communicate of that property which you have acquired, for those souls in whose behalf Christ endured incalculable anguish. Commit it to the custody of my missionary brethren.

At this season thousands of people, leaving their homes, accompained by their wives and children, are going on pilgrimage. In some places one hundred thousand assemble; in others eighty thousand; in others fifty thousand; in others thirty thousand; in others fifteen thousand; in others five thonsand; and in others three, two, or one thousand. Exceeding great sin is committed, and daily increasing. On this account, we say, *furnish us with religious books and we will distribute them*—so shall we free our garments from the blood of souls. The misssionaries will explain this matter to you. What more can I write? Accept from me, many, very many salutations. May blessings rest upon you.

Postscript—The last seventeen days, with the Rev. Mr. Sutton, I have been at Pooree. We go day by day to the bazaar, and preach to four, five, or six hundred people. Many acknowledge that our doctrine is true; others making various excuses, blaspheme. The people come from different countries—Oryias, Bengalees, Mahrattas, Telingas, Hindoosthanees. They experience great suffering through this pilgrimage. Many children are bereft of parents, and many people die of various diseases. Their skulls and bones lie scattered on the four sides of the city. On both sides of the great road also, from Pooree to their homes, their skulls and bones are seen. This God sees. This while I write, I also see. For them there is no cry, 'alas!' nor any to bury them. The birds of the air and dogs of the field devour them. It is for a sight of this Juggernaut at Pooree, all these miseries are endured. The Pundas go and invite and induce the people to come, that they may get their money and obtain presents from them. Taking all they possess, they send them empty-handed away. All the people receive, is a rag of cloth, a little dry rice, a stick, and a little sweet-meat (relics from Juggernaut). These taking, they return, begging along the road as they go. How much might be said! but were I to write it you could not endure it. My object in writing is that *tracts in Oriya, Bengalee, Persian, Hindooee, Maharatta, &c. &c. may be printed, and distributed among these ignorant and apostate people*. This would indeed be a good work. Who can tell but they may one day see, and hear, and understand, and turn to God? I think in my mind that in the last day they will say: 'It was by means of the dwellers in America, that, having obtained the divine word, we knew the Lord.' "

It is added in the English Report of 1843—"The American Brethren continue to act as fellow-labourers with your Missionaries, in an adjacent, but distant field of exertion. They have been encouraged by some pleasing instances of converting grace, and one of those gathered from heathen darkness to Christ, if not more, has become an assistant to them in preaching the glorious gospel. To their small band of missionaries they have made some addition, and, according to recent accounts, are expecting some others to join them."

An interesting letter from one of the American missionaries to the writer, may not improperly be referred to here, on account of the information which it contains. The reference to the connexion of the British Government with Idolatry is very important, and shews the magnitude of this evil in India. See G. B. Repository, 1844, pp. 250-51.

MIDNAPORE.

This station has been relinquished to the American Missionaries. The English Report for 1844 states,—The last Report announced that this Town had no longer a resident missionary. It has proved an unfruitful and barren spot, no one that has been occupied by the Society more so; and in consequence of the Oorea language been spoken here to a very small extent, the opinion was strongly and decidedly expressed to the Committee, that it would be advisable to relinquish this place to the American Brethren, who from its proximity to their stations, felt desirious of becoming its occupants. The Committee therefore adopted a resolution authorizing the Brethren in India to transfer the station to the American Missionaries if they deemed it desirable to do so, on receiving a reasonable sum for the chapel which belonged to the Society. Brethren Lacey and Sutton have adopted measures for carrying this arrangement into effect. The chapel having suffered much damage since it was unoccupied, they judged that four hundred rupees would be a reasonable compensation for it. They thought it improper to put this sum into the general treasury, but proposed to appropriate it as follows:

	Rupees.
To assist in rebuilding the Chapel at Berhampore	100
To assist in liquidating the debt on Cuttack Chapel......	100
To build premises necessary to commence a station eastward of Cuttack....................................	100
To build a Chapel at Choga, leaving the present small mud building for the accommodation of the native and European preachers at their visits	100

This branch of the mission has been honoured in the conversion of souls, the details of which as reported to the Society in America are doubtless interesting. The narrative of the conversion of Prasuram is of a highly encouraging nature. See G. B. Repository 1843, pp. 348-350.—"May the little one become a thousand, and the small one a strong nation, the Lord hasten it in his time."

The English Report of the mission for 1844 contains a brief reference to these zealous and beloved Brethren.—" The American Brethren have continued to occupy the field that your Missionaries resigned to them. The most harmonious feeling appears to exist between the Missionaries of the two Societies, who act as fellow-labourers, though acting distinctly. From the last Report of their Society it appears that Mr. Phillips was stationed at Jellasore, and Mr. Bachelor at Balasore. There were two native preachers, Prasuram and Rama, part of the fruits of the mission. A few converts have been baptized during the year, but some previously received have fallen. In September 1843, Mr. C. Dow was ordained as a Missionary, and was to sail from Boston for India in October. Mr. Noyes, who had been compelled by ill health to return to America, was then editing a publication designed to promote a missionary spirit."

CHAP. V.

Success of the Orissa Mission.

Its usefulness in the conversion of Europeans and Indo-British—Portuguese and Hindoos—Raising up of Native Preachers and Evangelists—Their ordination to the work of God—Students for the ministry—Brief accounts of Erun, Gunga-dhor, Ram-chundra, Krupa-Sindo, Doitaree, &c.

It cannot fail to be interesting, to refer particularly to various instances of conversion among the different classes of European and Indo-British, Portuguese and Hindoos, with whom the Missionaries both English and American come in contact, and to whom their labours, through the divine blessing have proved useful. In the early history of missionary operations, it is stated—" We have preaching regularly morning and evening, in English, on a Lord's day, though the congregations are small ; but we hope some good will be done, as the hearers are regular and serious in their attendance. A converted Samaritan may be the means of introducing the gospel to many." The "first-fruits" of Orissa unto God were among the Indo-British, the descendants of the Portuguese; viz. Messrs. Rennell, Baptist, George, De Santos, De Sozo, &c.

In the Report of 1827, it is observed by Mr. Lacey, after referring to the baptism of Mr. De Santos, "There are others whose minds are under serious impressions, and who seem hesitating and halting between two opinions: who, from the improvement in their deportment and particularly as it respects feasting, the observance of the Lord's-day, and their own observations, are evidently the subjects of a work of grace, and we hope we shall soon have the pleasure of informing you of their union with us. Among all those to whom we have access improvement is apparent. The Sabbath, till now neglected by them through the example of superiors and the imperious, commands of men, is now generally regarded; and if broken through the above causes, it is with much expostulation and difficulty, which will increase in proportion as the sense of obligation to God appears above that to man; and the Natives themselves have observed the change."

On Dec. 24th, 1826, three persons were baptized, in one of the rivers that skirts the city of Cuttack. One of these was a converted Jewess, the wife of Abraham, the native Preacher. Mr. Sutton wrote—"Her experience seems plain and satisfactory. Her mind has been convinced of her sinfulness for some time, and that the Lord Jesus Christ was the only Saviour; but within these last four months, from reading the third chapter of John her convictions have been much deepened, and she has fled in earnest to the blood of Christ. On being asked her reasons for wishing to be baptized, she said, that when a seapoy enlisted in the Company's service, *he puts on the badge belonging to their army, and she wished in the same way to enter into the service of the Lord Jesus Christ.* She is by birth a daughter of Abraham, and does not speak English." Another is the mother of Sunder, a native of Arracan, she had become a Roman Catholic. The third candidate baptized at that time was a steady youth, the brother of Sunder.

The same Report refers to the conversion of Mr. Beddy, who became a useful missionary. It is stated—"Four individuals of the Ordinance department went to reside at Cuttack, and of the four three appear to have felt the influence of divine truth."

Mr. Beddy laboured with considerable acceptance in Cuttack and Calcutta; and was subsequently accepted as a missionary by the Society belonging to the other part of the Baptist Denomination. See an interesting letter from him in the G. B. Repository, 1841, pp. 221. He has resided for some years at Patna.

An Ordinance day in 1832 is thus described, in grateful, glowing language.

"The more interesting service of this sabbath, however, was the evening service of the Lord's Supper. We sat down with a goodly number of dear native Christians at the sacred feast. There were Gunga, and his wife; Krupa Sindoo, and his wife; Koranasaw, and his wife; and the other Krupa Sindoo; Boodee, Purama, Radoo, and Betsies Maha, all natives won from satan and idolatry; celebrating the most solemn Christian ordinance, forming the foundation of the Church of Christ, which will spread wider and wider—forming a leaven which will work until it has leavened the whole lump. Yes, our hearts experienced no common emotion when we surveyed them in their various characters and bearings. Bro. Sutton administered the ordinance, and spoke in English, and Bro. L. spoke to the Oriya communicants. Another thing which gave no small interest to this pleasing opportunity, was, that two dear friends, one of the civil, and the other of the military service of the Hon. Company, requested to communicate with us. So here the highest and the lowest, the polished and honorable European, and the rustic humble native, dropping their distinctions, mixed in one communion, partook of one feast, actuated by one feeling, i. e. love to Jesus Christ, in whom there is neither Jew nor Greek, barbarian, Scythian, bond nor free."

One of the most remarkable features of primitive Christianity, was the ability of the converts to diffuse the gospel, and their readiness to engage in this sacred work. It is written, "They that were scattered abroad went everywhere preaching the word;" and again, "Now they that were scattered abroad upon the persecution, that arose about Stephen, travelled as far as Phenice and Cyprus and Antioch, preaching to none but the Jews only. And some of them were men of Cyprus and Cyrene, which when they were come to Antioch, spoke unto the Grecians, preaching the Lord Jesus. And the hand of the Lord was with them; and a great number believed and turned unto the Lord. Acts viii. 4, xi. 19, 21. It is a subject of devout thankfulness, that a goodly number of the converts have been blest with wisdom and utterance to make known the gospel of the grace of God. In the Report of 1829, after paying a just tribute to the memory of the lamented Cropper, reference is made to the raising up of the help for "the work of the ministry."

Ordination of Native Preachers.

The first ordination of Native Brethren to the work of the Evangelist in Orissa is very fully described in the Report of the Society for 1835, p.p. 18-21.

A third ordination was in 1841, when Bamadab was set apart to the work. "Messrs. Brooks and Stubbins conducted the former parts of the service. Mr. Sutton offered the ordination prayer, and Mr. Lacey delivered a charge."

It is stated "Thus after several years of trial, five have been ordained. Six are still employed as assistant preachers, and three are missionary students." Mr. Lacey states,—"Six native brethren have been entirely employed in preaching and disputing among the people, and others occasionally engaged. In the character of their ministry, I believe the native brethren have lately a good deal improved: their knowledge of christian truth has enlarged, and a corresponding improvement in their public administrations has exhibited itself. In the past year, moreover, their usefulness has been more apparent in several pleasing instances, wherein knowledge has been communicated and convictions implanted. Many of the native christians, and the enquirers have been able to bear testimony to their usefulness; and one instance of good to an idolater, now a candidate for baptism, is well calculated to encourage all who are interested in the labours of our native preachers." Several ordinations have occurred in late years.

As enemies to the Gospel have often urged that none but outcasts would embrace it, it may be stated that of these, three were Brahmuns.—Three Naiks.—One a pure Boisya.—One a Byragee. —One a Maharatta, son of the last Killadar of Cuttack.—One a Bengalee (unknown).—One a Farmer.—One a Mahantee or patovari.—There has been but one of a low caste baptized.

Native Students.

The Report of 1841 makes reference to this interesting class of Native converts.—These young men continued under Mr. Sutton's care till a special Conference in Oct. when it was agreed that the three should be received as assistant Preachers, Damadur to accompany Mr. Sutton to Calcutta, Sebo to go to Berhampore and assist Mr. Stubbins, and Somnath to remain at Cuttack. Mr. Lacey states,—"We have added three to the number of our native Preachers, who are all men of more than ordinary promise."

At the Conference held in Cuttack, April 25, 26, 1845, other native Brethren were appointed to aid in the great work of evangelizing Orissa.—Their names were Baligee, Subra Sahu, Subra Naik, Damadur, Somnauth and Bikhari. Dena Bundo and Prasu Rant were accepted as assistant native Preachers. (See G. B. Repository, March 1845, p 104.) The Lord give the word and increase "the company that publish it." The most recent information, speaks of the increase of these valuable labourers, and the establishment of an Academy at Cuttack, which was opened, with eight students, January 1st, 1846.

The following accounts of some of the most remarkable individuals among the Hindoos, who have been converted to God in Orissa, cannot fail to shew the friends of the Mission, both at home and abroad, the success of their efforts, and to lead them with the church of old to say—"*At this time it shall be said, What hath God wrought?*" The records both of the living and the dead, demonstrate the power of divine grace.

Erun.

Gungadhor was probably the first convert in Orissa; but the first Hindoo who broke the chain of caste, and put on Christ by baptism, was Erun, a Telinga, converted at Berhampore, by the labours of Mr. Bampton. The first reference to this person occurs in Mr. Bampton's Journal, in March 1827. He says—"On Tuesday evening a man came and said, with an apparent air of levity, that he would go with me and continue with me. From what I saw of the man I supposed that he was only in jest, and rather apprehended that he really meant to ridicule me. But as he seemed like a man with whom I could make free, I told him that if he went with me, he must wash the marks off his face and breasts. These marks were made, I suppose, with powder of sandal wood and water, and some of them were peeling off of themselves, so I took my finger nail and picked them off. The man seemed very careless about his marks, and I proceeded to say that, if he went with me, he must throw off and break his lingu. He expressed his willingness to do so, and not only expressed his willingness, but proceeded to take the case off his neck, and, taking out the little bit of wood, (the lingu,) laid it down, and gave me the liberty of breaking it. But as I did not know what effects it might produce among the people, I hesitated, and advised him to break it himself, on which he took my chair foot and did so. I did not then know that these little lingus are revered so much as I have since heard that they are; and it struck me that, as the case was silver, it might be of more consequence than its contents, so I advised him to break that too; to this he said that, it was silver, and he seemed to think that it need not be broken; but I said it was unclean on account of its use, on which he immediately laid it down, and taking the chair foot broke it!! I soon after saw a man exhibiting some parts of the broken thing, and requested to see them; they were immediately put into my hands, one of them was the principal part of the article, and the other a little bit that had been broken off; so I asked the owner if I might have them, to which he not only replied in the affirmative, but said that I might have the case too, and immediately gave it me.

"March 3rd. Erun, who broke his lingu, has been with me a good part of the forenoon. He says that the people are highly displeased with him for what he has done: they threaten to pull down his house and stone him. They say that the Sahib has given him forty rupees, and he may go with the Sahib, for they do not want to see his face in Berhampore. The man is afraid of them, and requested me to apply to the authorities for protection. Among other things my disciple (as the people call him,) told me that his father died at the age of 105, and his mother at 90. The old man, he says, retained his sight, hearing, and teeth to the last; his father despised the idols, but his mother did not."

His baptism and subsequent conduct are thus reported,—"Owing to the operations of various causes, the minds of Hindoos are generally weaker than the minds of Englishmen; but there are few, if any, English Christians who have been called to display so much Christian heroism as is displayed by a Hindoo who gives up his caste, especially if he be the first in the neighbourhood who receives the Gospel. And Erun's remaining fear, after again wishing to be baptized, showed itself in a proposal, that I should tell the truth if asked whether he had eaten with me or not, but say nothing about it if I were not asked. But this I felt myself obliged to refuse, and I told him that if he determined to remain unbaptized, no sum of money, nor any consideration whatever, should ever induce me to publish his having eaten with me; but that if he was baptized I would certainly publicly declare that his caste was gone. For I told him, the *caste was an enemy to Jesus Christ, which none of his friends could spare; and stood like a stone wall across the road to prevent the progress of the Gospel.* This firm but fair and honest way of treating him, manifestly pleased him, and he soon expressed his detemination to face every difficulty.

"*December 25th* was fixed for his baptism, and between three and four in the afternoon, to our no small satisfaction, he came to the tent, bringing with him a change of apparel; between four and five we proceeded to a tank called the Ramalingum tank, and on our arrival, including ourselves and servants there were not present perhaps above ten persons; before we had finished there might be twenty. In an address I delivered, I briefly pointed out the way of salvation; said that Jesus Christ required, first, faith, and then baptism—that my friend Erun had forsaken Hindooism—that he *had given up his caste*—that he believed in Jesus Christ and wished thus to connect himself with his followers. Then I asked Erun if it was not the case, and he said it was. I had not given him notice of my intention to ask him any questions at the water; but I proceeded to say that I should request his answers to a few, which, with his replies, I shall subjoin. 'Do you honour the Hindoo gods?'—'No.'—'What do you think of the Hindoo shastras?'—'They are all false.'—'Are you a sinner?'—'Yes.'—'Who saves sinners?'—'Jesus Christ.'—'What did Jesus Christ do to save sinners?'—'He died for them.'—'Who will be saved?'—'Those who rely on Jesus Christ.'—'Do you believe in Jesus Christ?'—'I do.'—'Do you wish to obey Jesus Christ?'—'I do.'—'Jesus Christ requires his followers to abstain from worldly business every Sunday, and devote the day to religious exercises: do you engage to comply with this requisition?'—'I do.'—'Do you wish to be baptized?'—'Yes.'

"We then prayed, and after prayer went into the water, when I said, *Peeta pootra dhurmatmar namorai ambhai toombokoo doobo dayee;* i. e. 'I baptize thee in the name of the Father, and of the Son, and of the Holy Ghost;' and my friend thought that as he was addressed it would be right to reply, so he said, Acha, i. e. 'Very good,' and I baptized him; and on coming out of the water much wished, that we had a host of Christian friends present to vent, in a song of praise, those feelings which the event could not fail to excite. After changing our clothes we returned to my tent, and Erun drank tea with us."

The consistent profession of this first convert is frequently noticed in terms of respect. In 1840 it is stated in the Annual Report—"Erun, who was baptized by Mr. Bampton, and was the first Hindoo baptized by the brethren, continues to pursue his spiritual pilgrimage. The probity produced by christian principles, has secured him the respect of his idolatrous neighbours; and, notwithstanding the opposition he once encountered, he is now much encouraged in his trade as a weaver. A little time ago he was employed to weave some beautiful cloth dresses for the Rajah. These were a kind of guaze about eight yards long, and an ell wide, some yellow, others a light or dark green, the middle parts plain, with gold thread woven into the sides and ends, and various pretty designs in coloured cotton.

"Erun is now aged, he cannot read, but his son reads the Bible to him; he dwells at times with much delight, on the kind instructions he received from Mr. and Mrs. Bampton. After a sermon on the judgment, Erun was asked by a friend, "Why he hoped to go to heaven?" He replied, "There was a flock of goats that the tigers and bears had seized, the good Shepherd rushed in among them, and brought him out; and now if he, till death, continued to love and follow that good Shepherd, he should be taken to dwell with him in heaven."

Gungadhor.

The first Oreah convert, whose conversion has been attended with the most important results, is the beloved individual whose history has now to be sketched. In the Society's Report for 1827, Mr. Lacey thus speaks of him. "I invited Gunga Dhor, our brahminical inquirer, to accompany me to the bazar, and he gladly acceded. He sung a geet, the '*Jewel Mine of Salvation,*' to a great number of people, who were astonished to hear such things from a brahmin. This piece exposes the ten incarnations of the Hindoos, and introduces Jesus Christ, as the Saviour of sinners; and speaks very feelingly of his sufferings and death. I have had it written on the tall potta for distribution, and was much benefited while putting it into Oreah from the Bengalee. Gungadhor dwelt particularly on some parts which mark his sense of their importance. Having finished the poem I put the catechism into his hand, when he read over the *Ten Commandments*, and made some severe remarks from them upon the moral conduct of the Hindoos, as, 'God here commmands you to worship himself alone and you have all worshipped wood and stone;—not to commit adultery, but you have all committed uncleanness with your neighbours' wives;—not to steal, but you have all stolen;—not to covet, but you are all full of covetousness, &c. &c. Will God endure this disregard of his commandments? nay, but he will not my brethren; and we all have sinned. But hear, Jesus Christ died to deliver us from the wrath of God, and let us believe on him: his is the true salvation.' While we stood and heard these things from an Oreah brahmin with such feeling and effect, we could not withhold the tear of pleasure, but tears involuntarily flowed from our eyes. We have experienced feelings not known

GUNGA DHOR.

before, and surely angels have ; and if ever they weep for pleasure, it must be to witness scenes like these. O that this dear man may have grace to continue steadfast even unto death :—should he do so, there is no doubt of his abilities as a preacher, and that of an acceptable kind. After this opportunity the people were almost mad for books : 'Give me the Ten Commandments, Give me the Ten Commandments,' was the cry from all sides."—He has returned from a visit to his family. Went out with us boldly in the evening, and preached the Gospel. Sat with him afterwards till about eleven o'clock, talking upon a variety of subjects. Giving up his cast and connections is a most serious obstacle, and it requires much prudence to lead him. I could not encourage him to do so till he is better established in his mind, for in the event of his forsaking us afterwards, the loss of his cast would produce a most unfavourable effect on the mind of the public."

Gunga's baptism took place March 23rd, 1828, a day that will be recollected with pleasure in the annals of the Missions. See Mr. Lacey's hymn on the occasion, G. B. Repository, 1829, p, 195.

Mr. Lacey during his visit to England, prepared "An account of the conversion of Gunga Dhor, the first-fruits of Orissa unto God," which is very interesting. See the Gen. Bap. Repository, 1836, pp. 192-95.

The writer was favored with an interesting letter from Gunga, in Nov. 1833, but want of room forbids its insertion. See G. Baptist Repos. 1837, pp. 185-9. The experience of this eminent servant of the Lord, is given in the Report for 1845, pp. 32-3, and is very striking.

Recently two interesting letters have been received from Gunga, addressed to the Rev. W. Pickering, of Nottingham. They are excellent, and expressive of a rich acquaintance with the word of God. G. B. Repository, 1845, p. 102.

The author finds it impossible to do justice to the character and labours of this and other evangelists, in the space which he has purposed to devote to this department of his history. He fears his book will prove too large, and on that account its circulation and perusal be too limited to do much good for the evangelization of Orissa.

Ram Chundra.

This individual is the second upon the list of Native Evangelists. His history is very fully told by himself, the perusal of which cannot fail very deeply to interest the reader. His father was killadar of the Fort of Cuttack, in the time of the Marhattas. His conversion and baptism are referred to in the Report of 1830, pp. 8-10.

A very full account of his conversion to the Christian faith, written by himself, and sent to his Christian brethren and sisters in England, is appended to the Report of 1834, and has appeared in the Quarterly Papers.

The following brief letter to the supporters of the mission, is very interesting.

"*Letter of Ram Chundra to Christians in England, giving praise to the Father of our Lord Jesus Christ. O all sincere brothers and sisters in Jesus Christ, to you Rama Chundra, a sinner and a Christian, now sends much salutation!*

"In former times I was involved in works of darkness, but, by the mercy of God, I obtained to hear of the great good news. After having heard it sin sprung up in my mind greatly, and my soul much dreaded the punishment of hell; hence, remaining in my house, I had much sorrow, and wept. My heart feared this world, and hence I prayed to the Lord in secret, and asked the Holy Spirit's help. The Lord, in mercy, granted me to obtain some help of the Holy Spirit. After this, calling my wife and children, my household and relatives, and my neighbours and acquaintances, I said to them, "I am dead to the customs of this your world; and by the death of Christ Jesus, I am determined to flee into the mercy of God! I will save my spirit from sin, and the torments of hell!" After I had said this, they wept and lamented with a loud voice; as when one is dead in a house so they wept. I came to Cuttack, and there many people attempted to convince me, but I disregarded their word. On the Lord's-Day I was baptized by Lacey padree sahib After this the people of the country, my own household and friends, abused and persecuted me much. None gave me a place to sit down upon; thus much affliction came on me, but the Lord kept me from all danger. All the rest left me, but my wife and children came and joined me.

From that day I have proclaimed the good news unto the people. What the Holy Spirit puts into my mind, that I proclaim. Every day I read the holy book, and worship three times; once in secret I pray unto the Lord, and twice, with my wife and children assembling, I bless and praise God. I pray with my mind always, and in this manner, through pain and pleasure, I have maintained life. I die to sin daily, and try to live to holiness. Satan daily condemns me before God, and creates difference between my brethren and sisters, and makes me without hope; but by the mercy and grace of God, the Lord Jesus daily increases my faith. From hence, with my body, I serve sin, but taking my spirit, I serve and praise God through our Lord Jesus Christ. Thus I daily live, and those days that I neglect to preach the good news, and do not pray, on those days my mind is in pain; on those days my spirit has no pleasure. Thus I have tried to tell you a little of my mind, and I will, hereafter, tell you my experience in full. Pardon my freedom in writing, and to the Lord, for our brothers and sisters in Orissa, you must pray, for we are all of weak minds.

Cuttack, Sep. 30, 1831.

KRUPA SINDOO.

The Report of 1830 gives an interesting account of the conversion of this native brother. Mr. Lacey wrote, "We have baptized Krupa Sindoo, a respectable man, a Khyetra, of Sutyabag. He was first disposed towards Christianity by hearing in the street at Pooree, of the love and sufferings of Jesus Christ for a sinful world. This is the gospel, and, as far as we can judge, after a year's trial and observation, it has been to him the power of God to his salvation. I have felt encouraged from this circumstance, to preach much, and indeed principally, the '*Cross of Christ.*' I have observed it to produce seriousness hundreds of times, and who can tell its effect on many whom we may never know. Krupa Sindoo maintains his family (eight persons beside himself) by dealing in a few articles. We are having some goods of him for our new school-house. He chose to reside at his own village, of which we were glad; he will be useful, for he is able to give a reason of his hope. His new religion, however, has made his neighbourhood very warm for him; he meets with the greatest opposition from his own mother, who tells him that he has sent his whole race to hell, and, 'O that he had died long since.'"

In reference to Krupa, who resides ten miles from Pooree, Mr. Sutton who resided there, furnishes some pleasing information;—"Krupa Sindoo, the last baptized, who lives within ten miles of Pooree, has been two or three times; he evidently grows in scriptural knowledge, but I fear he is in pecuniary difficulties, which hinder his growth in grace. He came up to me in the town one evening, and spoke boldly, and generally very evangelically, to the people assembled."

Grateful reference is made to the spirit of the native converts in their trials and preservations.—"They have, since their profession, conducted themselves so as to give us pleasure. Krupa Sindoo can read, and instructs his family and neighbours in his new religion. Rama is very zealous, and promises fair to become a useful preacher. They have suffered a good deal of persecution for the Gospel's sake, and are still persecuted. The washerman has refused to wash their clothes, and the barber to shave them, which, in this country, are some of the highest marks of disgrace, as these people are of very low castes. Krupa Sindoo bore this shame best, and wore his long beard and dirty clothes without a complaint; and as the persecution arose only from a spirit of malice, they soon came to him and proposed to assist him as usual. Rama felt this disgrace most keenly, and applied to a native officer for redress; but finding him of the same malicious disposition, he gave up, and submitted to the disgrace, and no doubt the difficulty will pass away. For some time Rama's mother, wife, children, and brethren, refused to eat or associate with him; they have now lost caste with him, and appear reconciled."

Doytaree.

Mr. Lacey furnishes the following account of this native convert. "Doytaree is a respectable man of some considerable learning and judgment. His caste is a naik, and his business a physician. He is of mature years, and has a wife and four or five children, three of whom, I believe, are at home. He has long since known the Gospel, and observed its ordinances, and, I have reason to trust, enjoyed its spirit and blessings; but his last married daughter was much beloved by him and his wife, and they found it difficult to give her up. He at length resolved to do so, and came on Saturday afternoon to be baptized. I had long considered him a fit subject, and as sending him back might involve him again in all his difficulties, we concluded to baptize him. I saw him in the morning, early, at the house of Ramara, and from conversation with him, on his views and from what I could judge of his feelings, I was confirmed in my hopes respecting his Christianity. Mr. Brown acceded. At five o'clock in the Afternoon, the natives, in a good number, the native Christians, some country-born, and some Europeans, assembled on the river's bank, below our compound, to witness the ceremony. Mr. B. gave out a hymn, and I addressed the people, and prayed in Ooriya; the people listened tolerably, and, towards the last, asked several questions and disputed, but behaved, on the whole, very orderly. The candidate then followed down into the water, amidst the laughs and hisses of the crowd. Arrived at a proper depth, he took off his mala, and and gave it into my hand, and I threw it down the stream; some said, Well, others groaned and hissed. He next broke his poita, and gave that into my hands, also, and after holding it up for a moment, it followed the mala down the stream. He was then baptized in the sacred names, repeated first in English and then in Ooriya. Coming up from the water, the people pretty generally hissed at him, but he went through all very well. It was a very

SEBO NAIK.

interesting baptism. Doytaree will, I hope, be very useful to us, being just the man we wanted for the native Christian Ooriya school. Of this situation we purposely kept him ignorant, before he was baptized, that he might not be influenced in his decisions by it. His wife is well disposed towards him, to say the least, and several others, at a village distant from the neighbourhood of our native Christians, are thinking of Christianity.

Mr. Sutton describes a visit to him when seriously ill. "Doytaree is very ill. Mrs. Sutton and I went to see him last evening. He spoke very feelingly of the contrast in the circumstances of his children, and his own youthful days. To what an excess of riot he ran, and how his children have neither the will, nor the power to do so, so delightfully had christianity changed the whole course of their life. He then sobbed out his thanks for the gospel, saying how he was enveloped in darkness, and we came sixteen thousand miles to shew him the way to heaven. "*You,*" said he, "*are Apostles to me, just as much as Paul was to the Corinthians and Galatians, &c.*" He added, "I often think when I first became a christian, of the time I spent in travelling with you and James Sunder. I then knew not how to pray, and was so ignorant I knew not what to do; but—blessed, blessed, blessed be the Lord."

To this affecting statement our brother adds, "Here I would rest the appeal for Missions. Let a man who can appreciate the change, look at the contrast between a living and dying heathen Hindoo, and a living and dying christian Hindoo, and he must exclaim, O what a precious boon to sinful man, is the glorious gospel of the blessed God."

The various Reports of the Society contain interesting details of the conversion and baptism of *Pooroosootum, Atmaram, Hurree, Rahhoo, Mahadab-das, Hurree Paree, Balogee, Sebo Sas, Rogurond, Damoodur, Rogubunduba,* * *Somnath, Damudar, Deenabunder,* &c. &c., but it is impossible to insert them in this History. The Lord God of our fathers make us a thousand times so many as we are, and bless us as he has promised.—Deu. i. 11.

---

* The writer feels peculiar interest in the conversion of this individual, on account of the recollections of the Idol of Honooman, near his own house, which he has passed hundreds of times. How delightful the thought, that its owner should have become a christian, and that on the site of the temple Gungadhor should be residing.—See Report, 1839, p. 13.

CHAP. VI.

MEMORIALS OF DEPARTED FRIENDS.

Brief records of departed Missionaries, both male and female—Christian Friends in Orissa, and Native Converts. Brief reference to departed Friends and Supporters of the Mission in England.

THE writer feels that he has advanced to a very important and solemn stage in his work ;—to review and record the career of departed brethren and sisters, with some of whom "he has taken sweet counsel, and walked to the house of God in company," is indeed a very solemn and affecting task. But "Who am I ?" and "What is my father's house ?" that I should be favored and honored to be present at the formation of the Society, one of the first missionaries, and now the historian of the Mission ? May the Lord enable his servant to perform this "labour of love" to the approbation of his brethren in Britain and America, in India and China; and greatly to "the furtherance of the gospel" both at home and abroad. Reflecting upon the *chronological* order of the events to be detailed in this chapter, it very forcibly occurred to him, that the *Infants* in the Mission family were the first martyrs—the first to take possession of "the lot of our inheritance," as Abraham's first possession was "a burying place." Will the kind reader excuse the insertion of the following

INFANT OBITUARY.

"Insatiate Archer! could not one suffice?
Thy shaft flew thrice, and thrice my peace was slain." YOUNG.

PARENTAL affection desires to rescue from oblivion, the names of the following dear children, who, for a short period, solaced the minds of the missionary family in India. They, like Abraham's beloved wife, Sarah, by right of sepulture, have taken possession of the land of our inheritance in the East. They were born and are buried at Cuttack.

FRANCES SMITHEE PEGGS, born May 14, 1822, died August 17, 1822.

ELIZABETH SMITHEE PEGGS, born September the 2nd, 1823, died July 28, 1824.

MARY SMITHEE PEGGS, born November 25, 1824, died May 14, 1825.

"*Verily thou art a God that hidest thyself.*" Thou destroyest the hope of man; but "Thou doest all things well." A seed shall serve thee, though not the first born of thy missionary servants; and these painful events shall best promote thy purposes of mercy to Orissa. May angels watch the dust of these infants! may myriads of saints slumber with them! and, in the morning of the resurrection, may multitudes of Oreah christians congratulate them as the first-fruits to God of the dust of Orissa.

AMOS SUTTON, the son of the Rev. A. Sutton, Missionary in Orissa, was born at Cuttack, April 3, 1825; and died and was buried in that city, September 16, following.

"Behold! happy is the man whom God correcteth: therefore despise not thou the chastening of the Almighty."

As Memoirs of a number of our departed brethren and sisters, and some of them of considerable length, have been published in the *Missionary Observer*, it is the less necessary that much space should be occupied by this department of the History. But the writer feels this a very difficult part of his undertaking, and with much anxiety throws himself upon the candour of his readers.

MRS. SUTTON.

Mrs. Charlotte Sutton was a daughter of Mr. James Collins, resident for a number of years at Wolvey, in Warwickshire. She was born at Smockington, near Hinckley, in Feb. 1801. Of her earlier years the writer knows little. She appears to have possessed naturally a cheerful, engaging and affectionate disposition To her parents she was loving, dutiful and kind; submissive to their instructions, and peculiarly a comforter in trouble. Her father, after her death, observed that in times of trouble he peculiarly felt her loss; as consolation administered by her had enabled him to bear many burdens with more patience than he could otherwise have done. As a sister and friend she was truly affectionate. Her mind was improved by reading, of which she was fond. In her nineteenth year, Charlotte Collins appears to have become decidedly pious. Her parents attending the Baptist Meeting at Wolvey, she probably felt religious impressions from her childhood, but passed a number of her youthful years before, under divine grace, she made the choice which fixed her happiness for time and eternity.

Scarcely had she felt the decided influence of real religion, before her desires were excited for the eternal salvation of others. The missionary cause soon engaged the attention of her ardent mind, and before she actually joined the Christian church she commended her efforts to promote its intrests.—In May 1821, Messrs. Bampton and Peggs, the first Missionaries sent out by the General Baptist Missionary Society, proceeded to India; the ordination of the former took place at Loughborough, on May 15th. The day was a day of peculiar solemnity and heart-thrilling emotions. Charlotte Collins attended the solemn services. Her impressions were deep, her attachment to the cause of Missions, strengthened to a desire to consecrate herself to its interests. A young man of respectable character and circumstances had previously sought her hand; but on the return from the ordination she absolutely declined receiving his addresses. Then and for some years afterwards, she had no prospect of devoting herself to Missionary services, but appears to have formed a determination not to enter into any connection, however flattering as to worldly circumstances, which would permanently bind her to her native land. Her correspondence in 1822 appears very scanty. In the only letter that year now before the writer, there appears an allusion to the circumstances mentioned above, as well as a description of her inward conflicts.

She accepted the hand of Mr. Sutton who was contemplating the missionary work. In June 1824, Mr. S. was ordained at Derby, and he and his beloved wife embarked for India, in the Euphrates Aug. 12. Many interesting circumstances occurred during the voyage. The Captain and passengers were peculiarly agreeable, and many opportunities of usefulness were enjoyed.

"Short as was the period of Mrs. Sutton's sojourn in India, (says Mr. Pike), yet her worth was highly appreciated there." A Baptist Brother at Calcutta observed,—"I assure you we have very seldom indeed seen a female in our view, more adapted for usefulness in this country than Mrs. S——, and we felt towards her and her husband the highest regard and esteem. We therefore affectionately sympathize with you in the loss you have sustained,—a loss, we feel, to the general interests of Christianity in this country. But he who knows best, and feels most deeply, the necessities of his Church, has removed her; and we humbly hope, he will raise up many more with equal zeal, affection, activity, and faith, to supply her place."

Mr. Peggs, in a letter recently addressed to the writer, remarks, —"I trust I shall never forget Lord's-Day, March 13th, when our mission family were at my house and we had worship at noon in my study. There were brother and sister Bampton, brother and sister Lacey, brother and sister Sutton, Sunder, Abraham, and Mrs. Peggs, and myself. That dear woman, whose early death we lament, was much interested with this interview; I recollect her attention to poor Abraham, and the very important advice she gave him—not to be unequally yoked with an unbelieving wife.

"In Orissa and Bengal, the memory of our valued sister is 'as ointment poured forth.' There was a vivacity, activity, sweetness, simplicity and piety in her, that were very pleasing. On arriving at Serampore in August 1825, I heard her spoken of in terms of much respect, and her death was greatly regretted. I know the spot near the detested temple of Juggernaut, where the first martyr to our Mission lies. But I correct myself, my first-born was the first martyr and Cuttack our first Station in Orissa, the spot where we first took possession of that land of our inheritance. Our beloved sister has not lived nor died in vain. The cause of Missions is endeared, when embalmed by the martyrdom of departed friends; and shall this cause decline in our estimation, affection and support? Visit the sandy grave of departed friends in the Mission field, and think, Has life been laid down in this cause? For this cause have Apostles, Confessors, Martyrs, and 'the noble army of martyrs, laboured and 'resisted unto blood,' yea, has 'the Captain of our salvation' 'poured out is soul unto death:' and shall I 'sit still,' and not go up 'To the help of the Lord, to the help of the Lord against the mighty?' What pious heart, what zealous mind, but must exclaim, as respects the promotion of the cause of Christ both at home and abroad, 'If I forget thee, O

Jerusalem, let my right hand forget her cunning. If I do not remember thee, let my tongue cleave to the roof of my mouth; if I prefer not Jerusalem above my chief joy.' Ps. cxxxvii. 5, 6, O may the great Head of the Church, who watches the ashes of his saints, 'till all that dust shall rise,' when he looks down upon the ashes of our sister, entombed near the Temple of Juggernaut—blast the system of Idolatry pursued within its walls—banish British support of its cruelties and obscenities, and in the morning of the resurrection, give our dear sister to rise, amidst myriads of believing Ooreahs; whose eyes have seen in successive ages, the desolations of that horrid shrine of idolatry;—

'O'er which the plough hath pass'd, and weeds have grown.'"

Mr. Joshua Mundy Cropper.

Joshua Mundy Cropper was born at Oxford, of religious parents, on December 10th, 1807. He was put to school very early in life, and cannot remember the period when he could not join with the family when reading the Scriptures; and read his chapter in his turn. At five years old, with his younger brother, he was sent to a boarding school about ten miles from Oxford, where he continued a twelvemonth. During this time he had frequent serious and striking ideas about religion; but getting among other children whose parents never thought of religion, nor ever pressed it upon their offspring, these impressions wore off as the early dew. Between the period of eight and ten years he had many serious convictions, particularly of the dreadfully awful state of the lost; frequently when rolling about his marbles, he would burst into tears at this tremendous state.

Led forward by the grace of God, Joshua Cropper became decidedly pious, and by a variety of circumstances, evidently taking place under providential direction, which he detailed verbally at his ordination, but of which no written account appears to exist, his mind was directed to missionary labours; and he became acquainted with the individual who subsequently was his tutor. On the 26th of June, 1825, he was baptized at Derby, with several other young friends, some of whom are still following the Saviour on earth, and some of whom, like him, have reached their eternal home. Soon after this he was admitted on probation as a missionary student, and placed under the instruction of the minister of the church to which he belonged. He was now in his eighteenth year; his heart was set on publishing the glorious Gospel, but he had not preached a single sermon. He applied, with considerable diligence, to study, and speedily became an acceptable and useful preacher.

This dear young brother was ordained to the work of the Mission at Leicester, April 25th, 1827. The Divine blessing upon his labours in his own country, were 'a token for good' that he would be a blessing to India.

Mr. C. arrived in India Oct. 10th, 1827. The vessel touched at Madras, where he spent a few days, and he had the pleasure of meeting Messrs. Bennett and Tyerman. He reached Calcutta November 2nd; and after spending a few weeks proceeded to Balasore.

The journals of this brother, display great devotedness to his work, but our space will not permit extracts from them. His early and lamented death may probably be traced to the following circumstance. He says—" Arrived at Cuttack, after a few mishaps. Going through a branch of the river on my horse, he sunk in the mud, and thus I was compelled to dismount in the midst of the stream, and I walked to the other side; coming to the shore I was obliged to wait a considerable time in my wet clothes, for a boat."—The following letter details the circumstance of his death.

Cuttack, Dec. 10th, 1828.

" Dearest Brother,

" I have heavy tidings to communicate; I cannot give you the particulars now, but will perhaps forward them to you in a few days. But I must tell you;—I would willingly spare my own feelings and yours, dear brother, and those of our dear friends in general, for he was, *dear, very dear* to us all; but what will be the use of withholding? it is true! you must hear it! It has so paralyzed our very hearts that we are almost dead to every thing but the dear, the amiable youth who has fled from us. I never felt such sensations before. His amiable disposition had attached our hearts to him with the strongest affection, and this was doubly strengthened by the promising and important character which he sustained in reference to the dear and sacred cause; this rendered him so dear, so desirable, that we feel lost, hopeless. Ah! perhaps here was a reason for the divine procedure: but should we not esteem piety, humility, goodness, zeal, ability, and universal amiableness of character? Our dear, our amiable Joshua is gone! is gone to the Saviour he preached; gone to that heaven where his heart had long been fixed; gone to realize all he believed: to enjoy all he hoped for. The dear fellow died of a jungle fever, on Monday last, Dec. 8, 1828, at 12 o'clock at noon. He died happy in Jesus, trusting for mercy in his atoning blood. He was favoured with the clear and full use of his powers of mind to the very last moment, which, in Indian fevers, is a wonderful circumstance. He had every possible assistance, both from the civil and military doctors of the station; but all human help was vain, for his fever advanced to its final consummation with awful strength and rapidity. He is a *vast* loss to us; there are few Joshua Croppers. We had ample opportunities of seeing him, nearly in every shade of character, but particularly as a Christian and a Missionary—we saw him and admired. He fled swiftly on his course, and soon has he arrived at the goal. Adieu.

Sorrowfully yours in Christ,

C. Lacey."

The Report of the Society for 1829, thus humbly acknowledges the mysterious character of this dispensation. "God often moves in a mysterious way: one of the mysteries of his providence has been this year seen at Cuttack, in the unexpected removal by death of Mr. Cropper. He had begun to travel through the villages of Orissa proclaiming the Gospel, and afforded fair indications of eminent usefulness. Not many weeks before his death a brother Missionary wrote,—"As far as I can judge, brother C—— promises to be eminent as a preacher in Oreah. I have observed his serious and affectionate addresses produce much effect on his hearers." Alas! the last of those affectionate addresses is finished. He, whose ways are not as our ways, has called the labourer to his rest. How much the Missionaries felt at his removal is evident from their correspondence. Short as was his course, that brief course contributed materially to advance the interests of that kingdom that will endure for ever. As far as India is concerned Mr. Bampton writes,—"With respect to our work it will perhaps appear eventually that our lamented brother Cropper, by turning our attention to one subject, has been of immense use; that subject is, *expectation of success.*" In England his brief Ministry was, it is known, blessed to the conversion of many individuals. In his short life the value of early Religion was impressively displayed. *He was a fervent Christian, a useful Minister, and a devoted Missionary; and all this before twenty-one years from the day of his birth had rolled away!* This Society was the favoured instrument in bringing him forward to public usefulness, as he had not preached a single sermon before his connection with the Society commenced. See Mr. Sutton's Lines on the death of dear Cropper, G. B. Repository 1829, p. 230.

Mr. Bampton.

"The immediate influence" says Professor Farish, "of the labours of a Missionary will, in all probability, be much less than he anticipates; he will perhaps go down to the grave as one disappointed of his hope. But, like Abraham, he must, *against hope, believe in hope.* He has planted a seed, which will push itself forth on all sides. He has excited a spark, which will raise a flame through a kingdom. He thinks he has done little; but he has, in fact, effected that which calculation cannot follow. We can scarcely entertain *too contracted an expectation of the immediate effect of his labours, and scarcely too exalted an idea of their ultimate efficacy.* The flame once excited, shall spread from breast to breast, from family to family, from village to village, from region to region; in time, from kingdoms to empires: and, at length, from empires to continents. But that flame must first be lighted from the fire that burns on the altar of God. How will the faithful Missionary rejoice before the Judge of quick and dead, when he shall meet at the right hand of Christ, not a straggling individual or two, whom he was the means of persuading, in the days of his flesh, to turn to God; but perhaps a nation of converts to whom his self-denial, and, at the time, unpromising labour, had been the original means of bringing salvation!"

The subject of this Memoir had the happiness of beholding a few, in one of the most benighted lands on the earth, gathered to the Saviour; what the whole result of his labours, under the divine blessing, shall be, the judgment day will discover.

William Bampton was born at Bourne, in Lincolnshire, in the year 1787, and was the son of parents in humble life. His first twelve years were spent under the parental roof; partly at Bourne, and at Thirlby, a neighbouring village, whither his parents had removed. He is described as having been, at this period, of a gay and volatile disposition, but strongly desirous of the acquisition of learning, in which he is stated to have made as much improvement as could be gained from the instructions of the village school masters, whose pupil he was. In his thirteenth year he left his father's dwelling, and obtained a situation at Boston. Here, for some time, he continued negligent of the great interests of eternity; but having been accustomed, with his parents, frequently to attend on the ministry of Mr. Binns, the Baptist Minister at Bourne, he was induced, at Boston, to attend on that of the late venerable Mr. W. Taylor, the Pastor of the General Baptist Church, whose instructions were happily rendered conducive to his eternal welfare, and whom he afterwards regarded as his father in the Gospel.

How solemn and important are the events that, in this transitory state, occur within a few short years. The pious Minister, whose instructions were thus sought, was then in the vigor of life, he has since felt the decays of age, and descended to the tomb. The awakened youth, that inquired for the way of peace, has since become a Christian, a Minister, a Missionary; has taught others the way to heaven, and has, like his revered Instructor, finished his labours, and sunk into the grave. These are events that extend an influence through the vast duration of eternity. Thus viewed, how momentous such events appear, when crowded into a span of time. Under the Ministry of Mr. Taylor his young friend was directed to the atoning death of the Son of God, as the foundation of a sinner's hope. He learned that

> "There is a fountain filled with blood,
> Drawn from Immanuel's veins;
> And sinners plung'd beneath that flood,
> Lose all their guilty stains."

Believing the ability and willingness of the Lord Jesus Christ to save to the uttermost, he sought peace in him, and found and enjoyed that peace which the world had never imparted, and which it could not take away. Having surrendered himself to the divine Saviour, he applied for baptism and communion with the church, and was cordially received into Christian fellowship.

In 1808, "at the request of a member of the church, he commenced preaching occasionally at Swineshead Fen houses near Boston," and in Jan. 1809, he was encouraged by the Church to exercise his talents for usefulness. In 1811 he took up his abode in the hospitable dwelling of the late Mr. J. Bissill, the Baptist Minister at Sutterton, who was then labouring under a protracted disease. There he continued for three years, being favoured with admirable opportunities for personal improvements, and ministerial usefulness.—On the recovery of Mr. Bissill's health, Mr. B. removed to Gosberton, when the writer first became acquainted with him in 1815. In 1818, he removed to Yarmouth in Norfolk, where the high resolve was formed, in the divine strength to devote himself to the missionary cause. After serious consideration, Mr. Bampton determined in Jan. 1820, to offer himself as a candidate for the Mission. So high was the estimation in which Mr. B. was held by his brethren, that on the receipt of his letter, offering to devote himself to missionary labours, a Committee Meeting was immediately summoned. The Meeting was held Jan. 18, 1820, and he was unanimously received. On the 29th of May, 1821, the brethren Bampton and Peggs, with their wives, in company with Messrs. Ward, and Mack, Mrs. Marshman, &c. sailed for India on board the Abberton. They touched at Madeira, landed at Madras, Sep. 25th, and safely arrived at Serampore, Nov. 15th, where they were entertained with much hospitality and affection. Orissa having being fixed upon as the scene of labour, the brethren embarked at Calcutta for Cuttack, Jan. 26, 1822, and reached that city, Feb. 12.

In Sep. 1823, Mr. Bampton removed to Pooree, the great seat of the Idolatry of Juggernaut. On this important step it has been remarked by one of his colleagues,—"After mature deliberation and prayer, he left Cuttack to form a new station at the temple of Juggernaut, distant fifty miles; the great emporium of idolatry to Orissa, and the surrounding countries. This important and eventful step is thus noticed by the writer, in his journal;—'*September 16th*, 1823; Monday. Yesterday brother B., determining to take advantage of water in the river, prepared to go to *Pooree*. The boat, with the furniture and books, was sent off to-day, and in the evening brother B. delivered his farewell sermon from, *I am pure from the blood of all men*. The attendance was considerable, and I felt the opportunity very impressive. The Lord give me grace to be faithful to the souls now left to my care, and succeed my brother in his new station.

"*September 17th.*—Eventful day; about three o'clock this afternoon, brother and sister Bampton parted from us, with much feeling, to go to the new station at Pooree. The river was unexpectedly full of water, and they took the opportunity of going. May the Lord not only 'lengthen our cords,' but 'strengthen our stakes.' May the complete triumph of Christianity over idolatry, at this 'seat of Satan,' render the record of this fact, in the future history of Christian churches in India, peculiarly interesting.

"The station of *Juggernauth or Pooree*, is one of peculiar difficulties and deep interest; a blow at Idolatry here, will prove 'a blow at the root.' No man in India, with whose character the writer has had any acquaintance, was so well adapted for this 'high place' of superstition, as the indefatigable Bampton. His firm, temperate, regular habits, and particularly his well-disciplined mind, rendered him peculiarly suitable to go on the forlorn hope, and plant the banner of the cross upon the battlements, or rather within the precincts, of Juggernaut's temple. A very inadequate idea can be conveyed of the singularly appalling aspect of this station. The few bungalows belonging to the Europeans, are built upon the sands which lie between the city and the mighty waters of the bay of Bengal; and four or five families, not unfrequently as many *individuals*, constitute the European society, during the principal part of the year. Here idolatry was found, regulated and pampered, by the mistaken policy of a Christian Government! Happy day! when Britain, in reference to Hindoo idols and their temples shall regard the divine admonition, '*Touch not, taste not, handle not!*' The poverty, misery, sickness, death, and brutal exposure of the dead, here exhibited, were enough to appal any heart but that of a man well taught in the school of Christ, and the writer can scarcely forbear to add, accustomed to the scenes in the anatomical rooms of a London hospital; yet in this 'Golgotha,' and this 'valley of the son of Hinnom,' from its numerous Suttees, did our departed brother and his estimable wife, of temper attuned to that of her beloved partner, reside from September 1823, to December 1830, when his labours closed by nobly falling upon the 'high places of the field.' Doubtless his 'reward is on high,' and his spirit, with those 'under the throne,' is crying, 'how long, O Lord!'"

Mr. Lacey, under date, Dec. 18 1830, describes the last, the closing scene.—"It seems to be my lot to bury our beloved dead, and to report their death and burial to you. It is now my painful duty to inform you of the death of our long afflicted and greatly loved Bampton; yes, he is gone at last! gone to Jesus, whom having not seen he loved—gone to be with his Lord, and where He is, there is fulness of joy;—gone to receive the reward of his privations and labours here—gone to hear the Redeemer say, 'Well done, good and faithful servant; thou hast been faithful over a few things, I will make thee ruler over many, enter thou into the joy of thy Lord.'—*Gone to join Charlotte Sutton, dear Joshua, and Brother Allsop, in glory!*—O! I can conceive of him now, having just emerged from the gloom of death into the light of life, surrounded with the light and glory of heaven—his Saviour smiles upon him—the glorified friends who loved him on earth, joyfully crowd around him to hear all the way through which he has been led to their bright abodes; while adoring angels at distance wondering stand! 'O blessed interview, how sweet!' But let me leave him there, and relate to you some particulars of his latter end on earth. About the 16th, all the symptoms which in his complaint indicate the fatal termination of the disorder appeared, as short breathing, diarrhœa, shaking, and fainting fits; with an increase of the hectic fever. The diarrhœa and fever, reduced his little remaining strength amazingly fast. He was carried from his study couch to his bed, that he might have more room. This was on the evening of the 16th; from seven o'clock that evening till near eleven, he slept soundly. About eleven he awoke, had three attacks of diarrhœa, from the first two he was able to reascend his bed by hanging on Mrs. Bampton's neck; but from the last his strength failed. However, with the help of a bearer she succeeded in getting him on the bed, from which he no more removed till I removed him into his coffin. After he was laid on the bed, Mrs. B. supported him, and he laid his head on her breast till she could sustain him no longer, and on his looking towards the pillow, she gently laid him down upon it. His breathing now became shorter and shorter, till just about three o'clock on Friday morning the 17th, when he calmly breathed his last. He suffered no convulsions whatever, but appeared to depart quite easily, insomuch that not one feature was distorted."

TOMB OF THE REV. WILLIAM BAMPTON.

Mr. Sutton thus briefly sketches the charater of this devoted man. "It may with truth be said of him, that 'he was a good man, and full of the Holy Ghost and of faith.' May all your missionaries be found at last with the spirits of Charlotte Sutton, of Cropper, and of Bampton. So far as earnest, faithful, persevering labours for the salvation of the Hindoos can render a man worthy of our esteem, our admiration, and our imitation, Bampton ranks with the foremost of Christian philanthropists, and deserves to be had in everlasting remembrance. What he was as friend and brother, the hearts of his colleagues can best testify. But this I must add, than beneath an aspect and address less prepossessing than many, was contained the kindest heart, and the most exquisite sensibility that ever a friend displayed."

Mrs. John Goadby.

The Report of the Society for 1835 contains an interesting account of this departed friend, from a Calcutta Periodical, and pays a just tribute to lamented worth.—"Marianne Goadby was the eldest daughter of the Rev. Robort Compton, of Isleham, in the county of Cambridge; she was born August 18th, 1809. At the age of seven she lost her mother, who died very suddenly; at the age of fifteen, the care of three brothers and a sister devolved upon her, towards whom her conduct was such as to gain from all of them the most ardent attachment. They regarded her as sustaining the place, and performing the offices, of their dearest relative.

From early life her mind seemed directed to things of eternity, and, as her character was developed, it became evident to all who knew her, that she had been affected by the precepts and doctrines of the gospel. Previous to her making a public profession of religion, she had been some years an active teacher in a sabbath school; she was baptized by her father, and added to the church under his pastoral care about Midsummer, 1827, from which time to her leaving England, her exertions became more general and extensive; distributing religious tracts, visiting the sick and dying, reading and praying with them, conversing with female candidates: in short, she was engaged in all those acts of piety and mercy which are proper for an active and devoted female.

In every department of her work she was the same zealous and indefatigable Christian; rain and cold were never obstacles in her way, if duty, or a prospect of being able to speak for Christ, led the way; and when asked why she exposed herself so much, she would answer, "That others may not be more exposed. Should my fear of getting wet and taking cold, or suffering a little inconvenience for a short time, prevent me from discharging my duty, and doing my Master's work? I think not, nor shall it, while I can go about." At the age of eighteen, her mind was directed to the heathen world by reading the Memoirs of Mrs. Newell; this subject for a time engrossed nearly the whole of her attention, until she came to the settled determination, should ever Providence open a way, that she would embark in the good and great work. When talking on missionary subjects, the question was started, Should you like to engage in that arduous work? She answered, her countenance beaming with divine benevolence, "Were I qualified, and had an opportunity, nothing would delight me so much."

Not till several months after the acquaintance between her and her now bereaved husband was formed, did she know that he had any desire on the subject; when she knew, her desire never varied; she would often say, "If this desire has been imparted from above, God will doubtless open a way for our going; to the present period I have all the evidence I desire, for he has directed to me one whose desires are like my own, though I knew it not at the time."

She was married on the 9th of May, 1833, and on the 9th July bid a final farewell to the shores of her beloved country. Her only object was to promote the glory of God and the eternal welfare of the deluded heathen; no other object could have reconciled her to breaking her earliest ties, and quitting without hope of return the land of her birth.

With feelings of peculiar pleasure she hailed her approach to the shores of India; full of anxiety to commence those studies which were requisite for future usefulness; high in hope of being the means, directly or indirectly, of alleviating distress and exhibiting the Lord Jesus as the only Saviour, to some of the wretched inhabitants of this wretched land. But alas! how shorted-sighted are the children of men; she landed at Calcutta on the 15th of November, and in less than eight months was numbered with the dead. Consumption, that always flattering and fatal disease, made its appearance in January. In her breast the spoiler nestled too firmly to be removed by any means art and experience could suggest; she gradually sunk under its influence, her vivacity left her, and gave place to a not unpleasant melancholy—a melancholy such as they feel who know they are declining to the tomb, and have nothing to fear for the future; but whose dejection, if it can bear the name, is for the dear friends they are leaving to mourn in this vale of tears. Such was hers; she feared not, nor mourned for herself, but for her beloved husband, and friends at home; but even this was mixed with hope of meeting them again in a better and infinitely happier world.

During the last six weeks of her life she conversed very little; her voice was quite gone, and she spake only in whispers; her cheeks became flushed, and pulse quick and feeble. Daily she grew weaker till the 7th of July; about mid-day on the 12th, she suddenly became worse. Towards evening she became delirious, but still continued at lucid intervals, to recognise all who were about her. On the 13th, the longest interval of sanity was about eleven o'clock, and it continued but little more than a quarter of an hour; during this time her husband told her, that her end was near; she was quite happy and resigned, had no doubt to becloud, and no fear to terrify her mind, but expressed her willingness to die, her confidence in the atoning blood of Christ, and her assurance that God would support her in the moment of dissolution. Her happy spirit took its flight to the regions of unclouded glory at 7 P. M. In labours, in practice, in perseverance, in piety, and in devotion to the work of the Lord, she was a pattern worthy of imitation. "There is no person," said a pious young minister, "whose removal from the church would be an equal loss, her father execpted; her equal in labour, perseverance, and usefulness will not be left behind."

Mrs. Stubbins.

Mrs. Stubbins was a native of Wisbeach, Cambridgeshire, and accompanied her husband as a missionary to India, in the summer of 1836. One fact is mentioned indicative of her zeal; "previously to leaving the ship, Mrs. Stubbins collected *Ten* Pounds for the mission."—Short as was her course there is very pleasing evidence of her usefulness. On arriving in India she addressed the following letter to her mother, but she had then departed this life, having died at Whittlesey, Nov. 14, 1836. She was thus spared the pain connected with the arrival of such intelligence. Mrs. Goadby was similarly favoured in reference to the death of her father.

"*Calcutta, Jan.* 12*th*, 1837.

"My very dear Mother,

"It is now six months since I saw you, and doubtless you have had many anxious thoughts concerning me, and have been ready to say,

Anne has forgotten me. But not so; and never, till this pulse shall cease to beat, and these now active limbs be still in death, shall I forget you. No: a mother's name is always new. I hope, ere this, you have recovered from your affliction, and can say with the Psalmist, 'It is good for me that I was afflicted.'

"On the 6th of August we left England, in the hope of reaching India's shores, with a nice breeze in our favour; but I soon began to be affected with the sickness from the constant motion of the ship, and continued in a sickly state five or six weeks. But it was a mercy, for which I felt very thankful, that Mr. S. suffered so little, that he was not prevented waiting upon me the whole time. We have indeed been the subjects of many mercies, and, through the goodness of our God upon us, we arrived at Calcutta in health and happiness, on the 4th of January. Our voyage was long but pleasant, not having experienced either storm or gale. The passengers were extremely kind: there were eight ladies on board, and most of them made me very handsome presents: their kindness opened my way for pleading that cause which I have espoused, and which I trust will ever lie nearest to my heart. One young lady appeared under very serious impressions; may the Lord deepen them, and may she be converted.

"We touched at the Cape—spent six days there, and enjoyed them very much. We boarded with a member of Dr. P.'s church; she is a most amiable woman. Mr. S. preached twice on the sabbath; but I cannot tell you how much I enjoyed meeting with christian friends, and in the sanctuary of the Lord, having been deprived of it for ten weeks. I was much delighted to see a number of the sable tribe sitting attentively to hear what the Lord had to say unto their souls. O that the time may soon arrive when all nations shall know the Lord. I feel sometimes ready to sink under the responsibility which lies upon me: may that God in whom I trust grant me grace and strength equal to my day. I cannot describe to you the sensation I felt at the first sight of the natives of India. They approached the ship in boats apparently ready to sink, and themselves almost naked. O what a degraded condition! Christian friends, send them the Gospel to change their inward and outward man: could you but see them you would not cease to pray and strive for them. Mr. Brooks has just come in. O how delightful to meet a dear christian brother and fellow labourer in a foreign land: he resides at Midnapore, about seventy miles from Calcutta. In a few days more we shall accompany them home, when I hope to see our dear sister B. And now, my dear mother, I commend you to God, praying that his presence may be with you in life, in death, and for ever. I intreat also an interest in your prayers, that the good Lord may establish the work of our hands, and make us a blessing to many. * * *

Your affectionate daughter,

ANNE STUBBINS."

Mr. Goadby remarks,—"During the whole of her affictions, which were heavy, she manifested the greatest patience and resignation; not a murmur escaped her lips. Sometimes she would exclaim, 'Oh my head, my head!' but she was, throughout the whole, uniformly peaceful and happy. Her confidence was strong and unshaken—her hope bright and cloudless to the last. She was much engaged in prayer, and her expressions of confidence in God, and submission to his will, were of the most pleasing kind. Our hopes of her recovery were never entirely gone until three hours before her death, when she appeared to sink very rapidly, but was still calm and peaceful, and said, with peculiar emphasis, 'The Lord is my help and my shield he is my strong tower,' and then, peaceful and noiseless as the falling dew, her redeemed spirit left its worn-out tabernacle to join the glorious assembly above. Death assumed his least repulsive form, and while we hung over, watching with painful and intense anxiety, we could not help feeling, 'Let my end be like hers.'

Mr. Sutton observes,—"My dear wife and I had been fondly cherishing the idea of welcoming them to a participation in our labours and trials at Cuttack. We had prepared our house for them, their goods and furniture had arrived, for they were to be stationed with us, when, as they halted at Balasore, sister Stubbins was attacked with fever: she lingered for about a fortnight in a most happy and peaceful state of mind, and then gently died in Jesus, on the Sabbath. Thus all our fond anticipations are cut off, and our plans again frustrated, at least to human appearance; and yet I have had too much experience in the results of these afflictive dispensations, not to know that God is often most favorable to our best hopes when he seems most adverse, and most kind when he appears to be most severe. Let not our friends despond, but still 'Onward, onward,' and so much the more as we see the day approaching.

"The words of Scripture have been much on my mind since this event first appeared probable: 'And his servants shall serve him.' Do they not seem to say, 'Mourn not that I have removed your affectionate fellow-labourer; I have another vineyard, and there, in a higher grade of service, I have appointed your sister to serve me. Think not then all is lost; far, far from this; did you know all, you would see that very much is gained.' This, dear brother, is another call to live and labour yet more diligently, seeking that honor which cometh from God only: so shall it be said, 'Well done, good and faithful servant.'

"You will doubtless pray for, and sympathise with, our afflicted brother: we expect a mournful meeting with the solitary widower, instead of a happy greeting with the beloved wife and husband. To my wife especially, this is a heavy disappointment: she is much over-worked, and has never yet been permitted to have a sister to labour with her. But not our will, but our Father's be done."

The Society's Report for 1838 contains much valuable information in reference to our departed sister, pp. 3—6.

Mr. Grant.

In the armies of Immanuel, as well as those of earthly princes, there are soldiers of various degrees, both as to their rank, their success, and the period of their service. As none who enlist under the banners of the cross, and are laudably ambitious to take the "high places" in the field, can possibly be excluded from public notice, a record of their names, and their spirit, even though they fall in the first onslaught, is due both to them, and the glorious cause to which they were devoted. Of this class, was the subject of this brief memoir. Though he was in the mission field for the short space of twelve months, he fairly entered on his work, and is now to be numbered with the honoured names of those who have borne the Gospel to the benighted inhabitants of Orissa.

Thomas Grant was born at the village of Burbage, near Hinckley, Leicestershire, Jan. 25, 1817. His parents were in the humbler walks of life, but his mother, whose maiden name was Clarke, appears to have been respectably educated. At the age of thirteen he was apprenticed in his native village. His Master was a Wesleyan, and Thomas was led by him to worship. About the age of sixteen he became united with that body of christians, and after a short time began to preach.

"I believe, (says one of his friends,) almost immediately after his conversion, he received a powerful impression, that the great head of the Church designed him for the work of the Ministry, and it appeared as though he could scarcely have lived did he not preach or promote the salvation of sinners in some way or other; and to the momentous work of saving souls he was soon called, not only by God, but also by his Church. But, before he was formally called to the work by the church, he did, in a sense, preach the Gospel every day; for he warned all who came in his way, of the folly and danger of sin, and earnestly and affectionately exhorted them to flee to Christ, as their only refuge from eternal death. And such was his zeal, such his solicitude to do good, that in less than twelve months, he was put upon the plan of the Wesleyan preachers in the Hinckley circuit, as a Local Preacher. The first time he went out to preach, I went with him. He commenced the great work in which he expired, on Christmas day, at Sharnford, a village about three miles from Hinckley. His text was "God is love;" and considering it was the first time, he preached with liberty and enlargement. I heard him several times after, and though I did not think he possessed first-rate abilities, I was quite convinced he was calculated to be useful."

Mr. Grant's views on the subject of baptism, became decidedly opposed to those entertained by the Wesleyan body, and he, with his master, united themselves to the General Baptist Church at Hinckley, and were baptized Aug. 7, 1836; after this, his venerable pastor states, "He continued to preach, and was well-beloved for his steadiness, as well as his punctual attendance on divine worship. His character was good. He was a pious young man, industrious, and for his opportunity, assiduous in learning." He soon manifested a desire to become a Missionary, and was received by the Committee in the latter end of 1840. He took for his companion in life, Miss Ross of his native village, to whom he was married in May, 1841. On the first of June, he was solemnly set apart to his work, at the Stoney Street Chapel, Nottingham; on the 17th of the same month, he bid farewell to his friends in England; and on the 26th of the following November, the "Pekin," cast anchor, in the Hoogly near Calcutta.

With commendable diligence, and considerable success, Mr. Grant applied himself to the study of Oreah, after his arrival at the missionary Station at Cuttack. He frequently visited the bazar, with brother Lacey, and in the Autumn of 1842, went a missionary tour with brother Wilkinson, and two or three native preachers. Before he returned home, Mr. Grant had symptoms of illness. On January 23rd, 1843, he was so far recovered as to preside at the Lord's table, and deliver a short address in Oreah. He afterwards visited a Hindoo festival with the native preachers; but, on Thursday, January 30, he was again afflicted. On Tuesday, recourse was had to more decided medical treatment, and he appeared to rally. But on Saturday, February 4th, he was suddenly seized with the pains of death, and in about half-an-hour, his liberated spirit winged its way to the regions of the blessed.

Thus, when he was entering on his sacred work, and the prospect of extensive usefulness was before him, Mr. Grant was taken from his labors, and another breach was made amongst our already too weakened Missionary band! May the Lord who does all things well, stimulate our Churches to increased zeal and devotedness in his cause, and raise up amongst us a succession of devoted Missionaries, who shall be his witnesses to the ends of the earth!

The Report of 1843 contains Mrs. G's. account of her bereavement, and Mrs. Lacey's testimony to the value of this departed labourer in the Lord's vineyard. Mr. Lacey writes,—"Brother Grant was a devoted Missionary; and, except on the score of his health, he promised to be useful. His acquisition of the language was not rapid, but very correct; every letter he could, and did properly pronounce. He had just commenced to address the people. He did not venture into large crowds, but conversed with six, or eight, or ten, on the subject of christianity. He had also commenced his labours in the instruction of the christian natives; and his address was understood, and liked. He had for some months, exerted himself in distributing tracts, and had given away some thousands. He has been permitted to sow some seed, which, by the divine blessing, may hereafter spring up and bring forth much fruit. O that this may prove to be the case."

Mrs. Phillips.

We have seen that the American branch of the Orissa Mission was first located at Sumbulpore. At the beginning the prospect was encouraging, but heavy afflictions befel the infant mission, and it was ultimately abandoned. Balasore was then fixed upon as the scene of its operations. At Sumbulpore the infant of Mrs. Noyes died, and afterwards Mrs. Phillips. The writer regrets that he has no account from her friends of her missionary course. The only information posessed is a short account appended to a letter of Mr. Sutton's, to Mrs. John Goadby, dated Cuttack Nov. 11, 1837. He says,—"Our Sumbulpore friends have been very ill, and when just recovering their little girl was suddenly taken from them. Since then Mrs. Phillips has finished her short course, a few days after a premature confinement. Poor Phillips seems greatly afflicted, and I rather expect, they will all come down to Cuttack for a season. Thus a dark cloud is passing over the brightning prospects of that long neglected region. Poor wretched, degraded, oppressed land. When shall the day of its visitation dawn? Is it to be now? So I hoped; but it is now hoping against hope. Yet I expect there would be great good done in that neighbourhood could the friends prosecute their labours. The people listen well, and Doitaree is very respectfully treated. Our friends in Calcutta are as bad off for labourers as we are. I cannot help thinking that the Baptist Society acts wickedly, in leaving their few men to sink into the grave neglected and unaided, while, to gratify a very questionable public sentiment, they send all their men and means to the West Indies. It is just so much practical infidelity."

Mrs. Bachelor.

Mrs. Bachelor, the wife of the American Missionary at Jellasore, died Jan. 20th, 1845. See an affecting account of her career in the General Baptist Repository, 1845, p. 251.

Mr. Allsop and Mrs. Hudson.

There are two more names dear to the friends of Missionaries in our churches, which cannot be omitted in this record. It does not fall within the limits of this History to give an account of the West

India Mission, and therefore, with great reluctance, but with feelings of much affection to the memory of his beloved brother-in-law, and of the wife of our valued Missionary now in China, he can do no more than refer to their interesting Memoirs by the Secretary of the Society, in the G. Baptist Repos. 1831 and 1833. May their children possess a 'double portion of their spirit.'

The Apostle Paul when recounting the deeds of departed saints, exclaimed—"And what shall I more say? for the time would fail me to tell of Gideon and Barak, and Samson and Jephtha, David also, and Samuel and the Prophets?" Thus the author is arrested in his labours, and much as he loves the memory of his departed friends, he finds it impossible here to present their memoirs and obituaries, though he had sketched many of them. Grateful is the memory of Messrs. Rennell and Baptist, Abraham the first native preacher, and Luckshmeebie, the wife of Ramachundra, Purama, Dalimba, Senjama, Cassia, Suttura, Lockindas, &c. It was once asked in a Missionary Meeting, rather abruptly, but very forcibly, by Mr. Rogers, of Fleet—"*How do they die? Tell us how they die.*" Well is it said—"Ask death beds, they can tell." Their simple, touching narratives, demonstrate the power of the Gospel to support the Hindoo in his conflict with "the last enemy." Surely we may adopt the language of the poet Lawson, in his 'Dying scene of the converted Bengalee," to several of the dear departed in Orissa.

"O, born too soon to die! eager to quit
This mortal state, careless of all its blandishments!
Tired, not of thy new life, but of its ills.
The wreck of thy old nature: thou aspiredst
To heaven to see thy Lord so lately known.
Enough to say of thee, thou livedst a life
Worthy thy Christian name, and diedst a death,
(Oh, may I die like thee) so calm, so still—
'Twas imperceptible! It came upon thee
Like the sweet dream of heaven, it caught thy soul,
And drew thee gently from the fading regions,
Stealing the breath that whispered the last hymn
Of praise to Him whose mercy saved thy soul.
'Twas night. The moon was in her course, and blest
With her fair glimmerings the wreathy cloud
That hung about her, and the breathless air
Found no disturbance, when they dug a grave
And laid him there. They loved him well, and wept
And hoped that soon (for they were Christians too)
Themselves should lie beside him, and await
The blessed judgment day."

The writer has felt much in erecting this monument to the memory of his departed friends in Orissa, and tears have flowed copiously, while he has been inscribing their names upon it. There is yet space for other names, and a thought has glided through his mind,—would it not be interesting both in this country and in India, to record the names of *the departed friends and supporters of the Mission?* But how can this be done? His space will not allow him to do it; his knowledge of the extent of the missionary spirit in the churches of our 'half tribe of Israel' is unequal to the task. The prevalence of the missionary spirit has been too extensive, deep, and effective, and many now sleep in Jesus whose names are and were to 'fortune and to fame unknown.' To discriminate, where so many have done well, is a very delicate and difficult duty. But their 'record is on high,' and the 'day shall declare' their love to Christ, their pity for the heathen, and the result of their labours for their good. The founders of the New Connexion deserve the first and most honored place in this record, viz.—Messrs. Taylors, Deacons, Tarratt, Smith, Thompson, Grimley, Donisthorpe, &c. &c. See the History of the General Baptist Denomination, by A. Taylor, 2 vols. 8vo., and J. Taylor's Statistics of the G. B. Churches, 1844. They possessed a missionary spirit, and were in 'labours more abundant,' though the state of the church required their energies to be employed at home, to be, as of old, 'a repairer of the breach, a restorer of paths to dwell in.' Mr. A. Taylor, in his history describes the character of these fathers of the Connexion. Truly, 'other men have laboured, and we have entered into their labours.'*

The example given by the other part of the Baptist Denomination had doubtless considerable influence upon the churches of this Connexion, and when Mr. Fuller declined the proposal to form a Society to be supported by both parts of the Denomination, Mr. Pike felt no rest in his spirit till the General Baptists came up 'to the help of the Lord, to the help of the Lord against the mighty.' In 1809 a letter upon the subject was read at the Association at Quorndon. Mr. Freeston of Hinckley, spoke of it in terms of high commendation, and Mr. B. Pollard of Quorndon, we have seen, is stated to have said—"he could almost have sold his coat from his back for the missionary cause." The writer cherishes an affectionate recollection of interviews with Mr. Felkin of Kegworth, and Mr. J. Deacon of Leicester in 1820, and particularly of the hospi-

* See Manasseh, pp. 41-3.

tality of the latter, and his lively interest in the missionary cause to which he was then devoted. Mr. A. Taylor, the editor of the *Repository*, speaking of the formation of the Missionary Society at Boston, Lincolnshire, in June 1816, states—"The zeal and liberality displayed at these meetings were highly encouraging, and afford good ground to hope well of the future success of this infant institution. As the noble efforts made by others, for carrying the religion of Jesus to the benighted nations of the heathen have always claimed the peculiar attention of the Editor of this Miscellany, it will certainly afford him greater pleasure to record the progress and success of the General Baptist Mission; and he trusts that the transactions of this Society will give additional interest to his future numbers." It is an interesting circumstance, that the venerable Founder of the Connexion, the Rev. Dan Taylor, then in his 78th year, presided at the Association when the Society was formed, and thus lived to see the dawn of foreign missionary operations among his people. He was invited to preside at "a general meeting of all the London Ministers," in reference to the persecution of the Protestants in the south of France, on Nov. 21, 1816. This was his last public service: in five days afterwards, he 'rested from his labours.' It is enough to say of him—'His praise is in all the churches.'

When the Society was enabled to commence actual operations by the ordination and departure of its missionaries to India in 1821, the zeal of its friends, both lay and ministerial, male and female, was highly encouraging. The ordinations of the first Missionaries at Loughborough and Wisbeach, and of other brethren at Leicester, Derby, Nottingham, Fleet, &c., demonstrate the ardour of ministerial brethren and of multitudes in the sacred missionary cause. And where are many of the honored ministers who assisted on these occasions, and who travelled scores and hundreds, and some of them thousands of miles to attend missionary meetings, and committees, and the embarkation of the missionaries and their wives? Where? And the echo pensively says, *Where?* Where are Thompson, Felkin, Deacon, Sexton, Hobbs, R. Smith, Stevenson, Goadby, Rogers, Hoe, Underwood, Binns, Cramp, Jarrom, Ingham, Bissill, Hardstaff, Wilders, Keeley, Orton, the Taylors, and the venerable Ewen? Ah! where? They are gone 'the way of all the earth.' They have 'finished their course with joy.' These names should be dear in Orissa, *for Orissa was dear to them.* Let them be familiar to succeeding generations, at home and abroad. They have 'served their generation :' may the present generation follow them 'as far as they followed Christ.'

But there is another column for names upon this mural stone, which is not yet full, and must not be filled, till Orissa, and India, and China, and the World need such benefactors no more. The writer refers to those who have assisted the Society by their property after death. Some of these deserve the most honourable mention, such as Mr. Parkinson, Miss Barnes, Mr. Radford, Mr. Payne, Mr. Newberry, &c. &c. These friends, as it is said of Abel, '*being dead, are yet spoken of.*' The kindness and liberality of these friends in death to the poor benighted heathen, must be most grateful to the native christians. Let them be informed of their names that they may supplicate blessings upon their children, their kindred, and their friends. May many of our people deeply consider "the responsibility of property," and weigh well our Lord's words, "*Make to yourselves friends of the mammon of unrighteousness, that when ye fail they may receive you into everlasting habitations.*" O for grace to be faithful!

There is doubtless another class of the friends of India whose names would adorn the column. The departed *Subscribers* and especially *Collectors* of the mission. But the writer cannot presume to undertake this work. Doubtless their names have been honored in answer to the prayer—

> "In thy fair book of Life divine,
> My God, inscribe my name;
> There let it fill some humble place,
> Beneath my Lord the Lamb."

Paul speaks of his 'helpers in Christ,' and declares 'whose names are in the book of life.' Let that suffice. 'The Lord knoweth them that are his.'—May every church possess such subscribers and collectors, as the claims of the perishing heathen and the resources of the Christian church demand; and some other historian of the Mission may transfer their honored names to this *Ebenezer*, upon which, at its base, is written—"HITHERTO HATH THE LORD HELPED US."

Some will probably be ready to expect a more full account of these dear departed friends, but as Dr. Cox forcibly observes in his History of the Baptist Mission,—"It does not belong to history, to give the details of biography, or to pronounce an oration over the grave of departed worth and greatness." Let what has been written suffice to shew the value of religion in the consecration of missionaries, the conversion of the heathen, and the divine support which the grace of God can impart in man's 'final hour.' "Here is the patience of the saints: here are they that keep the commandments of God, and the faith of Jesus. And I heard a voice from heaven saying unto me, Write, Blessed are the dead which die in the Lord from henceforth: Yea, saith the Spirit, that they may rest from their labours: and their works do follow them."

CHAP. VII.

PREPARATIONS FOR THE FINAL TRIUMPH OF CHRISTIANITY IN THE EAST.

Diffusion of education in the English and Native languages—Abolition of Infanticide—Suttees—Anti-colonization regulations and distinctions of color and religion—Pilgrim Tax abolition measure—Abolition of Slavery—Disallowance of the Grant to Juggernaut—Suppression of the Churuck Pooja—Grateful review of past progress—Decay of Idolatry and Mahomedanism—Diffusion of christian knowledge—Facilties of Britain for usefulness—Anticipations of the final triumph of Christianity in the East—concluding appeal.

It was written of Messiah's reign, "Wisdom and knowledge shall be the stability of thy times and strength of salvation." It is a most anomalous and extraordinary fact, that in the latter part of the last century, and even for a number of years in the present, the views of the Government of India were opposed to the diffusion of Christianity among the teeming millions of its subjects. This state of things aroused the powerful mind of the late Rev. R. Hall, who wrote an address on the subject of the renewal of the India Charter in 1813. He justly observed, "It must surely be considered an extraordinary fact, that in a country under the government of a people professing Christianity, *that religion should be the only one that is discountenanced and discouraged.* Every individual of the immense populatiou subjected to our sway, has claims on our justice and benevolence, which we cannot with impunity neglect.

The wants and sufferings of every individual utter a voice which goes to the heart of humanity. In return for their allegiance, we owe them protection and instruction, together with every effort to ameliorate their condition and improve their character. It is but fair to acknowledge that we have not been wholy insensible to these claims, and that the extension of our power has been hitherto highly beneficial. But why, in the series of improvements, has Christianity been neglected? Why has the communication of the greatest good we have to bestow, been hitherto fettered and restrained; and while every modification of idolatry, not excepting the bloody and obscene orgies of Juggernaut, have received support, have attempts to instruct the natives in the things which belong to their peace, been suppressed or discountenanced? It will surely appear surprising to posterity, that a nation glorying in the purity of its faith as one of its highest distinctions, should suffer its transactions in the east to be characterised by the spirit of infidelity, as though they imagined the foundations of empire could only be laid in apostacy and impiety; at a moment too, when Europe, convulsed to its centre, beholds these frantic nations swept with the besom of destruction!"

The efforts of the friends of religious liberty were so far successful as to obtain in the Act, the insertion of four clauses relating to "persons desirous of going to India, for the purpose of promoting the religious and moral improvement of the natives," beneficial in their results, though not such as to preclude absolutely the oppressions of a resolved infidelity and despotism.

Since this period, a brighter day has dawned upon the east. Missionaries are no longer forbidden to land upon the shores of India, but are rather welcomed to its glowing plains. As of old, 'the earth helped the woman,' a most important change has come over the authorities of India; and the interests of education, and the civilization and evangelization of our eastern dominions, obtain their cordial concurrence and support. One proof among many may here be noticed. A correspondent in March 1829, stated that the following notice appeared *daily* in the Calcutta Papers.—" The Governor-General invites the communication of all suggestions tending to promote any branch of national industry; to improve the commercial intercourse by land or water; to amend the defects of the existing establishments; to encourage the diffusion of education and useful knowledge; and to advance the general prosperity and happiness of the British empire in India!"

The late Rev. W. H. Pearce of Calcutta, on his visit to this country in 1837, thus describes the important changes in progress in India, and the desire of the Natives for education both in their own language and in English.

"It is evident to all acquainted with the state of native society in Calcutta, that a great and interesting change in the Hindoo mind has been long going on; but has been lately far more clearly and rapidly developed than before, and now requires corresponding exertions on the part of christians to give it a right direction. A new era, it is evident, is now bursting on India. The labours of former years are producing an extensive and beneficial influence, and an impetus has been communicated to the native mind which can never be repressed. In some places, the institutions of caste are generally, though not openly, violated; and in others, they have already fallen into contempt. A taste for European science and literature has been excited, which, in its influence, promises to be the most important. Such ridiculous statements with regard to geographical and astronomical facts are given in the sacred books of the Hindoos, that every youth who acquires only elementary scientific knowledge, soon suspects them to be false; his religious opinions being derived from the same works, doubt is gradually excited, which the increasing knowledge of every day tends to strengthen, till before his education is complete, Hindooism is discovered to be utterly an imposture. Hence the pupils who receive an English education, are all becoming, or have already become, complete unbelievers in the popular religion, and must either settle down as atheists and deists on the one side, or as christians on the other. Many thousands of youth are taught at the expense of different missionary institutions; these are all instructed in the great principles of christianity, and some almost every month acknowledge the Saviour. But many young people are in very different circumstances. Four colleges in Calcutta, and twenty-three colleges and superior schools in other large cities, have been established at the expense of government; in twenty-three of which, at least five thousand native youths are now receiving an English education of a superior order. No instruction in the principles of Christianity, however, is afforded in these institutions; so that as they begin to see the folly of Hindooism, they become acquainted with no better system of religion, and are thus exposed to the contagion of infidelity and vice.

"I may add, that their salvation or destruction will not take place alone,—it must involve that of many others. The late Governor-General, Lord William Bentinck, and his successor, Lord Auckland, having very judiciously encouraged the English language, in preference to to the Persian, in public business, the desire for education in this language throughout India, is greater than was ever known before. As an illustration, I may mention, that at the latter end of last year, when a new college was opened at Hooghly, a few miles above Calcutta, fourteen hundred native youths enrolled their names as English students within a few days! Several native princes, with their chief officers, are already learning our language, and are frequently applying to Calcutta for instructors. To supply the demand from all quarters, numerous teachers are required; and the pupils who are now under instruction in Calcutta, in the government as well as the mission schools, being the most advanced, will without doubt be engaged, and in a few years be scattered all over the country as instructors of their countrymen. Even now, almost every boy who receives instruction in English in the day time, communicates it to a class of his relations and acquaintances, at night; and several advanced pupils, who are still pursuing their studies, unite in superintending a large free school for the benefit of their countrymen. How lamentable will it be, if these young men, becoming infidels, should proselyte their pupils, as they emerge from heathenism, into the same destructive sentiments! How delightful will it be, if through the active exertions of missionaries, many of them should now be brought to God, and in various situations of influence, which from their superior information they must occupy, should widely diffuse among their countrymen, a saving knowledge of the blessed Redeemer!"

It is scarcely necessary to state, that, a similar movement is perceptible in Orissa; the Government School at Cuttack, in favor of which the Missionaries, though reluctantly, relinquished their own Benevolent Institution established in 1823, is one of the Schools above referred to, and that upon the whole, it is anticipated that the diffusion of general knowledge cannot fail of promoting the downfal of Idolatry and the diffusion of the gospel.

One of the most evident and pleasing features of the progress of Christianity in India, is the abolition, through its mild and humanizing influence, of various inhuman, impolitic, and mischievous practices. It appears important to place these triumphs of our common Christianity in detail, that the friends of Christian Missions may 'thank God and take courage.'

INFANTICIDE.—It is impossible here to enter into a description of the origin and nature, the extent and atrocities of this unnatural custom. The writer has endeavoured to do so in two editions of a Pamphlet on '*Infanticide in India,*' and in his '*India's Cries to British Humanity.*' This practice has chiefly prevailed at Saugur Island, near Calcutta, and in Western India, in the Provinces of Cutch and Guzerat. Dr. Carey, Buchanan, and other friends of India, presented a Memorial to the Marquis of Wellesley upon the subject, and in 1802, a Regulation was passed abolishing Infanticide at Saugur.† Colonel Walker exerted himself in Western India, to obtain the renunciation of Infanticide, in 1808.‡ It is a subject of deep regret, that on the departure of that philanthropic Gentleman from India, this important document became in effect a dead letter. More recently the British Government has shewn a very laudable zeal to abolish this inhuman and murderous custom. In October 1819, "A Treaty of Alliance between the Hon. East India Company and His Highness Maha Raja Mirza Rao Shri Desserljee, Chief of Cutch, was formed. The following clauses are very important.

"The Hon. Company engages to exercise no authority over the domestic concerns of the Rao, or of those of any of the Jahreja Chieftains of the country. That the Rao, his heirs or successors, shall be absolute masters of their territory, and that the civil and criminal jurisdiction of the British Government shall not be introduced.

"His Highness the Rao, his heirs and successors, at the particular instance of the Honourable Company, *engage to abolish in their own family the practice of Infanticide;* they also engage to join heartily with the Honourable Company, *in abolishing the custom generally throughout the Bhyaud of Cutch.*

"Previously to the execution of the deed of guarantee in favour of the Jahreja Bhyaud, according to the tenour of the sixteenth article, a written engagement shall be entered into by them to abstain from the practice of Infanticide; and specifying that, in case any of them do practise it, the guilty person shall submit to a punishment of any kind that may be determined by the Honourable Company's Government and the Dutch Durbar."

† See this valuable Document, Par. Papers on Infanticide, 1824, p. 29,30.

‡ Par. Papers on Infanticide, 1824, p. 49.

It is a subject of deep regret, that this practice is not yet fully extirpated. The Governor of Bombay addressed the Court of Directors in Nov. 1842,—"We now beg to solicit the attention of your Honourable Court to Lieutenant-Colonel Melvill's Reports, Dec. 8, 1840, and Jan. 11, 1841, submitting the first census that has yet been obtained of the Jahreja population of Cutch and Wagur; and explaining the measures which either have been adopted or are in progress for the suppression of Infanticide in Cutch, together with some observations regarding the custom of Suttee, which we regret to state is still permitted in this province. At the same time we request the notice of your Honourable Court to the memorandum, date April 28th, 1841, written by your political secretary, containing remarks and suggestions on these Reports. Your Honourable Court will regret to find in these documents a most lamentable account of the extent to which female Infanticide has during the last twenty five-years prevailed in Cutch; and that it is established beyond doubt that the practice is not simply confined to the Jahreja tribe, but that their evil example is followed by other Hindoos, and even by Mahomedan tribes residing in that province.

"The census submitted by Lieutenant-Colonel Melvill embraces the whole of Cutch and Wagur, (with the exception of Addooee,) belonging to the Chief of Moorvee, in Kattewar, and which is now included in the census of that province, and exhibits the following results:

Total number of houses or heads of families............	2,287
Ditto sons, grandsons, and great grandsons............	2,625
Ditto daughters, granddaughters, and great granddaughters,	335
Excess of males over female children	2,290

"Deeply as the results thus exhibited are to be lamented, it is, nevertheless, satisfactory to observe, from the observations contained in Lieutenant-Colonel Melvill's Report, Dec. 8, 1840, that the practice of Infanticide has lately diminished in a very sensible degree; and that the measures recently adopted for its suppression, although in their infancy, have already been rewarded with considerable success."

The prevalence of Infanticide in Goomsur, a district of Orissa, appears to have been very appalling. Lord Elphinstone, Governor of Madras, in a letter to the writer, dated Jan. 1842, speaks of a party of men being sent to abolish the practice. The *Friend of India*, Feb. 15, 1844, contains interesting intelligence upon this subject.—"We understand that Captain Macpherson has lately returned to the low country, from a month's visit to the sacrificing district of Goomsur, a tract about 30 miles long by 12 broad. Although his stay was curtailed by attacks of fever, and the extent of his operations necessarily thereby limited, yet, we believe, that his visit has been eminently successful. Our letters state, that all the tribes of Goomsur have been induced, not only to give up their victims, (already more than 80 in number,) but also to pledge themselves to the discontinuance of the rite of Human Sacrifice—the great social right of the Khund religion.

"Human Sacrifice has been abolished as a *public* rite throughout the whole district of Goomsur, though it may possibly be still occasionally practised in *secret*. To us this appears to be great and very gratifying success, and the abolition of the rite in the remainder of the Khund country, ought now to be comparatively easy."

SUTTEES.—Suttee is the name given in India to the woman who immolated herself on the funeral pile of her husband, or was buried with his body, and denoted that the female considered herself faithful to him even unto death; the term is also applied to the rite itself. Dr. Carey thus defines it in his Bengalee Dictionary,—"*Suttee.* From *sut*, good, chaste, pure, &c.; a woman who burns herself on her husband's funeral pile, that being thought an irrefragable proof of her chastity." Diodorus Siculus, who twice refers to the practice in the 103rd and 106 Olympiad, B. C. 327 and 314 years, supposes the practice to have originated in the unfaithfulness of the women to their husbands, and their taking them off by mixing deadly plants with their food. He observes, "This wicked practice increasing, and the punishment of the guilty not serving to deter others from the crime, a law was passed, that wives should be burned with their deceased husbands, except such as were pregnant and had children, and that the individual who refused to comply with this law should be compelled to remain a widow, and be for ever excluded from all rites and privileges, as guilty of impiety. This measure being adopted, it followed, that the abominable disposition to which the wives were addicted, was converted into an opposite feeling. In order to avoid that climax of disgrace, they not only took all possible care of their husbands' safety, but emulated

THE SUTTEE, OR THE BURNING A HINDOO WIDOW.

each other in promoting his glory and renown."* Strabo is of the same opinion.† Mandello, a German who witnessed a Suttee at Cambay in 1638, accounts for the rise of this singular custom in the same manner.‡ A practice similar to the Suttee exists among the Yarribanians in Africa, and its origin is very similarly accounted for.|| An intelligent Magistrate in India supposes it may have originated in "the voluntary sacrifice of a widow inconsolable for the loss of her husband, and who resolved to accompany him on the funeral pile." He supposes the Brahmuns commended the deed, and "the most esteemed authors of the age were induced to recommend it. Menu and the most ancient and respectable writers do not notice Suttee; it was therefore not known or not approved in their time.¶

The number of the Suttees in the three Presidencies of India, from 1815 to 1826, as far as they can be ascertained, was 7789. Probably a thousand poor unhappy widows have *annually* perished in Hindostan. And has this practice existed for more than twenty centuries? How noble the triumph when this horrible custom was abolished by the British Government in India. The late Sir T. F. Buxton, first drew the attention of the British Parliament to this evil in India, in 1819, and in July 1821, appeared the first volume of "*Papers relating to East India Affairs; viz. Hindoo Widows and Voluntary Immolations.*" These were continued to eight volumes, the last being dated June 1830. The first Pamphlet upon the Suttee was published by Dr. Johns in 1816. The Rev. T. S. Grimshawe followed in 1825, and in 1827 appeared the speeches of J. Poynder, Esq. and R. Jackson, Esq., and the Suttee's Cry to Britain. Bedford had the honor of being the first Town to petition against the horrid custom in 1823. Numerous petitions were presented in 1827 and 1828, and unexpected and great was the joy, when in Dec. 1829, that excellent and benevolent Governor-General Lord William Bentinck abolished the practice. The Regulation** is dated "Fort William, 4th December, 1829," and signed "W. Bentinck, Combermere; W. B. Bailey, C. T. Metcalfe." This magnanimous act will be mentioned in terms of high approbation by all succeeding generations. His Lordship and those who co-operated with him, have acquired honors in comparison with which—

"The laurels that a Cæsar reaps are weeds."

* Lib. xix. c. 32, 33. † Geogr. Lib. xv. Asi. Journal, May 1827.
‡ Asi. Jour. Jan. 1823. || Ecl. Rev. May 1832, p. 378.
¶ India's Cries, 3rd edit. p. 215. ** pp. 263-4, and G. Bap. Repository, 1830, pp. 279-80.

The Madras Government abolished the rite by a similar Regulation dated Feb. 2, 1830, and the Governor of Bombay abolished it before the close of the year. It is to be regretted that the Suttee still lingers, like a wild beast in the jungle, among the Seiks, in Gwalior, Cutch, and little Java, and some few independent States. It is hoped that the influence of the British power and example will effect its universal abolition. Haste happy day! when all the miseries of heathenism shall

"Be buried 'midst the wreck of things that were."

Anti-colonization Regulations and distinction of colour and religion in the Functionaries of the State have been removed. It was the singular policy of the East India Company for many years to discourage and prohibit the settlement of Englishmen in their eastern territories. A writer in an Indian Magazine uses very strong terms in reference to this policy, viz. "Never could insanity have devised any thing more utterly monstrous than the prohibition of Englishmen to settle in India." Hence Burke in his day thundered against his countrymen, exclaming,—"Were we to be driven out of India this day, nothing would remain to tell that it had been possessed during the inglorious period of our dominion, by any better than the ourang-outang or the tiger." Heber more temperately, but scarcely less cuttingly, observed;—"It was painful for me to think, if the English were now expelled from India, how few relics would be left behind of their religion, their power, or their civil and military magnificence. Still little, very little is done in comparison with all that there is to do." Rome held her conquest by colonizing them. Hume thus eulogizes Agricola, the ablest and wisest of the conquerors of Britain.—"He introduced law and civility among the Britons, taught them to desire and raise all the conveniences of life, reconciled them to the Roman language and manners, instructed them in letters and sciences, and employed every expedient to render those chains which he had forged, both easy and agreeable to them. The inhabitants having experienced how unequal their own force was to resist that of the Romans, acquiesced in the dominion of their masters, and were gradually incorporated in that mighty empire."

The New India Bill, the provisions of which took effect from and after April 22, 1834, contained three important clauses relative to the settlement of Europeans in India.

Lord W. Bentinck took away all the remaining restrictions Is India thus opened to settlers from every part of her Majesty's territories? Are many persons and families of property and talent, character and influence, removing to British America, the United States, Cape Colony, Australia, Van Dieman's Land, &c.? Are there no suitable persons in our Churches and congregations, who could settle in Bengal, and especially Orissa, and in various ways aid the cause of Christ? The Jews were scattered over the whole Roman empire, and they generally formed, as the seals of apostolic labours, the nucleus of Christian churches. Let our friends, our children, be taught to look forward to such an object, as important to the interests of commerce, morals, and religion, in Hindostan, and the whole of the Eastern world. A friend in trade at Nottingham has long had his mind directed to this object. Now the way is open. "Who is there among you of all his people? his God be with him, and let him go up to Jerusalem, which is in Judah, and build the house of the Lord God of Israel, (he is the God,) which is in Jerusalem. And whosoever remaineth in any place where he sojourneth, let the men of his place help him with silver, and with gold, and with goods, and with beasts, beside the free will offering, for the house of God, that is in Jerusalem." Ezra i. 3, 4.

The Despatch to abolish British Connexion with Idolatry in India. The reader must have noticed with painful interest, the obstacles opposed to the progress of the gospel by the impolitic and unchristian conduct of the British Government in India, in regulating, fostering, and deriving wealth from its deadly superstitions. The writer has felt this subject for these twenty-four years, and has prayerfully cherished the purpose to labour for their removal.

A correspondent in India writing from Manargoody, Dec. 1841, says—"*Christian England is the main support of the Idolatry of this country; and if that support be withdrawn, Idolatry in this land will soon fall.*" A Hindoo very justly inquired—"If the Government do not forsake Juggernaut, how can you expect that we should?" A Hindoo at Allahabad, (where a tax was levied by the Govt on pilgrims that bathed in the junction of the Ganges and the Jumna, and even stooped to the degradation of *licensing barbers* for the purpose,) inquired—"*I have paid the Company this morning a rupee for my salvation, and can there be a doubt of my safety?*" This evil has extended its ramifications into almost every part of Hindostan; and the evil is far from being eradicated in the Madras and Bombay Presidencies. In Feb. 1833, a very valuable Despatch upon this subject, said to be from the pen of the Right Hon. Lord Glenelg, then President of the Board of Control, was sent out to

India. The following summary of its provisions is peculiarly interesting.

1. "That the interference of British Functionaries in the interior management of native temples, in the customs, habits, and religious proceedings of their priests and attendants, in the arrangements of their ceremonies, rites, and festivals, and generally in the condition of their interior economy, shall cease.

2. "That the Pilgrim Tax shall be every where abolished.

3. "That fines and offerings shall no longer be considered as sources of revenue by the British Government, and they shall consequently no longer be collected or received by the servants of the East India Company.

4. "That no servant of the East India Company shall be engaged in the collection, management, or custody of monies in the nature of fines or offerings, in whatever manner obtained, or whether furnished in cash or in kind.

5. "That no servant of the East India Company shall hereafter derive any emolument resulting from the above mentioned or any similar sources.

6. "That in all measures relating to their temples, their worship, their festivals, their religious practices, their ceremonial observances, our native subjects be left entirely to themselves.

7. "That in every case in which it has been found necessary to form and keep up a police force, especially with a view to the peace and security of the pilgrims or the worshippers, such police shall hereafter be maintained and made available out of the general revenues of the country."

Excellent as are the provisions of this invaluable Despatch, it is notorious that it has not yet been fully carried into effect, in various parts of India. It is imperative in the friends of their country, and of Christianity in the east, to use every effort till our Rulers are "free from the pollution of Idols." Haste happy day!

Pilgrim Tax Abolition Measure. This unchristian system of making a gain of Idolatry has past under notice and received deserved condemnation, but like every improvement that involves the loss of money, many years rolled away before the friends of missions hailed the accomplishment of their long cherished desires, in reference to some principal temples. A few generations hence it will scarcely be credited that Britons, enlightened Britons, living in the nineteenth century of the Christian era, amassed wealth from the miserable votaries of superstition at Juggernaut, Gya, Allahabad, Tripetty, &c. At the temple of Juggernaut the mistaken policy of Government actually regulated *the fees of the pilgrim Hunters*, forgetting that these parties would not only take what the law prescribed, but as much more as they could get from their deluded votaries; who, beggared by these regulations and exactions, drooped and died by hundreds and thousands in their long pilgrimages. Oh my country! may God in mercy deliver thee "*from blood-guiltiness.*" The abolition of the Pilgrim Tax at Juggernaut, &c., is an important event. See the Act, in the G. Baptist Repository, 1843, page 312. It is dated April 20, 1840.

Abolition of Slavery. It is the genius of Christianity to promote the temporal as well as the spiritual welfare of mankind. Harris in his *Britannia*, has well observed—"It is the distinguishing feature of Christian benevolence, that while it aims chiefly at the highest good of man, it bestows a proportionate regard on all his inferior interests: resembling its divine Exemplar, *who on his way to the Cross to save a world, often stood still to heal the diseased and relieve the wretched.*" Slavery very extensively prevailed in British India. The slaves in Canara, Malabar, Travancore, Tinnevelly, Trichinopoly, &c. &c., amounted to 800,297. Some writers estimated them much higher. One extract from the voluminous Par. Papers on Slavery in India, will demonstrate its character.—"The treatment of slaves necessarily depends principally on the individual character of their owners; and when we reflect on those evils which are inseparable from even the mildest state of slavery, and consider how large a portion of our most industrious subjects are at present totally deprived of a free market for their labour—restricted by inheritance to a mere subsistence—and sold and transferred with the land which they till—policy no less than humanity, would appear to dictate the propriety of gradually relieving them from those restrictions which have reduced them, and must continue to confine them, to *a condition scarcely superior to that of the cattle which they follow at the plough.*"* The writer has long cherished an interest in the abolition of East India Slavery, and has often regretted that West India Slavery so much engrossed the sympathies of the friends of humanity. Great was the joy of every Philanthropist when tidings arrived of the suppression of Slavery throughout our territories in India. It was hailed by the Anti-Slavery Convention then assembled in London, with the greatest delight. It has been frequently observed of this measure—"In the grandeur of its conception it rivals those great measures of justice and benevolence—the Act for the Abolition of the African Slave Trade, and the Law for the extinction of Slavery in the British Colonies; so in the magnitude of its blessed results will it eclipse them both.

* See India's Cries, p. 364.

Its effects on all Asia will be immense! The States bordering on the British dominions in India must follow the example of emancipation, or their slaves will seek liberty in flight, and find it under the protection of our laws. The spirit of freedom is diffusive; like the light of heaven, it will find its way to the dark places of the earth, which are full of the habitations of cruelty."

The brevity and comprehensive range of this measure, viewed in connexion with its truly enlightened spirit, entitle it to universal imitation in legislative proceedings. See Gen. Bap. Repository, 1843, page 312.

Disallowance of the Government Grant to Juggernaut's Temple. The Poet justly observes—"'Tis lame kindness that does its work by halves." This very forcibly applied to the British Government in reference to the repeal of the Pilgrim Tax at Juggernaut. It was anticipated that all connexion with the Temple and its affairs would cease; judge how great was the surprise and regret of all interested in the question, to read in Lord Auckland's Despatch in Nov. 1838,—"I would therefore in wholly relinquishing the tax, make over to the Rajah of Khoordah as Superintendent, and to the Priests, the entire management of the ceremonies and affairs of the Temple, *on the understanding of the established pecuniary donation.* I would retain the *suttais hazaree mehal* (or Temple lands) in the management of our revenue officers, &c."

Lord Auckland conceived, from some erroneous statements made to him, that "we conciliated submission by binding ourselves to the accustomed maintenance of the temples of the country." Lord Wellesley thought otherwise, and during his administration, no support was given to Juggernaut's Temple, or any Tax levied. The friends of the Orissa Mission felt this "*established Government Donation*" to be a great abomination; and on June 21st, 1843, Memorials were presented to the Right Hon. the Earl of Ripon, President of the India Board, and also to the Court of Directors and Proprietors.*

At a Quarterly Court, held Dec. 18, 1844, the Chairman stated, "The necessary documents have been forwarded to India, to complete the severance of the Govt. of India from the idolatrous worship of the Natives in the temple of Juggernaut." The last Despatch is dated Dec. 18, 1844,† which is of a satisfactory character. Mr. Lacey wrote under date October 16th, 1844—"The endowment

* See this Memorial G. B. Repository 1843, pp. 256.

† G. B. Repository 1845, pp. 318.

DEATH OF HINDOOS ON THE BANKS OF THE RIVER GANGES.

lands have been given up." This does not appear to be yet complete—Alas!

In a letter dated May 1846, he speaks of a sum of money being given by the British Government, apparently, for the relief of the poor, miserable pilgrims. He says—"The sum of 36,000 rupees is conveyed by the officers of the Rajah, from the Collector's office, *before the multitude*—a most convincing proof that the Idol is the object of British support and patronage. Orders have, it appears, come out for the suspension of the donation, and it is acknowledged, that there exits no obligation or pledge. The seat of power is at home. The lever must be applied and worked there, and then the unsightly monstrous incubus will be rolled away." If this grant is for the relief of the pilgrims, it is highly exceptionable. Multitudes will be induced to take the pilgrimage for the sake of obtaining a trifle. Surely "the orders for the suspension of the donation" will be speedily obeyed; that Britain may be free from connexion with the pollutions of this 'high place' of idolatry.

The Churuck Poojah; *the Exposure of the sick on the banks of the Ganges, Burning the dead, &c.,* are all revolting customs which the mild influence of Christianity will remove. The former was prohibited in Calcutta in 1833, a happy commencement of its general suppression in Bengal and Orissa. One of the Hindoo Papers in Calcutta, called upon the Authorities to put down these disgusting exhibitions. The Editor says—"We earnestly implore our Rulers to rescue a deluded people from the thraldom of inhuman superstition. Let Pundits and other respectable independent Natives be consulted on the subject, and if Government find that the cruelties practised at this Poojah are not enjoined by the Shasters, let bye-laws be immediately made and promulgated among the people by beat of tom tom."

The Exposure of the Sick, it is apprehended has not awakened that deep attention which its real character demands. Ram Mohun Roy, in conversation with the writer in London, emphatically said of it—"*It is murder! murder!*" The Rev. J. Lacroix, in his speech at Exeter Hall, May 1842, solemnly declared, "The practice of exposing the sick on the banks of the Ganges is still murdering its thousands, and increasing the agonies of death in its tens of thousands." The Rev. W. Carey of Cutwa, in Bengal, in Nov.

1845, writes—" I hope the time is not far off, when Ghaut Murders will be abolished, and not only the bringing the dying to the river, but also their bringing the dead. Thousands are destroyed by being brought to the river before they are dead: but bringing the dead and burning them, or casting them into the stream, is a cloak by which thousands of murders have been concealed. Not only so, but at times the water is made so impure, I have no doubt thousands of people die by drinking it. A little river clay or water *taken to dying people would serve the same purpose;* therefore, to put a stop to all these practices would be no hardship to the Natives. O what a blessing would attend it!"

The abolition of this murderous custom is loudly demanded of the benevolent Rulers of India. Ram Mohun Roy stated in a letter, " From a reference to the decision on the Appeal to the King in Council, made by certain Hindoo inhabitants of Calcutta, against the abolition of the practice of burning Hindoo widows alive, it is evident, that *the local Government of India is invested with the power of abolishing any cruel practice without standing in need of parliamentary authority.*" May this power be speedily exerted on behalf of those who are daily 'drawn unto death and ready to be slain' by this horrid superstition.

The Cremation or burning the dead, or casting them into the river, it is conceived will disappear before the humane influence of the gospel. "The practice of burning the dead (says Mr. Ward) tends very much to blunt the feelings of the living, and the method of doing it is a striking contrast to the respect and tender feelings cherished in burying the dead among Christians. In the Hindoo funerals, no children or relations are seen weeping over the pile; the only persons present are two or three men, with bamboos in their hands, to keep the limbs and bones on the fire, and to facilitate their destruction. Even the ashes are washed away, or thrown into the Ganges, *not leaving a vestige that can remind the living of their deceased friends.*" Intelligence from India states, " The King of Bokhara has prohibited his Hindoo subjects from burning their dead. The order has been quietly submitted to."—When will the barbarous rite of cremation cease to brutalize the Hindoo people?

The review which has passed under the reader's notice, may be considered as affecting the *exterior* of Christianity; but the *interior* is scarcely less encouraging. Let us obey the command to the church in the wilderness—" Thou shalt remember all the way which the Lord thy God led thee these forty years in the wilderness."

"When a comparison has been drawn (says Dr. Cox,) between the operations of the mission in the East and West Indies, it has been frequently to the disadvantage of the former; so that the public mind, attracted by the splendid successes of the missionary and anti-slavery operations in Jamaica, seemed, for a long period, to be *cooling* in interest and sympathy with regard to the East. This was the more to be lamented, not only on account of that country being the primary seat of the mission abroad, and having for a long succession of years attracted universal attention by the unparalleled exertions of Carey and others, but also because the amount of good accomplished, though different in kind, was perhaps equal in degree to that of any part of the great undertaking. The results of labour were more immediate, more rapid, and, if it may be so expressed, more personal in the West Indies than in the East, as made known in converted thousands and tens of thousands, and in the far resounding victories over slavery; while in India, the work was, and still is, in a measure preparatory and prospective, as traceable, *in the cultivation of native talent, the extermination of native and european prejudice against the gospel, the improvement of the young, the diminution of the power of idol gods and their advocates over the popular mind, and above all, in the circulation of translated portions of the sacred Scriptures among the teeming myriads of Asia, in their vernacular languages.*" See Cox's History, vol. ii. p. 273, and vol. i. p. 96-102.

The review of a quarter of a century of christian exertion in Orissa is very encouraging. We have seen the chains of caste broken in numerous instances. The victory over language is scarcely less marked, as is demonstrated by the revision of the Scriptures, in the preparation of Tracts, the publication of valuable Dictionaries, and all the various labours of the local press, not to omit the ability of the Missionaries to preach the gospel with great power and effect. It is stated that a respectable Native at Cuttack, was observed at a little distance from the bazaar, listening to Mr. Lacey, and on being spoken to, he expressed his admiration at the fluency which he had acquired in the Oreah language. The work of conversion has been of the most decided and satisfactory character, as must have been evident from the history of the converts already perused. The number of Native Preachers is an encouraging proof of the influence of the gospel. Ten have been ordained to the work of the evangelist, and as many more as preachers or students are helpers in Christ. Mr. Ward's desire and prayer in 1799 have been fulfilled. The "new caste has arisen, and Brahmuns preach the gospel." The reflex influence of the mission at home has been most valuable. "Charity is twice blessed;" and this has been verified in the missionary enterprize. A new state and order of things has arisen; the scale of contributions in every good work has been increased, and we have seen that "There is that scattereth and yet increaseth." The value of the mission to the British churches is beyond calculation. The travels, labours, numerous works from the press, &c., &c., of its agents, missionaries, and active supporters, demonstrate the wisdom of the Great Head of the church, in his new axiom of christian morals—"It is more blessed to give than to receive." It has been remarked, "Man is built up on circumstances." And what circumstances so favorable as the promotion and advocacy of the Bible, Missionary, Sunday School, and Tract Societies? The General Baptist Churches have more than doubled their number and members since the commencement of their missionary operations. The Lord still "delight over his people to do them good," to "bless and to make a blessing."

The decay of Idolatry and Mahomedanism gives promise, as the scripture expresseth it, that, "that which decayeth and waxeth old is ready to vanish away." The efforts of the christian church to dispel the darkness of the east are still weak and few, compared with the wants of the population. As some one expresses it—"The idea that for thousands upon thousands of years idolatry has enslaved the inhabitants of that country is dreadfully overwhelming, but faith in our immutable Saviour affords the cheering hope, that small as is the little band there engaged, and weak as are our efforts, yet, they form the advanced guard of the army of the Prince of Peace; which shall one day conquer every opposition, and captivate every soul, and triumphantly exclaim, 'Thanks be to God who always causeth us to triumph in Christ, and maketh manifest the savour of his knowledge by us, in every place!'"

The following fact speaks volumes on the influence of education and the diffusion of christian light. It is extracted from a Hindoo newspaper called *Prubhakar*. "A few days ago, an inhabitant of Calcutta took his son with him to Kaleeghaut, to obtain a durshun of the divine Kalee. Having gone to a shop, and, after bathing, prepared his offering for worship, he approached the goddess, and, with all present, prostrated himself before her. But his sweet son offered no worship. This fool of a child, only saluted her who is worthy of the humble adoration of Brumha and all the gods, with —"GOOD MORNING, MADAM!!" On hearing this, many put their hands to their ears and fled, and as his father was about to chastise him, a worthy person prevented him, saying, 'Be calm, it is not proper to exhibit passion in this place.' The father, with grief, exclaimed, 'What crime had I committed, that I should have placed you in the Hindoo College, that, for your sake, my caste, honour, and every thing else should be lost? Alas! for this wicked son! I am a separated man, and cannot go to the Dhurma Subha.' Many hearing this lamentation, asked him, 'Sir, we have heard that the Hindoo College is under the direction of many respectable Bengalee inhabitants of Calcutta; how then is there such misconduct among the students?' He replied, 'Sirs, do not inquire into the merits of the great Bengalees; you can see how by donations of their money they are destroying the future welfare of all. How then can I speak of the merits of our Bengalee Baboos?'—A SERVANT OF KALEE."

The diffusion of Christian knowledge is attended with the most important results. It is an acknowledged maxim—*Ab hoste doceri, fas est*,—from an enemy to learn is right. Hear the following complaint of a Hindoo, addressed to the *Dhurma Subha*, which appeared in a Bengalee Newspaper in Calcutta, in 1842.

"O most holy men, do not boast any longer of being Hindoos! You think your children will remain faithful to the religion of their fathers, and join your religious bodies to defend Hindooism. Give up such hopes. The missionary gentlemen, who have left their own country and come to India, are now, whole bands of them, perambulating every lane and corner, in order to destroy the Hindoo religion; and foolish boys, like greedy fishes, being deceived by the hope of gain, are caught by the hook of their sorcery. In consequence of the exertions of Mr. Duff, many boys have given up their family, caste and religion; entered the family of Jesus; have been initiated into the mysteries of the Bible; and have destroyed their own nobility by their instruction. The leopard of the Hedo forest swallows up, one after the other, those children who in understanding, are not above beasts. Last week a child again lifted his wings, and flew to the tree of the love of Jesus Christ. What will happen hereafter nobody can tell. Like the sacrifical block at Kalighat, the blocks of the missionaries are day and night ready, and whenever they find an opportunity, they bring their oblation and kill their victim.

We are more afraid of the padrees than of cholera, fevers, or snake-bites; for these may be healed by charms and by medicines: but for the disease which the padrees inflict, neither charm nor medicine avails anything. This time Mr. Duff has returned from England with great design: he is very learned, and has a particular ability for instruction: it is therefore not to be wondered, when, by his instruction, senseless children are deluded, and plung into the ocean of Christ Jesus' religion.

We cannot find great fault with the padrees, for it is the glory of their own religion that they have crossed seven oceans and thirteen rivers, [a saying among the Hindoos] come into this country and are now spending immense sums in order to convert the Hindoos. Our religion, having no means of defending itself, is dying, and is going to its home, that is to say, to the house of Yam [the infernal regions]; and the holy men of Dhurma Subha will not even once apply the medicine of their endeavours for the restoration of their dying religion. Why do you quarrel with each other? If all the children join the white-faced Rishees [Sages] you will soon have nothing left to quarrel about?"

Great are the facilities possessed by Britain for the diffusion of divine light. " Many are the ties (says the Rev. J. G. Pike) which bind England to a British heart; many the excellencies which make her appear "the pearl of the ocean—the gem of the earth." To the Christian, however, the dearest attraction of his native land springs from the fact, that Britain appears appointed to lead the van, in preparing the way for the final and universal triumph of the Prince of Peace. Was the Gospel to be diffused through the countless Islands of the vast Pacific? England by her Colonies in Australasia prepared the way.—Did one hundred millions of Hindoos need that inestimable treasure? England has Hindostan committed almost miraculously to her care.—Did Birma reject the messages of gospel mercy? much of Birma is given to England; and a wide and effectual door is opened for introducing the rejected religion of the Cross.—Do nations, whose coasts extend through a space of many thousand miles, dwell around the Mediterranean, enveloped in superstition's darkest night—has the light of truth being extinguished in their dwellings, and death and darkness overspread their once favoured abodes? England has Malta given to her, whence that light has again begun to shine, which at length shall shine on every child of man. Feeble and inadequate indeed are all the exertions as yet employed to diffuse that light; yet in them British Christians have the happiness of taking the lead."

How commanding the position which Great Britain occupies among the host of nations. A French writer thus eulogizes it, " The British Empire may be considered as the greatest that ever existed; surpassing all others also in knowledge, moral character, and merit. *The sun never sets on its dominions!* Before his rays withdraw from the steeples of Quebec, his morning rays have enlightened the districts of Port Jackson; and while he is setting to the countries round Lake Superior, he is rising to those about the banks of the Ganges." How great the true glory of our country as described in the following glowing period. "If an Asiatic or a Roman of *the conquering ages of Asia and Rome*, could start from his grave, with what astonishment would he see an Island, once almost too trivial for his ambition, and too distant for his knowledge,—lording it over a dominion wider than all ancient empire, touching with her sceptre the eastern and western extremities of the earth, impressing her will on the councils of every kingdom, filling every corner of the earth with her arts, her benevolence, and her learning; gathering into her bosom the opulent products of every region; pushing her brilliant adventures to every spot where man can master the wild powers of nature; controling an empire in the heart of Asia: not less proudly conquering another empire from the swamps, and forests, and savage solitude of the western world; founding another empire in the new-born continent of the south; and in all, leaving vestiges of herself that no time will ever wear away; erecting altars that shall last when sword and sceptre are dust; founding institutes, not of harsh and sanguinary power, but like the pillars in the journeyings of Israel, bearing sacred evidences that their God had been their guide, and renewed his covenant with his people; planting her noble language, the old wisdom of her laws, the matchless security of her freedom, the incalculable knowledge of her religion!—England, the mighty mother of empires; the great dispenser of good; the intellectual sovereign of the globe!"

The extent of the British dominions has been thus graphically described on the occasion of the birth of the heir apparent to the crown "Salutes in honour of his birth will be fired—in America—on the shores of Hudson Bay, along the whole line of the Canadian Lakes, in New Brunswick, Nova Scotia, Newfoundland, in the Bermudas, at a hundred points in the West Indies, in the forests of Guiana, and in the distant Falkland Islands, near Cape Horn; in Europe—in the British Islands, from the Rock of Gibraltar, from the impregnable fortifications of Malta, and in the Ionian Islands; in Africa—on the Guinea Coast, at St. Helena and Ascension; from the Cape to the Orange River, and at the Mauritius; in Asia—from the fortress of Aden in Arabia, at Karrack in the Persian Gulf, by the British army in Affghanistan, along the Himalaya Mountains, the Banks of the Indus and the Ganges, to the southern point of India, in the Island of Ceylon, beyond the Ganges in Assam and Arracan, at Prince of Wales' Island and Singapore, and on the shores of China, at Hong Kong and Chusan; and in Australia, at the Settlements formed on every side of the Australian Continent and Islands, and in the Strait which separates the Islands of the New Zealanders! No Prince has ever been born either in this or any other country—in ancient or modern times—whose birth would be hailed with rejoicing, at so many different and distant points in every quarter of the world." O may our country seriously consider her high destiny, and the church of Christ in every part of our empire sedulously labour to fulfil her "high and holy calling."

An excellent writer has well said—"In the government of the Great Disposer of events, nothing is done without a reason, and that "the wisest reason." The reduction of so vast a portion of the earth under the Roman sceptre, was among the providential means of extending Christianity. What design inferior to this can be the ultimate cause of '*this mighty donative of supremacy*' to an Island in the German Ocean—the very end of the ancient world? Never was there a more significant emblem than has been grafted upon the royal escutcheon of England, by the accession of the house of Brunswick—*the white horse of triumph!* But who is its viewless rider? One whom heraldry knows not; whose form the political eye discerns not; but who not the less sways and directs, the apparently self-guided movements of the unconscious agents of His purposes. Whatever be the fate of England, she is planting in the desert, and stretching over both hemispheres, 'a kingdom that cannot be moved.'"

Let us cherish anticipations of the *final triumph of Christianity in the East.* The writer knows not better how to express this sentiment than in the glowing language of the late Rev. W. Ward, of Serampore—"It must have been to accomplish some very important moral change in the eastern world, that so vast an empire as is comprised in British India, containing nearly one hundred millions of people, should have been placed under the dominion of one of the smallest portions of the civilized world, and that at the other extremity of the globe. This opinion, which is entertained by every enlightened philanthropist, is greatly strengthened, when we consider the long-degraded state of India, and of the immense and immensely populous regions around it; the moral enterprise of the age in which these countries have been given to us; and that Great Britain is the only country upon earth, from which the intellectual and moral improvement of India could have been expected. All these combined circumstances surely carry us to the persuasion, that Divine Providence has, at this period of the world, some great good to confer on the East; and that, after so many long and dark ages, each succeeding one becoming darker than the past, the day-spring from on high is destined again to visit these regions, containing the birth-place of hnmanity, filled with all that is magnificent and immense in creation, made sacred by the presence of patriarchs, prophets, and the Messiah Himself, as well as the theatre of the most remarkable revolutions that have ever been exhibited on earth.

"At different periods it seemed doubtful whether Portugal, or Holland, or France, should obtain the ascendancy in the East. But on them it was not conferred. A day of trial was given to these powers, but they were found unworthy of the great trust, and incapable of accomplishing the good intended for India; they were therefore rejected. For a considerable period the power of Britain in India appeared very precarious; and, amidst such an uncertainty, but little opportunity for improvement was afforded. Latterly, however, our power has been so consolidated, in the decided preference of our sway in the minds of the governed, and in the complete dependence of every remaining power in India, that the improvement of the intellectual condition of the natives, as the means of uniting them to us from principle, has become the soundest policy, and a point of such paramount necessity and importance, that almost every one, at all conversant with the state of our Indian empire, is become a convert to this opinion.

"When it is considered that the intellectual condition of our Indian population is far lower than that of our ancestors at the period of the conquest; that there is not a single school or book in India by which the mind can be enlightened; that all the countries around Hindostan are enveloped in the same darkness; that the great mass of society in every country have emerged out of darkness by a progress so slow, as to be almost imperceptible; and that the population, to be raised into active and thinking beings in India, amounts to nearly one hundred millions,—all idea of the danger to the parent state, from attempting to improve the mental condition of society there, must be very extravagant. Many centuries must pass away, before India shall be in the condition of our American subjects at the commencement of their revolution; and after all these centuries shall have rolled over our country, if her power, and splendour, and foreign possessions, shall be retained so long, and she should, five or six hundred years hence, lose India, she will derive greater glory from having elevated into a mental and moral existence all these millions, than she would derive from adding all China and Tartary to her eastern possession: and India, thus enlightened and civilized, would, even in an independent state, contribute more to the real prosperity of Britain as a commercial people, by consuming her manufactures to a vast extent, than she does at present, or ever will do, remaining uncivilized.

"But let Hindostan receive that higher civilization she needs, that cultivation of which she is so capable, let European literature be transfused into all her languages, and the ocean, from the ports of Britain to India, will be covered with our merchant vessels; and, from the centre of India moral culture and science will be extended all over Asia,—to the Burman empire and Siam, to China, with all her millions, to Persia, and even to Arabia; and the whole Eastern hemisphere will be gilded with the rays of that Luminary, whose beams alone are the source of all the life and moral beauty found in our world. And when we consider that so many millions of the population of India are our fellow-subjects, what a stimulus to seek their good! What an imperative, what a paramount duty! Is it not manifest, that in the mental and moral improvement of this vast empire, Great Britain has a work of benevolence before her which in national glory, will eclipse all her other achievements, as much as the meridian sun exceeds in splendour the morning star. *Know then, the country of the Howards and the Wilberforces, thy high destiny!—Never were such miseries to be removed—never was such a mighty good put within the power of one nation—the raising a population of a hundred millions to a rational and happy existence, and through them, the illumination and civilization of all Asia.*"*
O Britain!

"Pursue thy glorious course. Be this thy art,
Not to corrupt, but meliorate the heart;
Where'er mankind in Gentile darkness lie,
Instruction's blessed radiance to supply;
O'er the oppress'd, soft mercy's dews to shed,
And crush with ruin the oppressor's head.
O haste your tardy coming days of gold;
Long by prophetic minstrelsy foretold!
Where yon bright purple streaks the orient skies,
Rise Science, Feeedom, Peace, Religion, rise!
'Till, from Tanjore to farthest Samarcand,
In one wide lustre bask the glowing land:
And, (Brahma from his guilty greatness hurl'd,
With Mecca's lord,) Messiah rule the world!"
"Then, while transported Asia kneels around,
With ancient arts, and long lost glories crown'd:
Some happier bard, on Ganges' margin laid,
Where playful bamboos weave their fretted shade,
Shall to the strings a loftier tone impart,
And pour in rapturous verse his flowing heart.
Stamp'd in immortal light on future days,
Through all the strain his country's joys shall blaze;
The Sancrit song be warm'd with heav'nly fires,
And themes divine awake from Indian lyres!"†

* Wrangham and Grant on the restoration of Learning in the East, 1805.
† Ward's View of the Hindoos, vol. iii. preface, pp. 17, 18, 51—54.

What more can the writer add in his concluding appeal, to "provoke to emulation" his brethren and sisters, to come up "to the help of the Lord, to the help of the Lord against the mighty?" Mr. Sutton, in his "Narrative," thus pathetically pleads for his beloved Oreahs. "And now beloved reader if thou hast been taught to feel the value of those privileges which a Christian land affords, pause I beseech you. Yes, look at dark, awfully dark, benighted Orissa! Gaze on its awful desolation and sin. Behold its impure temples, its bloody sacrifices, its shasters, unutterably obscene—the roads crowded with pilgrims hastening to the detested temple—the young untaught whatever most concerns immortal men—the aged uncheered—the afflicted without a comforter—the dying without a Saviour. On these hapless millions no Sabbath shines, an emblem of the Sabbath in the heavens—no Saviour's cheering voice diffuses gladness through their souls—no heaven opens its immortal portals to bid them enter in. Their religion is infernal—their hearts the seat of sin—their land the dwelling place of sorrow, and lamentation, and woe. And such it has been for ages. Time has thus rolled on through successive centuries, while millions, numberless as the dew-drops of the morning, have risen into life, spent its little day, and sunk into death; but all has been gloom and darkness, without one beam of heavenly light. Unhappy land! Can we be Christians and not lament its sorrows! Shall these sorrows always continue? Ah no!

Ten years ago our brethren began to proclaim the message of heavenly love to Orissa. A spark of light then entered those regions of darkness, that spark has since strengthened to a little flame, that flame will doubtless strengthen, and diffuse its light from village to village, from town to town, from hill to hill, till all Orissa sees its splendour, and the night of more than two thousand years vanishes before its brightness.

We are encouraged thus to speak and hope because similar has been the gradual increase of the gospel kingdom in every age. The blessed Redeemer declared, that it is to be compared to a grain of mustard seed, which being cast into the ground grows up into a tree, beneath whose branches the fowls of heaven find food and shelter. Or it may be compared to leaven which being cast into meal, ceases not to operate until the whole mass is leavened. "When the first missionaries of the gospel landed in the British Isles, they doubtless seemed a small and feeble band, yet few and feeble as they were, at length they triumphed over the superstition of ages, and the powers of darkness; and became the harbingers of eternal blessings to immortal myriads. The flame they kindled still continues to burn; and its splendour has cheered many while passing through the dark night of time to the bright day of eternity. The stream from the fountain they unsealed, has swelled into a river, and conveys the waters of life to multitudes that else would thirst and die. The first unnoticed British church has spread its branches over all the land: the little one has become a thousand, and the small one a strong nation!"*

The Indian Report of the Society, probably from the same pen, thus closes,—" In presenting this report and appeal to the Christian public in India the Orissa Missionaries feel strong consolation that they are not inviting attention to a new and doubtful enterprize. Imperfect indeed as is the sketch which is here presented, there is enough to show that their progress from the commencement has been onward, and their labours if perserved in, certain of been crowned with yet greater success. They have no misgivings as to the result of their humble efforts. They are disposed to view their actual success in making converts as bearing no greater proportion to the real progress made in the subversion of idolatry in Orissa, than does the light froth borne on the ocean's wave to the unfathomable depths that roll beneath. And they would extend these remarks to Missionary operations generally. "Father! thy word is passed, man shall find grace." India, with all her tribes, shall yet be blest in Christ, and oh! fellow christians, who read this appeal, may it be your happiness first to secure an interest in the Saviour of men yourselves, and then when your are removed to dwell with him whom your soul loveth, may you welcome to glory, through all the generations of time, successive multitudes who shall gratefully exclaim 'for our eternal salvation we are indebted to Christ, but for the means which brought us to him, we are, under God, indebted to you.' Amen."

How powerful is the appeal to Students and young Ministers, to devote themselves to the work of the Mission. Let the glowing language of the poet "stir up the pure mind."

Where the majestic Ganges swiftly pours
Her mighty streams along the eastern shores,
My hovering fancy dwells, and bears me hence
To India's burning climes, and plains immense;
Where darkness reigns I fain would spend my breath,
And toil to weave a never-fading wreath
To crown my Saviour's brow! O blissful thought!
To win to Christ a soul with darkness fraught!

* Sutton's Narrative, pp. 419-20.

Ye champions of the mighty God, arise,
And wave your floating banners to the skies;
With shouts proclaim a dying Saviour's love,
And, conquering and to conquer, onward move.
Shall not the clang of vile idolatry
Awake your souls to set the prisoners free,
And loose the dreadful chains that bind them fast
To superstitious rites and hellish cast?
Ye ministers of Christ, behold with grief,
The dying heathen panting for relief!
'Tis yours to break Oppression's cruel rod;
'Tis yours to point them to the Lamb of God:
Why then so slothful?—Why this long delay?
The work is God's—Immanuel leads the way!*

The Rev. C. Lacey, in a recent communication, refers to the state of the people, which was presented to him on his journey, and observes, "In passing through their native wilderness, I could not resist the following thoughts,—

O may these shades which own the tigers' sway,
And scarce admit at noon the light of day,
Where, if man treads, he treads with trembling steps,
And round the scene a watchful vigil keeps;
O, 'mid those shades may Christian dwellings rise,
And Christian temples emulate the skies.
From hill to hill may Christian anthems swell,
Roll down the rocks, and fill the lengthening vale,
'Till joy to frightful solitude succeed,
And nature's cheerful voice proclaim a gracious God.

In operating upon a mass of people like the Hindoos, a great deal of time and labour must be expended ere much can appear of pleasing and satisfactory results. The improvement is real, but apparently slow, and promises glorious results for the future rather than for the present time. We may, and do expect, occasional conversions; but the harvest will be gathered by our successors. The light of truth resembles the rising sun, which does not diffuse its beams on particular spots, but spreads everywhere, and at once enlightens the whole hemisphere, till darkness is banished. Of this gradual progress we enjoy many evidences. *Twenty-two years ago* it was not known that there was a God, by the Oreahs; *now*, this truth is everywhere acknowledged;—the name of Christ, as a Saviour, was not known, and could not be pronounced,—*now*, many, in every village throughout the land, know that *He* is the Saviour, and can pronounce his name, though with stammering tongues. It was not conceived that there existed an antagonist

* See G. B. Repository, 1841, p. 159.

system of religion, to Hindooism: *now*, the brahmins, the conservators of idolatry, feel that they are assailed, that their system has commenced to wane; and are called upon to step forward in defence of the faith which has made them, and supports them in their dignities and emoluments. No voice exhibited and explained the doctrines of Christianity—*now* tens of thousands have heard them from our lips, and retain a portion of the precious truth they have listened to. No doubt ever disturbed the mind of any among the mass of the population, that "*Perhaps Hindooism is not true*,"—*now*, doubts are everywhere discovered to exist; they set in from the sphere of our labours and ministry, and, like a wave of the sea, are spreading wider and wider:—not a book existed, but books of false religion and sin—*now*, every village in the country possesses many, and some of these are being daily read. The increasing light and influence of Christianity has already destroyed some of the monstrous institutions engendered by a dark, an infernal, and destructive system of idolatry. The flames of the suttee have been quenched; human sacrifices have been abolished;* brahmins are rendered amenable to the law of criminal jurisprudence;—punishment for embracing Christianity is done away with, and tax by government on shrines of idolatry abolished.

From east to west of the land,—*now*, we have *eight Churches and branch Churches, containing several hundreds of converted natives;* and our schools are rearing numbers of young persons of both sexes, who are forming families, and these families Christian locations among the people. The work has commenced, and has considerably advanced; and these testimonies are many of them among the means of facilitating its progress; so that every year the general improvement will be more and more strongly developed, till converts (for conversion is a degree of its progress) will, in large numbers, be brought into the fold of Jesus Christ. To promote the moral, intellectual, and spiritual regeneration of these degraded and miserable people, our efforts must be increased and continous. Our labours and sacrifices have already been crowned and rewarded, and converts from time to time will still come forth to encourage our efforts; but, in a while, thousands and tens of thousands will bless us for thinking of them, and labouring for them: and when the brief scenes of time shall close, we shall reap eternal and peculiar satisfaction for having brought the Gospel here. How glad should I be could I encourage the exertions of our friends at

* They still exist in the tributary states.

home by a relation of instances of conversion among the heathen, but I can only encourage them by the considerations with which I am myself encouraged. I enjoy the immediate approbation of God in spending my life and labours here; and so may they in sending us forth, and keeping us here;—we are, effectually though apparently slowly, demolishing a system of idolatry which has flourished for unknown ages, and has defied all other attempts;—the mighty superstructure is being undermined, and is cracking and splitting, preparitory to its fall, its fall to rise no more. These efforts they have largely contributed to produce; and, as the crisis comes on they do not think of slackening their efforts, much less of suspending them! How act the brave phalanx which assails the citadel of the foe? Every intimation of approaching success, serves but to stimulate their zeal and increase their efforts, and though many brave men may fall in the breach, they press on till the standards are planted on the conquered battlements, and shouts of joy proclaim the conquest effected. So we may fall, and our friends at home may fall; yet, seeing the intimations of approaching conqnest, we must press onward in our labours till the enemy is subdued, and Christ shall reign in Orissa.

Foremost in the band we write to tell our fellow-laborers, our help-fellows in the rear, that many and indubitable signs exist that the enemy is yielding, and the conquest is proceeding. Let them continue, and if possible, increase their efforts; and in due time, all these fair realms, at present blasted and cursed by Idolatry, will yield to our Lord, the Prince of peace; and his banner will wave throughout the land. I am often delighted with the grateful sense our native Christians feel and express for the Gospel and all its blessings, sent to them by, as they designate them, their brothers and sisters in England. We should like to see them much improved beyond what they are; but this improvement will occur as they recover from the physical, moral, and intellectual weakness, induced by idolatry. Meantime, they see and feel the value of the precious Gospel, and rejoice in its communications, and various privileges; and are especially thankful that our friends at home ever sent forth the tidings of revealed mercy to them. O how important it appears to me, that this precious plant has been placed in this soil! Happy are those who sent the seed, and happy are those who put it in the ground! *It is bearing the fruit of everlasting life, and must now multiply till it fills the land.*"

APPENDIX.

NAMES OF THE MISSIONARIES.

Missionaries.	Arrived.	Remarks.
Rev. W. Bampton	Feb. 1822	Died Dec. 7, 1830.
Mrs. Bampton	do.	Returned, 1831.
Rev. J. Peggs	do.	do. Nov. 1825.
Mrs. Peggs	do.	do. ———
Rev. C. Lacey	Dec. 1823	Furlough, 1835-7.
Mrs. Lacey	do.	do.
Rev. A. Sutton	March 1825	do. 1833-5.
Mrs. Sutton	do.	Died, May, 1825.
Rev. J. Cropper	Feb. 1828	Died, Dec. 1828.
Mrs. E. Sutton	July 1826	
Rev. W. Brown	Dec. 1830	Left, 1837.
Mrs. Brown	do.	Residing at Balasore.
Rev. J. Goadby	Dec. 1833	Returned, 1837.
Mrs. Goadby	do.	Died, 1834.
Rev. J. Brooks	March 1835	Returned June 1845.
Mrs. Brooks	do.	do.
Mrs. J. Goadby	April, 1835	Returned, 1837.
*Rev. Eli Noyes	March 1836	Returned 1842.
*Mrs. Noyes	do.	do.
*Rev. J. Phillips	do.	
*Mrs. Phillips	do.	Died, 1838.
Rev. J. Stubbins	Jan. 1837	Furlough 1843-5.
Mrs. Stubbins	do.	Died, 1837.
Mrs. E. Stubbins	March 1838	
Rev. H. Wilkinson	March 1839	Returned for health, Ap. 1846.
Mrs. Wilkinson	do.	

* Those distinguished by an asterisk were sent out from America by the Free-will Baptist Missionary Society, founded through the interest in India awakened by the visit of the Rev. Amos Sutton, in 1833.

Missionaries.	Arrived.	Remarks.
*Mrs. A. Phillips -	— 1839	- Died, 1840.
*Rev. O. Bachelor -	Sept. 1840	
*Mrs. Bachelor -	do.	
*Miss C. Cummings -	do.	
Rev. J. Grant -	Dec. 1841	- Died Feb. 1843.
Mrs. Grant -	do.	- Returned 1846.
Mr. W. Brooks, *Printer*,	do.	
Mrs. Brooks -	do.	
Miss Derry -	do.	
*Rev. C. Dow -	April 1844	- Midnapore.
Rev. J. Buckley -	Sept. 1844	- Berhampore.
Rev. J. Stubbins -	Sept. 1845	- Visited England and returned [June 1845.
Rev. W. Bailey -	do.	
Rev. J. Millar -	do.	
Miss Collins -	do.	

In addition to the above, the Rev. Messrs. Hudson, Bromley, and Allsop, with their wives, sailed for Jamaica in 1826 and 1827. It is with deep regret that the writer adds, Mr. Hudson returned on account of ill health; Mr. Allsop, his brother-in-law, died at Lucea, in September 1829, and the remaining missionary relinquished his connexion with the Society. In consequence of these painful events, and the very great expense of the mission, the stations so successfully occupied were tendered to the brethren of the other part of the Baptist Denomination, who entered into their labours. Happy day when "he that soweth and he that reapeth may rejoice together!"

ORDAINED NATIVE PREACHERS.

Gunga Dhor - - -	Doitaree - - - -	Denabundo
Rama Chundra - -	Sebo Saho - - - -	Balagee
Bamadab - - - -	Sebo Naik or Patna -	Damadur
	Bicarree	

NATIVE ASSISTANTS, NOT ORDAINED.

Somnauth - -	Boleram - -	Juggernaut -	Khumboo
Parasua - - -	Bonamallee -	Tamar - - -	Gunsham

OCCASIONAL PREACHERS.

Sunauthannee - Bhobanne - Hurre Je Jaik.

RECENT STATISTICS.

The Rev. C. Lacey, in a letter to the author, dated May 26th, 1846,—" You have often requested some statistics from me, and I shall close this letter with a few; they have reference to my own department.

Christianpore, 1 chapel, a school of 30 children, 17 houses, and 68 inhabitants.

Societypore. 8 houses and 33 inhabitants.

Laceypore. 11 houses and 42 inhabitants.

Khunditta. 9 houses, a school of 25 children, 1 chapel, preachers' house and mission bungalow, with 30 inhabitants.

Oodyapore, Choga. 20 houses, a pucka, chapel, and bungalow, a school of 16 children, 71 inhabitants.

Detached residences. 6 houses and 16 inhabitants.

Cuttack. Large mission chapel, printing office, &c.,

Total. Houses 72, chapels 4, christian schools 3, native christians 226, children in christian and heathen schools 71, asylum 93 children. No reference is made to the Indo-British nor European, whether belonging to the mission or otherwise. The Native christian community is fast increasing by birth and by conversion. We have been joined this year by about 25 from among the heathen." Berhampore and Ganjam report 53 members.

INCOME OF THE SOCIETY.

Year	£	s.	d.	Year	£	s.	d.
1820, April 1..	£1000	0	0	1833	£1227	2	6¾
1820, June ..	772	1	1¾	1834	1552	1	1¾
1821	1159	6	5	1835	1652	3	2
1822	1115	2	9½	1836	1307	2	1½
1823	1627	19	9	1837	1926	13	8¼
1824	1685	11	8¾	1838	1620	8	4½
1825	1763	7	2¾	1839	1647	17	3¾
1826	1595	12	2½	1840	1668	15	0
1827	1696	13	0¼	1841	1732	7	0¼
1828	1651	1	6	1842	1929	0	5½
1829	1286	18	0	1843	2450	16	8
1830	1212	6	8	1844	2478	18	8
1831	958	8	2¾	1845	2375	16	2
1832	1239	19	5¾	1846	2133	6	10

ILKESTON:—PRINTED BY JOHN WOMBELL, BATH-STREET.